Edited by
David Painting

Foreword by
Cindy Kent MBE

FRESH FROM THE WORD 2023

DAILY BIBLE STUDIES FROM AROUND THE WORLD

READ · REFLECT · GROW

First published in Great Britain in 2022

Society for Promoting Christian Knowledge
36 Causton Street
London SW1P 4ST
www.spck.org.uk

International Bible Reading Association
5–6 Imperial Court
12 Sovereign Road
Birmingham B30 3FH
www.ibraglobal.org

British Library Cataloguing-in-Publication Data
A catalogue record for this book is available from the British Library

ISBN 978–0–281–08751–8
eBook ISBN 978–0–281–08752–5
ISSN 2050–6791

1 3 5 7 9 10 8 6 4 2

Typeset by Fakenham Prepress Solutions, Fakenham, Norfolk NR21 8NL
First printed in Great Britain by Clays, Bungay, Suffolk, NR35 1ED

eBook by Fakenham Prepress Solutions, Fakenham, Norfolk NR21 8NL

Produced on paper from sustainable sources

Fresh from The Word aims to build understanding and respect for different Christian perspectives through the provision of a range of biblical interpretations. Views expressed by contributors should not, therefore, be taken to reflect the views or policies of the Editor or the International Bible Reading Association.

The International Bible Reading Association's scheme of readings is listed monthly on the IBRA website at www.ibraglobal.org and the full scheme for 2023 may be downloaded in English, Spanish and French.

Contents

Foreword

What a joy to be asked to write this foreword for *Fresh from The Word* – God has used these reading notes for many years, all around the world, and it's great that they can be used by anyone new to the faith or – like me – someone who's been a believer for a long time.

I have to admit to a bit of a struggle sometimes when reading the Bible – there are just too many temptations for my time. But when I do sit down and engage with the word I'm so pleased I did. I learn something about myself, the community I'm in and the world generally that I can take into the day. And helping us engage with the Bible is where *Fresh from The Word* comes in by not only providing notes but also ways to approach God's word.

Years ago, I was offered just such a helpful way of looking at a Bible passage; to put myself into the situation. So, for instance, I'm sitting on the edge of the well with the Samaritan woman and overhearing the conversation between her and Jesus. Or I'm next to Miriam, carrying home baby Moses to care for him. Other times I might be in the crowd jeering on the Via Dolorosa: how did I feel hearing the people curse Jesus – did I join in? The good thing about *Fresh from The Word* is that each writer starts from that position. They look at the text and then bring their own experience of God and his word, as it were, to shine a light on the passage, and, in doing that, they can help us to look at it with fresh eyes. In the dark days that we've just experienced, it can be so helpful to see through the eyes of someone else.

Another way that helps me is to use acronyms – I still remember the colours of the rainbow by reciting 'Richard Of York Gave Battle In Vain' (red, orange, yellow, green, blue, indigo, violet)! So, I have a couple of Bible-related ones that you might find useful: SOAP – Scripture, Observation, Application, Prayer. Scripture – read the passage and the accompanying notes, memorise the key verses or maybe write them down and remember them from time to time during the day. Observation – what is the main message and what does it prompt you to think about? Application – ask God how he wants you to apply this to your life today, and then Pray – either using the prayer provided or something that has inspired you.

And one final acronym to guide our response to the Bible passage: HEAR. Help each other; Encourage each other; Ask God to give you his guidance; and Relate this to those around you.

May God bless you on your daily walk with him.

Revd Cindy Kent MBE

Lead singer with The Settlers in the 1960s and early 1970s, Cindy Kent has appeared in pantomime and presented on BBC Radio 1, 2 and 4 as well as on commercial stations and Premier Christian Radio. An ordained priest in the Church of England since 2007, Cindy has been awarded an MBE for services to religious broadcasting and currently hosts a Saturday afternoon show on Serenade Radio.

How to use *Fresh from The Word*

How do you approach the idea of regular Bible reading? It may help to see daily Bible reading as spiritual exploration. Here is a suggestion of a pattern to follow that may help you develop the discipline but free up your mind and heart to respond.

- Before you read, take a few moments – the time it takes to say the Lord's Prayer – to imagine God looking at you with love. Feel yourself enfolded in that gaze. Come to scripture with your feet firmly planted.
- Read the passage slowly before you turn to the notes. Be curious. The Bible was written over a period of nearly 1,000 years, over 2,000 years ago. There is always something to learn. Read and reread.
- If you have access to a study Bible, pay attention to any echoes of the passage you are reading in other parts of the biblical book. A word might be used in different ways by different biblical authors. Where in the story of the book are you reading? What will happen next?
- 'Read' yourself as you read the story. Be attentive to your reactions – even trivial ones. What is drawing you into the story? What is repelling you? Observe yourself 'sidelong' as you read as if you were watching a wild animal in the forest; be still, observant and expectant.
- What in scripture or in the notes is drawing you forward in hope? What is closing you down? Notice where the Spirit of Life is present, and where negative spirits are, too. Follow where life is leading. God always leads into life, even if the way feels risky.
- Lift up the world and aspects of your life to God. What would you like to share with God? What is God seeking to share with you?
- Thank God for being present and offer your energy in the day ahead, or in the day coming after a night's rest.
- Finally, the † symbol is an invitation to pray a prayer that has been written for the day's reading. You are invited to say these words aloud or in silence with thousands of other readers around the world who will be reading these notes on the same day in dozens of languages.

Acknowledgements and abbreviations

The use of the letters a or b in a text reference, such as Luke 9:37–43a, indicates that the day's text starts or finishes midway through a verse, usually at a break such as the end of a sentence. Not all Bible versions will indicate such divisions.

We are grateful to the copyright holders for permission to use scriptural quotations from the following Bible versions:

THE MESSAGE	Scripture quotations marked *THE MESSAGE* are taken from *THE MESSAGE*. Copyright © by Eugene H. Peterson 1993, 1994, 1995, 1996, 2000, 2001, 2002. Used by permission of NavPress Publishing Group.
NIV	Scripture quotations marked NIV are taken from the Holy Bible, NEW INTERNATIONAL VERSION®, NIV®. Copyright © 1973, 1978, 1984, 2011 by Biblica, Inc.® Used by permission. All rights reserved worldwide.
NIVUK	Scripture quotations marked NIVUK are taken from The Holy Bible, New International Version (Anglicized edition). Copyright © 1979, 1984, 2011 by Biblica. Used by permission of Hodder & Stoughton Ltd, an Hachette UK company. All rights reserved. 'NIV' is a registered trademark of Biblica. UK trademark number 1448790.
NKJV	Scripture quotations marked NKJV are taken from the New King James Version. Copyright © 1982 by Thomas Nelson, Inc. Used by permission. All rights reserved.
NLT	Scripture quotations marked NLT are taken from the *Holy Bible*, New Living Translation, copyright © 1996. Used by permission of Tyndale House Publishers, Inc., Carol Stream, Illinois 60189, USA. All rights reserved.
NRSV	Scripture quotations marked NRSV are taken from the New Revised Standard Version of the Bible, copyright © 1989 by the Division of Christian Education of the National Council of the Churches of Christ in the USA. Used by permission. All rights reserved.
NRSVA	Scripture quotations marked NRSVA are taken from the New Revised Standard Version of the Bible, Anglicised Edition, copyright © 1989, 1995 by the Division of Christian Education of the National Council of the Churches of Christ in the USA. Used by permission. All rights reserved.
NRSVACE	Scripture quotations marked NRSVACE are taken from the New Revised Standard Version Bible, Anglicised Catholic Edition, copyright © 1989, 1993, 1995 by the Division of Christian Education of the National Council of the Churches of Christ in the USA. Used by permission. All rights reserved.

Introduction from the Editor

I love the film *Hidden Figures*. It's a story that combines two of my favourite things: space flight and overlooked people who turn out to be central to the plot. Katherine Johnson, an African American woman, marginalised and hidden because of her race and sex, ends up leading a team of 'human computers' whose calculations pave the way to earth-orbit and eventually to the Apollo moon landings and beyond. After years of obscurity, her ground-breaking work was recognised and, in 2016, NASA dedicated the Langley Research Center's Katherine G. Johnson Computational Research Facility in her honour. In a similar way, one of the themes in this edition of *Fresh from The Word* is 'hidden heroes and heroines', looking at characters in the Bible who are similarly overlooked, but who play a pivotal role in the unfolding of the kingdom. People like Siphrah and Puah, Zelophehad's daughters and the men of Issachar will step out of the shadows as we see the true significance and impact of their lives.

Alongside the mix of themes and consecutive readings (Matthew, Leviticus, James, 2 Corinthians, to name a few) we also explore the different types of literature in the Bible. With a week on each, we've asked our writers not only to unpack the daily passages written in that particular style, but also to provide an insight into how we can safely interpret scripture within each genre: poetry, law, prophecy, narrative and, of course, apocalyptic! Revelation is the most famous piece of apocalyptic literature, and we discover that 'revealing' is exactly its intent and it's our hope that these weeks will do just that – help you to see revealed that which was previously hidden.

I hope as you come to each new week that you will take time to look at the photo and read the brief biography of each of our marvellous writers so that they are no longer just a name, glanced over, but someone you get to know a little, and perhaps more so as you journey with them through the week – these too are perhaps 'hidden figures' whose significance God would have us notice and give thanks for.

Finally, in this theme of those who perhaps feel insignificant or marginalised, I would encourage you – the people for whom IBRA exists, the readers of *Fresh from The Word*. You are a daughter, a son, of God most high, a brother or sister – a friend of the King of Kings who died for you. You are not hidden to God – a truth that I trust will be reinforced time and again as you read this new edition.

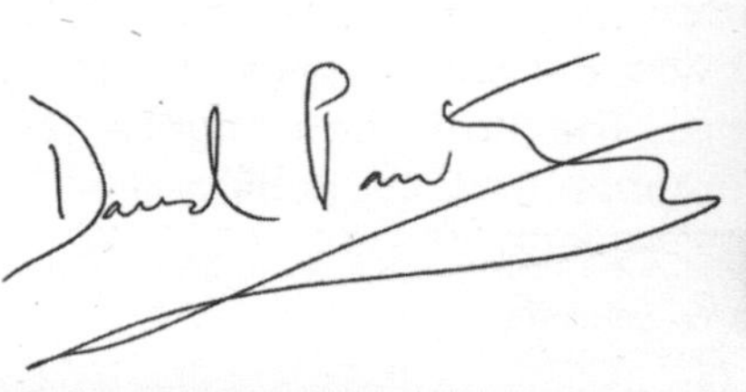

IBRA joins in to celebrate the 250th anniversary of the hymn 'Amazing Grace' today Sunday 1 January 2023

Rev John Newton was a former slave trade captain who came to faith when God saved him from a shipwreck and who later anonymously supported William Wilberforce in his successful campaign to have the UK Parliament declare the slave trade illegal.

Newton, deeply moved by his own redemption, wrote 'Amazing Grace' to accompany his sermon on Sunday 1 January 1773 in order to bring it to life for his congregation. Using thoughts rooted in 1 Chronicles 17, Newton, like David, reflects on his experience of God's grace in the past and the present and looks confidently to a future filled with his grace. The entire Christian life is in Newton's hymn:

- salvation ('saved a wretch like me')
- trials ('many dangers, toils, and snares')
- struggles with doubts and need for divine promises ('his word my hope secures')
- protection in spiritual battle ('he will my shield and portion be')
- ageing and facing death ('when this flesh and heart shall fail')
- hopes for re-creation ('earth shall soon dissolve like snow')
- a vision of the difference of living with God ('A life of joy and peace')
- and treasuring God for ever ('But God, who called me here below, / will be for ever mine')

From the beginning to the end of this autobiographical hymn, we are introduced to the unwavering grace of God throughout our lives on earth and looking forward to our eternal life.

This hymn has accomplished what we hope for *Fresh from The Word*: to cross boundaries and borders, to speak to everyone about the amazing grace that God offers. As you use these Bible reading notes through the year, we hope you will see the themes of this great hymn woven in the readings.

'Amazing Grace' has been sung for hundreds of years; it is well loved, and well known by Christians and non-Christians alike in many situations and for many reasons. Perhaps you could use this hymn today, 250 years since it was first sung, to tell someone of the grace you have found and that God longs to be theirs.

'Amazing Grace' was originally titled 'Faith's Review and Expectation'; it was first published in 1779 as hymn number XLI in *The Olney Hymns*. The music we recognise today was written by an American composer and first published with the hymn in 1847.

Extracts with permission from Tony Reinke: https://tonyreinke.com/2016/01/01/the-most-famous-new-years-day-hymn/

Getting ready

Notes by **Liz Clutterbuck**

Liz is a Church of England priest who combines parish ministry with a ministry-training role for the Stepney Area of the Diocese of London. Additionally, she has a research interest in exploring how church impact can be better measured, so that we can learn how missional initiatives work best and where. Liz is passionate about social media, film, baking and travel – and loves it when she manages to combine as many of her passions as possible! Liz has used the NRSV for these notes.

Sunday 1 January

Pause and take stock

Read Genesis 1:31; 2:1–3

So God blessed the seventh day and hallowed it, because on it God rested from all the work that he had done in creation.

(verse 3)

Happy new year! There is something particularly significant about the fact that the first day of 2023 falls on Sunday – the seventh day, the Sabbath day, when we are called to rest and consider the wonder of God's creation.

In many parts of the world, New Year's Day is a holiday. A day to pause and take stock before the work of January begins. Regardless of the day of the week, it can be seen as a time of Sabbath, a day to consider all that God has done in the year that has ended and what lies ahead.

Genesis reminds us not just of our creator God, but also that having created the world, God chose to rest. Our busy world does not always encourage us to take the time we need to recover, but today's reading makes it plain that we must follow in God's footsteps and honour the Sabbath.

Do you make space for sabbath in your life? Are you resting when God calls you to? As we explore scripture together over the first week of 2023, make space to consider what this year holds for you and your relationship with God.

† Creator God, I lift this new year to you. Grant me the space to rest in you today and to honour your Sabbath.

Monday 2 January

Wait for the right moment

Read Acts 1:1–5

While staying with them, he ordered them not to leave Jerusalem, but to wait there for the promise of the Father.

(verse 4)

Somewhat controversially, I do not believe in New Year's resolutions. You might think I feel this way because I've usually broken them before January is over – but that's not really the case. It's because I believe that we should make our resolutions to change or live differently when it is the right time for us to do that.

For those of us in the northern hemisphere, January is a terrible time to make a resolution along the lines of 'I will get up at 6 a.m. every day and run 5km' – because at 6 a.m. it's dark and cold, and in those conditions I'd expect most people to fail within the month! A resolution to do more exercise outside might be more successful if attempted in the spring instead. It's better to wait for the right time.

The emphasis on New Year's resolutions also overshadows the fact that there are multiple moments in the Christian year when we are called to consider our lives and make changes. Lent and Advent are two penitential seasons where we might fast or take on new commitments as a means of prayer and vocation. You might mark a 'new' year of Christian discipleship on a significant anniversary – such as baptism, confirmation or ordination.

At the start of Acts, the disciples are eager to get on with ministry. Jesus has returned and they are raring to go. But they are urged to wait. God's promise will be fulfilled, but they must be patient. It must be at God's timing that their ministry in the power of the Holy Spirit begins.

† God of promises, we pray for reassurance that your plans for us will be fulfilled in your time. Give us patience, and challenge us to live by your timing not ours.

For further thought

Look through your diary. Mark days when you will consider what changes God may be calling you into and what promises you are waiting to be fulfilled.

Tuesday 3 January

Get dressed

Read Colossians 3:12–17

Above all, clothe yourselves with love, which binds everything together in perfect harmony. And let the peace of Christ rule in your hearts, to which indeed you were called in the one body. And be thankful.

(verses 14–15)

In the UK, today is the first day back at work for many people who have spent most of the last two weeks celebrating the Christmas season with friends and family. The alarm clock and early commute will be a shock to their system.

I am categorically not a morning person! I really wish I was as it would make my life so much easier, but for me, getting up and out of the house is a struggle. There will often be days where I will have done the bare minimum in order to get out of the door.

This passage from Colossians provides us with a blueprint for how we can include God in our morning routines, even when we are chaotic and running late. The metaphor that Paul uses of followers of Christ 'clothing' themselves with compassion, kindness, humility, meekness and patience is an excellent model for prayers that we can say as we prepare for the day.

As you physically get dressed, allow yourself to spiritually clothe yourself in the Christian qualities that you should embody today. Who are you struggling with? Where is forgiveness needed? Who do you love? Where in your life do you need peace? What are you thankful for this morning? What song is rising from your throat as you prepare for the day ahead?

Perhaps there's a spot where you could place these verses where you'll see them in your morning routine – on a bathroom mirror or the kitchen fridge? Ground your working day in the discipline of Christ and see what impact it has.

† Loving God, break through into our busy lives. Give us space to look to you at the beginning of each new day and clothe us again in the Christ-like gifts we need to do your work.

For further thought

How could you incorporate clothing yourself for Christ into your morning routine?

Wednesday 4 January

Trust for the future

Read Proverbs 3:5–8

Trust in the LORD with all your heart, and do not rely on your own insight. In all your ways acknowledge him, and he will make straight your paths.

(verses 5–6)

On New Year's Day 2021, I marked the new year with friends by walking a labyrinth. If you've not encountered one before, it is a physical representation of a spiritual journey. Its path winds in and then out in a beautiful pattern. It might look similar to a maze, but it is not for getting lost in, it's for physically entering into a journey with God.

This particular labyrinth is made of chalk, on some reclaimed wasteland next to a railway line that carries commuters into central London. It's on the edge of Tower Hamlets cemetery, a Victorian graveyard in the heart of East London, which is now a park and nature reserve.

The day of 1 January 2021 dawned grey and cold and London was in the midst of another Covid-19 lockdown. As we walked into the centre of the labyrinth, we brought before God those things we wanted to lay down; on the way out we concentrated on what God was saying to us in light of what we'd laid down. We walked slowly, at a distance from each other. It gave me space to straighten out some of my thoughts.

I find the psalmist's words a little misleading. The path we travel with God winds up and down, through light and darkness. A straight path could get rather dull! But the important message is that we do not need to rely on our own insight. Our thoughts get muddled and we can blind ourselves to God's path – but if we take time to listen, our insight can be clarified by God.

† Find a labyrinth – online there is a directory of ones open to the public; you can also print one off and trace the journey with your finger. Take yourself on a spiritual journey with God today.

For further thought

If there isn't a labyrinth near you, research how you could create one (permanent or temporary).

Thursday 5 January

The way ahead

Read Isaiah 43:18–21

Do not remember the former things, or consider the things of old. I am about to do a new thing; now it springs forth, do you not perceive it?

(verses 18–19)

Do you still use a paper diary? Have you started a brand new one, full of empty pages, this week? I transitioned to an electronic diary some years ago (it's much more convenient for my life) but I do miss the physical symbolism of empty pages, ready to be filled with the activities of the coming year. Perhaps you journal and, like me, love the feeling of starting a new notebook, ready to be filled with thoughts and encounters with God. To me, blank pages bring a sense of optimism for the new.

Scripture contains a series of reminders of God's gift at bringing about the new – right from creation in Genesis 1; through the land promised to Israel; and the new covenant embodied in Christ's resurrection. While history and tradition are key elements of salvation history, so too is God's ability to do a new thing again and again.

We can sometimes get too attached to the things of old – whether it's old patterns of behaviour, old beliefs, or things that simply weigh us down. It is a human failing that we have seen throughout history. But God calls us to forget the old so that we can recognise what is new. Isaiah is speaking to those who have been captive in Babylon so long that they have lost hope in anything new. A way will be made for them in the wilderness.

† God of the new, help me to let go of the things of old that hold me back. Open my eyes to see the new thing you are doing before me.

For further thought

On a blank page, write out the 'former things' that are weighing you down. Offer them to God in prayer.

Friday 6 January

Start small

Read Luke 13:18–21

What is the kingdom of God like? And to what should I compare it? It is like a mustard seed that someone took and sowed in the garden; it grew and became a tree, and the birds of the air made nests in its branches.

(verses 18–19)

Last year, my 3-year-old niece brought home a broad-bean seed planted into a small plant pot. It was placed on the kitchen windowsill and its progress was monitored. My sister hasn't inherited our parents' green fingers (neither have I!) so photos and questions were regularly sent to 'Grandad' so he could advise on next steps – like planting it in a bigger pot and adding a stake for support as it grew. In just a few weeks, this plant had grown taller than my niece. Within a couple of months, it bore fruit.

From something very small, and with very little effort or skill, a fruitful plant was produced. Mustard trees or bushes are not common in the UK, but in their natural habitat they're planted as a means of providing shade in dry climates and very little is needed for the tiny seed to grow into a tree that is over 20 feet tall.

I know enough about gardening to know that low-maintenance plants are rare. But this is precisely why Jesus uses it to demonstrate the nature of God's kingdom, and how it can grow from even the tiniest seed.

At the start of this year, it's a good opportunity to review what you are doing to plant tiny seeds of the kingdom. Evangelism can feel like a massive challenge, but Jesus' illustration of the mustard seed reminds us that God's kingdom can grow from the smallest start.

† Creator God, please continue to cultivate the seed of faith within me and show me the times and places where I might plant the seeds of your kingdom.

For further thought

Take a walk in your neighbourhood and look for signs of new life and growth. Where can you see God at work?

Saturday 7 January

'The work of Christmas begins ...'

Read Luke 4:16–21

The eyes of all in the synagogue were fixed on him. Then he began to say to them, 'Today this scripture has been fulfilled in your hearing.'

(verses 20b–21)

At Christmas, the image of Jesus that is at the forefront of the celebrations is a baby lying in a manger. God became human in the form of a helpless baby. It's a very easy image to get on board with as babies are almost universally adored.

But Jesus the Messiah is not meant to be palatable. His incarnation was intended to be a disruptive event in the history of salvation, not a crowd-pleaser. We begin to understand this in scripture when Jesus speaks in the temple in his home town.

Before the people of Nazareth, Jesus reads the words of Isaiah 61 – a prophecy of the long-awaited Messiah. There is no doubt what Jesus intended by doing this, as he tells them that the prophecy has been fulfilled in front of them.

Jesus is not the Messiah that Israel was expecting. They had not anticipated a baby born in a humble manger. Nor did they expect it to be the local carpenter's son. They wanted a king, a warrior who could free them from Roman imperialism.

Part of our challenge in more secular societies is to help people get beyond baby Jesus and understand who the meek and mild child grew into. Talking about Jesus and our faith can feel easier at Christmas, but Jesus is for life, not just for Christmas!

† Jesus, Son of God, help us to demonstrate your identity to those around us all year round, not just at Christmas. Especially where there might be opposition to him.

For further thought

Go back and read Isaiah 61 to remind yourself of the ways in which Jesus fulfilled Isaiah's prophecy.

Biblical library (1)

Poetry: singing the Lord's song

Notes by **Catherine Williams**

Catherine Williams is an Anglican priest who works as a freelance Spiritual Director, Retreat Conductor and Writer. She writes biblical reflections for a variety of publications and is the lead voice on the Church of England's Daily Prayer App. Living in the English town of Tewkesbury, Catherine is married to Paul, also a priest, and they have two adult children. For leisure, Catherine enjoys reading, singing, theatre, cinema, and poetry. She keeps chickens and is passionate about butterfly conservation. Catherine has used the NRSVA for these notes.

Sunday 8 January

Thanksgiving and praise

Read Exodus 15:1–18

The Lord is my strength and my might, and he has become my salvation.

(verse 2)

This week we explore the genre of poetry within biblical writing, as seen in poems and songs. During the week we will encounter passages written to give individual and communal expression to a wide range of responses to God, including lament, celebration, restoration and love. Today's song from Exodus is sung by Moses, Miriam and the Israelites as they stand on the far side of the Red Sea, safe from Egyptian oppression and freed from slavery. What starts as an individual response – 'my salvation' – becomes communal as the singers recognise that the whole people of Israel have been redeemed and led to safety. Songs are for singing together. They unite us as we mourn, rejoice, praise and give thanks to God. They also function to keep alive stories and events from the history of our family, community or nation. Those who were liberated from Egypt taught the song of Moses and Miriam to their children and children's children so that the generations to come remembered God's steadfast love towards their ancestors and thus themselves. Biblical songs and psalms, together with hymns and contemporary worship songs, help to build, renew and sustain the body of Christ throughout the world.

† Lord God, thank you that your people find faithful expression in poetry and song. Keep each of us singing your songs of praise, thanksgiving and lament, so everyone may hear of your steadfast love.

Monday 9 January

Bless the Lord!

Read Judges 5:1–12

… you arose, Deborah, arose as a mother in Israel.

(verse 7b)

Today we join with Deborah, judge and prophet, to sing a great song of victory. Seated under her palm tree, Deborah summoned Barak, offering him the Lord's commission to lead the Israelites into battle against the Canaanites. Barak agreed to go if Deborah went with him. Together they entered the battle, but it was another woman – Jael – who brought about the victory by despatching the enemy leader, Sisera, with a tent-peg. Deborah's song records the victory, which is framed as cosmic. The elements – rain and earthquake – herald Yahweh's arrival from Mount Sinai to win this great battle. Deborah is lauded as a 'mother in Israel': one who leads, teaches and nurtures her people, with wisdom and spiritual guidance. Several times, Deborah sings: 'Bless the Lord.' This song is one of the earliest songs in the Hebrew Bible. Written to celebrate a particular event, some of the references are now obscure. But we can appreciate the confidence and delight that celebrates the victory of two courageous women.

Do you have a great moment in the story of your family, clan or tribe that you recall when together? Perhaps it is a miraculous survival, a fresh beginning in a new place, a resolving of a significant matter, or a triumph of some sort, where someone has overcome difficulties and been brave and steadfast. We all have moments of celebration in our lives. At such times, it's important to remember that little phrase: 'Bless the Lord' – acknowledging God who is with us in good times and bad, promising not to let us go, come what may.

† O God, you are with me throughout life's joys and challenges. May I bless your name in all things, trusting your power to save.

For further thought

Think of the women you know in leadership roles. Give thanks for them and, if appropriate, contact one to show your appreciation.

Tuesday 10 January

Far from home

Read Psalm 137:1–9

How could we sing the Lord's song in a foreign land?

(verse 4)

Carried into captivity in Babylon, the Israelites gathered by the river to worship and weep.

Weeping for the death of loved ones. Weeping for the loss of everything they owned. Weeping for the destruction of Jerusalem. Weeping over the agony of their captivity. Weeping for a future that seemed bleak. Their captors tormented them, saying: 'Sing us one of your great songs from home.' Remembering this, the Israelites recalled: 'How could we sing the Lord's song in a foreign land?' Psalm 137 is a psalm of lament, a communal outpouring of grief, loss and anger. Those who are being oppressed in Babylon voice their longing for revenge, wishing violent death on the generations to come. This can be hard for us to hear, but we need to appreciate the context of intense suffering in which this psalm was conceived.

People oppressed or enslaved have often developed songs to express their condition, lament their slavery or cry out to God for liberation. African American spirituals, blues, soul and reggae all take their origin from slavery, oppression or colonialism. People have learnt to sing the Lord's song in difficult and challenging places, far from home, and have discovered in so doing that songs infused with suffering and grief have a new key, tone or rhythm, as God is experienced in fresh ways or more deeply. How is suffering or oppression expressed in your culture? Are there particular songs or poetry that resonate with these experiences in your life, or the life of your family or nation? What does your song of oppression sound like?

† Lord, help me to stay faithful when times are challenging. Wherever I find myself, may I always sing your song of love and freedom.

For further thought

Play some music that has its origins in suffering and lament. Think about ways in which you or your community could help relieve suffering in your area.

Wednesday 11 January

From tears to laughter

Read Psalm 126

The Lord *has done great things for us, and we rejoiced.*

(verse 3)

Today's song is one of the Psalms of Ascent that pilgrims to Jerusalem would have sung as they approached the temple. It's a song that records a journey – the movement from sorrow to joy, from tears to laughter. It's a song of restoration, celebrating the liberation and return of the Israelites from captivity in Babylon. They remember all the 'great things' that the Lord has done, and recognise that in God's economy seeds sown in adversity can lead to an abundant, joy-filled harvest. In Judaism, this psalm is sung as grace after meals, on the Sabbath and at festivals, giving thanks for God's provision.

This psalm also prefigures the Christian experience of the journey from crucifixion to resurrection: death to life. The tears of the disciples on Good Friday are turned to abundant joy on Easter Sunday, as God makes the impossible possible, raising Jesus to new life. Do you have a story in your family or community history where God has intervened during a time of great difficulty and sorrow to bring a fresh start filled with new life? God may have acted creatively or surprisingly, in ways you couldn't possibly imagine, bringing life, healing and restoration. These are the stories we need to celebrate. Such stories enable us to carry hope both for ourselves and for others when times are challenging. Reminding ourselves that God is at work even in the darkest of places, when a way forward seems impossible helps us to remain steadfast and faithful. Tiny seeds sown in cold earth really can become a harvest of great blessing.

† Lord God, teach me to watch for, celebrate and join in with your renewing action in the world.

For further thought

What are you grateful for? Make a list of all the 'great things' that God has done for you and your family. Take time to give thanks for each one.

Thursday 12 January

Unmuted praise

Luke 1:68–79

And you, child, shall be called the prophet of the Most High; for you will go before the Lord to prepare his ways.

(verse 76)

Recently I undertook the full Spiritual Exercises of St Ignatius, which required me to spend almost five weeks in silence. It was an extraordinary experience, and when I returned to my everyday life I found that, for a while, I was very thoughtful about what I said. My words were measured and centred on Jesus, with whom I had walked very closely. I didn't say more than I needed to, and I have continued to enjoy periods of deep silence, peppered with gratitude and praise to God.

Previous to today's passage, Zechariah has been silent for nine months, struck dumb for questioning the angel Gabriel's seemingly impossible good news. Now that his son has been born and Zechariah has confirmed his name as 'John' in writing, his tongue is set free and he immediately praises God long and loud. Filled with the Holy Spirit, Zechariah utters prophecy, singing of the role his son will fulfil in preparing the way for the Messiah – Jesus. This song, like Mary's earlier in this chapter of Luke, acts as a bridge between the Old and New Testaments, looking back to promises made and forward to their fulfilment. How wonderful that after so many months of silence Zechariah's first words are used to praise and exalt God, celebrating the birth of his son and the beginning of a new era of prophecy. Hope has been kept alive. In what ways can you see God's promise of love and new life being fulfilled in yourself, your family and your community? Which song is God calling you to sing?

† Lord God, thank you that we see your promises fulfilled in Jesus. Help us to share this hope with all those we meet.

For further thought

Spend some time in silence listening to God, and thinking about the way you use words. End your time of silence by singing your favourite hymn or song of praise.

Friday 13 January

Seeking a comforter

Read Lamentations 1:1–22

For these things I weep; my eyes flow with tears; for a comforter is far from me, one to revive my courage; my children are desolate, for the enemy has prevailed.

(verse 16)

Today's passage takes us back again to the time when the Israelites have been taken into captivity in Babylon, and the great city of Jerusalem ransacked. The writer imagines Jerusalem as a woman grieving the loss of her children. She weeps bitterly and nothing brings consolation or comfort. The passage is full of emotive language, with words such as 'groaning', 'suffering', 'tears' and 'sorrow'. It's written as an acrostic poem, each of the twenty-two verses beginning with a different letter of the Hebrew alphabet. It's as if the pain and mourning run on for ever: from A to Z. The poem is a lament in which Jerusalem pleads to God for mercy, as she mourns over all that has brought her to this place of desolation. She longs for a comforter.

The devastation of Jerusalem in 587 BC was a catastrophe that significantly shaped the history of God's people. Modern-day catastrophes such as terrorist attacks, floods, famines or the Covid-19 pandemic shape our generation and call forth from us questions and concerns as we puzzle over suffering and evil. Before rushing on to rebuilding lives and communities it's important to pause and lament, expressing our pain and distress and calling for comfort and reassurance from God, who promises to bring resurrection and new life from the most devastating of events, both personal and communal. Moreover, as Christians, we have the gift of the Holy Spirit with us and for us, bringing guidance, counsel and comfort. This precious gift of God the Comforter is to be shared with those around us, keeping hope alive and bringing healing and new life.

† Holy Spirit, breathe your comfort and counsel into the broken and despairing places of our world.

For further thought

In what ways have you experienced the Holy Spirit as Comforter? Think of ways to show this comfort to those in your community who are grieving or broken at this time.

Saturday 14 January

A love song

Song of Solomon 2:10–14

The flowers appear on the earth; the time of singing has come.

(verse 12)

After a week of laments and songs of celebration, victory and restoration, we end with a love song. The Song of Solomon (also known as the Song of Songs) is a collection of passionate love poetry that can be read on a variety of levels. On the one hand, it is the simple poetry of two lovers; on the other, it is the allegory of the soul on its journey to union with the Divine, and a foretaste of the love Christ has for his beloved bride, the church. Today's beautiful passage is often read at weddings, Jewish and Christian.

The lover calls to his beloved to rise up and come away. The season is changing. Cold, damp, fruitless winter is over, and the air is full of the promise of new life. Flowers appear, the birds are calling, fruit ripening and it's a time for singing with joy and delight. The lover tells the beloved that her voice is sweet and her face lovely. We can hear the joy and excitement of fresh love given and received. Lovers long to be together and can't help but gaze on each other.

How does this poem make you feel? Can you identify with the lovers? Is this something you have experienced with another person? Are these feelings of love and longing present in your relationship with God? We are God's beloved. God calls us to rise and come, to seek deeper experiences of divine love. God gazes on us, sees the beautiful person we are becoming, and loves us utterly. How do you respond to this love?

† Thank you, Lord, that you love me without beginning or end. Help me to love you in return with trust, passion and commitment.

For further thought

Play or sing your favourite love song. Imagine yourself and God singing this song together. Now imagine God singing similar love songs to the whole of creation.

The Gospel of Matthew (1)

1 Starting afresh

Notes by **Peter Langerman**

Peter is a pastor in a Presbyterian church in Durbanville, Cape Town, and from 2018 to 2021 he was the Moderator of the General Assembly of the Uniting Presbyterian Church in South Africa. He is married to Sally, and they have four daughters. Peter is passionate about the dynamic rule and reign of God. He believes that God invites all to be part of God's transformative mission through love, and that the most potent and powerful agent for the transformation of local communities is the local church living out faithfulness to God. Peter has used the NIVUK for these notes.

Sunday 15 January

Repent

Read Matthew 3:1–6

In those days John the Baptist came, preaching in the wilderness of Judea and saying, 'Repent, for the kingdom of heaven has come near.'

(verse 1)

When I was much younger and a member of the Boys Brigade, we had to do an orienteering badge. In order to earn this badge, we were dropped off in an unknown area in the bush, given a map and a compass and we had to find our way from point to point until we arrived at our destination. The plan was simple, but what was not known was that the person who had drawn up the orienteering points had made a mistake. So our small group ended up a way away from where we should have been, completely lost, and those who had responsibility for us had no idea where we were. We eventually managed to find a farmhouse and phone for help. All's well that ended well and we got our badges.

I was reminded of this as I reread this passage. The Jewish people had not had a prophetic word for 400 years and they must have felt spiritually lost. That's like no new music being written from the time of Bach's Brandenburg Concerto until today. What John offered to the people of his day was new beginning.

What a great way to begin a new year.

† Lord, thank you for the opportunities to begin again at the start of this year. Help me to understand that the best is yet to come.

Monday 16 January

Holy Spirit and fire

Read Matthew 3:7–12

I baptise you with water for repentance. But after me comes one who is more powerful than I, whose sandals I am not worthy to carry. He will baptise you with the Holy Spirit and fire. His winnowing fork is in his hand.

(verses 11–12)

People wondered if John was the Messiah and it's not hard to see why. Cruelly suffering under Roman occupation, struggling to rediscover their national identity, surrounded by political chancers and charlatans, they longed for someone who would set them free and restore them to greatness. John seemed to promise all that. A wild man who preached repentance and offered a brand-new start ticked all the boxes. John, however, was quick to pop that particular balloon and to point to the one who would come after him. He says that he is but the forerunner, the messenger for the Messiah who would baptise people in the Holy Spirit and fire.

After just over a hundred years of Pentecostalism we're now quite familiar with the phrase 'baptized (or filled) with the Holy Spirit', and, depending on your particular tradition, we either welcome it or we're wary of it. But do we ever think of what it means to be baptised in fire?

In Cape Town, where I live, we often have devastating fires, driven by high winds, and it is frightening to watch. Could God really want to subject us to the ravages of fire? Sometimes fire is necessary to clear the ground and create the opportunity for new growth. Sometimes we can't make a new start because there is too much dead wood that needs to be burnt away before the new can come.

† Lord, help me to understand that when you put me through the fire it's to cleanse and make space for you to do a new work in and through me. Help me to trust you when the going is tough.

For further thought

When you have gone through the fire, how difficult was it to keep your focus on God? What helped you to do so and what made it more difficult?

Tuesday 17 January

God is really pleased with you

Read Matthew 3:13–17

As soon as Jesus was baptised, he went up out of the water. At that moment heaven was opened, and he saw the Spirit of God descending like a dove and alighting on him. And a voice from heaven said, 'This is my Son, whom I love; with him I am well pleased.'

(verses 16–17)

John did not expect Jesus to come to him to be baptised. In the first place, John was clear that he was preparing people for Jesus – if anything, Jesus should baptise John and not the other way around. Second, John knew that Jesus was sinless and there was nothing for which Jesus had to repent – why then would Jesus need to be baptised?

So John is taken aback, but we may also wonder at this scene – why would Jesus have to go through this? For at least two reasons. First, Jesus is baptised by John to identify fully with sinful humanity. Just as the sin was washed off the people as they went into the Jordan, Jesus picks up their sin and carries it with him to the cross. Second, Jesus is baptised by John because even Jesus needed to be filled with the Holy Spirit in preparation for what he was to face, and even Jesus had to hear the words of affirmation from God the Father before he launched into his public ministry.

It is a such comfort for us to know, when we feel weak and alone, that even Jesus needed strengthening and affirmation to be able to accomplish the tasks that were ahead for him. And to know that the words of affirmation spoken to Jesus are spoken to us as well.

† Lord, help me to hear your word of affirmation and acceptance over all the clamour and noise that keep telling me that I'm not good enough.

For further thought

Take a look in a mirror and look closely at yourself. Instead of seeing all the flaws and imperfections, hear God say, 'I love you and am well pleased with you.'

Wednesday 18 January

It is written ...

Read Matthew 4:1–11

It is written: 'Man shall not live on bread alone, but on every word that comes from the mouth of God.' ... It is also written: 'Do not put the Lord your God to the test.' ... Away from me, Satan! For it is written: 'Worship the Lord your God, and serve him only.'

(verses 4, 7, 10)

The fact that Jesus was tempted by the devil, immediately after having been filled with the Spirit, could either comfort us or frighten us. It is comforting to know that Jesus can identify with us when we are tempted since he was tempted in the same way that we are. It is frightening to think that Jesus was tempted immediately after he was filled and empowered by the Holy Spirit. When we pray for an empowering or infilling of the Holy Spirit, we seldom reflect that when God does answer that prayer, we might face incredible temptations afterwards.

What should also give us hope is that Jesus overcame the temptation by quoting from the Hebrew Bible – three passages from two chapters in Deuteronomy. When we are faced with temptation, Jesus gives us the way in which to deal with temptation: being grounded and assured of God's word. The impression is that Jesus had been meditating on these portions of scripture and, as a result, when he was tempted by the evil one he was prepared to answer in a way that sent the accuser away with his tail between his legs. All of this leads to the obvious question: when we are tempted, how steeped are we in scripture and to what extent are we filled with the Spirit so that we are able to deal with the temptations and not fall prey to them?

† Lord, help me when I am tempted to rely on your word and the indwelling of your Spirit, instead of my own willpower, to carry me through.

For further thought

How good is your biblical knowledge? Have you ever thought of doing a course or signing up for a programme to deepen your knowledge of the Bible?

Thursday 19 January

The unexpected God

Read Matthew 4:12–17

When Jesus heard that John had been put in prison, he withdrew to Galilee ... From that time on Jesus began to preach, 'Repent, for the kingdom of heaven has come near.'

(verses 12, 17)

Jesus' behaviour might strike us as a bit strange. John was his cousin, a person with whom he must have been quite close as they grew up together. John, being slightly older, began his earthly ministry before Jesus, but Jesus came to John to be baptised. After this, many of John's disciples became disciples of Jesus, something John welcomed, saying famously, 'He must become greater and I less.'

John's message was a message of repentance in the light of the coming of God's kingdom. Now John has been arrested for speaking truth to power, but Jesus does not go to him. In fact, Jesus heads as far away from John as he can get, heading north to Galilee while John was in prison in the south. Then Jesus begins his public ministry with exactly the same words as John. Was Jesus not coasting on John's success and popularity while John languished in prison?

Sometimes God's ways seem strange to us and we struggle to find a reason behind God's actions. We have no indication of whether John struggled with any of these thoughts. Probably he did not. He knew that Jesus was the Messiah who had been promised and he knew that his task had been completed. Now he awaited the outcome with a sense of peace, knowing that he had done what God required of him. How wonderful it would be if each of us could face the end of our lives with such peace and calm. Assured that we had done what God called us to do and that we had finished the tasks God had given us to do.

† Lord, help me never to envy the success of those I have mentored and trained and become bitter when they appear to do better than me. Help me to genuinely celebrate their successes.

For further thought

Is there someone of whom you have been jealous because they seem to be doing better at life than you? What would it take to admit that to yourself and let it go?

Friday 20 January

The cost of non-discipleship

Read Matthew 4:18–22

'Come, follow me,' Jesus said, 'and I will send you out to fish for people.' At once they left their nets and followed him ... Jesus called them, and immediately they left the boat and their father and followed him.

(verses 19–20, 21b–22)

You have to feel for the fathers of Peter and Andrew, James and John. Being fishermen themselves, they must have both been thrilled when they had two sons each. Their legacy was ensured, their business's future was guaranteed. They would train their sons in their own trade, how to fish in the unpredictable waters of the Sea of Galilee, and one day they could retire, secure in the knowledge their sons could take over and run the business. They had a sound business model and a structured succession plan in place. They might have felt a little troubled when their sons showed some interest in John the Baptiser, but they returned when John was put in prison and life went on as it had done before. Then Jesus arrives, calls the two sets of brothers, and they leave everything just there and follow him.

Perhaps this story scares you a little and perhaps it should. We have become so used to watering down Jesus' call to discipleship that in many cases we have a model of discipleship that costs us nothing. This is not what we find in the Gospels. The disciples knew too well that the decision to follow Jesus and become his disciple meant leaving behind all other attachments. And what if they had not done this? They would have missed out on the greatest adventure of their lives. The cost of discipleship may be high, but the cost of non-discipleship is incalculable.

† Lord, help me to see that when you call me it's always to a future that I can't see but you already know. Help me to follow you even when I don't know exactly where I will end up.

For further thought

Is there anything keeping you from making the decision to lay it all down and follow Jesus? Are you prepared to give all up and follow him today?

Saturday 21 January

Proclamation and demonstration

Read Matthew 4:23–25

Jesus went throughout Galilee, teaching in their synagogues, proclaiming the good news of the kingdom, and healing every disease and illness among the people.

(verse 23)

Many people who are not people of faith or church people are often intrigued by Jesus, as they are by many other significant historical figures. They are often interested in the teachings of Jesus; they are fascinated by him as a person worthy of a certain amount of attention. When asked, they will say something along the lines of, 'Well, I don't have much time for Christians, but I do like Jesus. He is such a great historical figure and an insightful teacher.' They would stop short of according to Jesus the biblical status of the Son of God and, while they may acknowledge his death, they will certainly baulk at any suggestion that he rose from the dead and is alive today.

The odd things is that 'great historical figure' and 'insightful teacher' are not anywhere close to the view of Jesus we get from the New Testament. Yes, Jesus did teach, but in almost every case the Bible tells us that in addition to his teaching he went about healing the sick, casting out demons and even raising people from the dead. These were not sideshows in the ministry of Jesus, but part and parcel of his mission. The other interesting thing is that when the disciples began to preach salvation in and through Jesus, they did not focus on his teachings at all. Their sole focus was on his resurrection from the dead and it was this claim that got them into trouble. So let's put aside the romantic notion of who we think Jesus is and assess him on who he claimed to be: the Son of God and God in human form.

† Lord Jesus, help me to remember that you are the one who changed human lives while you walked the earth, and you still do that today. Help me to trust you for a miracle today.

For further thought

Can you trust Jesus enough to present him with the burdens you carry and allow him to take them from you, leaving you free and unencumbered?

The Gospel of Matthew (1)

2 Teaching the kingdom

Notes by **Tim Yau**

Tim Yau is a Pioneer Missioner for the Anglican Diocese of Norwich, encouraging missional practice: 'not trying to get people to go to church, but trying to get the church to go to the people'. He's one of the few Chinese heritage priests in the Church of England and wants to see more minority ethnic vocations, believing, 'To be it, you have to see it.' Often found immersed in the latest sci-fi epic, he dreams of being a superhero. Tim has used the NIVUK for these notes.

Sunday 22 January

Happiness Hill

Read Matthew 5:1–12

Now when Jesus saw the crowds, he went up on a mountainside and sat down. His disciples came to him, and he began to teach them. He said: 'Blessed …'

(verses 1–3a)

This week we will be exploring the 'Sermon on the Mount' (Matthew 5 – 7): Jesus' response to the religious teaching of the day on various moral issues and how he envisaged them through the lens of the kingdom of God. The writer of the Gospel tells us that Jesus has been teaching, proclaiming and healing, and that large crowds from across the nation followed him (Matthew 4:23–25). Now Jesus climbs a mountain, reframing Moses' Sinai ascension to receive God's commandments, yet this time the multitude are brought near to hear God's new revelation directly. Now God's people don't need a prophet mediator because Jesus *is* Immanuel, God with us (Matthew 1:23), and therefore his words are the living law.

However, Jesus doesn't open with ten renewed commandments but nine blessings, which is where we get the word 'beatitude', deriving from the Latin *beatus*. These blessings are characterised by happiness and promises of being highly favoured by divine grace. But they're not an aspirational tick-list of things to do to achieve spiritual enlightenment, comparable to the Buddhist Noble Eightfold Path. Instead, they're saying that those who already are like that are inhabiting God's kingdom way; therefore they should be happy and celebrate.

† Lord Jesus Christ, help us to recognise God's kingdom working in our lives and embrace your blessed promises to us now and in eternity. Amen

Monday 23 January

Live the light

Read Matthew 5:13–16

In the same way, let your light shine before others, that they may see your good deeds and glorify your Father in heaven.

(verse 16)

The night air temperature was dropping and it was getting darker by the minute. What had started as an evening stroll was beginning to get treacherous. I stumbled over the loose rocks and ragged heather knowing full well that the Cornish cliff tops were nearby and that I'd lost the path some time back. My shins were scratched from the thorns and the reality of my self-made predicament was creeping in: at this hour no one would see or hear me fall, and no one knew where I was.

Thankfully, a faint glimmer of light bled through the bracken and brambles piercing my shadowy reverie; it was coming from the top of the hill. I pushed on upwards, getting stung by nettles but spurred on by hope. Finally, I crested the hill and found myself at a bright and welcoming pub next to a well-lit road and a safe way back to my holiday accommodation. I was saved.

The UK is well illuminated at night, so much so that we talk about 'light pollution', and some parts of the country are being designated 'dark sky discovery sites' so that we can experience the stars and give nocturnal creatures space. However, in first-century Palestine light at night was a precious commodity, something to be shared.

God declared that the people of Israel had a role as a light to the nations (Isaiah 42:6; 49:6). In John's Gospel, Jesus describes himself as the light of the world (John 8:12); now he passes on the light of hope and salvation to his followers, and subsequently to us.

† Lord Jesus Christ, Light of the World, shine for us, in us and through us, so that as we are blessed by your divine light, we might bless others too. Amen

For further thought

When you share your light through words and actions, whose image and reputation is highlighted – God's or yours? What's stopping you from shining your light?

Tuesday 24 January

Living law

Read Matthew 5:17–20

Do not think that I have come to abolish the Law or the Prophets; I have not come to abolish them but to fulfil them.

(verse 17)

In 1977 a new British comic book character made his debut in the science fiction world – Judge Dredd. Since then, he's starred in two eponymous Hollywood movies, several computer games and still remains a print favourite of fans. Dredd inhabits a dystopian future city called Mega-City One, where street Judges are law enforcement and judicial officers empowered to arrest, convict, sentence and execute criminals as they see fit. Dredd is the toughest and strictest of all the Judges and his catchphrase is 'I am the law!'

Dredd embodies a heartless penal code: there are no grey areas in his worldview; there is no appealing to his humanity, once you cross the line, you're a criminal and legal justice is served.

In today's reading, Jesus says that he has come to fulfil the law – thankfully it is not the way of Dredd but the way of love. At the time, Jewish law was the Torah, the 'five books of Moses', the first five books of the Old Testament. However, it also became shorthand for the whole developing Jewish legal tradition, written and oral. The Pharisees and the teachers of the law gave these wider teachings an elevated, almost divine, status. This is what Jesus challenged.

Jesus was the incarnation of the law, but not of excessive adherence to a set of rules, but a life of God's grace pointing to a time of God's rule on earth – the kingdom of God. This will not be achieved by slavishly following religious regulations to acquire righteousness but by transformed hearts that overflow with love for God and humanity.

† Almighty God, you did not send your son into the world to condemn the world, but to save the world through him. Help us to live in that freedom for the sake of others. Amen

For further thought

How do you feel about God being judge? How do you deal with guilt? How does God's unconditional love change your perceptions of divine judgement?

Wednesday 25 January
Appetite for anger

Read Matthew 5:21–26

But I tell you that anyone who is angry with a brother or sister will be subject to judgment.

(verse 22)

He looked ashamed. There was no defiance or anger in his eyes, just regret. A night on the town led to hasty words and an altercation where an angry outburst escalated to an impulsive punch being thrown. This scenario is often repeated, where young people are letting off steam after a week of work. However, this time it ended with a dead man and a young life in prison.

I'd known the offender since he was a boy, he'd grown up in a Christian family and I'd been his youth leader at church. He'd always been impulsive; I remember taking him to hospital when we were away at youth camp. We'd been playing a night game that involved hiding and being caught. He was surrounded, but instead of surrendering he'd leapt out of a tree to evade capture and damaged his ankle.

As he got older, he'd drifted away from church and with it the loving relationships and accountability structure. When impulsiveness connects with a flash of anger, regrettable things can happen. The book of Proverbs says, 'A quick-tempered person does foolish things' (Proverbs 14:17a).

In one sense there's nothing wrong with anger, it's a normal human response to unfair or unjust circumstances – see Jesus' turning over the tables in the temple (Matthew 21:13). However, when anger is unchecked and actions impetuous, then problems occur. Nevertheless, Jesus goes further than the teaching of the day, prohibiting anger altogether. The anger he refers to is the brooding bitterness against a fellow believer. This is a sin because it violates God's command to love one another.

† Jesus, help us to get rid of all bitterness, rage, anger, brawling, slander and every form of malice. So that we can be kind and compassionate, forgiving each other, just as you forgave us. Amen

For further thought

What do you do with your anger? Who can you open up to about it? Who in church do you need to make peace with?

Thursday 26 January

Lust and love

Read Matthew 5:27–32

But I tell you that anyone who looks at a woman lustfully has already committed adultery with her in his heart.

(verse 28)

'Look at this!' We gathered around the magazine we'd found; there was an air of excitement and puzzlement over the glossy images of naked women. This was something beyond our juvenile, naive understanding, but somehow we knew it was illicit and something to be hidden.

Today pornography is endemic, sexual images and films are free and easy to access over the internet. The lust economy is booming, it's a global multi-billion-dollar industry. Where once it used to be something shameful, now it is often celebrated as the emancipation of sexual appetites.

I had a conversation about pornography with a reasonable and articulate young man. He argued that using pornography doesn't really hurt anybody. How wrong could he be! There's a common misapprehension that the actors are willing participants. However, because the majority of online content is unregulated, it is wide open to abuse and the coercion of mainly young women being manipulated to perform. The industry seems to be built upon damaging damaged people.

Also, the effect of objectifying people in a purely sexual framework dehumanises them and therefore the consumer. The concept that this is not a person but a method for sexual gratification infects our psyche. Lust is unsatisfiable, it always wants more. Lust diminishes our capacity to love, because lust consumes while love creates.

Again, Jesus goes further than the teaching of his day and highlights the hidden lust in our hearts. He uses figurative language to state the seriousness of his teaching, but the meaning is clear: do not tolerate unchecked lust in our lives as it'll destroy us.

† Lord Jesus, you said blessed are the pure in heart, for they will see God. Help us to pursue love and not lust; open our eyes to see your divine image in all people. Amen

For further thought

What do you do with your lust? Who can you open up to about it? What can you do to help free people from pornography?

Friday 27 January

Rethink revenge

Read Matthew 5:33–42

But I tell you, do not resist an evil person. If anyone slaps you on the right cheek, turn to them the other cheek also.

(verse 39)

In adolescence I grew up on a diet of Hong Kong, straight-to-video, kung-fu movies with exciting titles like *Snake in the Monkey's Shadow*. The stories usually followed the same basic plot: a young man's family or girlfriend or kung-fu teacher is violated, killed or dishonoured, so the inexperienced protagonist sets off on a martial arts journey of self-discovery. The hero finds a new kung-fu master. Then there's a long, arduous and complicated training montage, followed by prolonged elaborate and acrobatic fight scenes, where finally the newly trained disciple delivers his deadly technique and revenge is served.

Revenge films are not just the premise of Chinese kung-fu films; you're also likely to see it in a Bollywood musical or a Hollywood action blockbuster. Seemingly, the common response to violence, hatred and injustice is revenge – get them back as good as, or even better than, they got you. We see this played out not just in fiction but from childhood sibling rivalry all the way up to international geopolitical hostility.

Jesus quotes the 'law of retaliation' (Exodus 21:24), the like-for-like punishment was supposed to limit vengeance. However, you can't legislate for the human heart, and bitterness around injustices easily becomes a legacy of unresolved dispute. So, Jesus subverts this teaching on religious restitution by urging his hearers not to 'resist'. At face value this teaching seems to be giving in to persecutors. However, Jesus calls us to rise above signs of contempt and not pursue our legal rights, thus breaking the cycle of violence – the way of the cross instead of the way of revenge.

† Lord Jesus, give us courage to stand up to intimidation and break cycles of injustice and violence with the fruit of the Spirit: with love, joy, peace, forbearance, kindness, goodness, faithfulness, gentleness and self-control. Amen

For further thought

God says: 'It is mine to avenge; I will repay' (Deuteronomy 32:35a). How will you trust God with your historic and present injustices and injuries?

Saturday 28 January
Friending foes

Read Matthew 5:43–48

But I tell you, love your enemies and pray for those who persecute you, that you may be children of your Father in heaven.

(verses 44–45a)

I'm an Anglo-Chinese, Anglican priest living in an affluent middle-class suburb of a secular Western democracy. So, who are my enemies? Well, as far as I'm aware there's no one who personally and openly hates or opposes who I am or what I do. However, there are many groups out there who disagree with some of the aspects of my identity.

Depending on who you listen to there's a long list of possible ideologies I should fear: racists, multiculturalists, the far right, the liberal elite, anti-clericalists, Islamists, Christian fundamentalists, humanists, secularists, new atheists, anarchists, anti-establishmentarianists ... the list goes on and on.

Thankfully, these groups aren't trying to kick down my door in the middle of the night to drag me away, so any talk of Christian persecution in the UK should be taken with a pinch of salt. In many parts of the world, our Christian brothers and sisters face real threats and opposition to practising their faith, sometimes ending in martyrdom.

British culture is transitioning to a post-Christendom society, where the church is no longer at the centre of power; therefore the pains of disentanglement are being felt and the truth of Christian principles are being eroded and challenged, but it's not persecution.

Jesus flipped the received wisdom of his day, commanding his hearers to love their enemies and not hate. We're called to God's kingdom way, one that is impossible to reach without the help of the transforming and empowering Holy Spirit. This love is the overflow of God's love in us that breaks the chains of hate and turns enemies into friends.

† Lord Jesus, you embodied divine love, you stood up to aggression and opposition with grace and truth, and you forgave your executioners with your dying breath. Help us to follow your way of love. Amen.

For further thought

Who are your enemies? What would loving your enemy look like? How can you and your church support persecuted Christians around the world?

Healing divisions

1 Divisions in the Old Testament

Notes by **Immaculée Hedden**

Immaculée Hedden is from Rwanda. She worked for African Revival Ministries, serving as National Intercession Co-ordinator, and then with Youth With A Mission (YWAM) Rwanda before relocating to the UK to work with YWAM England. There she served in reconciliation ministries and in counselling. In England she met her husband Richard, and together they wrote the story, called *Under His Mighty Hand*, of how she survived the 1994 genocide against the Tutsi. They are currently based in Rwanda with YWAM. Immaculée has used the NIV for these notes.

Sunday 29 January

Jacob and Esau

Read Genesis 33:1–11

He himself went on ahead and bowed down to the ground seven times as he approached his brother.

(verse 3)

Jacob showed humility in the face of an encounter with his brother Esau, whose relationship had been broken years before because of his deception. Esau ran to him, and they were reconciled.

Humility, whether expressed through spoken apology, acts of kindness and reparation, or specifically requesting forgiveness, is powerful. It can hold the key to disarming resentment and other barriers to reconciliation with our loved ones.

As I read this scripture, I am reminded of a friend I called who had fled the violence in Rwanda to come and see me again. She came in fear because she was associated with those who carried out the genocide. She feared anger, hostility and revenge because of the killing and violence that had gone on. When I saw her, I hugged her and was so pleased to see her. She was my sister in Christ. After she had gone back to Kenya, she wrote to me and said meeting me had been a healing for her. She knew that not all Tutsi hated her, despite the atrocity of the genocide.

When Jacob and Esau hugged, both wept. This showed the pain of the broken relationship and that healing had begun. God's way never changes. Let us permit ourselves to express these emotions.

† Lord, give us humility, like Jacob. Help us realise we hold an important key to the healing of divisions we experience in our relationships.

Monday 30 January

Joseph and brothers

Read Genesis 50:14–21

What if Joseph holds a grudge against us and pays us back for all the wrongs we did to him?

(verse 15b)

Injustice and violation cause anger, distress and wounding in varying degrees. Joseph was greatly distressed by the betrayal of his brothers when he was sold into slavery, but his subsequent response is a great lesson to us all. His brothers didn't know of his inner transformation and were expecting revenge and payback for their wrongdoing. But there was no feeling of ill will or resentment in Joseph for their past offence. He had the bigger picture of what the Lord had done and was doing through him. There was no room for any grudge. He had won those battles against bitterness, anger and resentment and now was leading his people out of famine and hardship.

Shortly after the genocide ended in Rwanda a pastor came up to me, full of anger and bitterness. He said, 'I don't think God can forgive those people for what they have done to us. Those who are unclean will remain unclean.' 'Well,' I said, 'if they repent, the Lord can forgive them.'

He left angry and didn't even say goodbye.

A couple of years later I met him again. He said, 'Daughter, I was so upset and angry then. I have now forgiven those people who did so much killing. I understand what you meant then, but before I was so hurt.'

I was so pleased that this pastor was not carrying a grudge. Together as the body of Christ we need the godly vision of our lives and nations. What the enemy intends for harm, the Lord intends for good to accomplish what is now being done.

† Lord, open the eyes of our heart to see you and your purpose for our lives. Help us to see the impact of our past injustices. Help us release forgiveness and heal relational divisions that exist.

For further thought

When God forgives us we are fully forgiven. As human beings we sometimes don't forgive ourselves and have slave attitudes. We misunderstand the nature of grace.

Tuesday 31 January
Samuel and Saul

Read 1 Samuel 15:24–31

I was afraid of the people and so I gave in to them.

(verse 24b)

One main root cause of Saul's downfall was his fear of what people might think or do. When Samuel went to anoint him king he hid among the baggage. Later we read that he feared David. This root helps explain much of his subsequent behaviour that caused division in relationships. The fear that should be cherished is the fear of the Lord. If Saul had walked consistently in this, we would have celebrated a different outcome.

That Saul asked forgiveness was great, but we don't read of this being combined with a wholehearted repentance of his fear of people that led him to overcome in this area and which would have allowed reconciliation between himself and David.

Immediately before the genocide against the Tutsi in Rwanda ignited on 6 April 1994, I spent three days of prayer and fasting for my country. During that time the Lord spoke to me on the theme, 'Who are you that you fear mere mortals, human beings who are but grass, that you forget the LORD your Maker, who stretches out the heavens and who lays the foundations of the earth?' (Isaiah 51:12–13). As the Lord spoke to me in such a personal way, it enabled me to keep a fear of the Lord during the time of tribulation and danger I was about to enter.

† Although the reasons we fear people may be understandable, Lord help us to choose to die to that tendency for the better reality of life lived in the fear of the Lord, and set the foundations for the healing of divisions in our relationships.

For further thought

Saul wanted to be honoured before human beings. This was more important for him than to please God. Spend some time considering ways in which we choose to look good to other people rather than to God.

Wednesday 1 February
Saul and David

Read 1 Samuel 19:1–18

As surely as the Lord lives, David will not be put to death.

(verse 6b)

Saul's fluctuating moods made his behaviour inconsistent and at times confusing. The oath he made to David, in the verse we have just read, was no guarantee for his future behaviour.

With my counsellor's hat on I might ask about Saul's childhood, where unresolved wounds might be lurking, or identify insecure attachment that needs fixing. As an intercessor, I seek the strongholds in Saul's life and where he or his ancestors created an open door to evil.

Ultimately there was no healing of the division between David and Saul. No amount of God-fearing behaviour from David was able to bring that about. At some point we may all need to look evil in the face and reconcile ourselves to that reality in this world. We need to leave it to God to deal with it.

The Lord had a plan for David: as surely as the Lord lives, he would not be put to death. Despite the actions that belied these words of Saul, it was the Lord's plan that prevailed.

Midway through the one hundred days of the genocide, when I had to move from my cousin's house to an orphanage 500 meters away, a bomb exploded next to a heavily guarded roadblock. All the militia ran off and I walked through and took refuge at the orphanage. Within half an hour, a lot of killers went to my cousin's house searching for us, but we were not there. God had spoken to me, saying that he would protect me with his right hand (Isaiah 41:10). I am here to testify that he is able to do the same for you.

† Pray for the protection of all those who are in danger because of the evil intent of other people, especially the persecuted church. May the Lord protect us with his right hand.

For further thought

Jonathan and Michal stood against the evil their father intended towards David. In your generation, how can you do the same?

Thursday 2 February
David and Absalom

Read 2 Samuel 14:21–33

Then Joab went to Geshur and brought Absalom back to Jerusalem. But the king said, 'He must go to his own house; he must not see my face.'

(verses 23–24a)

Joab negotiated the return of Absalom from his exile, but division between father and son was not healed. Absalom was not even permitted to see his father for two years after he had returned.

Absalom had murdered his half-brother Amnon as reprisal for the rape of his sister, Tamar. Their father burned with anger at what the sons had done. But Absalom must have felt aggrieved at his father's passivity towards Amnon.

The root of David's problems, his adultery and subsequent murder to cover it, continued to haunt him even though he humbled himself before the Lord. He can be a lesson to us all. We need to be aware of what happened to David's house; the same sins of sexual immorality and murder were repeated in the next generation, and this was a primary cause of the lack of reconciliation.

When these things happen to us, we need to humble ourselves before the Lord and people. Admitting and uncovering our sins brings healing. In Rwanda, I have seen powerful reconciliation when people humbled themselves and took responsibility for what they'd done. One man killed a mother's children and husband. He sent a letter from prison, admitting what he had done and asking for forgiveness. She replied saying she forgave him but took it further. She went to the prison to say that she wanted to adopt him as her son. The government released the man and said, 'Who are we to keep this man in prison? The one he has done wrong to has forgiven him.' He was released and became her son.

† Lord, bring authentic reconciliation and healing to our families and nations.

For further thought

What do you need to do to bring heaven in action and manifest God's grace in divisions around you?

Friday 3 February

Elisha and Naaman

Read 2 Kings 5:1–15

Now I know that there is no God in all the world except in Israel.

(verse 15b)

Elisha's display of power over Naaman's leprosy awakened him to the reality that the God of Israel is the true God. His leprosy was healed. He believed. Jesus later compared this with the unbelief of those inside Israel where no leprosy was healed (Luke 4:27).

The fear, prejudice and mistrust of the King of Israel at Naaman's arrival, and the national pride of Naaman when asked to wash in the Jordan, nearly prevented the healing from occurring. He required humility and obedience, rather than Naaman's expectation of honour and no action on his part. It was the faith of Elisha that brought the miracle, he knew God was able to do something for Naaman.

Some people say that God forgot the land of Rwanda during the terrible days of 1994, but I disagree. I always knew the Lord was with me. Even during the most desperate times when I was holed up in an orphanage seeking refuge and did not have food or water for three days, I knew deep down inside of me that God was making a way for us. As people around me shook with fear and lamented that we were going to die, I said, 'We need to give thanks to the Lord that he has kept us alive until now; we don't know what he can do.' He did make a way for us, and I survived to tell the world of God's display of power on us. Let Naaman's story be a wake-up call for us, so we see what the Lord wants to do and pray it into being.

† Lord, help us to witness to the world that there is no God in all the world other than Father, Son and Holy Spirit.

For further thought

Consider things in your life that may have become other gods. If so, what will be required to remove them?

Saturday 4 February

Daniel and the officers

Read Daniel 6:1–23

Daniel answered, 'May the king live forever! My God sent his angel, and he shut the mouths of the lions.'

(verses 21–22)

At the height of the genocide against the Tutsi a militiaman came to me intent on killing me. He had just said he was going to finish my life, but as I said to him, 'Peace be with you,' I had this scripture from Daniel, 'May the king live forever', in my heart. Knowing that this man was not my enemy, but the real enemy that wanted to kill me also wanted to kill him, I prayed silently in my heart: 'Lord, if this is my time to come to you, receive my spirit. But if it is not, then I rebuke the evil spirit at work in this man so that he will not touch me, in Jesus' name.' After checking my ID card, which clearly told him I was on the death list, this man walked away, saying he would be back in half an hour. But he never came back.

As in the case of Daniel, my God had sent his angel and shut the mouth of the lion. Divisions in relationship can be healed by knowing who is our true enemy and rebuking the evil at work behind the person in front of us trying to bring that division. God can make a way where there seems to be no way.

† Lord, may we stand on our authority as believers to be the agent of healing in our relationships.

For further thought

Today, where are the Daniels? Those the world would try to accuse of corruption, but would find nothing to implicate them? Can we, by grace, be the ones?

Healing divisions

2 Divisions in the New Testament

Notes by **Paul Nicholson SJ**

Paul is a Roman Catholic priest belonging to the Society of Jesus, a religious order popularly known as the Jesuits. He currently works in London as Socius (assistant) to the Jesuit Provincial. He edits *The Way*, a journal of Christian spirituality, and is author of *An Advent Pilgrimage* (2013) and *Pathways to God* (2017). Since being ordained in 1988, he has worked principally in ministries of spirituality and of social justice, and was novice master between 2008 and 2014. Paul has used the NRSVA for these notes.

Sunday 5 February

United we stand, divided we fall

Read Luke 11:17–20

Every kingdom divided against itself becomes a desert, and house falls on house. If Satan also is divided against himself, how will his kingdom stand? … But if it is by the finger of God that I cast out the demons, then the kingdom of God has come to you.

(verses 17-18a, 20)

Snap a twig. It's easy, something you can do without difficulty. Snap twenty twigs in quick succession – perhaps you're preparing a fire – and still you won't find it challenging. But if someone ties those twigs together beforehand, and then tells you to break the entire bundle, without separating them, you may struggle.

The idea that strength comes from being united seems common in many cultures. Conversely, division can bring weakness. So Jesus exposes muddled thinking on the part of his opponents here. Evil only has power in so far as its forces are united. It makes no sense to accuse him of casting out devils, those agents of evil, by employing the strength of evil itself.

Yet if evil united is strong, the good news is that Jesus is stronger. The kingdom of God has come to us. United with that kingdom, we share its strength, and need have no fear of the forces of evil. As we pray this week with stories of divisions in the New Testament, and of attempts to heal them, it's worth remembering why this is important. We all need the strength of God in our lives, and that strength is more accessible when we are united.

† In whose company do you find the strength to live the Christian life more fully? Pray especially for each of those people today.

Monday 6 February

Jesus, bringer of division

Read Luke 12:49–53

I came to bring fire to the earth, and how I wish it were already kindled! ... Do you think that I have come to bring peace to the earth? No, I tell you, but rather division! From now on, five in one household will be divided, three against two.

(verses 49, 51–52)

The Roman headquarters of the Jesuits, the religious order to which I belong, has a statue of Ignatius of Loyola, our founder, in its main corridor. To one side is painted the quotation, 'I have come to bring fire to the earth', words of which he was fond. On the other side of the statue is a prominent fire extinguisher! An accidental reminder, perhaps, of our tendency at times to want to damp down the flames of the Spirit.

I suspect that Jesus, at the start of his public ministry, didn't intend to set family members at loggerheads with each other. There is, after all, so much in his teaching that speaks of peace, unity and harmony. Clearly the disciples, to whom these words were addressed, were surprised by the constant opposition that he seemed to encounter wherever he went. Yet at some point Jesus must have noticed that his could be a divisive message, and perhaps later came to see that this was an inevitable consequence of his radical view of God's loving acceptance of all people.

The church has never been without its divisions, internally as well as between itself and the world. The only way these could be wholly avoided is by dampening down the radicality of Jesus' teaching. Accepting the truth of that, even when the divisions are between ourselves and those closest to us, is part of what it means to be a disciple of the divisive Christ. Undoubtedly, we should work to overcome division, but it is also necessary to recognise that this work will not always be successful.

† Lord Jesus, who prayed that all your followers should be united, help us to work to overcome our divisions, while holding strongly to the sometimes divisive truths that you have shown us.

For further thought

Who is it that the gospel has divided you from? Are these the sort of divisions to be accepted, or healed, or both?

Tuesday 7 February

How can we best worship God?

Read John 2:13–22

In the temple he found people selling cattle, sheep, and doves, and the money-changers seated at their tables. Making a whip of cords, he drove all of them out of the temple, both the sheep and the cattle. He also poured out the coins of the money-changers and overturned their tables.

(verses 14–15)

It is unlikely that animal sacrifice is central to the religious observance of anyone reading these words. Certainly, it won't have the key role that it played in the Jerusalem temple. So, it takes a bit of an effort of imagination to understand what is going on here. Animal sacrifice requires animals, and money to buy them with, and all the commotion that goes with this. Jesus isn't here attacking something peripheral to the temple, as we might clear out a bookshop from a church. He is launching an assault on the heart of the worship practised there.

Yet this form of worship had sustained the people of God for centuries, and was painstakingly restored whenever the temple was destroyed. It is understandable if many of the Jews weren't ready to abandon it lightly. Nor, we may assume, did Jesus attack it without good reason. After all, at the age of twelve he stayed on in the temple to learn from the teachers there.

Now, years later, clearly he finds some aspects of the worship offered in the temple to be impediments between people and the God he calls Abba, Father. In his judgement, only radical action can demonstrate his vision. He knows such action will be divisive. Indeed, some have suggested it was this action that finally led the religious authorities to work for his death.

Once again, we see a Jesus who accepts divisions as at times necessary if he is to be true to his own message, one who is prepared to pay the price for bringing these divisions to the surface.

† Lord, help us to find those ways of prayer and worship that will most help us, individually and collectively, to unite ourselves with the loving God whom you called Abba, Father.

For further thought

What patterns of prayer do you find most useful? Are there ways of praying that you have outgrown or abandoned?

Wednesday 8 February

Discretion in reporting divisions

Read Acts 15:36–41

Barnabas wanted to take with them John called Mark. But Paul decided not to take with them one who had deserted them in Pamphylia and had not accompanied them in the work. The disagreement became so sharp that they parted company.

(verses 37–39)

The first chapters of the Acts of the Apostles present an idyllic picture of the early Christian community, united heart and soul, praying daily together and ensuring that none of their members was ever in need. Only later on does the writer, Luke, admit that things didn't always run so smoothly. But he does so with discretion, not wanting, I imagine, to deepen any divisions that he is aware of.

As a result, we don't know exactly what is going on in this passage. It is clear that Paul and Barnabas disagree, and that their disagreement centres on another disciple, John Mark. There is the suggestion that when John Mark left the missionary group earlier on to return home (as recorded in Acts 13) Paul, at least, felt that he was guilty of desertion, while Barnabas was more understanding. In fact he ends up travelling with Barnabas. Much more than that we do not know.

Two lessons, perhaps, can be taken from this. The first is that divisions, even among well-meaning Christians, are to be expected. The honeymoon period of early Acts can only last so long. The second comes from the attitude shown by Luke. He is not going to fan the flames of the dispute for the sake of a gripping story. He is not writing Acts to spread gossip! He records the disagreement, sides with neither party, and then moves on with his story. In an age where the internet thrives on provoking and deepening disagreement, Luke's example here is worth pondering.

† I remember before God any fellow Christians with whom I disagree, and pray that God will help me to understand more fully the situation as they see it.

For further thought

How do you think that Paul might have told this story? And what might Barnabas' version have looked like?

Thursday 9 February

Whose side are you on?

Read 1 Corinthians 3:3–9

When one says, 'I belong to Paul', and another, 'I belong to Apollos', are you not merely human? What then is Apollos? What is Paul? Servants through whom you came to believe, as the Lord assigned to each. I planted, Apollos watered, but God gave the growth.

(verses 4–6)

Whose side are you on? This question can be as life-threatening as defending your nation in time of war, or as innocuous as picking teams in a friendly soccer kickabout. Yet there seems to be a tendency deeply ingrained in human beings to pick sides, dividing the world into 'us' and 'them'. I am myself a Jesuit, a follower of Ignatius of Loyola, and not a Franciscan or a Dominican.

It's unsurprising, then, that the early Christians identify themselves with whoever had the major role in bringing them the gospel message. Unsurprising, but also unhelpful, if this attitude prevents that message from reaching others. If the followers of Paul won't work with the followers of Apollos, God's work is impeded, just as it is if Catholics won't work with Protestants (or Jesuits with Dominicans, for that matter!).

The prayer of Jesus that his followers may remain united is in part a prayer for the credibility of Christian witness in a world often ready to exploit any signs of division. Paul has different ways of promoting this unity where he finds it threatened. Elsewhere he argues forcefully for the complementarity of different gifts or approaches, likening them to different parts of the one body. Here, by contrast, he invites those who hear his words to recognise that all these various gifts and approaches have a single source, God. It is by keeping our eyes first on God that we may hope for other divisions, in time, to be overcome.

† I make my own the prayer of Jesus recorded in chapter 17 of John's Gospel: 'May [they] be one, as we are one ... so that the world may know that you have sent me.'

For further thought

List a number of ways in which you identify yourself as different from other people. Where is this identification helpful, and where less so?

Friday 10 February

Diplomacy or hypocrisy?

Read Galatians 2:11–21

When Cephas came to Antioch, I opposed him to his face, because he stood self-condemned; for until certain people came from James, he used to eat with the Gentiles. But after they came, he drew back and kept himself separate for fear of the circumcision faction.

(verses 11–12)

Is it fair to feel sorry for Cephas (Peter) in this passage? He has tried to tread a fine line, keeping both Jewish and Gentile converts to the gospel message on board. But what others might see as careful diplomacy, Paul judges to be rank hypocrisy. So, Paul not only challenges him, but challenges him in public. I'm sure there are areas of my own Christian living that wouldn't stand up well to Paul's insistent scrutiny.

Two things might be said in Paul's defence. First, this is a crucial point to be resolved in considering how this new faith in Jesus is to be lived out in practice. Was it to be constrained by the stipulations of Jewish law, or did Christian discipleship offer new freedoms? The way the church developed would look very different, depending on the answer to that question. And second, Paul goes on to explain carefully, clearly, and in detail, the rationale for his decision. This isn't simply a personal whim or arbitrary decision on his part. Rather, it goes to the very heart of understanding how Christ continues to work in the world.

Living a life according to precise, unchanging rules can be comforting in the security that it offers, yet risks being blind to the new things that the Spirit of God continually brings into being in the world. Discernment is the name given to the specific gift enabling Christians to recognise where the Spirit is at work today, and the implications for everyday living. The way Paul opposes Peter here offers a worked example of discernment in action.

† Spirit of God, give me your gift of discernment, so that I may recognise you at work in the world each day, and respond in loving service to what I see.

For further thought

We only have one side of the story here, of course. How do you think that Peter might have responded to Paul's challenge?

Saturday 11 February

Coming to know God more deeply

Read Philemon 8–21

I am appealing to you for my child, Onesimus … Perhaps this is the reason he was separated from you for a while, so that you might have him back for ever, no longer as a slave but as more than a slave, a beloved brother.

(verses 10, 15–16)

One of the divisions to be found in reading scripture is not so much internal disputes or debates within the books at the times when they were written, so much as the divide between those times and today. The early church is sometimes criticised for its seeming acceptance of slavery as an institution. A number of Jesus' parables, for example, speak of the relations between slaves (or servants) and their masters, urging generosity and justice, but without condemning the social system of which these relationships form a part.

In the letter to Philemon, Paul, while not rejecting slavery outright, does at least recognise that there are better ways for human beings to treat each other. He asks (rather insistently) that Philemon frees Onesimus, to treat him as a 'beloved brother', rather than as a slave. Paul recognises that this may cost Philemon something. Yet he is confident that he will respond positively to Paul's request.

Cardinal Newman, the great nineteenth-century English churchman, spoke of the 'development of doctrine'. The church, over the centuries and under the guidance of the Holy Spirit, comes to understand more fully the radical implications of Christ's teaching. No Christian institution today founded on slave labour would be acceptable. Now many Christians are becoming more fully aware of the need to show better care for creation as a response to the global message.

If there are truly divisions here between older, more restricted patterns of thought, and a fuller understanding of God's will for our world, they are surely divisions that we can be grateful for.

† Grant me, O Lord, to see everything now with new eyes, to discern and test the spirits that help me read the signs of the times.[1]

For further thought

Can you recognise places or situations where you see the implications of God's call more clearly than your parents or grandparents did?

[1] Prayer of Pedro Arrupe SJ, from Michael Harper SJ (ed.), *Hearts on Fire: Praying with Jesuits* (Chicago, IL: Loyola Press, 2005), p. 97.

The Letter of James (1)

Notes by **John Proctor**

John is a minister of the United Reformed Church. Now retired, he has served in a Glasgow parish, a Cambridge college and the URC's central office in London. John has written commentaries on Matthew (BRF, reissued 2022) and the Corinthian letters (WJK, 2015), also several Grove booklets on New Testament themes, including the Letter of James. John is married to Elaine, and they live near Cambridge. John has used the NRSVA for these notes.

Sunday 12 February
Pressure points

Read James 1:1–12

My brothers and sisters, whenever you face trials of any kind, consider it nothing but joy, because you know that the testing of your faith produces endurance; and let endurance have its full effect, so that you may be mature and complete, lacking in nothing.

(verses 2–4)

Jesus' brother James led the church in Jerusalem in the 40s and 50s. He was martyred in AD 62. This letter appears to be a circular, to Jewish followers of Jesus living in the Gentile world. The writing is practical and direct, and crosses the centuries with striking power and clarity. Today's verses, at the start of the letter, set the tone.

Life was tough in that era. It often is for migrants and minorities. Early followers of Jesus faced poverty, prejudice and persecution. 'Do not be afraid' is James' message. Difficulties can be stepping-stones to growth. The word 'testing' (verse 3) suggests a proving process, quality control, pressures that both refine and reveal a person's inner strength.

A first goal is 'endurance' (verses 3, 4, 12) – steadiness under pressure, stamina to bear life's hardships and hurts, and resilience to go on living wisely and faithfully. The longer-term aim is to be 'complete' (verse 4). Jesus spoke in the same vein: 'Be perfect' (Matthew 5:48). James wanted his friends to aim for maturity and wholeness, to love God deeply and actively through thick and thin. Such a life is truly blessed. This is love that God will return in kind (verse 12).

† Do you know any Christians who have grown stronger through a time of serious difficulty? Pray that God will keep their faith steady and secure.

Monday 13 February

Welcoming the word

Read James 1:13–27

[God] gave us birth by the word of truth, so that we would become a kind of first fruits of his creatures ... welcome with meekness the implanted word that has the power to save your souls. But be doers of the word, and not merely hearers who deceive themselves.

(verses 18, 21–22)

Life gives birth to life. But the world contains many kinds of life, and today's verses speak of two very different sorts of birth. On the one hand, temptation kindles desire, then desire gives birth to sin, and sin to death (verses 14–15). Pursuing every impulse, and carelessly chasing our aspirations without restraint or boundaries, will do fatal damage to our well-being and personal integrity. By contrast, '[God] gave us birth by the word of truth' (verse 18). God's word generates new and fruitful life in a person, shaping attitudes and deeds that are good for neighbour and for self.

Therefore welcome the word (verse 21). Give God's message hospitality, attention and time. Be comfortable in its company. Let it express itself in the practice of our days – in our habits, commitments and relationships. Discover the gospel's full meaning, by treating it as a word to live by, and by putting it into action.

What did James mean by 'the word'? I think he had the teaching of Jesus in mind, which echoes often in this letter, more obviously than in other New Testament epistles. Indeed, James mentions 'the perfect law, the law of liberty' (verse 25), and Jesus too talked of fulfilling the Old Testament law (Matthew 5:17). Israel's ancient covenant was gaining new energy and direction – 'completeness', James might say – through the wise teaching of the Messiah Jesus. And this wisdom could give new life to the people who 'welcome' it in their hearing and doing. That takes 'perseverance', says James. But, as we have already heard, perseverance brings much blessing (1:12, 25).

† Remember people you know who share God's word with others – perhaps at church, or among children or young people, or in singing, broadcasting or writing. Pray for God's word to be welcomed through their work.

For further thought

Is there one practical step you could take today that would feel like doing God's word rather than forgetting it?

Tuesday 14 February

On the level

Read James 2:1–13

If a person with gold rings and in fine clothes comes into your assembly, and if a poor person in dirty clothes also comes in, and if you … say, 'Have a seat here, please', while to the one who is poor you say, 'Stand there', or, 'Sit at my feet'.

(verses 2–3)

Yesterday's reading urged us to welcome God's word. Today we focus on welcoming God's people. Long ago, when a million pounds counted for even more than it does now, I was told that a certain visitor to our church was 'worth a million'. It would be important, was the suggestion, to make this man feel at home among us. And I hope he did feel welcome. But surely every person in that congregation was worth a million – friend and stranger alike, any with wealth and many without. Church is one place where privilege, rank, riches and social class should not define, divide or distract us. Gathering as Christians puts us all on the level (verse 1). God welcomes us in Jesus' name, and expects us to share that welcome with one another.

By way of motivation, James describes the poor as 'heirs of the kingdom' (verse 5). If Jesus treats such people with honour, his church should do the same (Matthew 5:3; Luke 6:20). James remembers too that powerful people have sometimes given Christians a hard time (verse 6–7). And he knows that Israel's law resists partiality or favouritism, with its concern for neighbour love (verses 8–9; Leviticus 19:15, 18).

In church we represent the friendship and welcome of Jesus, not our own prejudice or preferences. We are to love the people he favours – all of them, without deference or distinction. That makes the church different from most other groups in society. The weak are welcome. The fearful find a home. No one is more important than the next person. Friendship in Jesus' name invites, involves and includes.

† Think about poor people in your neighbourhood – those you know, and perhaps many you don't. Pray for them, and for what the church might be and do for them.

For further thought

For a newcomer or stranger in your local church, how good, honestly, is the welcome? Could you do anything to improve it?

Wednesday 15 February
Faith in action

Read James 2:14–26

If a brother or sister is naked and lacks daily food, and one of you says to them, 'Go in peace; keep warm and eat your fill' ... what is the good of that? So faith by itself, if it has no works, is dead.

(verses 15–17)

Today's verses pursue two themes that we met earlier this week. Meeting is one, coming together as church, from our different personal situations. Meeting commits us to equality. It also commits us to practical care for one another. Church is family. We rejoice together and weep together, and if support is needed we try to help.

Many churches do this very well. You find them involved in food banks, help for homeless people, credit unions, elderly care, and much else. They know how to share support, within the fellowship and beyond, in ways that enable rather than embarrass. Jesus is evident in their works, not just their words.

Which leads to the second theme: word and deed. For James these go together. God's word comes alive when it is put into practice. Welcoming the word (1:21) means living it out, not just taking it in. Hearing must lead to doing (1:22–25). Today that point is made in terms of faith and works. Insulated belief, with no contact point in living, is inert belief. Contained belief, like a lake without outflow, becomes stagnant and stale. Such faith is dead. It does no good to others, and it will not help the believer either.

James mentions Abraham and Rahab from the Old Testament (Genesis 22 and Joshua 2). Abraham's faith, which began much earlier (Genesis 15:6), was 'activated and completed' by what he did (verse 22). Rahab too was 'justified', shown to be a woman of faith, by her actions (verse 25). And active faith, grown and proved through faithful deeds, is what this letter asks of you and me.

† Can you think of two places, one local to you and one far away, where Christian care is meeting human need? Pray for the various people involved.

For further thought

Do you agree that outflow keeps faith fresh? Have there been times when this was true in your experience?

Thursday 16 February

Speech matters

Read James 3:1–12

Not many of you should become teachers, my brothers and sisters, for you know that we who teach will be judged with greater strictness. For all of us make many mistakes. Anyone who makes no mistakes in speaking is perfect, able to keep the whole body in check.

(verses 1–2)

We read yesterday about words and deeds. Now James writes about the power of words in themselves. Speech matters – what we say and how we say it. Words build relationships, but often break them too. They can be tools of trust, or of terror. They can deal healing, and hatred. James gave advice about speech early in the letter – 'be quick to listen, slow to speak, slow to anger' (1:19) – and he develops the theme here, in a series of pictures.

Words direct. Like a horse's bit or a ship's rudder, speech often gives life its course and direction (verses 3–4).

Words can damage, like fire running ravenously through a forest in the dry heat of summer (verses 5–6).

Words are defiant. The human tongue sometimes behaves like a wild animal (verses 7–8). It moves to its own rhythm, a tune we can neither fathom nor follow.

Words can deceive. Few of us are really straightforward and consistent in what we say. Moods, situations, company or fear, all affect us. We can be sweet and sour, almost in the same breath (verses 9–12).

Much of this observation has parallels in the Old Testament, and indeed in the writings of other peoples and cultures too. James' distinctive insight will appear in tomorrow's reading, about God's wisdom. But a first step towards wisdom is to recognise speech as a serious challenge. All of us need God's help with this, especially any who teach (verse 1).

† Do you know people who have to use words a lot – teachers, preachers, writers, lawyers, sales staff, councillors? Pray for them to be honest, clear and careful.

For further thought

Could you say one thing today in a conversation, letter or phone call that would bring some healing to a difficult situation?

Friday 17 February

Two kinds of wisdom

Read James 3:13–18

But the wisdom from above is first pure, then peaceable, gentle, willing to yield, full of mercy and good fruits, without a trace of partiality or hypocrisy. And a harvest of righteousness is sown in peace for those who make peace.

(verses 17–18)

Yesterday's warnings about speech find an answer in today's words on wisdom. Wisdom is not the same as mere knowledge. It is more concerned with the way we act, how we relate to other people, and what sort of character we reveal to the world. Wisdom is the life we live with God amid the complex mesh of human activity, opinion and need.

So James talks of two different kinds of wisdom. One kind always strives to get ahead, to gain position and power, to undermine and manipulate other people. James calls this wisdom 'earthly, unspiritual, devilish'; it leads, he says, to chaos and conflict (verses 15–16). Whereas God's kind of wisdom will build peace, bridge across divisions and disputes, and bring care and compassion in places of stress and sorrow.

This second kind of wisdom comes 'from above' (verse 17). It's a gift, growing out of a person's relationship with God. This wisdom is truthful, trustworthy, unprejudiced and generous. It can listen, negotiate and give ground to others. It knows how to keep silent, and how to speak peace in times of tension.

There are echoes here of the teaching of Jesus. He blessed the gentle, the merciful, the pure and the peacemakers (Matthew 5:5, 7, 8, 9). He challenged hypocrisy (Matthew 6:2, 5, 16). He described God's work in the world as sowing for a harvest (Matthew 13:3–9). And God's wisdom too is like the fruit of the earth – beautiful to behold, nourishing to take in, and strengthening when we share it with one another (verse 18).

† Lord Jesus Christ, thank you for the wisdom we see in your life among us. Please help me to grow in wisdom, and to follow it in the living of today.

For further thought

Can you remember a time when God's wisdom impacted on your life, through another person? What can you learn from that encounter?

Saturday 18 February

Come near to God

Read James 4:1–12

'God opposes the proud, but gives grace to the humble.' Submit yourselves therefore to God. Resist the devil, and he will flee from you. Draw near to God, and he will draw near to you ... Humble yourselves before the Lord, and he will exalt you.

(verses 6–8, 10)

We read yesterday of the peace and mercy that God's wisdom can bring to human relationships. But today's verses plunge us into a very different atmosphere, of selfishness, conflict and resentment. Clearly times were far from happy, and people – Christians included, by the look of it – had responded bitterly and badly. So James points his readers back to God. They will only handle matters well if they draw on their spiritual roots.

Life involves loyalty, he reminds them. We must choose our friendship – to God, or to the habits of 'the world' (verse 4). Even if coveting, grasping and quarrelling are thought of as normal, Christians are to resist the pull of this 'devilish wisdom' (3:15; 4:7). God wants us to take a different way through life. The entry point, where we 'draw near to God' (verse 8), is the 'narrow gate' (Matthew 7:13) of humility and repentance – knowing and naming our smallness, reviewing and redirecting our life. That's the aim of the commands in verses 7–10.

Taking this teaching seriously will surely involve a long, hard look at ourselves. But we will discover there not just the depth of God's goodness but the strength of God's power (verse 10). If God casts us down, the purpose and intention is to raise us up. More than that, humility and repentance have a practical effect. Though they start within us, they make a difference outwardly – in the words we use about other people (verses 11–12) and, as James goes on to explain, in the ways we handle our resources, our plans and our pains (4:13 – 5:11).

† God of grace and pardon, I want to draw near to you – humbly, honestly and hopefully – in times when I pray and in the ways that I behave. Please help me. In Jesus' name.

For further thought

Is there one 'devilish' habit that you could resist more resolutely than you have done? Could you start by acknowledging this in conversation with God?

The Letter of James (2)

Notes by **Delyth Wyn Davies**

Delyth is a Learning and Development Officer for the Methodist Church in Britain, based in Wales. She has worked as the National Children's Work Officer for the Presbyterian Church of Wales and as Wales Co-ordinator for BMS World Mission. She has translated over thirty-five Welsh-language Bible story books for children, edited Welsh language Christian song books and is involved in gobaith.cymru, a Welsh website with downloadable hymns and song lyrics. Delyth has used the NRSVA for these notes.

Sunday 19 February

Less boasting and bragging

Read James 4:13–17

Instead you ought to say, 'If the Lord wishes, we will live and do this or that.' As it is, you boast in your arrogance; all such boasting is evil. Anyone, then, who knows the right thing to do and fails to do it, commits sin.

(verses 15–17)

Today's reading presents some challenging contrasts. James rebukes those who are presumptuously boasting about their future plans by reminding them that even what happens tomorrow is unknown. Such arrogance shows a lack of humility and self-awareness. Then as human lives are compared to the fleeting appearance of mist, we sense a recognition in James' writing of how small we are in comparison to God's eternal greatness. We are, in fact, completely dependent on God for everything, including matters relating to daily living. It seems to echo much of Jesus' teaching, in particular his parable of the rich man in Luke 12:16–20.

James offers an alternative attitude, of humbly acknowledging God and of putting him first before ourselves and our own gains. His directive suggests the possibility of someone being aligned to God and his purposes and seeking to live in communion and partnership with God.

Boasting about yourself is evil, says James emphatically, but in a sharp twist he turns our ideas about sin upside down. Sin is not just about doing wrong, such as boasting, but is also the lack of doing what is right. I find this the most challenging contrast of all.

† Lord, create in me a humble heart so that I live my life completely for you, doing all the good I can.

Monday 20 February

Let your 'Yes' be yes

Read James 5:1–12

Be patient, therefore, beloved, until the coming of the Lord ... Above all, my beloved, do not swear, either by heaven or by earth or by any other oath, but let your 'Yes' be yes and your 'No' be no, so that you may not fall under condemnation.

(verses 7, 12)

Are you familiar with the saying, 'When the going gets tough, the tough get going'? Yet when things get tough our focus can shift and we can find ourselves doing and saying things we don't mean. James was aware of tough times – of oppression and suffering – and he reminds us of where our focus should be.

Without naming Jesus, James places him firmly at the core of his teaching. First, three references are made to the coming of the Lord in verses 7–9. This was important in the context of the early church as Jesus' second coming was believed to be imminent. But there were tensions and impatience, with believers turning on each other. James gently encourages them to be patient and to be of strong heart, with his beautiful analogy from the familiar world of farming.

Second, this passage draws on material from Jesus' own teaching from the Sermon on the Mount – just as you would expect from a good preacher! There are echoes of Jesus' teaching on storing treasures on earth (Matthew 6:19), on rejoicing in the face of persecution (Matthew 5:12) and on swearing oaths (Matthew 5:33–37), with verse 12 close to quoting Jesus' own words, telling us to simply say yes or no. In New Testament times, swearing on oath was commonplace outside of the legal world, and using God's name seemed to make it more binding. James reiterates Jesus' teaching that swearing by God's name or by anything relating to God is forbidden. It is truthfulness and trustworthiness, not an oath, which gives integrity to Jesus' followers.

† Lord, help me keep focused on you, even when times are tough. Give patience and strength to your followers under persecution today. May I honour their integrity and courage by always telling the truth.

For further thought

Verse 12 starts with the words 'Above all', suggesting that this teaching is of upmost importance. What is the significance of this to you?

Tuesday 21 February

The prayer of faith

Read James 5:13–20

The prayer of faith will save the sick, and the Lord will raise them up; and anyone who has committed sins will be forgiven. Therefore confess your sins to one another, and pray for one another, so that you may be healed. The prayer of the righteous is powerful and effective.

(verses 15–16)

One cannot doubt the importance that James gives to prayer in today's reading and that Christians should be praying in all circumstances, however they feel. Here we see praying is for both the individual and for the community. Having referred to suffering earlier he tells those afflicted that prayer should be the natural response. And if they are cheerful, whether in the absence of suffering or in good heart in the face of suffering, James recommends joyful prayer. Prayer is for all of life's experiences, as Paul wrote: 'Rejoice always, pray without ceasing, give thanks in all circumstances; for this is the will of God in Christ Jesus for you' (1 Thessalonians 5:16–18).

When praying for the sick, elders should be called in by the sick person to pray for healing, and the promise is that the prayer of faith will lead to healing. This is a team effort. It doesn't depend on one person but on people of faith praying together in the name of the Lord. The outcome, as James puts it using words such as 'save' and 'raise', could be interpreted in two ways, either physical healing or eternal salvation. Healing is for the whole person. Notice also the link between healing and forgiveness of sin, which also featured in Jesus' ministry. Sins are to be confessed to one another as well as to God, not to the elders but those who were sinned against, leading to forgiveness. The power of prayer is experienced not because of what the pray-er does but because that person demonstrates an alignment to God's will.

† Lord Jesus, you are with us in times of suffering and of joy. We pray for healing and forgiveness for all who cry out to you. Lord, give us faith and hear our prayers.

For further thought

John Wesley encouraged Methodists to confess their sins to one another and pray together. Is it easier to confess sins to God than to people?

Exploring the Lord's Prayer

1 Pray in this way

Wednesday 22 February (Ash Wednesday)
Act discreetly

Read Matthew 6:1–6

Beware of practicing your piety before others in order to be seen by them … whenever you pray, do not be like the hypocrites … go into your room and shut the door and pray to your Father who is in secret; and your Father who sees in secret will reward you.

(part of verses 1, 5, 6)

Today is Ash Wednesday, a day when Christians from many different traditions mark the first day of Lent, a forty-day period of devotion and sacrifice in preparation for Easter. The day is observed in different ways, but one tradition is that ashes of the previous year's palm leaves and crosses are ceremonially placed on people's foreheads as a reminder of our sinfulness and the need to repent. There is a real sense of self-denial associated with this day and the weeks that follow. It is fitting that this is reflected in today's reading.

The words are those of Jesus from the Sermon on the Mount. He sets the scene by warning his followers not to practise their piety or good works in order to be seen and praised by others and then cites examples from three areas of religious life, almsgiving and praying and, later, fasting. He warns people not to be like the hypocrites, acting out their faith publicly in order to seek praise, but to act discreetly. It may seem to contradict earlier teaching in the Sermon on the Mount about being salt and light and 'letting your light shine before others, so that they may see your good works and give glory to your Father in heaven' but the key difference is the motive. Doing these things to gain reward is futile, even if they do receive praise. Jesus was not telling people to stop charitable giving, praying and fasting, nor to do them anonymously, but to think carefully about why we are doing them and who we are really trying to please.

† Let the words of my mouth and the meditation of my heart be acceptable to you, O Lord, my rock and my redeemer.

For further thought

Many Christians practise Lenten disciplines through abstinence or intentional acts of good works. How will you mark Lent this year both publicly and privately?

Thursday 23 February
Pray in this way

Read Matthew 6:7–15

When you are praying, do not heap up empty phrases as the Gentiles do; for they think that they will be heard because of their many words. Do not be like them, for your Father knows what you need before you ask him. Pray then in this way.

(verses 7–9a)

A clergy colleague in Wales often expresses his amazement that when people pray the Lord's Prayer simultaneously in Welsh and English we always finish together! It does have a certain rhythm and pattern to it, and listening to the words of 'Ein Tad/Our Father' being shared together in more than one language is an uplifting experience.

The words of this prayer were given by Jesus to show his disciples how to pray. Just as they had been told not to show off in prayer like the hypocrites, they are then warned not to babble on like the Gentiles, with many words and no meaning. 'Pray then in this way,' Jesus said, offering a template, outlining all the essential elements of real, meaningful prayer. It is both a model for all our prayers and a prayer in its own right and can legitimately be used in both ways. The pattern of three petitions glorifying God through his name, kingdom and will, followed by three petitions concerning us – our material needs, the need for forgiveness, and asking for guidance and protection – encompasses every part of life and our relationship with God. The focus is always on God, and consequently our dependence on him as creator, redeemer and helper. William Barclay says that it 'teaches us to bring the whole of life to the whole of God and to bring the whole of God to the whole of life'.[1] There are real implications for our lives if we take this prayer seriously. Jesus is not just teaching his disciples to pray meaningful words but to really mean them.

† Thank you, Jesus, for giving us the words of this prayer. We delight to pray them with others and cherish them when we struggle to know what to pray. May we always live by them.

For further thought

Jesus follows the prayer with further reference to forgiveness. How important is forgiveness to you and what do you find challenging in Jesus' words?

[1] William Barclay, *The Daily Study Bible: The Gospel of Matthew, Volume 1, Chapters 1–10*, rev. edn (Edinburgh: The Saint Andrew Press, 1987), p. 200.

Friday 24 February

Treasures in heaven

Read Matthew 6:16–24

Do not store up for yourselves treasures on earth, where moth and rust consume and where thieves break in and steal; but store up for yourselves treasures in heaven … For where your treasure is, there your heart will be also … You cannot serve God and wealth.

(part of verses 19–21, 24)

In today's reading, Jesus introduces a series of short pieces of teaching on priorities that affect the whole of life. The first section on fasting follows exactly the same format as his earlier teaching on almsgiving and praying (Matthew 6:1–6), reminding his listeners not to be like the hypocrites but to act discreetly within the privacy of their relationship with God.

The three bite-size pieces that follow also offer contrasting ways of thinking and doing. There is always a choice and always a consequence. The message is clear – one cannot have it both ways.

In offering those alternatives, Jesus gives us the opportunity to compare and contrast. As we consider the treasures on earth with treasures in heaven we learn of the real value of attitudes in life. Treasures on earth are short-lasting and can easily be taken away from us, whereas treasures in heaven have eternal consequences. What we value and give our attention to now express where our heart's real desires are and where we find fulfilment.

This is reinforced further in the challenge regarding the eye. The word eye here is used to mean mind or spirit. Just as healthy physical eyes allow light to illuminate things around us, our vision, the focus of the 'lamp of the body', can lead to being in the light or in darkness spiritually.

The most striking of Jesus' illustrations is the third. In Jesus' time slaves were owned by their master. It was therefore impossible to serve two masters. It cannot be any clearer. We cannot give our all to God and also to something else.

† Lord, I give you my heart. May I store treasures in heaven. Lord, I give you my mind. May I live in your light. Lord, I give you my will. May I serve you alone.

For further thought

The three illustrations in verses 19–24 seem to focus in turn on the heart, mind and will. In what ways can these things be enslaved?

Saturday 25 February

Don't worry

Read Matthew 6:25–34

Therefore I tell you, do not worry about your life, what you will eat or what you will drink, or about your body, what you will wear … But strive first for the kingdom of God and his righteousness, and all these things will be given to you as well.

(part of verses 25a, 33)

How often are you told not to worry? We are all prone to worrying over things big and small. Perhaps we need to be reminded by others so that we can put things in perspective and focus our energy on the things that really matter. This is what Jesus does in today's reading.

Having challenged his listeners about heart, mind and will choices in previous verses, Jesus takes his teaching further in practical terms by telling them not to worry about material needs such as food, drink and clothes. He isn't implying that we shouldn't plan for things but that we shouldn't be preoccupied by worrying about them. God knows what we need, and we can be assured of this as we look at the created world around us. Sadly, we are aware that worry for daily needs is the stark reality for many people all over the world who are living in poverty, in war-torn regions and disaster-struck places. It's natural that they worry. Jesus' words were addressed to Jews awaiting God's reign.

They were about kingdom values, and those values throughout his teaching included meeting the needs of others. In telling us to strive for God's righteousness he is not only talking about being right with God but is challenging us to take action to bring about God's righteousness for all.

The message is clear that God's kingdom comes first in the here and now as well as for the future. If we strive for that, we will receive the other things we need. This is where we should put our energy.

† Lord, thank you for life's blessings, and for your care for everyone's needs. As we seek first your kingdom and righteousness, we commit ourselves to striving to make them a reality for all.

For further thought

What strategies could you have when you find yourself worrying about something? What does this passage have to offer to those who are feeling anxious?

Exploring the Lord's Prayer

2 Our Father in heaven

Notes by **Mark Mitchell**

Mark manages emergency logistics for World Vision. He has been engaged in the aid and development sector over the last twenty-five years and is inspired to demonstrate God's love through practical application of his reading of scripture and an understanding of God's love for the poor. Mark is based in New Zealand and lives with his wife and two daughters in their late teens. Mark has used the NIV for these notes.

Sunday 26 February

Our Father in heaven

Read John 1:14–18

The Word became flesh and made his dwelling among us. We have seen his glory, the glory of the one and only Son, who came from the Father, full of grace and truth.

(verse 14)

Ask yourself this: how often have you read 'Our Father' but internally, unconsciously, read this as 'My Father'? I know I have. After all, it's a personal relationship, a personal salvation.

And yet, the Lord's Prayer reminds us right from the start that he is *our* Father. He is Emmanuel – God with *us* – and he came to dwell among *us*. In the historical sense, he chose to come to a region that was the conflux of cultures at a time of the Roman Empire with greater movement than ever before. It was a diverse society with some who knew he was the coming Messiah and others who knew nothing of him at all; still others who completely rejected him.

As this reading reminds us, we have all received his grace and we can all call him 'Father'. What's more, if he is Father to all, then we are all his sons and daughters.

At a time when society seems to divide us we must remember that whoever we are, wherever we are and whatever we believe, we are, first and foremost, brothers and sisters to each other. Should not the grace we have received extend to each other?

† Lord, help us to remember that we are all united by the fact that we can call you Father.

Monday 27 February

Father and son

Read John 17:1–5

After Jesus said this, he looked toward heaven and prayed: 'Father, the hour has come. Glorify your Son, that your Son may glorify you.'

(verse 1)

'Glorify your son.' It's a strange thing to be praying for when condemned and on the way to the ultimate punishment. Yet Jesus was praying this on the way to the ultimate punishment. Many, like Jesus, had faced crucifixion and I'm sure they didn't feel as if they were being honoured or glorified. No, Jesus was about to receive the world's rejection. As we read in Isaiah 53:3, he was despised and rejected, held in low esteem. Not only that but he went on to experience what looked like rejection by the Father, his Father, as he died on the cross.

Of course, this was no ordinary crucifixion and no ordinary sacrifice. He would indeed be glorified through his death and his resurrection. He knew the sacrifice he was to make and why he was making it. He knew that through the power of his death and his resurrection he would be restoring humanity to himself and he was being obedient to the Father. What looks like rejection from the outside, with human eyes, did, in fact, bring glory from the Father. As a result we now esteem him. Furthermore, it was through this obedience and ultimate sacrifice that God the Father was glorified.

Our sacrifices, too, may bring about rejection and loss of honour among our peers. However, it is when we are obedient to God that he honours us, but more importantly that he is truly glorified.

† Lord, help us to know your will and be willing to truly sacrifice that you may be glorified.

For further thought

What does the idea of being a 'living sacrifice' (Romans 12:1) mean to you?

Tuesday 28 February

Hallowed be your name

Read Exodus 3:1–6

'Do not come any closer,' God said. 'Take off your sandals, for the place where you are standing is holy ground.' ... At this, Moses hid his face, because he was afraid to look at God.

(verses 5, 6b)

In the last couple of days we have spoken about God the Father. We are reminded that as a Father we can come before him with boldness and out of relationship. Here, in the story of the burning bush, we see that while God beckons Moses, there must remain a distance, a reverence and, yes, a fear. As we follow the life of Moses, we see a tension played out – a maintained distance but a calling for greater connection. In chapters 19 and 20, God reminds Moses (and the Israelites) that he is holy and powerful, not to be taken lightly. However, throughout, God allows Moses to approach. Fascinatingly, though, as Moses relates to God through the story of Exodus, we see him develop from a timid individual who has run away, who doesn't know how to speak and is scared of what might happen, to one who grows in his understanding of the power and glory of the Lord and is able to do and achieve all that the Lord commands him to.

Likewise, Jesus demonstrates this paradox in the first line of the Lord's Prayer. God is our Father and he is also hallowed, greatly revered and holy. As we deepen in our understanding of this paradox we also grow in his righteousness. James 4:8 reminds us that we are to 'Come near to God and he will come near to you'. It is not until we incline to this that we learn to trust and be obedient to his calling.

† Lord, help us to remember that you are holy and to be revered.

For further thought

Take a few minutes to meditate on God's holiness and why he should be revered.

Wednesday 1 March

I made your name known

Read John 17:6–10

I have revealed you to those whom you gave me out of the world. They were yours; you gave them to me and they have obeyed your word. Now they know that everything you have given me comes from you.

(verses 6–7)

Who has God given you? Based on today's reading, it seems fair to believe that just as God the Father gave specific individuals to Jesus so he has given us a range of people in our lives – friends, family and colleagues. As I read this, I think first of the team around me, some of whom I manage, some I report to. I'm sure, for each of us, it puts a different focus on how we engage with our teams and the relationships we have with them, particularly when we are reminded that not only are they God's first and foremost, but also that he has given them to us. Our team mates are a gift from God. Yes, even those that we don't necessarily see eye to eye with. Certainly, when I look at the mix of individuals who made up Jesus' team, I can imagine some terse words at times. Jesus' response was to listen to the Father and impart the Father's wisdom to the lives of his team. And then he prayed for them, specifically and individually. I can imagine him praying through them all by name, for their specific needs, and for the team dynamics.

Again, Jesus' response was to pray specifically for those the Father had given him. How much more should we pray for those God has given us?

† Lord help us to remember that those we spend our time with are a gift from you. We pray for them now.

For further thought

God's gift of people extends to the church too. Yet there seems to be an increase in division across the church. Are we too often divided about what should unite us?

Thursday 2 March

Your kingdom come

Read Isaiah 2:2–4

In the last days the mountain of the LORD's temple will be established as the highest of the mountains; it will be exalted above the hills, and all nations will stream to it.

(verse 2)

From his position looking out over time, Isaiah prophesies of a coming end time where Jesus is enthroned over his kingdom, where the nations are drawn to him and learn from him. It is a picture again, however, of the character of God. Even here, in this final kingdom, where he is enthroned as King of Kings, we see evidence again of the humble King and a God of peace. It is a beautiful picture of heaven, where all wars will cease.

But what is the application for here and now? God calls us to himself and in our acceptance of his Lordship over our lives we are obedient to his command; to 'turn from evil and do good; seek peace and pursue it' (Psalm 34:14)

How often do we argue, disagree, rant and rave compared to how much time we spend investing in others, bringing peace to a very confusing world? As we are reminded in Romans, 'If it is possible, as far as it depends on you, live at peace with everyone' (12:18). In this call to be peacemakers we are to put down divisiveness and weapons of destruction, and pick up the tools that will produce a harvest.

† Lord, you are the Prince of Peace. As we are drawn to you, let us also be bringers of your peace.

For further thought

Pray for peace in the world; for those in authority and for those who are seeking to find peaceful solutions.

Friday 3 March

A throne in the heavens

Read Psalm 103:19–22

The LORD has established his throne in heaven, and his kingdom rules over all. Praise the LORD, you his angels, you mighty ones who do his bidding, who obey his word.

(verse 19)

These verses remind us that God is truly Lord over everything. He is the King of Kings, Lord God almighty. Lord of all he has created. All heavenly hosts and angels do what he commands and act in accordance with his will.

As I read this, however, I have a confession to make – I am acutely aware that sometimes I am guilty of reducing God to fit into my life and expecting him to align with my agenda. Instead of obeying his word, I dip into it like a fortune cookie, expecting a pithy phrase that will be a blessing for my day. A pocket god, if you will.

Don't get me wrong, Jesus has left us with the Third Person of the Trinity, the Holy Spirit to teach and to guide. He is indeed a constant companion, a source of encouragement and a comforter, who advocates on our behalf. We can call on him and he will intercede for us and guide our prayers.

However, we are created to worship and to praise his name and to be obedient to him; to raise him up and exalt him above all else. More than this, we are to give him our all. As Jesus said in summarising the commandments, we are to love the Lord our God with our all. It's time for me again to flip the narrative and to remind myself that he is Lord. What about you?

† Praise the Lord, my soul; all my inmost being, praise his holy name.

For further thought

Read the whole of Psalm 103 again and use the words as a prayer for your own life.

Saturday 4 March

A different kind of kingdom

Read John 18:33–37

Pilate then went back inside the palace, summoned Jesus and asked him, 'Are you the king of the Jews?'

'Is that your own idea,' Jesus asked, 'or did others talk to you about me?'

'Am I a Jew?' Pilate replied. "Your own people and chief priests handed you over to me.'

(verses 33–35)

'Is that your own idea?' Jesus asked this because, of course, Pilate did not know. Jesus was not a threat to the Roman Empire. If the kingdom that Jesus was about was coming to overthrow the Roman occupiers you can be sure that Pilate would have known about it. However, as we know, God's kingdom isn't like that. In spite of what many Jews were hoping for, God's kingdom did not come by force but rather to demonstrate a different way of life, one initially envisaged in the garden of Eden where Adam and Eve walked with God.

Interestingly, the reason Jesus had come to Pilate's attention was because the people and chief priests had handed him over. The people who saw Jesus as the biggest threat were the religious leaders. Jesus was messing with their 'kingdom'. They had lost sight of the kingdom of God and made it about power, and they used this to their own advantage, ultimately separating people from a personal relationship with their God

Jesus was about turning the whole world order upside down, reducing the power of rulers and raising up the humble and filling those who are hungry. A true demonstration of our relationship with God the Father will bring about this different kind of kingdom. Jesus preached that the greatest in God's kingdom are those who love the poor and who demonstrate God's kingdom by loving their enemies and blessing those who would persecute them.

† Heavenly Father, help us to seek your kingdom and to demonstrate your love to those the world forgets.

For further thought

The church is God's plan to extend his kingdom. Are we living out that plan or are we like the religious leaders at the time of Jesus, more interested in building and defending our kingdoms?

Exploring the Lord's Prayer

3 Your will be done

Notes by **Gail Adcock**

Gail is the author of *The Essential Guide to Family Ministry* (Bible Reading Fellowship, 2020) and continues to advocate enthusiastically for families and intergenerational church life, both in her role as Family Ministry Development Officer with the Methodist Church and in her local setting with St Mark's Church, Hitchin. She recently started ordination training with the Church of England, and welcomes having strong ecumenical credentials! She's married to Matt and enjoys being the parent of adult sons who continue to bring a whole bundle of joy into their lives as family together. Gail has used the NRSVA for these notes.

Sunday 5 March

Your will be done

Read Psalm 40:4–8

Then I said, 'Here I am; in the scroll of the book it is written of me. I delight to do your will, O my God; your law is within my heart.'

(verses 7–8)

Over the past few years, I've been exploring my sense of calling and vocation. For most of my life it has been clear that God has called me to ministry with children and families, something I've found hugely satisfying and enjoyable. Yet there was a creeping sense for me that there was something else. That God was whispering, 'There is a new thing on the horizon', but I simply wasn't willing to pay attention! I wonder how many of us have found ourselves in a similar situation?

It started to dawn on me that God was asking me to step into a bold new season of ministry, one that I wasn't sure I could sign up for. Instead of willingly saying, 'Here I am, Lord', I chose a strategy of avoidance – if I ignore God for long enough maybe it will go away. Yet my experience would say that God simply finds a host of other ways to grab my attention.

Reflecting on your own sense of calling, how have you experienced God speaking to you? Maybe that's not been something that's part of your faith journey recently. Either way, why not find a few moments to consider what it might be that God is asking you to respond to by saying, 'Here I am.'

† Lord God, help us to trust you completely, with courage and confidence that you work towards the good of all things in our lives.

Monday 6 March
God's will fulfilled

Read Colossians 1:15–20

For in him all the fullness of God was pleased to dwell, and through him God was pleased to reconcile to himself all things.

(verses 19–20a)

In conversations with children about faith, we often pose a question to which there seems to be an obvious answer. In fact, this has become something of a cliché, so that whenever a question is asked in a Christian setting, someone is bound to put their hand up and answer 'Jesus?' (regardless of what is being asked). In this instance, though, the answer is definitely, absolutely and without doubt: JESUS! Everything begins and ends with Christ.

When God's intention is distilled down to its essence, it was always to live in peace and love with all that has been created. Jesus Christ made that possible – what an extraordinary thing has been done for us to know and be reconciled to God! God acts generously and with infinite love to bring us back into relationship, to no longer be estranged but to draw close to our maker and the lover of our soul.

Have we let that knowledge seep into our bones and brains, making its way to our heart and finding a dwelling place in our being? We can respond in a wide range of ways, from feeling unworthy or undeserving through to embracing deep gratitude and giving God our heartfelt thanks. What stirs in you now as you read this passage?

† Loving God, we praise and thank you that your will was fulfilled in Jesus, that it is possible for us to know you and be known. Help us to absorb the wonder of calling you friend.

For further thought

Consider your own response to all that Christ has done for us. How easily do you feel able to believe and receive God's invitation?

Tuesday 7 March

The will of the Father

Read John 6:35–40

Everything that the Father gives me will come to me, and anyone who comes to me I will never drive away; for I have come down from heaven, not to do my own will, but the will of him who sent me.

(verses 37–38)

Spending so much more time at home during the pandemic gave me a greater appreciation of our garden, a space I've always loved and tried to cultivate with my not very green fingers. I've taken endless photographs of things that have caught my eye, zooming in on my phone camera to try and capture the minutiae and intricacy of what I see. Zooming in and zooming out seems to be what we're encountering in Jesus' words here too.

There's an interesting pair of ideas in this passage from John's Gospel: from talking of bread to eternal life. From talk of everyday needs to mention of life after death; the tangible here and now to the more abstract thought of what lies beyond once our mortal selves are no more. We're able to connect that Jesus will both care and provide for us in the here and now (zooming in) while seeing the bigger picture and longer term (zooming out). All of which is God's will and in turn Jesus' will too as he works out God's purposes on earth. Jesus comes to give life to our ordinary everyday with the sound hope that our futures are also taken care of. In the midst of trusting Jesus wherever we find ourselves today, we can know we shall never be lost, for eternal life awaits anyone who believes.

† Generous God, we bring our needs before you for this day, however big or small they may be, giving thanks in the knowledge that our lives and futures are secure in your hand.

For further thought

Reflecting on your current circumstances, how might your view be impacted by knowing that through Jesus you have eternal life?

Wednesday 8 March

On earth

Read Acts 2:43–47

All who believed were together and had all things in common; they would sell their possessions and goods and distribute the proceeds to all, as any had need.

(verses 44–45)

In the town where we live there are a number of food-focused initiatives – one is intended to support households and individuals on low incomes and another rescues food that would otherwise be thrown away, offering it for voluntary contributions that ensure it still gets used to fill up tummies. When reflecting on today's passage, there's a question that lingers – what about the non-believers?

Here's an image in Acts of wonderful fellowship in this fledgling group of Christians, of everyone sharing their resources, worshipping together and building one another up. I can cast my mind back and recall many experiences in my life when church friends have gone above and beyond. Times when folk have cooked and contributed to group meals, stepped in during pressured times and gathered to worship together as people of all ages. There have been moments when I've looked round a room and been so thankful for the people assembled there and their willingness to give in a host of different ways!

All of which is vital and supportive for those of us part of church, but it begs the question: how does our life together as believers impact our wider community? We don't exist in isolation, so how does that generous spirit we demonstrate to each other find expression with our neighbours beyond faith community lines? As I notice need in the lives of people who live nearby and all around me, how do I respond to the challenge to take goodwill to others? So that they too have the joy of belonging to a neighbourhood that also seeks to share, care and be kind to others.

† God of justice, help us to see those who are in need and long to belong. May our churches be places where generosity is normal and everyone knows they'll receive a warm welcome.

For further thought

Spend time finding out where support exists locally for those who have little and feel disconnected from their wider community, or begin such an initiative if one doesn't already exist.

Thursday 9 March

As in heaven

Read Isaiah 25:6–9

It will be said on that day, Lo, this is our God; we have waited for him, so that he might save us. This is the Lord *for whom we have waited; let us be glad and rejoice in his salvation.*

(verse 9)

Words of hope. Words of comfort. Words of promise. In the majestic poetry and prophecy of these verses we're transported to a heavenly and uplifting place of abundance. A place where God acts decisively to welcome, nourish and finally bring to an end the hurt and pain humanity has experienced. How do you respond to this incredible image of God's actions on our behalf? Is it possible to sense the quality of God's expansive love running through all that is done? Actions motivated only by a desire to draw us close, to be at peace and know God's unfathomable grace and hope. What an occasion that will be.

Yet, I recognise my own impatience: 'God, why must we wait?' my heart cries out. 'Act now, step in, do what only you can do!' Some of you may not relish waiting either; these past couple of years have been so full of uncertainty that we may be craving some certainty for the here and now. I am learning to sense the quality of God's immutability – that God is unchanging in the covenant promises made to us, always a place of refuge and safety and security. When all else may be raging or shifting around, God will still be our sure foundation.

† Eternal God, help us to see beyond our current circumstances to a time when you will act to remove pain and heartache. Be our comfort and ever-present help today.

For further thought

Spend some time meditating on these verses and invite God to show you his extraordinary love through the events of the day.

Friday 10 March

Give us today our daily bread

Read 1 Kings 19:1–8

Suddenly an angel touched him and said to him, 'Get up and eat.' He looked, and there at his head was a cake baked on hot stones, and a jar of water. He ate and drank, and lay down again.

(verses 5b–6)

We meet Elijah at a seriously low ebb in life. His life is endangered, he is depressed and hopeless. 'It is enough,' he laments to God; after everything that has happened, his resources are depleted and resolve drained. It must have been bewildering to arrive at this point in time, to be seemingly out of answers and profoundly drained in his spirit. Surely this is a moment for God to act powerfully, to intercede and act dramatically on Elijah's behalf? Do we expect thunder, lightning, plagues, grand mountain-top experiences that instantly revive and empower him? It brings to mind the scene in the film *The Incredibles* where havoc breaks out around the dinner table and Helen shouts to her distracted husband Bob to 'engage' and do something!

It's time for God to intervene with a grand gesture, and yet almost the opposite of this is what occurs: a very simple meeting of need in that precise moment – to feed and refresh. To be provided with bread and water; that is exactly what is required to revive Elijah's weary mind and body. Give us this day our daily bread, we utter in the Lord's Prayer, which at its simplest level asks God to give us what we need. Here and now. Enough to sustain us, like Elijah, for the journey ahead.

† Provider God, you know our needs so well; help us to trust that you will give us what we require, especially in moments when we may not even know what that looks like for ourselves.

For further thought

Look ahead to the coming week and consider what simple needs or 'daily bread' might look like for you.

Saturday 11 March
Bread in the wilderness

Read Exodus 16:13–18

But when they measured it with an omer, those who gathered much had nothing over, and those who gathered little had no shortage; they gathered as much as each of them needed.

(verse 18)

At the youth event I help to plan and organise in my role with the Methodist Church, we imagined a townscape for children and young people to explore and encounter God. It has familiar landmarks, such as a health centre, theatre, town hall and marketplace: all spaces where issues of life and faith can be discussed and reflected on during their time together over the weekend. One of the additions is a place described as 'The Wilderness', somewhere that offers an opportunity to consider those arid and barren periods of life, the times we feel distant from God or God feels distant to us. Times that often feel desolate and bleak. It felt important to offer children and young people this space to explore, as they're not immune to having wilderness experiences of their own.

As adults, these times can unsettle and disturb us, prompting big questions and maybe even challenging God's place in our lives. I wonder if you reflect on your own journey whether you recognise times that could be described as 'desert experiences' and what they were like. Were we able to catch glimpses of hope in unexpected things? In this passage, God provides just enough for the needs of the people on that day. It doesn't last for long but there is the promise that God's provision will come again at the break of the new day.

If you find yourself inhabiting a wilderness time right now, may these verses be a gentle reminder that God is present and will provide. Let this thought spark some quiet comfort for you.

† Lord God, as we wander in our own times of wilderness, we ask that you give us what we need. Help us to trust you day by day.

For further thought

From your own wilderness experiences, what were the things that God gave you or that made a difference each day?

Exploring the Lord's Prayer

4 Bread of heaven

Notes by **Catherine Sarjeant**

Catherine describes herself as living in a messy place. A place where she is being treated for PTSD and still has the effects of trauma playing out. She lives in this messy place with Jesus – a place where she is weak and he is strong. She co-leads a small house church, helping others meet Jesus in their messy places too, and learn that he walks with us to bring order to the chaos. Catherine has used the NRSV for these notes.

Sunday 12 March
Eternal provision

Read John 6:48–51

I am the living bread that came down from heaven. Whoever eats of this bread will live forever; and the bread that I will give for the life of the world is my flesh.

(verse 51)

'Give us our daily bread' recognises that food is the difference between life and death. But in the context that we all die, therefore, this passage is not a guarantee of prosperity nor even that we will physically have enough. Of course, God longs for us to have all we need practically and has promised his ongoing provision for us globally ('there will always be a springtime and harvest'). But what he gives even more than this is the image of himself; we have choice, as individuals and corporately.

The fair distribution of his provision is dependent on us making good choices at both levels. If some do not have enough, we must act justly – we can't rely on the miraculous as a church to make up for the inadequacies of our sinful choices.

So, the promise isn't to miraculously provide for us physically, though of course there are times when this happens. Beyond this is an eternal provision. Not just satisfying the immediate need, but our deepest needs: security, identity, belonging, love – life in all its fullness. Communion is a reminder of this provision; what you eat becomes part of you, and when we partake of the bread of life, Jesus becomes entwined with us, a part of us, and he transforms what is perishable into the imperishable.

† Lord, we cry out 'Give us our daily bread' and mean more than 'Give us food and clothing'. We recognise that our daily bread is your daily presence in our lives. Without that we are truly dead.

Monday 13 March

Eternal living: restoring the broken relationship

Psalm 103:8–17

The Lord is merciful and gracious, slow to anger and abounding in steadfast love. He will not always accuse, nor will he keep his anger forever ... As a father has compassion for his children, so the Lord has compassion for those who fear him.

(verses 8-9, 13)

One of my children left the bathwater running. They realised they had made a mistake when water poured through the ceiling – and were upset about what had happened! It was a mess and potentially dangerous – wooden floors, electrics and plaster are not the best materials when water is poured over them.

As parents we know that there are two extremes in responding to such mistakes: one is to absolve the child from any responsibility: 'It doesn't matter, go to bed we will sort it.' The other extreme is to castigate and punish and condemn. What you really want is for them to know they got it wrong, learn from the mistake and do what they can to repair the damage. In reality, it was too big to undo by themselves and, painful though it was, we all helped together till the early hours of the morning to mop and dry. Ironically, the subject in church the week before was Noah and the flood!

God, as our Father, longs for the same when we get things wrong. He longs for us to own our sin, come to him with it and work with him to repair what we have broken. When we do this, he is honest about the choices we have made and the damage they have done, and, while we might not be able to fix it all ourselves, he joins with us to do the bits that we cannot.

This is the start of forgiveness, acknowledging and agreeing together the reality of what we have done.

† Lord, search me and show me where I am putting up barriers to coming to you honestly. Show me where my view of you needs changing.

For further thought

Does my view of God hinder my ability to safely come to him and own my sin, and relate to him in a healthy way?

Tuesday 14 March

As we forgive those ...

Read Acts 7:54–60

While they were stoning Stephen, he prayed, 'Lord Jesus, receive my spirit.' Then he knelt down and cried out in a loud voice, 'Lord, do not hold this sin against them.' When he had said this, he died.

(verses 59–60)

Stephen had spoken of the love of Jesus and demonstrated it by feeding the poor. The authorities, stirred up by Saul, decided to silence him. Yet he had such a soft heart in the face of evil that he calls it sin, not as a condemnation but with a desire that they would own it as such and therefore receive forgiveness not just from him but from God.

How could he have that attitude in the face of such injustice?

For Stephen, on this day, the vision of eternity with Jesus (verses 55–56) was his 'daily bread' and, as daily bread always is, it was enough. He has met with perfect love – Jesus – and this 'casts out fear'. It is in that place that he is able to speak forgiveness. To release forgiveness can only come from a place of love, of meeting Jesus.

I wonder if this event was Saul's turning point, where his sins began to become apparent to him. He would later write that his present trials were as nothing compared to the weight of glory that was waiting for him – just as he had heard Stephen express. And maybe this is a key for us too – the presence of Jesus becoming greater than the injustice, the sin; his presence with us in the pain of the injustice. It doesn't minimise the hurt or the consequences of the sin done to us – Stephen still died – but it gives us a bigger picture, a bigger love from which to own our sin and to forgive that of others.

† O Lord, help me meet with you today, and discover more of your love and grace.

For further thought

Reflect on the depth of Stephen's love of Jesus. This must have been a process. Are there things that we can't yet forgive? How do we engage with this journey?

Wednesday 15 March

Restoration in forgiveness

Read John 21:15–19

Peter felt hurt because he said to him the third time, 'Do you love me?' And he said to him, 'Lord, you know everything; you know that I love you.' Jesus said to him, 'Feed my sheep ... when you grow old, you will stretch out your hands, and someone else will fasten a belt around you and take you where you do not wish to go.'

(verses 17, 18b)

There are two words used in this passage, both translated as 'love', but with very different meanings. *Agape* is the all-giving, unconditional love, while *philo* is the love found in friendship.

Peter had claimed an *agape* love that was deeper than anyone else's, a love that will allow him to die for Jesus, even when others won't. But his claim wasn't based in reality, and he ends up denying rather than dying. Now, in this first personal meeting after these events, Jesus asks him if he really loves him in that *agape* way. Peter, speaking from a more honest place, responds by only claiming the love of friendship. Jesus asks the question again and Peter reaffirms that he loves him as a friend. Finally, Jesus asks him if even this is true – 'Do you love me as a friend?' Peter is hurt by the question and looks even deeper inside asking himself, 'I know I'm not who I long to be, can I claim even this?' and concludes that he can. 'You know all things, you know that I am your friend.' In that place of authenticity, the relationship is reset and Jesus goes on to tell Peter how his life will now unfold – a journey from friendship to the very *agape*-type love he had first claimed. One day, Peter will indeed die for Jesus.

A lack of authenticity damages relationship. It can't go deeper, and in the end will break. On the other hand, owning who we are, owning what we've done, leads to unity and restoration.

† Lord, help me to be honest about who I am right now, knowing that that is enough.

For further thought

Being authentic about who we are means that we can be fully present with God. How might this change your day, the way you live?

Thursday 16 March

Lead us not into temptation

Read Psalm 27:7–12

Hear, O Lord, when I cry aloud, be gracious to me and answer me ... Do not give me up to the will of my adversaries, for false witnesses have risen against me, and they are breathing out violence.

(verses 7, 12)

If we don't start from where we are, if we can't acknowledge where we are or who we are, we become vulnerable to temptation. Authentically crying out to God about our situation, about our weaknesses, is an act of warfare against those who would seek to lead us astray – including ourselves! The moment we hide temptation is the moment sin is in progress.

I carried shame. I carried a sense within me of my badness. Abuse does that to you. The thought of God was frightening to me. I lived a life hiding who I was because of that. I would do the correct things, behave well, serve in a way that looked good, but all to avoid the deficiency that I felt inside. I wasn't authentically me; I barely knew who I was.

I tried to change it by reciting words from the Bible. 'You are a new creation ... the old has gone, the new has come', but the new didn't seem to be there. If I'm honest, church advice didn't always help: 'It's still true even if you don't feel it; you just need to believe.' But that only fed my sense of inadequacy – I obviously wasn't good enough at this faith thing, tempting me towards increased perfectionism, trying from a place where I wasn't.

I was fighting the battle all wrong – if you don't start from the place you are at, how can you battle – it's like fighting a battle from your living room when the battle is happening in a field, miles away! Nothing will ever change like that; battles are fought from where we are.

† Search me, O Lord, and reveal where I am not being honest about myself, my strengths and my weaknesses.

For further thought

To what extent do we use rules made by human beings to defend us from temptation rather than being real about ourselves in order to be transformed by God? Rules can't defend us from temptation.

Friday 17 March
Stand firm

Read Ephesians 6:10–20

For our struggle is not against enemies of blood and flesh, but against the rulers, against the authorities, against the cosmic powers of this present darkness, against the spiritual forces of evil in the heavenly places ... Pray also for me, so that when I speak, a message may be given to me to make known with boldness the mystery of the gospel, for which I am an ambassador in chains. Pray that I may declare it boldly, as I must speak.

(verses 12, 19–20)

Paul was in the heart of the battle despite being in prison, in chains. We can be in the battle while housebound, ill, recovering – because the real battle is not about physical location, it is in the heavenly realm. 'Our Father, who is in heaven' is the beginning of the Lord's Prayer. I love the way God places himself in the heart of the battle.

Nor is the battleground about us being close to the apparent out-workings of sin – the battle is everywhere, not just in the places of obvious evil. Equally, our safety doesn't come from removing ourselves from those out-workings as a means of protection. Real safety only comes from being at the heart of the battle, wearing the armour provided. We're safer on the front line with God than hiding at home without him.

But sometimes we hide in different ways, wear armour that is humanly made, not from God. The armour of rules, human institutions, human good ideas. And sometimes we seek to fight battles that we want to win, that we see as necessary, or that others want us to fight. If God isn't calling us to that battle, we will not be protected in it.

Because God is in the place of battle, if we are not in the battle we have moved away from God. Of course, within life, there are times of green pastures and still waters – but these are refreshments for the battle, not a replacement of it. They are not the goal, the presence of Jesus is the goal.

† Lord, where do you want me to stand?

For further thought

We need to be engaging in the battles God is calling us to, not those that others would have us in, or even some of those we would like to be in!

Saturday 18 March

Protected by the name

Read John 17:11–14

And now I am no longer in the world, but they are in the world, and I am coming to you. Holy Father, protect them in your name that you have given me, so that they may be one, as we are one.

(verse 11)

As a survivor of abuse, feeling safe is tricky. In this world I was not safe. In this world I was not protected by those who should have been safe. Some things caused great harm. When people say to me, 'Just turn to God, he will protect you', meaning physically here in this world, I want to scream that that is not a given, not what is promised. In our earlier reading, Stephen, who loved God, who had turned to him and trusted him, died as a martyr. Peter would eventually be crucified upside down. Jesus died. We live in a place groaning. We live in a world where sin causes harm to people.

So, God must mean something more here. What is it, then, that God promises to protect, to keep safe? One day, our current body will die and we will have a new one. One day, we will have fully renewed minds that far surpass our current one. But our spirit that was brought alive in Christ, the essence of who we are, the uniquely amazing person that God loves and created, is eternally protected. This is what is safe, what is inseparable from the love of God. The safety of our spirit knowing he is with us, the safety of knowing ultimately what is to come, the safety of knowing that even in death or in harm coming to us physically, the essence of who we are is safe with God.

This is safety; that he knows, he weeps, and he says one day all will be well.

† Lord, show me today that all will be well.

For further thought

Maybe the treasures of safety are not out of reach for me. Maybe the treasure of feeling safe is not about being safe in the here and now, but rather knowing that all that is eternal will be protected, all that is good is safe.

Exploring the Lord's Prayer

5 Deliver us from evil

Notes by **Jessica Hewitt**

Jessica is a family woman with one young daughter. She has a personal understanding of mental health issues, the complexities surrounding diagnoses and how this affects people's views on spirituality and the world. She loves deep spiritual debate through the lens of someone with complex mental health challenges and uses this to spark discourse on social and political issues. Her religious upbringing has developed into examining other branches of faith and beliefs in recent years, which has broadened her understanding of Christianity as a theology. Jessica has used the NIVUK for these notes.

Sunday 19 March

But deliver us from evil

Read Psalm 56

Record my misery; list my tears on your scroll – are they not in your record?

(verse 8)

My immediate thoughts while reading this extract were of resonance and sympathy. Have we not all been fleeing from the enemy in some way or another, desperate for relief and mercy? King David, author of this psalm, may have had literal foes at his heels in the Philistines, but it strikes me how similar his cries for help are to those in spiritual and mental turmoil. Feeling trapped, betrayed, schemed against. Wronged.

There have been more than a few instances where I have had these exact feelings about people or organisations in my life. Over the course of the pandemic, it has become increasingly difficult to feel safe within ourselves and our lives when so many intangible and insidious forces are threatening our security. Turning to, throwing ourselves at God's mercy is often all we feel we have the power to do. Yet sometimes even that feels like a failing, for shouldn't we have the strength to face our worldly problems with worldly solutions? More and more often as I grow and learn, I realise that accepting spiritual help when my earthly tools just don't cut it *is* the stronger option. God doesn't have limits, but he knows ours and is there with his strength when we reach them.

† Lord, when I feel surrounded by evil I can rely on your love and strength to help me through. I pray that I remember to trust in you in my dark moments.

Monday 20 March
The Lord my keeper

Read Psalm 121

My help comes from the LORD, the Maker of heaven and earth.

(verse 2)

Have you ever been whittled down by life? Sometimes it's just a bad day. Others, it could be a week, a month or even longer that you've been trudging on, trying to make things work. Suddenly, just as you hit a wall, the sun breaks through the clouds ahead of you and you find peace surveying the skies. It feels like a personal message, an indicator of the continued caring. You matter. The Lord thinks you matter. It can be hard to remember this as we get on with our mundane tasks, the day-to-day business. So much of our day is made up of small moments of neutral, and we can lose ourselves in the blah. But even in that ebb and flow, we have been picked out by God. He sees you, cares for you, and you are important. Try and take a moment to savour one small task today, even if it's just making yourself food or organising something around the house. Take your time to be intentional. Feel every part of it carefully, intensely, and imagine how God is doing that for every single moment of your life. You were crafted with care and intention because he meant for you to be here.

† Lord, wherever I am in my life, I trust that I am a part of your plan and that you are my keeper. I pray to see the truth of your love and care today.

For further thought

If you don't keep a gratitude journal, have a go at finding five things today to be thankful for and write them down.

Tuesday 21 March

Keep them from the Evil One

Read John 17:15–19

For them I sanctify myself, that they too may be truly sanctified.

(verse 19)

The phrase 'Be in this world, but not of it' has echoed through my Christian upbringing somewhat emptily. It was often spoken by elders trying to pass down wisdom, but it fell on the deaf ears of the youth. How could I be a part of something if I wasn't fully immersed in it?

Social anxiety and peer pressure have untold power when you're too young to set your own boundaries and appreciate those of others. The consequence of that is that we risk being damaged, tainted by the world of others – and the knee-jerk response might be to isolate ourselves away from that world.

But as a Christian we are supposed to be influencing the world with the goodness of God, so, how can we protect ourselves from 'evil' while being in its midst? Perhaps the key is to 'sanctify yourself' – which doesn't have to be a religious ritual or rite, it can be as simple as taking the time to check your own state before a God who loves and knows you. And that includes your mental health as well as your spiritual and physical needs and safety. You might need to 'check out' of the world for a few minutes, to re-centre yourself. No one is exempt from needing to take care of themselves, just as no one is exempt from needing to be taken care of. We all have spiritual, emotional and physical needs within and without, and 'keeping ourselves from evil' is about ensuring those needs are met from healthy sources.

† God, I know setting healthy boundaries for myself pleases you. Please help me to stand up for myself when they are crossed by those who would do me harm.

For further thought

Is there someone in your life who may need help taking care of their needs? Can you reach out to them today?

Wednesday 22 March
For the kingdom

Read Psalm 145:10–13

Your kingdom is an everlasting kingdom, and your dominion endures through all generations.

(verse 13)

What would you consider your kingdom to be? The things in your life that you have authority over and have value for you? For me, it used to be my family and my social circles. I worked very hard to make sure I was considered a good, worthy person. Some of my diagnoses, ADHD and anxiety in particular, made me focus far too hard on how I might have come across to other people. It took many years and months of self-reflection and evaluation, unboxing the reasons why I felt the need for this outward validation, before I could come to any semblance of peace about who I was to others.

With this definition, my kingdom these days is my daughter and my husband. I now see reflections of who I am through my daughter, every lesson (intentional or not!) an insight into my behaviour and pathology. I've never had such a clear and honest mirror. Some generational trauma can be hard to face, and the efforts, and failings, of our own parents become more apparent. It can be both uplifting and painful to see your own strengths and weaknesses so obviously. In the same way, this psalm reminds us that the work of good Christians is apparent to the world. Our personal kingdoms reflect the work of Christ within us, and it's plain to see when God is the centre of our lives. His kingdom is our kingdom.

† Heavenly father, I know how important it is to have Christians visibly working for God. I pray that all I do is for the benefit of your kingdom.

For further thought

What does your personal kingdom look like? Do you think others can see the values you hold most dear from outside?

Thursday 23 March

The power and the glory

Read 1 Chronicles 29:10–13

Wealth and honour come from you; you are the ruler of all things. In your hands are strength and power to exalt and give strength to all.

(verse 12)

My house is a fairly traditional one, even if its members couldn't be less 'traditional'! My partner brings an income from outside the home, while I manage the home from within. One of my most important roles is of household accountant, which I recently discovered is how a lot of traditional Japanese families manage their money. Wives are given their husband's salaries, and the wives give them an allowance each month. I find this fascinating on many levels: sociologically, psychologically and economically. Most importantly, I resonate with it. Early on in our relationship, it became apparent that my money management was going to be one of the keys in us building our future together.

That task, though, has been made more and more difficult through job losses, navigating the welfare system and subsequent cuts, having a young family and moving houses all in the space of just over a year. While as an adult I no longer have a wish for excessive wealth, that glimmering fantasy has been replaced by a simpler desire that I might not have to worry about where our next food shop is coming from. Every day, I pray and use affirmations for many things, but financial stability is still a fundamental aspect of that.

That being said, here's what we've experienced. No matter how troubling the political and financial climate, my family has been taken care of in some way. The kingdom of my spiritual family has made sure of that. I'm more than grateful for the wealth that has been provided and I can safely say my wealth comes from God also.

† Pray today for the people who do not have comforts and have to rely on others for their basic needs.

For further thought

Maybe you are not wealthy, but you may still be blessed. In which ways do you feel this, and do your blessings flow from God?

Friday 24 March
Glory and unity

Read John 17:20–26

Then the world will know that you sent me and have loved them even as you have loved me.

(verse 23)

Social media has become a mental health haven for me since the lockdowns were first initiated. I used to fight the draw, desperate not to be another social media junkie, but slowly and surely I opened up to a few particular platforms after finding my 'tribes' on each one. These 'tribes' are groups of people who make you feel at home, safe and not judged, usually with shared interests. I use one for my pole fitness tribe and another has become my ADHD tribe. It started as just a community of likeminded people with similar symptoms and ended up feeling like family – a group journey towards understanding ourselves better. I never thought I would be a part of an online community this deeply, but it truly helped me to feel united in a world where disconnect became the norm. These platforms have become sanctuaries of normalising the chaos that I thought was unique to me and my life, and, even though everyone has their own colour of chaos, the shades are similar.

Unity can be found in surprising places, and that feeling is truly glorious. God has always meant for us to be united through him and through his love, wherever and whatever that looks like. It may be a Bible study group, a Sunday service or a pole fitness tribe, but our love for one another through Christ is the embodiment of unity.

† I pray for a united world, and strive to bring people together through Christ.

For further thought

Social media can be a positive tool with the right intentions. How can you use your social media presence to help someone, or yourself, today?

Saturday 25 March

Now and for ever, amen

Read Revelation 11:15–19

Then God's temple in heaven was opened, and within his temple was seen the ark of his covenant.

(verse 19)

'New beginnings are often disguised as painful endings.' I first heard that in the group I was attending while attempting sobriety. I was confident, but not certain, it would be my last attempt – that was five years ago now. All five years have been sober, and none of them have been smooth! Revelation feels so final, with good reason. I used to love reading about the certainty of how everything would end, especially when I felt like my world was crumbling around me. Regularly I couldn't see how anything would ever improve. I was convinced other people were pretending to be happy; it was absolutely inconceivable to me that anyone was truly walking around just being OK.

True crime documentaries were my lullabies, and horror films were my safe space. I know now that this is a shared habit of traumatised people; the endings of such media, however dark and horrible, resonate with the outcomes that our trauma taught us to expect, and as such provide comfort and succour. It is healthy for me to sometimes revisit the deep, complex sadness of those moments in order to remember how peace is often born of chaos.

The seventh trumpet preceded the revelation of the ark of the covenant, God's reminder of his presence. I've been through many personal apocalypses and without a doubt, every single time, if I give myself time and grace, God's light shines through at the end. It's taken me thirty years to learn to give myself the same grace God gives us every day, but it is worth the learning curve!

† We know that your love is now and for ever. Thank you for your everlasting promises that give us certainty all the time.

For further thought

Is there something in your life right now that you deserve to give yourself time and grace for?

The Gospel of Matthew (2)

1 Passiontide: the coming of the kingdom

Notes by **Angharad Davies**

Angharad is married to Simon and they have two delightful children. She is a full-time home-educating mother and it's her dream job! She has a BA in Welsh literature and worked as a missionary with YWAM for eleven years, four in England and seven in South Africa where she helped found an NGO called The Dignity Campaign. She is in the process of publishing a book about her testimony of overcoming eating disorders and suicidal depression, the first of its kind in the Welsh language. Angharad has used the NIV and *THE MESSAGE* for these notes.

Sunday 26 March

Out with the old and in with the new

Read Matthew 24:1–14

Jesus left the temple and was walking away when his disciples came up to him to call his attention to its buildings. 'Do you see all these things?' he asked. 'Truly I tell you, not one stone here will be left on another; every one will be thrown down.'

(verses 1–2, NIV)

The temple has been a cornerstone for Jewish culture and religion for hundreds of years; a statement of reverence and awe for Yahweh, something to be honoured and respected. But Jesus simply says that this historic piece of architecture that stands so solidly will crumble and tumble to the ground in a heap of ruins. Just like the Jewish system of religion is about to.

Why would the disciples not be freaked out? Jesus doesn't elaborate or give a detailed plan. He simply says that everything is about to change. What was to come would be far worse than what they could anticipate, in terms of their personal suffering, and yet far more glorious for humans than all their wildest dreams.

We suffer. We all suffer. We suffer for Jesus because we know we live in a world that is full of crooked and perverse people and systems. We suffer by swimming upstream and being light in the darkness. We suffer because of our own blindness and sin. He has established and will establish a new order, where he himself is the temple and the people of God are his temple.

† Jesus, help us make peace with the paradoxes in our lives, which we suffer here on earth, yet also see the future glory in you.

Monday 27 March

From bad to worse, then glorious

Read Matthew 24:15–28

For as lightning that comes from the east is visible even in the west, so will be the coming of the Son of Man.

(verse 27, NIV)

I have lived to hear people say that Jesus will come again in their lifetime, and those people have died without that happening. I think it is fair to say that Jesus is quite clear: it's going to be awful. If you think it's awful now, just wait until it's as awful as Jesus means.

Having worked as a missionary in other nations and seen all kinds of suffering, and having educated myself as to the abominations that happen to children and so forth, it can really feel like the end. The evil that is being allowed to reign on earth right now makes me want to vomit and to see Jesus come now, today, as I'm writing this passage! At times my own personal suffering, grief and loss have been so deep that I have longed to be delivered from my life instantaneously.

Perhaps he will come tomorrow, perhaps it won't be for a few hundred years. 'Soon' to God is usually not as soon as we interpret. And 'short' for God may seem long for us. But he is sovereign, and he knows that our present sufferings will be put to death once he has come to make it right. This is incomprehensible to us, but we must cling to it by trusting in his character, his nature and his promises.

He will come! He won't needlessly drag it out. He will cut the suffering short for our benefit. We will be terrified and horrified; then mesmerised, captivated, and captured by love, justice and righteousness.

† Jesus, you are coming. I long for you to come. The days are evil, and I fear for so many people. Help us wait well, to wait with eager anticipation for what you will fulfil.

For further thought

Ask the Holy Spirit to speak with us when we hear of things changing in our world; discern and take appropriate action.

Tuesday 28 March
Unaware of the abyss

Read Matthew 24:29–44

The arrival of the Son of Man will take place in times like Noah's. Before the great flood everyone was carrying on as usual, having a good time right up to the day Noah boarded the ark. They knew nothing – until the flood hit and swept everything away.

(verses 37–38, *THE MESSAGE*)

When we came back from South Africa, to live in the UK, we had serious culture shock. I was shocked at how far our culture had slipped, seeing the layers of make-up worn by young girls and kids acting like teenagers. I was depressed by the grip of consumerism and materialism and so forth. I was saddened by the pain felt as a result of gender and identity confusion.

Even though I had come from a beautiful nation that sadly has an astronomical amount of corruption, sexual violence, aggressive violence and poverty, it was coming back to my own nation that made me realise how far we have strayed from any biblical moral compass.

It can feel very odd to know that there's more to life than what everyone else is prioritising and to be living by a completely different set of values than the culture you're surrounded by. It's also quite eerie or scary to be feeling, 'Why can't they see what I see?'

I cannot escape my culture or the world systems, but I can live with intention every day. I can set up my internal and external life in such a way that I wholeheartedly pursue God, regardless of everyone around me. There is pressure and temptation, and I will make mistakes, but I can determine to set my course and deviate as little as possible.

† God, have mercy on all who are living in these times and open our eyes when we are blind to you and your kingdom principles.

For further thought

How do we make our life count? We need to budget our time, allocate it, and invest it in things that God values.

Wednesday 29 March

Who you are, behind the scenes

Read Matthew 24:45–51

Who then is the faithful and wise servant, whom the master has put in charge of the servants in his household to give them their food at the proper time? It will be good for that servant whose master finds him doing so when he returns. Truly I tell you; he will put him in charge of all his possessions.

(verses 45–47, NIV)

Getting married and having children are the two life experiences that God has most used to show me inconsistencies in my own life. There are many other situations that God can use to highlight these in our lives: living in community, friendships with work colleagues, working with people we go to church with, and so forth.

It can be easy to project being a certain type of person in certain situations. But push comes to shove when we are under pressure and given responsibility. And the true test comes when we choose to act with good character, even when there's no one else in the room.

I could burn out all my energy on being a good missionary, feeding the hungry and clothing the poor. But if I come home and treat my husband like a doormat then I am not trustworthy. I can be life and soul at a Home Education meet-up, giggling with and wooing the other mums. But the true test is when I am home alone with my kids, in the winter, in the rain, in the darkness, in lockdown, and we are all being pushed to our limits. Can I then display the type of character that makes me worthy of being given responsibility over others and over significant tasks?

My husband, children and friends need to know they can depend on me to be of consistent character. I am a life in process and a work in progress. But my aim is to have integrity.

† Jesus, help us co-operate with the work you want to do in us, to become like you in character.

For further thought

We can all listen to the still small voice of the Holy Spirit who will gently point out our inconsistencies and help us make the right changes.

Thursday 30 March

Choose wisdom or folly

Read Matthew 25:1–13

Therefore, keep watch, because you do not know the day or the hour.

(verse 13, NIV)

I can't say that I intentionally set out to be foolish. But I can say that I have naive wishful thinking; a vague notion that it'll all work out somehow. Now, I do like planning and organising, but I don't have practical foresight. This is where I am indebted to my husband who always reminds me to fill up the car with fuel, because you never know when … My husband doesn't live in fear of 'what if', but he is extremely prudent when it comes to taking care of the practicalities of life, so that life can go smoothly and so that we will be OK in an emergency. His maturity in this area is wearing off on me and it makes me feel more secure in life! His wisdom reduces anxiety and panic. If we are to live prepared for the normal stuff of life, then how much more so do we need to be prepared for life-and-death issues such as salvation and the second coming of Christ?

We hear a lot about decluttering and simplifying and living mindfully. This is all ace but should not be limited to material possessions alone. How about our mental, spiritual and emotional energy and capacity? Or are we using them up on God and his priorities? Are we filling up the tanks of our hearts with his love and discernment? Are we so closely connected to him that we can laugh without fear of the future? We need to!

† Jesus, help us live our daily lives, fully aware of you and fully prepared to meet you face to face.

For further thought

Drifting from Jesus can give us an ache and a sense of impending doom. May we always listen to that empty feeling inside and let it drive us to him.

Friday 31 March

Who is God?

Read Matthew 25:14–30

Then the man who had received one bag of gold came. 'Master,' he said, 'I knew that you are a hard man, harvesting where you have not sown and gathering where you have not scattered seed. So I was afraid and went out and hid your gold in the ground. See, here is what belongs to you.'

(verses 24–25, NIV)

As a woman who is a full-time home-educating mother, earning no income and therefore not being valued or validated by society as someone contributing to the economic purposes of our country, I can struggle with the generosity of God.

I have lived on a tight budget since I left my parents' home. I understand scrimping and saving. I can shop at charity shops and find second-hand bargains. I struggle with the opposite: paying to have a holiday, buying treats for my kids at a cafe, purchasing brand new items, choosing a food of my heart's desire at the supermarket and so on.

And this is just a material manifestation of a sense of deprivation. Am I starving myself from God's love because it's too good to be true? Do I reject comfort from a spouse because I don't feel worthy? Can I not receive compliments from friends because 'if only they knew'? We could go on!

God wants us to suck the marrow out of life and to be fully alive and engaged in the life he has given us to live. He wants me to love deeply, grieve deeply, give freely, invest wisely, make my life count so that it overflows and blesses those around me, yielding fruit and profit.

It all boils down to who I think God is – a hard master or a generous father? Let's invest what our good Father gives us!

† Jesus, show us what gifts, talents and resources you have given us, and help us multiply it.

For further thought

I love words and I longed to write a book about my testimony to help others. So, I did! What talents can you bring to life to bless the world?

Saturday 1 April

Masterful motivation

Read Matthew 25: 31–46

Then the King will say to those on his right, 'Come, you who are blessed by my Father; take your inheritance, the kingdom prepared for you since the creation of the world.'

(verse 34, NIV)

We all know that being criticised is not an impetus to work harder, do better, be kinder. I'm sure we can all remember being at school and the teacher returning our carefully crafted work, but now it's covered with corrective red ink. This did not inspire me to rewrite my work, it discouraged me.

In this passage we see both sides of the coin. It feels like Jesus reiterated himself to get the weight of his point into our hearts. It's quite alarming to think that if I reject someone or refuse to provide help that is within my means to give, I am saying no to Jesus himself. What a high price he places on human life; that he will compare the beggar on the street, the starving prostitute, the man suffering from AIDS to himself. How humbling!

God may want us to give to those who are obviously poor; at other times the rich will need our help, and at other times there will be people who seem rich but who may secretly be poor, who will also need our assistance. All human beings are of such worth to Jesus that he will compare himself with them and reward us for helping because it's as if we have helped him. We do not help others merely to get a reward, but Jesus values other people so much that he longs for us to have our hearts so transformed that we can also love, value and respect others, as does he.

† Jesus, help me notice others, notice when they are in need and be quick to offer appropriate assistance.

For further thought

I can be quite unloving when I am interrupted. I daily need to remind my heart and mind that God places infinite worth on each human soul.

The Gospel of Matthew (2)

2 Holy Week: the way of the cross

Notes by **Orion Johnson**

Orion's Christian faith was nurtured at the Anglican church where she grew up in the London suburbs. After marrying, she moved to Warwickshire in the UK Midlands and raised two sons – now young men. Her career has been in publishing – which included printing tens of thousands of children's Bibles that were distributed around the world, in a host of different languages – and marketing. She now works for IBRA and RE Today, on their publications. Orion has used the NIVUK for these notes.

Sunday 2 April (Palm Sunday)

The perfect gift

Read Matthew 26:1–16

When she poured this perfume on my body, she did it to prepare me for burial. Truly I tell you, wherever this gospel is preached throughout the world, what she has done will also be told, in memory of her.

(verses 12–13)

We now call it 'Holy Week' but these few days in the gospel accounts bristle with all manner of very human responses to Jesus and his impending fate. As drama, the twists and turns, scheming and threat are gripping: highly charged politics that *still* kick around in our divided world.

Today's passage is skilfully balanced: rising political and religious tension start and end it, framing a central moment of beauty, generosity, even calm. As it is Palm Sunday, let us focus on the positive bit – we have six more days to ponder the plotting, betrayal and execution.

I like to know that Jesus had good friends to call upon. John's Gospel identifies the woman presenting a luxurious perfume as Mary, sister of Martha and Lazarus. At this house in Bethany, Jesus is among friends. Mary anoints Christ's head as he reclines: you can almost smell the scent and feel the sense of ease.

But even this foreshadows Christ's death. The extravagant gesture echoes the gifts of the magi described earlier in Matthew. A close friend in Bethany and strangers from the East perceived the value of the expensive gift, when well chosen, and perhaps Jesus' destiny too.

† Teach me to be like Mary: may I listen to, learn from, understand and adore my friend Christ Jesus.

Monday 3 April

A traitor unmasked

Read Matthew 26:17–35

And while they were eating, he said, 'Truly I tell you, one of you will betray me.'

(verse 21)

What I warm to in this passage is witnessing the establishment of Holy Communion, with the familiar phrases and elements we share at a Sunday service. Those gathered even sing a hymn at the end, before departing for the Mount of Olives.

But an atmosphere of betrayal is present at this particular communion, and Judas embodies many typical characteristics of the sort of treacherous 'friend' we might still encounter.

Judas made up his mind to help Jesus' enemies following the 'wasteful' perfume incident we read of yesterday. When contemplating something that goes against our conscience we often need to 'give ourselves permission' for it: the justification that manages to override better judgement. I can sense how an argument over money for the poor could allow Judas to persuade himself it was a good idea to abandon his leader.

But Judas doesn't just disagree and go; at the Last Supper he maintains the appearance of a loyal follower. He is now scheming and flatly lying.

For a moment, the imagery is intense: Judas dips his hand into the bowl at the same time as Jesus. A film-maker would probably fade the other disciples into the background, puzzled and muttering, while Judas and Jesus are close. Judas has the bold nerve to share in the bowl with the teacher he is plotting to betray. Their eyes lock as each knows the other's thoughts.

Jesus makes his accusation plain, but Judas still pushes back: 'Surely you don't mean me, Rabbi?' A common deflective strategy makes out that the assertion is ridiculous or outrageous (without actually denying it).

† We all fail you at some time or another, Lord. Forgive me when I do. Teach me faithfulness and give me the strength and courage to follow you.

For further thought

Is there something that repeatedly draws you away from following God? Can you think of a way to avoid or overcome it?

Tuesday 4 April

Overwhelmed with sorrow, to the point of death

Read Matthew 26:36–56

Going a little farther, he fell with his face to the ground and prayed, 'My Father, if it is possible, may this cup be taken from me. Yet not as I will, but as you will.'

(verse 39)

How many times have you and I prayed: 'Please, God – make it stop'? I'd guess it's one of the most common prayers of all.

It is our human lot to be tested mentally, emotionally and physically, sometimes to our limits. I don't have the capacity to explain satisfactorily why that is so (and if I could, I doubt there's room to do it here). Reading the Gospels, it seems even more mystifying that Christ – the divine – had to be put through the impending torture. Surely God could make the 'rules' of how human sin could be forgiven and this could pan out differently? Try explaining to a child (they inevitably ask) why Jesus had to die in such an awful way. Deep down, I have a dreadful sense that nothing less than Christ's suffering would have been enough.

God becoming human is an amazing and wonderful gift to us, but now it means that Jesus experiences terror. No 'legions of angels' arrive to waft him painlessly through this ordeal, yet he will face it.

For us, perhaps God will take the terrible thing away. If not, it might be some advantage to make it our own decision to undergo the challenge, with God's help and as much faith in him as we can muster. Strength and wisdom have a tendency to spring from surviving adversity, even if all we feel we've gained is a lesson in trusting God.

It is human to fear and to hope that what we fear can be avoided: and it is what Jesus did.

† Father, you know my fears. Give me the courage to face the things I must deal with, and the reassurance of your presence when I struggle or doubt.

For further thought

Read a reassuring psalm – one that sings of the care, help or protection we receive from God; one of my favourites is Psalm 121.

Wednesday 5 April

The show trial

Read Matthew 26:57–75

The chief priests and the whole Sanhedrin were looking for false evidence against Jesus so that they could put him to death.

(verse 59)

A few years ago, my church presented a dramatisation of the Holy Week events, from Palm Sunday to the crucifixion.

The part of Caiaphas was given to our vicar: with his priestly bearing and authoritative delivery, he seemed aptly cast. Close to performance, we were no longer fumbling with scripts and noting where to enter, but had learned lines, taken direction about speech and movement, were interacting with the other characters and getting used to props and costumes. By then, we could sense each part more thoroughly and I remarked how it must have felt very alien to a man whose life and profession were dedicated to Christ to stand in his own church denouncing the young man playing Jesus as a blasphemer, calling for his death. And I don't think it was entirely comfortable for one of the churchwardens, playing Peter, to deny Jesus three times over. I was Mary, mother of Jesus, and knew from the off there would be certain emotions to convey but had not expected the feelings of anger and disappointment that emerged.

Some disapprove of using drama in church, but I find watching or acting allows you to walk in someone else's shoes and, boy, can that give a different perspective – be it in sympathy, revulsion or just sparking a new idea about what happened and why.

One undeniable feature that performance made evident was that Jesus' appearance before the Sanhedrin was no fair trial.

† Lord, I pray for those who face accusation or punishment without a fair right of reply or trial. Guide all who have the power to judge or condemn.

For further thought

Think about the words that people speak in this or another Bible passage and read them aloud. What does it feel like to say them?

Thursday 6 April

Desperation

Read Matthew 27:1–26

Early in the morning, all the chief priests and the elders of the people made their plans how to have Jesus executed. So they bound him, led him away and handed him over to Pilate the governor.

(verses 1–2)

Where can you turn when the very people who claim authority to interpret God's law and ensure it is upheld are the ones who disregard it? The death of an innocent man is the design and demand of those who ought to behave better: the priests and elders.

A desperate figure, Judas has comprehended the unjust, fatal consequence of switching allegiance and is torn up with guilt. The man whose name remains a byword for 'traitor' confesses his sin. Yet his new allies don't provide any consolation or reassurance, let alone a route to redemption. These are the holy men, men of the temple, but now that Judas' help is no longer needed, they will not even bother with a civil word. Instead, they crush him further by turning responsibility for their cruelty back on him.

I'll repeat: these are (meant to be) the holy men, the men of the temple. When Judas hurls his bribe back in disgust, I wonder whether the predicted temple's destruction is already being brought to pass by those very men. Blood money lies on the floor of the temple: have the priests and elders themselves ensured that its days are numbered?

So, where now? Might state law offer protection? Questioning Jesus, Governor Pilate realises there is no crime to answer. A politician, he alights on a seemingly clever political 'democratic' solution. But when the priests and elders contrive to free a murderer to secure Christ's execution, Pilate's response is indeed political: knowing it wrong the governor concedes to the mood of the crowd to dispel riot.

† Lord, thank you that you offer us mercy; grant us your loving protection as we turn to you, and remind us to put our faith in you, even when human judgement and power fail us.

For further thought

How can you act wisely in your responsibility towards others? Can you use what authority you have to help others and honour God?

Friday 7 April (Good Friday)

Despised and rejected

Read Matthew 27:27–44

They stripped him and put a scarlet robe on him, and then twisted together a crown of thorns and set it on his head.

(verses 28–29a)

Matthew's account of Good Friday is utterly brutal: an unremitting catalogue of violence, humiliation and scorn. Crucifixion was never going to be pleasant, but there's no moment of respite and his supporters are at a distance or absent. Jesus is surrounded with hate.

People often like to 'kick down'. By that, I mean trying to feel better about themselves by hurting (physically or verbally) someone they consider an inferior or more vulnerable. How many of the people listed here have an actual quarrel with Jesus? The priests might feel threatened by what they consider his 'heresy', but I can't imagine the soldiers even know who he is. And I wonder if any of the jeering passers-by had been among those happily waving palms a few days before.

The Roman soldiers hardly live up to the honour of the regiment: mocking, spitting, stealing, then beating their tied-up prisoner. Did that make them feel superior for a little while, when normally they'd be the ones taking orders? They even pick on a bystander, forcing Simon of Cyrene to carry the cross (had that been me, I'd have been terrified of ending up on the cross myself).

In Matthew, there is no repentant thief alongside Jesus and even those executed around him hurl insults from their own crosses. That really is 'kicking down': they are guilty, condemned and dying, surely at rock bottom, but still find a harmless victim to abuse.

We readers know that Jesus is undergoing wretchedness and death for the sake of these persecutors, and out of love for us all.

† Thank you, Jesus. I know that you suffered and died because you love me. Help me always to remember that and honour you.

For further thought

Do you ever gain satisfaction or self-importance by hurting someone who can't hit back?

Saturday 8 April

Christ broken for you

Read Matthew 27:45–66

And when Jesus had cried out again in a loud voice, he gave up his spirit.

(verse 50)

Birmingham in the UK boasts much beautiful Victorian stained glass, including prominent pre-Raphaelite examples; the window there that moves me most is preserved in the city's Museum and Art Gallery, donated from a church upon its demolition in 1983. Artistically, it is not unlike countless depictions of Christ crucified in churches around Britain and Europe, but it is the *damage* to this one that sets it apart.

On its central panel Jesus hangs on the cross, his eyes closed. His right ribcage has been pierced by the soldier's sword. Christ has surrendered his spirit and is dead. In the window's history, perhaps while in place during its eighty-five or so years at the church, or during removal to the museum, the panel has sustained many cracks yet remains whole. Fracture lines cross the figure's abdomen and passive face. Somehow, I'd love to know how, a star crack was made (as when a stone hits a windscreen), its fracture lines radiating out from a central impact point, that centre point being just over Christ's heart.

It brings to mind Christ's heart, broken at the moment when, after hours of daytime darkness, the earth shook and the temple curtain was torn in two. Were the window's artist (G. F. Bodley) to see it now, rather than frowning at its damaged state, might he be astonished that this accident has enhanced the poignancy of his artwork?

Christ broken, with a spirit 'given up', was the act of sacrifice which enabled us to be forgiven, meet with God once more and hope for eternal life with him.

† I praise you and acknowledge that Christ took upon himself the pain of my sin so that I might be reunited with God, and that his body was broken for me.

For further thought

Is there an artwork or image which conveys to you Christ's passion or triumph over death? Bring it to mind, or look it up.

Celebrations

Notes by **Jane Gonzalez**

Jane is a Roman Catholic laywoman. Retirement has offered her opportunities to spend more time in Spain, where she and her husband have a home, but also to indulge her creative side. She is currently writing haikus (seventeen-syllable poems) and illustrating them with her own photos. Projects for the future include weaving and collage. In between all this, she remains an active member of her local parish, particularly in the Justice and Peace Group. Jane has used the NRSVACE for these notes.

Sunday 9 April (Easter Sunday)

You never walk alone

Read Luke 24:13–35

So he went in to stay with them. When he was at the table with them, he took bread, blessed and broke it, and gave it to them. Then their eyes were opened, and they recognized him; and he vanished from their sight.

(verses 29b–31)

The lockdowns we endured during the Covid-19 pandemic heightened our awareness of the human need for companionship. Isolation and loneliness are, perhaps, the hidden pandemic of modern living. We all need somebody to turn to when we are at our lowest ebb – a soul friend, mentor, guide or companion. Somebody who shares our struggles and our joys.

The Emmaus story highlights the absolute importance of companionship and sharing. Jesus joins two travellers and shares their walk home. He shares their anxieties; he shares his wisdom; and lastly, he shares an evening meal which is blessed and transformed by his presence. In the breaking of the bread, they recognise him. Immediately, confusion and sadness vanish. This intimate moment of companionship means they can do now what seemed impossible only minutes before – return to Jerusalem, full of hope and promise. By walking, talking and sharing, Jesus transforms sorrow and isolation, even as he disappears from the table.

Jesus engendered hope and trust when all seemed lost. He has continued to do so over the course of two millennia. We are never totally isolated or alone because he walks with us. The impossible is within our grasp because we are never without him.

† Father, I thank you for my companions, all those who have walked with me so far. Bless all our journeys and teach us to walk in your ways.

Monday 10 April

Sufficient unto the day ...

Read Leviticus 23:4–14

These are the appointed festivals of the Lord, the holy convocations, which you shall celebrate at the time appointed for them.

(verse 4)

Every week I sit down with my husband and we 'do' our diaries. We look at our joint and individual commitments and plan so that there are no double bookings. It is an opportunity to take the long view of the weeks and months ahead so that we can properly honour the 'appointed festivals' of both the secular and religious spheres.

Every year, academic, calendar, financial or liturgical, has its own rhythm – its high days and holidays, its fallow periods. The liturgical seasons of the Christian year apportion time according to the different rhythms of human life – birth, death, anticipation and waiting, fulfilment, joy, sorrow, growth and decay, feast and fasting.

It is important that we remain faithful to these seasons and resist the temptation to seek the 'highs' all the time. Celebrations can become impoverished if we gorge ourselves before the appointed day – there can only be a real feast if it follows a famine of some kind. Thus, the observance of Advent prepares us for Christmas; the abstinences of Lent, the sombre rituals of Holy Week, enable the explosion of joy at Easter; Ordinary Time mirrors 'normal' life as it jogs along.

Jesus came to bring us life in all its abundance. And abundant life is there – hidden and often unrecognised and uncelebrated in the ordinary and commonplace. There are blessings in the present moment, in the small treasures of the mundane. We can find these if we allow ourselves to celebrate and savour each day. If we let the weeks and months unfold at their own pace and in their own time.

† Father, I thank you for the gift of today. I know you are beside me always and everywhere. Give me the grace to see you at work in all that I do.

For further thought

Reflect on Ecclesiastes 3:1–8. Where do I need to pay more attention to the rhythms of life?

Tuesday 11 April

The writing on the wall

Read Daniel 5:1–12

King Belshazzar made a great festival for a thousand of his lords, and he was drinking wine in the presence of the thousand ... They drank the wine and praised the gods of gold and silver, bronze, iron, wood, and stone.

(verses 1, 4)

This year, among my family and friends, we have celebrated a wedding and some significant birthdays and anniversaries. It was wonderful to have the opportunity to celebrate together, in large numbers, and to 'eat, drink and be merry', as the saying goes. Seeing and socialising with loved ones brought us all great joy, even in the humblest of meals.

Human beings, throughout the ages, have come together and shared a meal, a feast, a banquet, as a means of recognising and remembering important people and events in their lives. Even in times of sorrow following a death, the human reaction is still to come together for a 'wake' – to eat and drink together in memory of the loved one who can no longer share our table but whose presence remains. For the powerful, throughout history, sumptuous meals have often played a significant role in cementing alliances and rewarding fidelity and service. And they have served (and still do in many societies) to emphasise who is 'in' and who is 'out'; who has favour and who has not; who is rich and who is poor.

Belshazzar's is one such feast: he is surrounded by his people and they, the *haves*, the victors, sate themselves on food and wine. It is then that the writing on the wall appears – *you have been weighed in the balance and found wanting* – as Daniel will explain later. God is not mocked. He celebrates with us as we feast but he sees the hungry at our door, even if we choose to ignore them.

† Father, sometimes I am so bound up in my own concerns that I fail to recognise those in need. Give me the strength to be more giving and less selfish.

For further thought

Check out Mary's Meals at www.marysmeals.org, or a similar charitable concern. What can you do to show your gratitude for God's abundance in your life?

Wednesday 12 April

Party time

Read Luke 15:22–24

'And get the fatted calf and kill it, and let us eat and celebrate; for this son of mine was dead and is alive again; he was lost and is found!' And they began to celebrate.

(verses 23–24)

When I was an undergraduate, I spent an academic year living in Barcelona, perfecting my language skills. It was a year of total immersion in all things Spanish. This was years before mobile phones, the internet, globalisation. It was a complete culture shock! Spain was still ruled by the dictator Franco, and although tourism was increasing, even a big city like Barcelona showed little outside influences. I loved it, however, and participated fully in the life and customs of the people I lived with. But, not unnaturally, there were things I missed: Mars bars, proper tea, and steak and kidney pie. The latter was my mother's speciality and I wrote and asked her to make it for me on the day I arrived back in the UK. It was to be the celebratory meal of my homecoming.

The young man who returned to his father's house never dreamt that there would be the equivalent of steak and kidney pie on the menu – he was grateful for anything that wasn't acorns or pigswill. I was certain of my welcome when I returned home, of my place in my family, whereas he anticipated a different reception: rejection maybe or reluctant readmission to a lowly place in the household. Instead, he is greeted, as I was, with joy and thankfulness.

So is it with our father God whenever we turn back to him. He is eager for us to find our way back, to be reconciled with him, no matter how long we have been absent from home. God awaits us with open arms and a fatted calf.

† Father, I often stray from the path. I stumble and fall. Thank you that you are always there to love me, embrace me and welcome me home.

For further thought

Take some time to look back at your faith journey. Can you identify moments of grace when the Lord lifted you up from distress or sorrow? Give thanks for those.

Thursday 13 April

It's a family affair

Read Luke 5:27–32

Then Levi gave a great banquet for him in his house; and there was a large crowd of tax-collectors and others sitting at the table with them.

(verse 29)

There are some books to which I return time and again. I love the stories about the twelfth-century sleuthing monk, Brother Cadfael, who features in a series of mysteries by Ellis Peters. Often the actual 'whodunnit' element is slight – what makes the books enjoyable is the interaction between the characters and the humane wisdom demonstrated by this Christian from so long ago.

I've been rereading *The Devil's Novice*,[1] and was struck by the scene where Brother Cadfael goes to visit a local family but refuses the offer of food. He forswears 'a midday meal with a household with whom he felt no kinship'. I suppose we have all felt the discomfort of having to be at table with people with whom we have little in common.

Jesus, on the other hand, never seemed to feel such reservations. He looked for and found common ground with everyone. Meals were central to his ministry and the foundation of his teaching and outreach. They also were the source of conflict with the pious who failed to understand the ease and comfort he felt sitting among the outcasts and rejects of society. How could he 'welcome sinners and eat with them'? Jesus wasn't choosy when it came to sitting down at table. He could just as happily have supper with Levi as with Simon the Pharisee. Anyone who was open to his message was somebody with whom he could claim kinship and friendship.

Can we say the same of our Christian communities today? For whom is our welcome reserved or withheld?

† Father, it is so easy to judge others. Help me to seek what unites me to those I fear or mistrust rather than dwell on what divides us.

For further thought

Whose opinions or beliefs challenge you? Read or research them and try to understand where they are coming from. Can you find common ground of any kind? And if not, why not?

[1] Ellis Peters, *The Devil's Novice* (London: Futura Books, 1988).

Friday 14 April

Practice makes perfect

Read John 2:1–10

When the wine gave out, the mother of Jesus said to him, 'They have no wine.' And Jesus said to her, 'Woman, what concern is that to you and to me? …' His mother said to the servants, 'Do whatever he tells you.'

(verses 3–5)

This year we celebrated our daughter's wedding. All our family and friends were there; after a week of rain, the sun shone all day, and the service was a reverent and Spirit-filled occasion. There were some minor glitches but all in all it was a *perfect* wedding.

What constitutes 'perfect' will differ from bride to bride, but everybody wants all aspects of the celebrations to go without a hitch. The pressure to have everything 'just so' is unremitting from the moment the date is set. Two thousand years ago, it was no different. The perfect wedding is threatened because the bar has run dry … and the mother of Jesus wants to avoid embarrassment for the couple involved.

Of course, it is not just the society we live in that seems to impose unrealisable notions of perfection upon us – the perfect body, home, career, etc. As Christians, we are commanded to be as perfect as our heavenly Father is (Matthew 5.48), a task that seems as much beyond us as turning water into wine. How can mere human beings attain perfection?

The way of perfection surely lies in what the mother of Jesus says: 'Do whatever he tells you.' Do as he tells you in the daily struggles that you face. Be the good news that others can read. Embrace and celebrate the sufferings, hopes and joys of life, seeing them, as Jesus did, as situations pregnant with opportunities to grow spiritually. Ask yourself in every situation, 'What would Jesus do?' – and do it as best you can.

† Father, help me to do your will in all I do. Help me to accept with grace the daily bread of joys or disappointments that come my way.

For further thought

When you pray the Lord's Prayer this week, dwell on 'Thy will be done'. Where is God calling you, or your faith community, to genuine conversion or change?

Saturday 15 April

Where two or three are gathered

Read 1 Corinthians 11:23–26

For as often as you eat this bread and drink the cup, you proclaim the Lord's death until he comes.

(verse 26)

Some of my husband's family are from the Hebridean island of Lewis. When we visit we are very aware that the Sabbath is still strictly observed. Shops are closed, ferries do not sail and housework is frowned upon. It must be one of the few remaining places in the UK where the 'traditional' Sunday still exists. Elsewhere, Sunday seems a day just like any other. There is one custom that still seems to hold fast, however – that of Sunday lunch. Whether at home or in restaurants or pubs, the tradition of coming together for a Sunday roast dinner steadfastly persists. In my parish, once a month, a Sunday lunch cooked by volunteers is offered to those who would otherwise be eating alone.

Our Sunday gatherings as Christians are rooted in a traditional shared meal. We may celebrate in different ways and with different emphases but essentially we come together like our sisters and brothers at Corinth to remember who we are – companions in faith and mission.

The early church believed that *solus Christianus, nullus Christianus* – a Christian alone wasn't a Christian. Ours is a faith and practice centred on being together, in a place and a space of equality where our lives are sanctified by the presence of Jesus in the ordinary and the everyday. As at Emmaus, when we started this week, he is revealed in the small but precious moments of our lives, the simple joys of shared meals and fellowship, the toasts to absent friends and the hospitality we extend. And he calls on us to do the same.

† Father, I thank you for all the friendship and love that I have received over the years. May I, in my turn, extend hospitality to any who are in need.

For further thought

Try over the next few weeks to say a grace, before and after meals. Check out websites like www.living-prayers.com for contemporary blessings.

Judges of Israel

1 Deborah and Gideon

Notes by **Terry Lester**

Terry has been an Anglican priest in Cape Town, South Africa, for almost four decades, currently serving in Constantia. Widowed a few years ago, he has three adult children and four grandchildren. Conscious that racial discrimination has had a devastating effect on the lives of most South Africans, Terry is a vocal advocate for justice. To this end, he is engaged in projects aimed at restoring dignity and building reconciliation in his fragmented community. Terry has used the NRSV and NLT for these notes.

Sunday 16 April
Starting over

Read Judges 2:6–23

Then the Lord raised up judges, who delivered them out of the power of those who plundered them.

(verse 16, NRSV)

Whereas Moses represented leaving Egypt and Joshua their arrival in the 'promised land', Joshua's death brought about a period of uncertainty and insecurity for God's people. Each tribe had settled in a different part of the land and each decided their own modus vivendi (way of living) with the Canaanite tribes they encountered. Their once common experiences – slaves to the Egyptians, sojourners through the desert wastelands – no longer bound this motley group. Each now forged their own path as most chose assimilation and immersion into the local customs and culture, avoiding confrontation. Others kept to themselves, which often led to suspicion. The result was a disconnection from their common story and God of Israel, while also blurring the distinction between their God and the gods of Canaan. It also left them militarily vulnerable and easy pickings for their enemies. This in-between time, after settlement and before the Davidic monarchy, is the period of Judges where Yahweh raised up leaders in the face of these challenges they faced. The God of Israel seems ready to start again on their journey of discovering what should be jettisoned and what retained, what was essential and unique to their relationship and what needed discarding. Our journey with God requires much the same.

† Lord God, you are the beginning and the end, the Alpha and Omega. You are also everything in-between; enable me to remain in you through it all. Amen

Monday 17 April

The ways of God

Read Judges 3:12–31

But when the Israelites cried out to the Lord*, the* Lord *raised up for them a deliverer, Ehud son of Gera, the Benjaminite, a left-handed man.*

(verse 15, NRSV)

The Latin word for left is *sinister.* Growing up, I heard stories of how some teachers used punitive means to force left-handed learners to write right-handed, as some considered it sinister to write left-handed! In Middle Eastern communities, the right hand is used for eating, greeting and welcoming activities, while the left hand is used for personal hygiene and washing. This remains so in many communities. There still remains some superstitions that encourage avoidance of left-handedness although many have changed their view these days and believe differently. Left-handed or left-footed sportspeople are feted as possessing a natural weapon. The writer includes this peculiar but curious detail about Ehud, together with other unique qualities which describe his stature, strength, ability to think quickly and fearlessness. By listing these, the writer links Ehud to other illustrious biblical figures before him, who, likewise, accomplish great feats for Yahweh. Note also the Benjaminite link, for one day a man born of the Benjaminite tribe would redeem Israel.

These 'hero' stories have ancient roots and appear from time to time as a reminder of the qualities found among God's people. It serves to invite people to keep an open mind for they know not who the next significant instrument of God's salvation might be.

† Dear Lord God, it is often easier to find reasons that disqualify a person as a likely instrument of your love and grace. Help me keep an open mind. Amen

For further thought

Prejudice is often taught, most times also caught! Identify one in yourself and decide what you will do about it.

Tuesday 18 April

Breaking the yoke and freeing the captive

Read Judges 4:1–24

Barak said to [Deborah], 'If you go with me, I will go; but if you will not go with me, I will not go.' And she said, 'I will surely go with you.'

(verses 8–9, NRSV)

Living all my life in Cape Town, I have witnessed the debilitating effects of fear on communities where daily life has become more and more difficult and dangerous to navigate. Children hardly play outside or walk to their local shop. Grandmothers no longer walk to collect their pension or to visit and have a cup of tea with a friend up the road. The prevalence of gangs, mostly youngsters, many who have dropped out of school, often with hard-core addiction to drugs, creates fear and uncertainty. They, however, fear neither death nor the law and are pitted mostly against any form of authority. Despite their tender years, some have been responsible for heinous acts. It takes huge courage to stand up to them, as often they have access to deadly weapons and are unafraid to use them. But more and more we see pushback. We hear of communities where mothers are standing together and of women who refuse to live in fear or as targets to those who terrorise them. Many are breaking the stranglehold these gangs exert and are finding ways to free their children from their grip.

In today's reading, Deborah and Jael, two unlikely heroes of a terrorised community, outsmart Sisera, the general of King Jabin's army. Barak finds courage in Deborah's assurances, knowing that he does not have to face these tormentors with their vast resources alone.

† Give courage and strength to all whose lives are lived in fear and paralysed by threats of harm and encourage them. Amen

For further thought

Find out about girl and women empowerment groups in your area and ask how you can support them.

Wednesday 19 April

God puts a song in our hearts

Read Judges 5:19–31

She put her hand to the tent peg and her right hand to the workman's mallet; she struck Sisera a blow, she crushed his head, she shattered and pierced his temple. He sank, he fell, he lay still at her feet; at her feet he sank, he fell; where he sank, there he fell dead.

(verses 26–27, NRSV)

All over the continent of Africa, and certainly in the country of my birth, people sing. They sing at funerals, at weddings, in droughts, during floods, in good times and in bad. They sing in times of peace and in war, often listing gruesome details of raids, of cruel deaths which frequently leave the hearers wondering how on earth these lyrics have made their way into song.

The song of Deborah highlights a common feature in scripture where narrative is infused with poetry and prose cast in a rhythmic pentameter. I remember singing 'Ring-a-ring-o'-roses' and 'Atishoo, atishoo, all fall down' in a kid's game. Little did I know that it referred to the period of the pneumonic plague and of people dying in vast numbers with an innocuous sneeze being the tell-tale sign. Music, like humour, helps to ameliorate the harsh effects of devastating events, often enabling the participants to distinguish between victim and perpetrator, thereby creating memory and remembrance into the future.

Central to Israel's life was the psalter. It reflected their prayers, their praises and their laments in daily life, as well as communal experiences of deliverance and triumph. During the Covid-19 pandemic we were not allowed to sing at services. It was a tough call to make, knowing it was very un-African and went against the established traditions of liturgy. For when the faithful gather, they vent in song about how God is experienced in any given situation.

† Lord God, put a song in my heart that I may pray and praise aright and serve you in all I do. Amen

For further thought

Music and song carry a people and strengthen togetherness. Write songs of praise, sing and join in where you can.

Thursday 20 April

Worshipping in spirit and in truth

Read Judges 6:11–32

Gideon answered him, 'But sir, if the Lord is with us, why then has all this happened to us? And where are all his wonderful deeds that our ancestors recounted to us, saying, "Did not the Lord bring us up from Egypt?"'

(verse 13, NRSV)

Relationships have to be two-way streets to be real and remain healthy. It should be safe to express how you feel to one to whom you are committed. Gideon is committed to God, but things are very bad for him and his community. They live in fear of the Midianites who raid their stores at will; as we see Gideon beating out the wheat in an empty winepress and with no wine, it means nothing to celebrate! But it is a defiant act, not only to provide food but also as he addresses the angel, and not a cowering by Gideon. Hence the address: 'Hail, mighty warrior!'

If there is anything we learn from this book, it is that God often sees in people what they often do not see in themselves, nor do others. The book is an invitation to the reader to see what God sees. No matter how unlikely. Gideon is not at ease with God, who seems to have abandoned them to the whims of their enemy, and expresses this dis-ease to the angel. It is a dis-ease reflected in the community, too, as many have turned away from God and turned to Baal, a foreign god who seems to have replaced the One who brought them up from Egypt. By the end of our reading, Baal's altar is destroyed and the Lord's peace is established not just in Gideon but also in the community.

† Lord our God, life for so many is a daily struggle for survival. Open doors for those who need and rely on the help of others to survive, and raise up those who feel beaten down. Amen

For further thought

Often the need is not far away – next door, across the road. How will you live more consciously and respond more meaningfully?

Friday 21 April

Silencing the noise and shedding the excess

Read Judges 7:1–21

But the Lord told Gideon, 'There are still too many! Bring them down to the spring, and I will test them to determine who will go with you and who will not.'

(verse 4, NLT)

We live in an age of accumulation. Multi-storey buildings are being erected just to provide storage for what is excess for many. In Cape Town, with a chronic housing shortage, more buildings are being converted into storage spaces than living units. Is it due to our need for self-reliance and holding on to excess possessions that gives us some assurance? Is more, better? In the Gospels, Jesus' teaching on faith suggests that it is not how much faith we have but, rather, who that faith is in – even if it is the size of a mustard seed. Our reading suggests that God is more than capable of performing the task – the fewer, the better! The process of jettisoning numbers and the image of soldiers lapping water like dogs is quite hilarious. Maybe the writer is suggesting that Gideon's, and our, reliance on vast numbers other than on God is equally hilarious! God is teaching Gideon about the essentials needed for trust and life. Also, the comedic image of soldiers smashing jars and blowing trumpets, thereby sowing fear and mayhem among the hardened Midianite ranks of soldiers, all fully kitted out, yet fleeing from the sound of innocuous objects, highlights their vain and inexplicable insistence on placing their trust and reliance on things. Dare one suggest therefore that we are much the same? That the more we have, the less likely we are to trust God for our life and survival? Trust is about letting go too.

† Teach me, my God and King, reliance and trust and faith in you my God and Creator. Amen

For further thought

When last did you engage in decluttering? Maybe start with a cupboard and clothing and give to charity shops or others in need.

Saturday 22 April

In weakness, strength

Read Judges 8:22–35

Then the Israelites said to Gideon, 'Rule over us, you and your son and your grandson also; for you have delivered us out of the hand of Midian.' Gideon said to them, 'I will not rule over you, and my son will not rule over you; the LORD will rule over you.'

(verses 22–23)

For the first time the reader is introduced to what is to follow for God's people – kingship. Whereas anyone could be selected as a judge based on the needs of the time, kingship would be a pre-ordained, predictable and predetermined selection. The people had had many encounters with the kings of Canaan who adversely dominated their life. Now they begin to toy with having their own king. The passage is ambiguous and suggests that Gideon is against it, yet he names his son Abimelech, meaning 'my father is king'! The ground, though, is laid for what would be an acrimonious debate in Israel on whether they too should have kings like the other nations. Gideon had been an extraordinary saviour, judge and possibly even a king. Yet, in the end, he displayed the same weaknesses as others before him, demonstrating that he too was only a mere human with feet of clay. Earlier in the book he considers himself weak because of inexperience and diffidence, yet God uses him mightily. Now, though, as his confidence and power grow and his might is felt among the Midianites whom he subdues, his weakness for self-aggrandisement shows. He, like the people of Israel, has forgotten that Israel's true King, Judge and Saviour is the Lord.

† Dear Lord, though I may forgetful be, may I never forget you, our King, our Lord and our Saviour. Amen

For further thought

List the times when you acknowledged your own powerlessness yet discovered a strength beyond your imagining: in weakness, strength.

Judges of Israel

2 Jephthah and Samson

Notes by **Nathan Eddy**

Nathan is Director of the Council of Christians and Jews, the oldest interfaith charity in the UK. He also teaches Hebrew and helps lead a small United Reformed Church congregation. He lives with Clare and their daughters on a housing estate in London, and edited *Fresh from The Word* for several years from 2014. Nathan has used the NRSVA for these notes.

Sunday 23 April

Who shall go up for us?

Read Judges 10:6–11:11

Go and cry to the gods whom you have chosen; let them deliver you in the time of your distress.

(verse 14)

'Who shall go up for us?' The book of Judges asks in chapter 1, verse 1. Last week we saw the up-and-down fortunes of Israel under the leadership of Deborah and Gideon. This week our hopes turn to Jephthah and Samson. Will they be the ones to rescue their people?

With pointed clarity, today's reading portrays Israel's ongoing intransigence in unflinching terms. Israel has followed other gods, and God's response is to leave them to face the natural consequences of their actions. It makes for painful reading; but God is grieved for his people (verse 16). There is yet hope.

Unlike in the cases of Deborah and Gideon, Jephthah's birth is described. Here is a special leader, these details suggest. Like King David and other leaders of Israel after him, Jephthah's story is one of scrappy determination, grit and questionable integrity. The son of a prostitute, a woman in those days of no rights and low social standing, his beginnings are not auspicious. Disinherited by his brothers and, seemingly, his townsfolk, he gathers a band of outlaws and makes his own fortune. He is an unlikely candidate to return Israel to the ways of God. What will come of his leadership?

† When our loyalty is broken, O God, let yours sustain us.

Monday 24 April

A rash vow

Read Judges 11:29–40

So there arose an Israelite custom that for four days every year the daughters of Israel would go out to lament the daughter of Jephthah the Gileadite.

(verses 39b–40)

The parallels are disturbing: Abraham had only one son, whom God asked him for no reason to sacrifice, yet God held off and the child of the promise was spared. Jephthah had but one daughter, whom he promised to God; God was silent and the child was sacrificed by her own father. On the one hand, the obedience of Abraham, the ancestor of Christians, Jews and Muslims, shines through. On the other, the senselessness of human folly and the silence of God. Nowhere is Judges more bleak than here – except, perhaps, in the story of the Levite's concubine that concludes this week.

Even the oft-repeated name Mizpah takes on ironic significance. The root for this place-name means 'to look out' or 'see', and it probably refers to a mountain lookout or defence. Yet Jephthah is a leader who definitely does *not* 'look out'. He vows his vow rashly, with no clue about the impending calamity. Abraham, by contrast, looks up to the starry sky and sees his descendants.

Moreover, Jephthah seems to miss the Israelite truth that in fact sacrifice, as necessary as it is in the ancient world, is offered freely; it cannot change the mind of the God of Israel. In giving up his only daughter to this God he betrays his own misplaced trust.

God's silence in the face of Jephthah's folly is unsettling – but the responsibility for his daughter's death is Jephthah's alone. Yet Jephthah refuses to accept responsibility for his errors and displaces them on to the victim. Like many other women in Judges and down to today, this unnamed woman pays for the guilt and errors of another.

† Loving God, we hold in our hearts today all victims of violence, and all girls hurt at the hands of their families.

For further thought

What other options did Jephthah have? Can this story encourage us to challenge traditions that do harm?

Tuesday 25 April

A wise woman

Read Judges 13:2–25

You shall conceive and bear a son. So then drink no wine or strong drink, and eat nothing unclean, for the boy shall be a nazirite to God from birth to the day of his death.

(verse 7)

Although she is not named, Samson's mother takes centre stage today as a woman who perceives and collaborates with a messenger of God. Like Sarah in Genesis as well as Elizabeth and Mary in the New Testament, Samson's mother is a willing participant in the mysterious and miraculous ways of her God. Indeed, the story follows a familiar pattern that shaped the form of the later New Testament stories.

It also provides relief from the narratives of sin and brokenness in the Jephthah cycle. Here, we encounter a world open to the holy presence of God. Telling Samson's parents of their son's future role, the messenger rises in the flames of the sacrificial fire. The parents-to-be are terrified to realise they were in the presence of God (verse 22), as Elizabeth and Mary will be in a later age.

Twice in this story, the word for 'wonders' or 'wonderful' is used in relation to the messenger from God (verses 18 and 19). It is the same word used in Exodus 15:11 to describe the miracle of the rescue at the Red Sea. And it appears three times in Psalm 139, when the psalmist marvels at God's 'wonderful' ways and that the psalmist, too, is a 'wonderful' creation (Psalm 139:6, 14).

The name 'Samson', *Shimshon* in Hebrew, is perhaps related to the word for the sun, *Shemesh*, meaning 'little sun'. As with Samuel, David, John the Baptist and Jesus, the spirit of the Lord is present in this one (verse 25). Will he be the one to wonderfully redeem his people?

† God of all, open our eyes to see all around us who might be unnamed and invisible – and help us imagine that they are central to your redeeming purposes.

For further thought

What parallels can you see between Mary, Samson's mother, Jesus and Samson?

Wednesday 26 April
Samson the trickster

Read Judges 14:1–20

Out of the eater came something to eat. Out of the strong came something sweet.

(verse 14)

Our hopes of redemption under Samson are dashed as we read on. Instead of a wise and discerning leader – one as perceptive as his mother or as hospitable as his father – Samson obeys only his baser urges, demanding a beautiful Philistine woman he sees (verse 2). Renowned as the 'strong man' of the Bible, Samson is in fact one of the weakest, blind to his own rampant urges.

Eating, strength, sweetness ... the words of Samson's riddle in verse 14 evoke the sensuality of the wedding feast. The words also evoke Song of Songs 8:6: 'love is strong as death, passion fierce as the grave'. 'Strength' and 'sweetness' speak even more broadly to the experience of Israel as a whole. The God of Israel is strong to save (as at the Red Sea in Exodus 14) and gives a way of life, the law, which is sweeter than honey (Psalm 19:10).

In this broader sense, Samson represents his whole people. Like Samson, Israel has lusted after foreigners and their gods, in the view of Judges. Like Samson, Israel has acted impulsively, without thinking. Like Samson, Israel has neglected cultic duties and the covenant itself.

Is this a deliberate strategy of Judges, to show us again and again the frailty of Israel's faith? Judges challenges any naivety about human goodness. The future is always open and repentance always possible, but the people of Israel and its leaders continually close the doors that God would keep ajar. We the reader – indeed God, as well – are helpless onlookers as Israel flounders.

And yet: the love of Israel's God is strong as death.

† God of life, teach us to delight in your word and guide our lives by it.

For further thought

Riddles are characteristic of the Bible's wisdom literature, like Proverbs, Song of Solomon and many psalms. Does the riddle need to have only one meaning?

Thursday 27 April

Samson in love

Read Judges 16:4–22

She let him fall asleep on her lap; and she called a man, and had him shave off the seven locks of his head. He began to weaken, and his strength left him.

(verse 19)

Again, Samson is smitten with passion – but here he falls in love (verse 4). Will this time be different?

Undeniably, Judges is not a kind book towards women. Although it features the strong women leaders in Deborah and Jael, it also features horrific violence towards women, as in Saturday's story of the Levite's concubine and Jephthah's daughter.

Yet Delilah and other female characters offer a counterpoint. Although Samson is endowed with divine strength, Delilah's human cunning easily outflanks him. Delilah shows herself, as did the unnamed wife before her, to be more loyal to her people than to her husband. These women, in a sense, show Israel what loyalty looks like. Samson's mother, too, although unnamed, shows the kind of trust and faith that can serve as a model for her people.

Samson and Jephthah, by contrast, although strong warriors, are revealed to be weak. Masculinity, leadership and faith are playfully undermined by the examples of Delilah and the other women. In the end, Samson's strength came from a surprising source: his nazirite vow, not his innate power or God's charismatic gifts of the spirit. Ignored for most of the narrative, the vow, like a covenant, is a source of power. In this way, Judges challenges us to look beyond the obvious and discern God at work in less likely individuals and means.

Samson's life turns tragic. In Gaza, Samson visited prostitutes (Chronicles 16:1); in Gaza he was also imprisoned in chains. He is reduced to grinding grain like a brute animal (verse 21). Blinded by his passions, his eyes are gouged out by his oppressors. Will our sight be any more true?

† Gracious God, teach us to lead faithfully, fully and fairly, that your rule might be known.

For further thought

Delilah's weaving of Samson's hair suggests magic. What are the positive and negative ways women are portrayed in this story, and all this week?

Friday 28 April

Prayer warrior

Read Judges 16:23–31

Lord God, remember me and strengthen me only this once, O God, so that with this one act of revenge I may pay back the Philistines for my two eyes.

(verse 28)

In one final act in this high drama, Samson avenges himself at the hands of torturers. The man who in his life never showed much regard for his own vow, or for morality in general, destroys a symbol of idol worship, a temple to another god.

His imprisoners call him out to entertain them. The mighty hero is reduced to party tricks. But he has a last trick of his own up his sleeve. He prays to God for one last gift of strength and topples the whole structure down on himself and thousands of Philistines.

Blinded, shackled, weakened, Samson kills more Philistines in his death than in his life. As a man of prayer – surprisingly, a figure resembling Daniel's piety in the face of persecution – Samson is far more effective than he ever was as a man of muscle.

Is his life a triumph or a tragedy? Is he a hero or a buffoon? Is he a mighty man of God or someone crippled by lust and passion?

In a sense, Samson is all of these; an enigma open to as many interpretations as the riddle he told. Strength and sweetness, love and passion, death and life: all these are spun out of the example of his life. Tragedy, comedy, faith: the saga of Samson is one of the most alluring and well crafted in the whole Bible.

His kinsfolk retrieve his body and bury him in his father's tomb. In death, although not in life, Samson rests with his people.

† God of all strength, our lives are an enigma to ourselves. Teach us to seek you in all we do.

For further thought

The fact that Samson's kinsfolk, rather than his own progeny, retrieve his body suggests that he had no offspring. If we live like Samson, does this mean that there is no lasting legacy?

Saturday 29 April

A broken woman

Read Judges 19:10–30

Has such a thing ever happened since the day that the Israelites came up from the land of Egypt until this day? Consider it, take counsel, and speak out.

(verse 30)

Following the death of Samson, there is no leader for Israel. And the ensuing chaos is crystallised in a story of almost unspeakable horror: the Levite's concubine.

A Levite from the hill country of Israel journeys to win back his wife (a concubine in ancient Israel is a kind of second-tier spouse) after an argument. On their return, night has fallen and they seek accommodation urgently. In the town square in Gibeah they are met by a welcoming local. He takes them in – but after nightfall, others from the city bang on the door, demanding the Levite guest. Their intentions become clear when the host offers to the mob the concubine and his own daughter instead. The concubine is thrust outside, apparently with the consent of the Levite; she is raped and abused all night, and in the morning summons her strength to fall at the door of the house, her hands on the threshold. When morning comes, her husband discovers her, apparently dead. He takes her home and, in a grisly climax, takes a knife and cuts her in pieces to be distributed throughout Israel.

As with Jephthah's daughter, the story of the Levite's concubine features senseless violence inflicted on unnamed women. Both stories also seem to relate to Abraham's near-sacrifice of Isaac in Genesis 22, and the story today horribly prefigures Saul's summoning of Israel with a dismembered ox in 1 Samuel 11:7.

The story issues a challenge. Should the events be shrouded in silence? Is Israel's lawlessness acceptable in the eyes of God? 'Consider it, take counsel, and speak out.'

† Gracious God, we lift up to you all women who suffer anonymously at the hands of men and pray for healing and justice.

For further thought

Name all of the women who have appeared in our stories this week and hold them in your heart.

Biblical library (2)

History

Notes by **David Painting**

David's passion is to see people encounter God more profoundly. A science graduate, David has held senior roles in industry and commerce alongside a pastoral ministry in Baptist churches in the UK. Having spent time in YWAM leading and teaching on Discipleship Training Schools in the UK and overseas, he currently divides his time between software development, co-leading a house church, teaching and writing. He was a theological advisor and data contributor to the Infographic Bible project. David has used the NRSVA for these notes.

Sunday 30 April

After Joshua

Read Judges 6:1–10

I said to you, 'I am the Lord your God; you shall not pay reverence to the gods of the Amorites, in whose land you live.' But you have not given heed to my voice.

(verse 10)

I love reading stories, like the narrative parts of scripture that we're looking at this week. But I quickly get bored with books that have lots of detail: pages of descriptions, endless dialogue, lots of flashbacks to flesh out the characters. I just want to know what happens next, to keep the plot moving, the action unfolding. It's no different when I come to reading stories in the Bible: genealogies, lists of arcane rules, repetition – just tell me what happens next!

Today's passage precedes the story of Gideon: the people are hard pressed and have cried out to God for help. But I rush through to the meeting with the angel, the 'Hail mighty warrior', the fleeces, the tearing down of the Asherah pole, the army lapping the water.

But in truth, the help that the people cry out for does not begin with the miraculous deliverance from evil by Gideon, but with a recognition of how that evil has arisen. 'You have not given heed …' Without acknowledging why they are in the mess, there can be no escape from it.

Are you crying out for help from God? Don't rush past the 'boring' bits of lament, confession, repentance, restitution. Don't race to the destination and miss out on the journey.

† O Lord, help us not to rush over what you have said now in order to get to what we think is more exciting.

Monday 1 May

Where you go, I will go

Read Ruth 1:1–19; 4:11–17

But Ruth said, 'Do not press me to leave you or to turn back from following you! Where you go, I will go; where you lodge, I will lodge; your people shall be my people, and your God my God. Where you die, I will die – there will I be buried.'

(1:16–17a)

What a fabulous story the book of Ruth is! But how much we miss if we just read it as story. It begins with a famine in Bethlehem – but read more deeply. Bethlehem means 'house of bread', so, in the place renowned for bread, there was no bread. Next, they went to Moab. But stop, look up 'Moab' – it's a place forbidden to Jews earlier in the Old Testament: now we see perhaps why Elimelech and his two sons die – they have wandered from God's protection, from the place of blessing to the place of curse. Finally, Naomi returns home – but pause and consider: when the men were alive, they made those catastrophic choices, the women were powerless. But the moment Naomi has the right to choose, she leads her daughter-in-law to God. And that's just chapter 1!

But chapter 4 ends with a genealogy – why? Ruth is the story of ordinary people living ordinary lives, often powerless, sometimes misunderstanding God, but faithfully following his ways. It's the story of how God takes these ordinary, otherwise unnoticed lives and transforms them into the extraordinary. A story of refugees, an unexpected wedding and a baby. A nice story which ends there for Ruth. But we get to see the real end through the genealogy. Out of Obed comes Jesse and out of Jesse, David: the first king Israel will know. But even that isn't enough for a God, who magnifies our small steps and makes us 'more than conquerors'. For out of Ruth, from David's line, comes the redeemer of humankind, the King of Kings and Lord of Lords.

† O Lord, give me the patience to wrestle with scripture, to see the fullness of you in it.

For further thought

When the blessing stops, what do you do? How easy it is to run away from that which God has blessed and fulfil our needs in the place of curse. How can we avoid this practically?

Tuesday 2 May

Anointing the king

Read 1 Samuel 16:1–23

But the Lord *said to Samuel, 'Do not look on his appearance or on the height of his stature, because I have rejected him; for the* Lord *does not see as mortals see; they look on the outward appearance, but the* Lord *looks on the heart.'*

(verse 7)

'Appearances can be deceptive' is a very English truism. For speed, we once used a packet of powdered milk to make a sauce to go on a dessert. We mixed it with water and chocolate powder to make a lovely chocolate sauce. Unfortunately, the packet also contained savoury flavourings for use on cauliflower cheese. Onion flavoured chocolate sauce: not one of our better recipes!

Moses and Joshua had been appointed as permanent leaders. The period of the Judges had been different; God raising up leaders as and when needed. The people had been called to be different – formed to reflect God's image, not simply mirror the nations around them. But they rejected that calling and demanded that God give them a king, to be like the other nations. And graciously, God gave them Saul, who had every appearance of being like a king.

But appearances can be deceptive! Whether it's a story with hidden depths (as we saw yesterday), a man who looks like a king but isn't kingly – or a chocolate sauce that has invisible onion. We have to learn to look with God's eyes at situations and people, to look beneath the obvious. Otherwise, we misread the story, misjudge the person and end up, as with the sauce, with a bad taste in our mouth!

Look behind this story, then. Hannah is Samuel's mother, and we know how that story began. With a man looking at the outward appearance – Eli looking at Hannah's distress and judging her as a drunk. Hannah insists that he look beyond the appearance to see her broken heart. And now her son Samuel must do the same – and so must we.

† O Lord, search me and know me, reveal to me anything that is hidden; shine your light that I might see more clearly the truth about myself and others.

For further thought

Are there people you have judged by appearance? Do you need to apologise to anyone?

Wednesday 3 May

Solomon

Read 1 Kings 1:1–48

Now Adonijah son of Haggith exalted himself, saying, 'I will be king'; he prepared for himself chariots and horsemen, and fifty men to run before him. His father had never at any time displeased him by asking, 'Why have you done that?' He was also a very handsome man, and he was born next after Absalom.

(verses 5–6)

As we've seen this week, when we look beyond the appearance of the plot, we see patterns of repeating themes and a picture that is bigger than the immediate story. This is the nature of Hebrew storytelling, and we see it again today.

David uses his power to fulfil his lust for Bathsheba, leaving her with no choice; he rapes her. Then he seeks to cover up his crime and ends up murdering Uriah. As we look beyond the surface for the patterns, we see that David's son Amnon rapes Tamar (his half-sister) and David does nothing about it, effectively covering it up. Another son, Absalom, then murders Amnon to do what David wouldn't. Rape, cover-up, murder. Like fathers, like sons ...

In today's reading, two of David's remaining sons fight for the throne because David has not publicly made clear who will succeed him. He has privately told Bathsheba that it will be Solomon but has never disciplined Adonijah, giving him the impression of being the king's favourite. Again, we can look deeper and see how little parental discipline David had – his father Jesse didn't even remember that he had a son called David! The seeds of this generation's issues are sown in the previous generation.

Our passage begins with David having yet another beautiful woman come into his life, the last in a succession of inadvisable or inappropriate relationships. At the end of Solomon's life he had 700 wives and 300 concubines. Two sons fought over the throne of David, the kingdom divides into two after Solomon. When we see the patterns, we see more of the grace and heart of God.

† Holy Spirit, please open my eyes to the deeper truth in the stories of the Bible.

For further thought

What patterns from previous generations do I need to break? What seeds am I sowing into the lives of the next generation?

Thursday 4 May

Into exile

Read 2 Chronicles 36:1–23

The Lord, the God of their ancestors, sent persistently to them by his messengers, because he had compassion on his people and on his dwelling-place; but they kept mocking the messengers of God, despising his words, and scoffing at his prophets, until the wrath of the Lord against his people became so great that there was no remedy.

(verses 15–16)

Jehoahaz, Jehoiakim, Jehoiachin, Zedekiah – the last four kings of Judah, each more evil than their predecessor. As you read Kings and Chronicles, it is easy to fall into the rhythm of the narrative: there is a king, and he does evil and dies. He is succeeded by someone who does even more evil. He dies and is succeeded by one who is even worse. And so on, until God intervenes with a prophet or they rediscover the law, or they are oppressed and turn briefly back to God. Followed by an evil king who leads the people astray, then he dies and is succeeded by an even more evil king …

All of 1 and 2 Chronicles, chapter after chapter, follows the same pattern. God's mercy, his patience, his grace on constant display, despite their fecklessness. Until the very end of the book. God's heart is still the same, but there is nothing more that he can do. He has done it all, to no avail. And so, the full consequences of their choices down the centuries must be felt and this generation will be the ones to feel it. Even in the infinitely loving and creative heart of God, there comes a point where, tragically, there is no remedy.

Ultimately, with great anguish, God gives them what they had set their hearts on. From 'give us a king' to the final king, they have chosen to be less and less distinct. Now they get what they wanted, to be so like other nations as to be absorbed into their culture, taken into captivity and assimilated.

† O Lord, help us to keep our hearts soft towards you, always responsive to your Spirit convicting us of sin, that we might be holy and distinctively like you.

For further thought

Look beyond the story, investigate the meanings of the names of the last four kings. What story does this tell, to what does it point?

Friday 5 May

Return

Read Ezra 1:1–2:70

The whole assembly together was forty-two thousand three hundred and sixty, besides their male and female servants, of whom there were seven thousand three hundred and thirty-seven; and they had two hundred male and female singers. They had seven hundred and thirty-six horses, two hundred and forty-five mules, four hundred and thirty-five camels, and six thousand seven hundred and twenty donkeys.

(verses 2:64–67)

Are these the bits you tend to skim over, as I am tempted to do? Why has God included such detailed lists? What does it add to our knowledge of God or ourselves? (If you're interested, that's 49,897 adults and 8,136 rides – about six people to every animal.) Perhaps a good starting point is to ask, 'What does this connect with, what does it remind me of?' For me it brings two thoughts: first, I am reminded of Jesus telling us that God 'numbers the hairs on our head'. He is into the detail of our lives. He values each person enough to count the hairs. He knows each name of everyone of that 49,897; knows their history, whose family they belong to, which donkey they got to ride ... and he wants us to value and honour them as well; they went back when it was much easier not to.

Second, it reminds me of other counting – in Exodus 12, for example, Moses records the number of people who left Egypt (for the land to which these 50,000 are returning). Six hundred thousand people. More than ten times the number who are going back. A remnant. And, in that, I am reminded of God's faithfulness. Even after all the centuries of evil kings and unrepentant people, even after all that God had done to win them back, only for them to reject him time and again, even though it broke his heart, he holds back the full consequences of their rebellion in order that some might be saved.

And now, after generations of captivity, this remnant pack their belongings, load up the mules and begin the journey back to the place of peace – Jerusalem.

† O Lord, thank you for counting me, for knowing me, for loving me in the detail of who I am.

For further thought

Are there people you 'skim over' when you see them, but you don't really see them? Pause and ask God for insight – how does he know them, how can you love them?

Saturday 6 May
Rebuild

Read Nehemiah 6:1–16

[And] so the wall was finished on the twenty-fifth day of the month Elul, in fifty-two days. And when all our enemies heard of it, all the nations around us were afraid and fell greatly in their own esteem; for they perceived that this work had been accomplished with the help of our God.

(verses 15–16)

As we've looked at different stories this week, we've seen how recurring patterns link them together like the interlocking pieces of a jigsaw puzzle. But what is the picture they make when put together?

Our readings end unexpectedly. God speaks to a non-Jew, a man at the head of the empire that is oppressing the remnant of Judah, and out of reverence for God he invites the people to return and rebuild Jerusalem. He even funds the project, returning the plundered items from the temple. It's an extraordinary story of restoration, of unity and courage in the face of opposition. Opposition that grows verse by verse so that when I read the 'and so' of verse 15 my mind wants to add 'and so they were defeated'. But Nehemiah doesn't write that. Despite the centuries of evil, of rebellion, despite the generations in exile, despite the unbearable opposition to the rebuilding work, he simply writes 'it was finished'. God completes the work he began. And in that phrase we hear echoing through eternity another 'It is finished' and we see where all scripture points – to a cross, to Jesus, to a God who redeems and restores.

Jesus is the picture on the box! That's how we make sense of the sometimes puzzling pieces of the Bible. Of course, each individual piece, each scripture, is significant, but only if it is in the right place, connected to the right other pieces, revealing Jesus.

† Thank you, Lord, for your faithfulness, that you are able to complete the good work begun in me.

For further thought

Are you facing opposition as you seek to rebuild walls of peace in your life? Be assured, with Jesus, they will be finished.

Places of worship

Notes by **John Birch**

Based in South Wales, John is a Methodist Local Preacher, writes prayers and Bible studies for faithandworship.com, and is amazed at where these are being used and how God has blessed lives through them. Some prayers have been adapted for use within choral and more contemporary worship settings. John has several published books and in his spare time sings folk songs and, with his wife Margaret, has an allotment, walks and explores the country in a campervan called Lola. John has used the NIVUK for these notes.

Sunday 7 May

Worship in a tent

Read Exodus 33:1–11

As Moses went into the tent, the pillar of cloud would come down and stay at the entrance, while the LORD spoke with Moses. Whenever the people saw the pillar of cloud standing at the entrance to the tent, they all stood and worshipped, each at the entrance to their tent. The LORD would speak to Moses face to face, as one speaks to a friend.

(verses 9–11a)

Moses was having a bit of a nightmare with the people he'd brought out of Egypt. They had lost patience with him and were worshipping a golden calf. He needed to talk things over with God.

So, Moses made his way to the Tent of Meeting, outside the main camp and somewhere he could go, be still and hear God's voice. Remarkably, when Moses went inside this tent, a cloud representing God's presence rested overhead. Seeing it, people would stop for a while to offer worship outside their own tents. In the chaos of life, a moment of calm.

I remember a large tent in a field where, with the family and a few thousand others, we gathered for worship at a festival. Onto a stage came 15-year-old Becky, and in her wheelchair, smiling broadly and using an electronic talker, she gave an inspirational message that not only brought a tear to every eye but a standing ovation. It reminded us not only of God's love but that God can use and speak though all of us, bringing hope, confidence and strength to face each day.

There was no cloud over the tent, but God was surely there.

† Loving God, you know the things that are troubling me at this moment. I bring them to you and ask for your help and guidance through the coming days. Amen

Monday 8 May

Worship in high places

Read 1 Kings 3:1–9

The king went to Gibeon to offer sacrifices, for that was the most important high place, and Solomon offered a thousand burnt offerings on that altar. At Gibeon the Lord *appeared to Solomon during the night in a dream, and God said, 'Ask for whatever you want me to give you.'*

(verses 4–5)

This is the wonderful moment where Solomon, offered anything he wants by God, chooses wisdom rather than riches, as this will help him govern the people. The divine encounter takes place during worship on a hilltop just north of Jerusalem, a 'high place', and a practice frowned on by many, as these were places where pagans had altars. But the first temple had yet to be built, and God was happy to be with Solomon as he worshipped in that place.

It is not uncommon to hear hilltops and other remote locations called 'sacred spaces' where God's presence seems close. Living in Wales with its fair share of hills and mountains, I can understand this, having found places where this experience is profound. Near to us is Ffald y Brenin, which translates as 'Sheepfold of the King', a hilltop with a large cross at one end and a retreat centre nearby, where thousands have experienced God's presence and healing touch over the years. Our local churches have been there on day visits, and it really is a special place to spend time in God's presence, as did Solomon at Gibeon, and find both wisdom and inspiration.

So, reading about Solomon having this extraordinary experience of God's presence on a hilltop seems quite affirming, and a reminder that when, and wherever, we pray we should think not only about ourselves but about how we might best serve those around us.

† Lord, I pray for those working in government, local or national, that they might find, like Solomon, the wisdom they need in making decisions that affect the lives of others. Amen

For further thought

How do we 'experience' the presence of God, and can it be in many and various ways?

Tuesday 9 May

Worship in a temple

Read 2 Chronicles 7:11–22

Now my eyes will be open and my ears attentive to the prayers offered in this place. I have chosen and consecrated this temple so that my Name may be there for ever. My eyes and my heart will always be there.

(verses 15–16)

Solomon worshipped happily on a hilltop, but that was nothing compared to the joy of entering the temple in Jerusalem, seven years in the making and magnificent in appearance. His father David had wanted to build it, but God refused his request and told him this would be a task for his son. Within the new temple was the ark of the covenant, along with all the silver, gold and furnishings that David had already sourced and dedicated to this project.

The temple was indeed a beautiful and holy place, sadly destroyed in 587 BC. I confess I had always thought of it as a very Jewish place and not so relevant to my faith, but then I discovered that one of Solomon's prayers was that any foreigners, drawn to it after hearing of God's greatness and love, would be welcome there. It was Solomon's desire that this building might be a focus of faith for all people.

The nearest we have here would be a cathedral and I am reminded of a visit to Brecon Cathedral in Wales, its site a focus of worship stretching back to the ancient Celtic church. It might not be full of gold and silver, but somehow the fragrance of worship through the centuries has permeated its walls, and those of faith and no faith are welcomed through its doors, encouraged to be still, sense God's presence and make their own response.

† Gracious God, I thank you for the knowledge that the prayers I offer, for myself and others, are not said in vain but heard and answered. Amen

For further thought

How might the scale or design of a place of worship contribute to the experience of regular worshippers and visitors?

Wednesday 10 May

Worship in a synagogue

Read Acts 17:1–4

As was his custom, Paul went into the synagogue, and on three Sabbath days he reasoned with them from the Scriptures, explaining and proving that the Messiah had to suffer and rise from the dead. 'This Jesus I am proclaiming to you is the Messiah,' he said.

(verses 2–3)

The daily routine of a synagogue is different from that of the temple, as its Hebrew name means 'house of assembly'. It is a place of gathering, a time to pray, study, draw the community together and help others. In the Gospels, we find Jesus teaching regularly in the synagogue, and Paul, on his missionary journeys, used them as opportunities for teaching and evangelism. Here in Thessalonica, we hear that Jews and Gentiles, men and women, were convicted by his powerful words and joined the group of believers.

Following a service I took some years ago, an elderly church member took me aside and explained that at one time they used to meet afterwards to discuss the sermon, and how he missed that opportunity to engage with the message. At the time, I thought this might be quite intimidating and was rather glad they had stopped, but my opinion has gradually changed, along with my confidence in preaching, and now I would gladly embrace this practice as part of our worship. So much better than a congregation sitting there quietly listening to the message, only to forget it shortly afterwards!

Connecting with God's word regularly is such a good discipline, as Jesus, Paul and others who frequented those synagogues knew only too well, and an important element in our own worshipping life, whether delivered by sermon, discussion groups, Bible studies or daily notes.

† For the joy of reading my Bible, the wisdom, strength and guidance received, even the questions needing further thought and study, I thank you, loving God. Amen

For further thought

Should we think more about discussing the Sunday sermon, if not after a service, then through the week? What could be the benefits for the worshipping community?

Thursday 11 May

The house church

Read Romans 16:3–5

Greet Priscilla and Aquila, my fellow workers in Christ Jesus. They risked their lives for me. Not only I but all the churches of the Gentiles are grateful to them. Greet also the church that meets at their house.

(verses 3–5a)

Paul knew Priscilla and Aquila well, a friendship going back several years to when he stayed with them during his mission work in Corinth. They then moved on with him to Ephesus, and from there to Rome, supporting Paul as he taught about Jesus and establishing a small worshipping fellowship within their home. There are many examples within the New Testament of believers meeting together for prayer and worship in houses, and there were practical reasons for meeting like this, when the church was growing so quickly and believers wanted to meet for fellowship, prayer, the breaking of bread and study, even if they continued their regular worship in the temple.

Meeting in homes has been an important element of church life across denominations for centuries. I'm part of the Methodist Church, and its founder, John Wesley, encouraged weekly class meetings in homes comprising worship, sharing and learning together. We hosted one of these many years ago, and I can affirm how good it was for the life of the local church. Growing together in faith, learning to trust each other, and sharing joys and sorrows within that secure environment helped many a faith to grow and blossom. We recently revisited that church, and almost forty years later it is still a vibrant, loving fellowship.

† Loving God, for all those meeting today in small groups to enjoy fellowship, study and discussion of your word, may their faith grow and blossom along with their knowledge of your word. Amen

For further thought

What are the opportunities for members of your own church to meet together in small groups?

Friday 12 May

It's not about a building

Read John 4:19–24

Yet a time is coming and has now come when the true worshippers will worship the Father in the Spirit and in truth, for they are the kind of worshippers the Father seeks.

(verse 23)

Jesus is talking to a Samaritan woman at Jacob's well, and as the conversation gets a little too personal and challenging, she changes the subject and asks Jesus if their worship should take place on the mountain close to where they were sitting, or where the Jews insisted, in Jerusalem where Solomon's temple had stood?

Jesus did not want to get drawn into what was a historic controversy. In his answer, he alludes to her ancestors trying to blend the worship of foreign gods and idols with the God of the Jews, but his key point is simply that it is not where you worship or offer a sacrifice that matters. If God is spirit, we cannot confine him to one place, and certainly not within an object. True worship, in the power of his Spirit and in truth, will find God wherever we are.

This week we have seen worship taking place in a tent, on a mountain, in a temple, a synagogue and a house. In these places we have seen God's people gather to offer sacrifices, sing, pray, hear God's word, discuss its meaning, break bread together and become a fellowship that is outward looking, mission focused. That is what God desires from us, and that does not limit us to location, as comfortable as we may be in our current spiritual homes!

† Dear Lord, may it never be about where we meet, and how magnificent or humble is the building, but how we meet, as your children gathering to worship in Spirit and in truth, meeting with their God and Saviour. Amen

For further thought

Where in your local area, with its shops, cafes and meeting places, might a small group of Christians gather for fellowship and perhaps even outreach to the community?

Saturday 13 May

Worship in heaven

Read Revelation 21:1–3

And I heard a loud voice from the throne saying, 'Look! God's dwelling-place is now among the people, and he will dwell with them. They will be his people, and God himself will be with them and be their God.'

(verse 3)

So far, we have focused our thoughts on the past and present, but in Revelation, the vision is of a new heaven, new earth and new Jerusalem. We might find this book and its language difficult to comprehend, but we find its reflection in countless artistic and musical compositions, and within the soaring architecture and stained-glass windows of so many cathedrals, because this passage has echoes of one of Ezekiel's visions, picturing the glory of the Lord entering and filling the temple. He is told that it is here that God will live among the Israelites for ever. However, John's vision here does not include a temple in the New Jerusalem because God's presence will be wherever his people are.

And this is where we can connect the readings of this past week. God's desire has always been to be where his people are, and yet we find so many stories in the Bible of people rejecting or rebelling against God, the cause of a painful separation. We may not yet have seen a new heaven, earth or Jerusalem, but as we meet for worship in cathedral, church, chapel, community room, cafe, tent, mountain or home, acknowledging our sin and offering our lives in service, God's dwelling place is with us, this we know, and John's vision is, in part, being fulfilled.

† God of all time and place, we offer our thanks and praise that the worship we enjoy now is merely a foretaste of what is yet to come, within the fellowship of all believers. Amen

For further thought

What does the word *worship* mean to you?

The Gospel of Matthew (3)

1 Healer and teacher

Notes by **Bruce Jenneker**

Bruce is a retired South African Anglican priest living in Cape Town. During thirty-five years of ministry, worship, liturgy and Christian formation were his primary occupation. He served as Canon Precentor at Washington National Cathedral, St George's Cathedral, Cape Town, Precentor at Trinity Church Copley Square, Boston, Director of Liturgy at Trinity Church Wall Street in New York City and as Rector of All Saints Church in Durbanville. He taught Liturgy at seminary and led conferences and retreats. Bruce has used the NRSV for these notes.

Sunday 14 May

Words of life

Read Matthew 7:1–12

In everything do to others as you would have them do to you; for this is the law and the prophets.

(verse 12)

The readings for this week are from Matthew 7–9, central to chapters 4–16 which recount Jesus' teaching and healing ministry in Israel and its rejection of him. For the early church, the first Gospel served as a textbook to form and guide new Christians in the way of Jesus Christ.

While it is assumed that it was initially addressed to a diverse community of Jews and Gentiles, its knowledge of and dependence on the Hebrew scriptures suggest an earnest intention to present Jesus as the Jewish Messiah in whom all God's promises are fulfilled.

As it served the early church, so it serves us, laying before us the good news of Christ, its promises and demands, a lamp to our feet and a light to our path.

Following the way of Christ involves commitment and belief, conviction and practice. Christians are to be generous in their dealings with others, reserving judgement, offering the benefit of the doubt. Christians will have a profound respect for what is holy, hallowing the sacred in all they say and do. Christians strive to live with complete confidence in the loving-kindness, grace and presence of God, here and now, everywhere and always.

† Lord Jesus Christ, inspire my mind, fill my heart, and guide me in all I say and do, that your gospel will shape my life.

Monday 15 May
Confident living

Read Matthew 7:13–29

A good tree cannot bear bad fruit, nor can a bad tree bear good fruit … Thus, you will know them by their fruits. Not everyone who says to me, 'Lord, Lord', will enter the kingdom of heaven, but only one who does the will of my Father in heaven.

(verses 18, 20–21)

Jesus was eager for his followers to understand the demands and the cost of living the gospel. It is a world-changing and counter-cultural way of life, based on a radical conversion to Christ and Christ's good news.

Jesus' way of life was not understood or valued by the community in which he lived and taught. They took religion for granted. For many of them it was a nominal acceptance of conventions, not a sincere commitment of the heart and a deliberate choice of behaviour. Jesus condemned this attitude as hypocritical.

Contemporary secular societies also pay lip service to values they readily abandon. All over the world, on personal, social and political levels, vice abounds and corruption is rife. As individuals, we present ourselves as people of integrity, eager witnesses of righteousness but almost always choose self-interest over the common good; as societies we mouth the words of fairness and justice but are apathetic in the face of poverty and violence; most politicians make grand promises but inevitably yield to greed and corruption.

Following Christ and living Christ's gospel is living in faithful imitation of Christ's life: authentically owning who we are and committing ourselves to patterning our lives on Christ's. To align our words and deeds with Christ's requires choosing light when darkness threatens, identifying with hope when despair reigns, acting with compassion and generosity when indifference and greed are the order of the day.

As Christ is the light of the world, so Christ's followers are called to be a lamp set on a hill and the salt of the earth.

† Lord Jesus Christ, break through the walls of indifference that enclose me, claim, redeem and restore me; make your way my way, make your will my will, make your love the meaning of my life.

For further thought

Examine your recent actions. Consider the social and political choices that are made by you and on your behalf. Are these congruent with Christ's gospel?

Tuesday 16 May

Living whole and healthy

Read Matthew 8:1–13

Many will come from east and west and will eat with Abraham and Isaac and Jacob in the kingdom of heaven, while the heirs of the kingdom will be thrown into the outer darkness, where there will be weeping and gnashing of teeth.

(verses 11–12)

Archaeological research has found that infectious diseases were prevalent in first-century Palestine. Both the poor and the wealthy were equally at risk when an aggressive pathogen struck. Infant mortality was high, leprosy and tuberculosis were widespread, and infection by tapeworm was debilitating and often fatal.

For the community in which Jesus lived, taught and healed, disease and death were familiar and constant threats – as indeed they are for us as we live with the consequences of a devastating and, as I write, a still-threatening pandemic.

Nothing defines our daily lives as totally as sickness, dying and death. Despair takes up residence within us when disease renders us powerless and death looms. Hope is impossible in the face of the facts. Panic lays hold of us. We are caught in the downward spiral of anxiety and alarm. Calm serenity is impossible. Moments of denial and false hope assail us when consuming dread and the awful truth become too much to bear. Ostrich-like we bury our heads in the sand and choose unreality over truth.

For those of us who live in, by and with Jesus Christ, Christ is not our insurance against disaster, illness, dying and death. Rather, for us, life in Christ is having the all-provident, unconditional, never-failing grace of God present with us as we face the inevitability of disaster, illness, dying and death. All our arrogance and misguided confidence to the contrary, our human condition is weak, vulnerable and mortal. Pain, illness, suffering and death are inevitable. But thanks be to God, with Christ none of it can ever overcome us.

† Lord Jesus Christ, be my constant companion when I am overcome by more than I can bear; carry me through the storm to the safe harbour of your love and peace.

For further thought

Examine your response to disaster. Are you self-reliant and confident in your own resources? Where do you find your ultimate support?

Wednesday 17 May

Saving power

Read Matthew 8:14–27

That evening they brought to Jesus many who were possessed by demons; and he cast out the spirits with a word and cured all who were sick. This was to fulfil what had been spoken through the prophet Isaiah, 'He took our infirmities and bore our diseases.'

(verses 16–17)

Who is this Jesus, that even the winds and the sea obey him? This is one of the most profound questions in the Gospels – and for the life of faith.

When Jesus taught, the people asked, 'Who is this Jesus, who teaches with authority?' When Jesus healed the sick, the people asked, 'Who is this Jesus who has the power to cure?' When Jesus performed miracles, the people asked, 'Who is this Jesus who has this supremacy over the wind and the waves?'

And the answer? Jesus is the covenantal promise of God, made flesh in human form, present in our history, transforming every place and time into the very presence of God – and humanity into the chosen and redeemed people of God. In the beginning of Israel's history God made a covenant with the people – to be their God and they to be God's people. God pledged to be with them for ever. To make that promise irrefutably clear, in the fullness of time, God took human form and dwelt among us, one of us in every way except for sin.

In Jesus, God embraced and made God's own our every infirmity, and bore all our diseases. In this supreme act of love, God utterly identified Godself with humanity, with each and every child, woman and man. No more would anything whatsoever have the power to separate us from the safety, security and blessedness of God's love.

† Lord Jesus Christ, keep calling to me when I am distracted by fear and pain: pierce my defences, penetrate my hard heart and unlock my stubborn brain.

For further thought

Examine your relationship with Jesus. Who is he? Is he an article of faith, a theological proposition? How do you enter into relationship with Jesus?

Thursday 18 May
Confronting dis-order

Read Matthew 8:28–9:1

The whole town came out to meet Jesus; and when they saw him, they begged him to leave their neighbourhood. And after getting into a boat, he crossed the water and came to his own town.

(verses 8:34; 9:1)

Jesus and his companions left the Jewish side of the Sea of Galilee and crossed to the other more Gentile side, a region of significant diversity. This diversity probably accounts for the presence of the pigs in this incident.

Jesus 'came to the other side'. Christ does not choose the confines of the familiar, but moves beyond it to encounter and embrace the wider world, no part of which is outside the divine economy of salvation.

Immediately, dis-order is threatened by Christ's redemptive authority. The demoniacs cry out against his presence. However, grasping his irresistible healing and saving power, they beg Jesus to cast their demons into the swine.

Dis-order is always percolating in society, threatening our individual and social health. There are many causes for it, most of which were unrecognised in Jesus' time. Genetical, psychological and hormonal causes are better understood today, as are the consequences for mental health of violence, trauma and substance abuse. Dis-ordered spirits appear in our families and communities, and sometimes it is our own spirit that is dis-ordered.

Neither the unfamiliar 'other' world of radical diversity, nor the painful world of mental illness is beyond the reach of Jesus and his saving embrace. The universal, unconditional, unreserved saving love of God, made real and revealed for all time in Jesus Christ, is at the heart of the gospel.

Dis-ordered mental health threatens us and fuels our prejudices against those different from us. We are called to live in absolute congruence with the gospel truth of the unreserved saving love of God, in every encounter and in all our attitudes.

† Lord Jesus Christ, let your grace keep my body well, your spirit enlighten my mind, and your love fill my soul, that by your grace I may be whole and holy.

For further thought

Examine whether your life and attitudes are aligned with God's universal, unconditional, unreserved saving love. Do you harbour prejudices that need to be redeemed?

Friday 19 May

Called and re-ordered

Read Matthew 9:2–17

Neither is new wine put into old wineskins; otherwise, the skins burst, and the wine is spilled, and the skins are destroyed; but new wine is put into fresh wineskins, and so both are preserved.

(verse 17)

New insights come, sickness is healed, dis-order is overturned, inaction is invigorated, resolutions are formulated. All good and well. But the real question is, 'What happens next?'

Repair, restoration and healing are doors that invite a new future, each a conversion from destruction, damage and illness. Yet it is an undeniable truth about the human condition that we immediately forget the bad as soon as it is reversed. Our horror at suffering is acute, and yet with its relief comes an all-consuming amnesia.

Old habits die hard. We persist in them even when they endanger our health and well-being. A new insight is eagerly embraced, only to be lost to well-worn attitudes. Sickness is cured, only to be undermined by a speedy return to the lifestyle that caused it. Dis-order is identified, and a curative therapy prescribed, only to be abandoned in the false security of feeling better. Putting new wine into old wineskins is careless, wasteful and dangerous. We 'stand up and walk' only to fall more dangerously.

Authentic religious practice requires rigorous and constant alignment with its standards, principles and values. Acquiring the habit of this discipline demands intellectual assent and continuing commitment. Jesus condemned the hypocrisy of those who paid lip service to religion but whose lives were far from its commitments.

The first flush of easy and enthusiastic assent to new truths requires the follow-up of systematically re-ordering the whole of our lives. To say 'Yes' to Jesus Christ is to lay one's whole life open to renewal by Christ in order to conform to Christ in all things.

† Lord Jesus Christ, by your grace, strengthen my will and keep me faithful to the promises I make, that I may be yours, wholly and for ever.

For further thought

Examine your fads, enthusiasms and commitments. Are you conscious of the differences among them? Consider how to become more disciplined about your commitments.

Saturday 20 May

Redeemed, restored, recruited

Read Matthew 9:18–38

[Jesus] had compassion for them, because they were harassed and helpless, like sheep without a shepherd. Then he said to his disciples, 'The harvest is plentiful, but the labourers are few; therefore, ask the Lord of the harvest to send out labourers into his harvest.'

(verses 36–38)

Jesus Christ came into the world to be the loving, saving presence of God among us. God creates us in love, yearning to be loved by us. In Jesus Christ – one of us, like us, living among us – God seeks us, finds us, and seals our relationship with him.

Jesus Christ breaks into history, our here and now, to rescue us from all that threatens to diminish and destroy us, in order to redeem and restore us. Christ comes to us as teacher, healer, liberator and friend. In this multidimensional embrace we learn the power of God's love, from which nothing whatsoever can ever separate us.

In Jesus Christ, God assumes all that we are, all our infirmities and diseases, all our griefs and sorrows. In loving compassion, Christ embraces us where we are, as we are, supports us, and in our brokenness makes us whole.

While the gospel of Christ proclaims the fullness of God's love and the perfect redemption that is ours in Christ's loving self-sacrifice, the gospel is in fact incomplete. God's work of creation is ongoing, and we are recruited as God's partners in the renewal of creation. This vocation is particularly pressing in the global crisis of climate change. God's work of our redemption and preservation continues as we bear witness to the good news of the gospel. This vocation is our Christian commitment to be the presence of Christ in word and deed. God's work of sustaining us with all the blessings of this life continues as we take up the responsibility of being our neighbour's keeper.

† Lord Jesus Christ, move in and among us who bear your name and use us to be present as you are, to serve as you serve and to love as you love.

For further thought

Examine your role as God's partner in creation and as a herald of the gospel of Christ. Are you a faithful steward of creation and a bold proclaimer of Christ's gospel?

The Gospel of Matthew (3)

2 Lord of the Sabbath

Notes by **Louise Jones**

Louise lives and works in Winson Green, Birmingham, in an embedded, community-based organisation (Newbigin Community Trust), which aims to create a sense of family, purpose and social cohesion in a community that is often overlooked, forgotten and misunderstood. Louise has a passion for empowering, resourcing and loving those that have slipped through the cracks of our systems to help people see their immense value and worth in Jesus. Louise has used the NIVUK for these notes.

Sunday 21 May

Showing up in the arena

Read Matthew 10:1–15

... first, Simon (who is called Peter) and his brother Andrew; James son of Zebedee, and his brother John; Philip and Bartholomew; Thomas and Matthew the tax collector; James son of Alphaeus, and Thaddaeus; Simon the Zealot and Judas Iscariot, who betrayed him. These twelve Jesus sent out.

(verses 2–5)

When I read the passage, the fact that Matthew records all the disciples that Jesus sends out to spread the good news by name struck me as significant. It would make sense in our world that prizes success to have only named the disciples who did a good job of displaying God's love, but Matthew doesn't do that. He includes everyone, even Judas, who it would be safe to say didn't do the best job at serving Jesus well. But God isn't interested in only praising those who do perfectly; he cares that we have the faith to show up and have a go. The disciples were flawed individuals who consistently fell short of the heavenly standard set before them. But the important part is that they don't let perfectionism paralyse them, they show up and have a go. This week we will look at specific ways Jesus advises us on how to live, and some of them are quite challenging and seem very difficult. It is important to remember that God's love for us is not hinged on our performance. Like the disciples, our name gets remembered and recorded when we faithfully step into what God calls us to.

† Jesus, we pray that you would release us to make mistakes without condemnation as we faithfully show up and show your love to others today.

Monday 22 May
Being strategically loving

Read Matthew 10:16–33

Therefore be as shrewd as snakes and as innocent as doves.

(verse 16b)

I think it's important to read this verse by giving equal weighting to being 'shrewd' and 'innocent'. Part of my job role is doing work with young people in the community who come from challenging home situations. I have learnt that sometimes being 'shrewd', or strategic, in how I work with teenagers who have had little parental input is vital. Often their language or behaviour was unhelpful (and shocking to me as someone from a middle-class background with two Christian parents!). It would have been easy for me to seek to impose my learned ideas of what was appropriate, but part of being 'shrewd' is sometimes a willingness to step back and see what is really important. In any case, I quickly learnt that they did not respond well to being directly confronted or challenged. I had to be 'shrewd' and use a more coming-alongside approach, genuinely befriending and earning their respect, becoming an accepted part of their world. As I did so, I discovered that their behaviour was often the result of trauma they had experienced at home or elsewhere during childhood. They needed loving healing as well as healthy behaviour.

But what about 'innocence'? How do you enter into the world without becoming tainted by it? Alongside being shrewd in my engagement with my teenage friends, how can I remain 'innocent', not allowing their attitudes or behaviour to influence mine? How did Jesus engage with publicans, prostitutes, every type of 'sinner' according to the world, while remaining 'without sin'? Perhaps the beginning of an answer is that we are to be as 'innocent as doves'; knowing and being filled with the Holy Spirit, allowing him to lead and guard.

† Lord, reveal to us areas where we could be more strategic in how we live and interact with others so that we can love others in the ways they need us to.

For further thought

It is said that if you judge people, you have no time to love them. When have you judged someone where you could love them?

Tuesday 23 May

God revealed in everyone

Read Matthew 10:34–42

Anyone who welcomes you welcomes me, and anyone who welcomes me welcomes the one who sent me.

(verse 40)

My daily prayer is that I may learn more about who God is through the people I see that day. I love the fact that we are created in God's image and, even though that image has become less clear, we all reflect part of who he is. So, rather than being scared when we are confronted by the difference we see in others, wouldn't it be beautiful if we saw it as a wonderful discovery of another part of who God is?

Winson Green is hugely diverse, but a common thread is that its people have been pushed to the margins. The organisation I work with uses a local community centre as a place of first contact for anyone seeking our help. I love the way they are welcomed, seen as valued individuals, irrespective of their outward appearance or needs. As the reading tells us, because we carry the image of God, welcoming people in this way is welcoming God.

I am privileged to live in a community where I am constantly surrounded by those who are different from me. It encourages me to look beyond the differences and to value them. And as I do that, I begin to see different aspects of God that I might never have otherwise discovered. I can learn about God's motherly, protective instincts through an asylum seeker as she fiercely fights for her family. I can encounter God's sense of humour as an ex-convict shares something amusing, despite their pain and suffering. My life is made much richer by meeting God in my diverse community.

† God, show me something new about who you are through my interaction with somebody new today.

For further thought

Challenge yourself today by interacting with someone who is very different from you and let God reveal parts of himself that you haven't met before.

Wednesday 24 May

Actions rooted in love

Read Matthew 11:1–19

For John came neither eating nor drinking, and they say, 'He has a demon.' The Son of Man came eating and drinking, and they say, 'Here is a glutton and a drunkard, a friend of tax collectors and sinners.' But wisdom is proved right by her deeds.

(verses 18–19)

Unlike the Pharisees, Jesus never lets sticking to the letter of the law get in the way of loving people well. In this passage, Jesus shows how it is not the specifics of what we believe (feasting versus fasting) but what we do, how we love and who we spend our time with that is more important.

I was confronted with the reality of this when my housemate and I came down with flu. My housemate's mum invited us to her home so that she could cook dinner and look after us. She told us she believed we were ill because of bad luck, so she wanted to tie pieces of string that had been blessed at the gurdwara (her family is Sikh) on our ankles to ward off evil spirits. I have never been a superstitious person and my faith means that I don't feel it necessary to have a black piece of string around my ankle to prevent me from harm. It would have been easy, therefore, to have insisted on my beliefs and to have rejected the anklet, to have rejected the love that had been so generously offered. But Jesus teaches us that our actions speak louder than words, and my beliefs about the string were irrelevant when compared to the love shown by this woman in risking her own health by taking me into her home and cooking me a warm meal. I gladly received the anklet as a token of her love and received her love as a token of God's love for me. Wisdom is proved right by her deeds.

† God, help us to see the heart behind people's actions and words today, and help our actions and words be rooted in your love.

For further thought

What would it look like to let someone love you today regardless of your differing beliefs?

Thursday 25 May

God's counter-cultural heart for the unqualified

Read Matthew 11:20–12:8

At that time Jesus said, 'I praise you, Father, Lord of heaven and earth, because you have hidden these things from the wise and learned, and revealed them to little children. Yes, Father, for this is what you were pleased to do.

(verses 25–26)

So often we only follow and trust people in positions of power, people who are well trained. However, this passage shows us that God isn't interested in our definition of 'being qualified' but instead chooses to entrust and empower 'little children' over those who are 'wise and learned'. This is something I have witnessed happening first-hand as my boss Anji created a 'lived experience' policy in our organisation. She chooses to employ people with lived experiences of addiction, homelessness, social services intervention, or time in prison. Where most places would let their fear and distrust of these people get in the way of employing them, Anji chooses to see their negative experiences as their assets in helping the next person in crisis to overcome their problems.

Our lived experience workers are anecdotally more successful in finding people housing, getting people on to drug rehabilitation programmes and inspiring people to take healthier steps to recovery. They've been through it all themselves and know how the system works much better than me or Anji. Jesus seems to be talking about not letting our arrogance of being 'wise and learned' get in the way of letting others guide us. God's heart is always for the 'little children', those we least expect, whose humbleness and openness allow them to be more useful to God than anyone who claims to have more wisdom or training. In this passage we are invited to join in with God's plans for the downtrodden in our communities rather than blindly following those who claim to have the answers.

† God, open our eyes to those around us who have been overlooked, and help us to trust and empower them to live to their full potential.

For further thought

It has been said that loneliness and being unwanted is the most terrible poverty. What can you do today to alleviate that poverty for someone?

Friday 26 May

Permission to withdraw

Read Matthew 12:9–21

Then he said to the man, 'Stretch out your hand.' So he stretched it out and it was completely restored, just as sound as the other. But the Pharisees went out and plotted how they might kill Jesus. Aware of this, Jesus withdrew from that place.

(verses 13–15a)

In my contributions to this book last year I wrote about Sophie, a single mum who had been diagnosed with terminal cancer and the tragedy of coming to terms with that. Only a month before writing this year, Sophie sadly passed away, leaving her three children scattered among various family members. Even though we knew this was coming and had prepared ourselves and the community as well as we could, the blow of her passing away unexpectedly hit me like a tonne of bricks. I had to withdraw.

In the lead-up to today's passage, Jesus explains the Father's heart; that compassion is at the root of Sabbath and that therefore healing on the Sabbath is lawful. He heals someone's hand and the Pharisees plot his death, rejecting him and his view of God. I find it reassuring to read here that Jesus has to withdraw as a response to this. I might expect him to push on, but it is comforting to see that even the Son of God has to stop and process his disappointment and sadness.

Like Jesus, I had to take a day or two to take stock of Sophie's death. I wasn't expecting my body to react in such a physical way, as I felt very prepared. But as this passage shows, sometimes things don't make sense and the best thing to do is to pause, withdraw and bring your pain to God.

† Help us, God, to know when our body, mind and spirit need a break and to rest in you. Thank you that you are a safe place to bring our pain and confusion.

For further thought

Is there a moment in your forthcoming day where you can withdraw and retreat to rest with God – especially in the difficult moments of today?

Saturday 27 May

Choose hope

Read Matthew 12:22–37

Jesus healed him, so that he could both talk and see. All the people were astonished and said, 'Could this be the Son of David?' But when the Pharisees heard this, they said, 'It is only by Beelzebul, the prince of demons, that this fellow drives out demons.'

(verses 22b–24)

I was struck in this passage by the two options of how to react to the miracle Jesus performs. Neither group can comprehend how Jesus has performed this miracle. One group transforms their awe and confusion into hope and trust that Jesus is who he says he is. The other group lets their lack of understanding lead to scepticism and judgement.

We always have a choice when confronted by something we don't understand: to hope for its validity or to listen to our doubts and reject it. I am regularly inspired by the way people in my community hold on to hope. Specifically, those who have had children removed and continue to hope and fight for them to be reinstated into their custody. Having journeyed with a few families who have had children removed or returned I have been able to see how unpredictable and subjective decisions made by social services can be. It is not a system I would easily put my hope and trust in. However, time and again I find myself inspired by the tenacity and optimism the parents show as they choose to believe that the hopeful story – that their children will be returned to them – is the one that will come true.

During the coronavirus pandemic, I became a more cynical person, but I've been encouraged by the families in my community who continue to choose hope in the most challenging circumstances. I want to be like the people in the passage who choose the hopeful story, the story that says Jesus is who he says he is.

† Lord, when I feel despairing and confused by the world around me, help me to hold on to hope. May your constant love be a source of hope for myself and others.

For further thought

What are the situations you are facing where you need a new sense of hope? Or where can you bring hope to others today?

Social responsibilities and love in action

1 Display his glory

Notes by **Helen Van Koevering**

After living in Mozambique for twenty-eight years, Helen, raised in England, moved to the USA with her family. Helen had served as a parish priest and Director of Ministry within the Anglican Diocese of Niassa, where a church-planting and people movement doubled members and congregations between 2004 and 2014. As Rector of St Raphael Episcopal Church in Lexington, Kentucky, where her husband serves as bishop, she experienced the 2020–21 Covid-19 pandemic highlighting the church's missional responsibilities to show God's love in action. Helen has used the NRSV for these notes.

Sunday 28 May

Good news for the oppressed

Read Isaiah 61:1–3

The Spirit of the Lord God is upon me, because the Lord has anointed me … to give them a garland instead of ashes, the oil of gladness instead of mourning, the mantle of praise instead of a faint spirit.

(verses 1a, 3)

Today's passage holds the beginning of Jesus' reading in Nazareth's synagogue, when he announced to his hometown, 'Today this scripture has been fulfilled in your hearing' (Luke 4:18, 21). Jesus proclaimed this good news as release, recovery and freedom for those captive to oppression, for those lacking vision, and those lacking fullness of life. The good news is transformative for both the oppressed and the oppressors. The good news is life-giving for the whole community of creation to be as God intended.

To speak of the oppressed and oppressors receiving garlands for ashes, gladness for mourning, praise for faint spirits, is to speak of forgiveness. When South Africa was emerging from the apartheid years, Nelson Mandela instituted, in 1995, the Truth and Reconciliation Commission (TRC) to hear apartheid-related crimes with the aim of healing, uniting and rebuilding the nation. Archbishop Desmond Tutu, the chair of the TRC, embodied the principles of reconciliation, forgiveness and restitution that he believed would deal with the truth-telling of atrocities of those years of apartheid. Tutu wrote of the TRC in his book, *No Future without Forgiveness* in 2000. South Africa's need for healing and transformation taught him that restitution was important, where possible, but also that forgiveness was vital good news to free both the oppressed and the oppressors.

† Jesus, you showed us the way of good news for the world. May we be that good news today. Amen

Monday 29 May

Generosity to the poor

Read Deuteronomy 15:7–11

Give liberally and be ungrudging when you do so, for on this account the Lord *your God will bless you in all your work and in all that you undertake. Since there will never cease to be some in need on the earth, I therefore command you, 'Open your hand to the poor and needy neighbor in your land.'*

(verses 10–11)

Today, in a discussion of the sabbatical year and the remission of debts, we see the trust the Israelites were invited to live within. What a shift to go from many generations of slavery to a generation of absolute dependence on God in the wilderness – both being rigorous but clear-cut ways to live – to now owning land, having power, shaping and living in a society with all the complications and messiness that brings. In case the wilderness manna wasn't enough, in case the practice of resting every seventh day isn't enough, God says every seventh year all debts will be erased. But the call to attend to those in need remains always.

God recognises how insidious the mindset is, how sin creeps in and entices us to build ourselves up at others' expense, to guard and protect ourselves and ignore others' need. A clean slate every seven years ought to prevent the consolidation of power and the disempowering and dehumanising of others. It ought to help them keep seeing each other as mutual caregivers, belonging to each other and always helping one another as God helps us. And it's so pragmatic and honest – calling out the temptations of being tight-fisted and hard-hearted, resenting those in need as if they are taking something away from you.

There will never cease to be need upon the earth, so be open to the poor and needy, and join with God in the way of freedom and trust that meets one another's needs.

† Lord, may we follow you on this path of attending to the needs of others, and have our eyes opened to see opportunities to meet other people's needs wherever we find ourselves today.

For further thought

Whoever you meet today, take note of each person. Pray for what is hidden from sight, for a need unspoken. It could be as easy as offering them a smile!

Tuesday 30 May

Redeeming the enslaved

Read Deuteronomy 15:12–15

Remember that you were a slave in the land of Egypt, and the Lord *your God redeemed you.*

(verse 15a)

These verses in Deuteronomy come in the midst of a chapter about relationships: relationships to our time, talent, treasure and everything else we have. There are principles to follow in how we invest our whole lives in our relationship with God, other people and all creation. It is all about opening the eyes of our hearts to God's way that helps us fulfil the two greatest commandments: love the Lord your God with all your heart, soul, mind and strength; and love your neighbour as yourself.

Money is to be loaned to those in need. Debt is to be forgiven after seven years. Property will be returned after fifty years. We are pleasing God when we care for one another and are open to the needy, and we are to recognise God's blessings on us. Personal connections between people are very different in these days of social media and greater geographic distances even between families. Online services during the pandemic distanced us all from our ministers and doctors. But human relationships have always been vital to the well-being of all creation. The Hebrew scriptures show us that our focus of care is to be for the needy. The sabbatical year set even indentured servants free, their needs attended and blessings shared. Empathy reminds us to live differently. As Nelson Mandela, the first President of post-apartheid South Africa, said, 'To be free is not merely to cast off one's chains, but to live in a way that respects and enhances the freedom of others.'

† Jesus Christ, Son of God, remind me of when I have needed the time, the support and the encouragement of others. May I now do likewise. Amen

For further thought

Turn to someone who needs your care and support today. Find some way to release them from their need. Pray for them.

Wednesday 31 May
Look after the earth

Read Psalm 8:1–9

You have given [humanity] dominion over the works of your hands; you have put all things under their feet, all sheep and oxen, and also the beasts of the field, the birds of the air, and the fish of the sea, whatever passes along the paths of the seas. O Lord, our Sovereign, how majestic is your name in all the earth!

(verses 6–9)

Psalm 8 is a psalm of praise, unique in that it is addressed directly to the Lord – no asides calling us to participate, no passages in the third person, or even any inward conversation on the psalmist's part ('O my soul') as in other psalms. This is intimate connection that gently invites us to listen in to the writer's private prayer and meditations as our own. 'O Lord, our Sovereign, how majestic is your name in all the earth!' God's overarching sovereign care frames the context of this psalm – a view of humanity's vocation, seen in two relationships, that between humankind and the rest of creation, and that between the Creator and his human creations. We are caretakers within a dynamic, living community of creation. The earth is our common home. God's *oikos* is for all creation.

Oikos is the root of the word *oikoumene* (ecumenical), *oikonomia* (economy) and *oikoslogia* (ecology). Ecology studies relationships between animals, plants, organisms and minerals, and the way that each plays a vital role in maintaining the balance and biodiversity of this beloved ecosystem, community and 'home'. Humanity is made from the same stuff of the earth and our relationships have ecological significance. Economic, social and political relationships affect the balance of creation. Everything that we fabricate, use and produce has its origin in the earth, and sustainable relationships require our faith, reason and wisdom. The earth is a gift, held in trust, and we are to safeguard conditions for life, create systems, technologies, consider natural systems and inherited traditions, boundaries and limits rooted in the ecological limits of our common, shared home.

† For this home, we thank you, God. Teach us how to live sustainably with all your creation. Amen

For further thought

Try writing a psalm of praise to our common home.

Thursday 1 June

Speak up for the voiceless

Read Proverbs 31:8–9

Speak out for those who cannot speak, for the rights of all the destitute. Speak out, judge righteously, defend the rights of the poor and needy.

(verses 8–9)

Today's verses from Proverbs 31 are part of the context offered before we hear the ode to a capable wife, the match of her husband. Proverbs 31:1 explains that the unnamed mother of the unknown King Lemuel composed this poem: the description of the woman the Queen Mother seeks as a royal match for her son may reflect how she sees herself. At one level, the text is a royal woman's articulation of the characteristics she wants in a daughter-in-law. At other levels, the text is part of the often patriarchal, always androcentric (male-centred) scriptures.

This poem is much more than a patriarchal text about the idealised woman as entrepreneurial, industrious, generous, a wise craftswoman, caring, considerate and attentive to the needs of others. This text is revered by many Jewish and Christian readers as the wifely ideal, and recited on Shabbat (Friday evening), as well as featuring as the subject of Women's Day sermons, marriage retreats and women's devotional literature. In truth, the heart of the poem is the essential character trait of the woman: fear of God. Various text translations have constructed a stereotypical 'femininity' that ignores the context of the Queen Mother seeking a woman for her son who will match him strength for strength. What we learn from today's verses is that speaking out for the needy voiceless, the rights of others and defence of the marginalized is a praiseworthy fruit of the knowledge and fear of God.

† Holy God, may we seek to be the people you call us to be. May we know your strength in all we do, know and say in our communities. Amen

For further thought

Who needs your voice in your community today?

Friday 2 June

Defend the oppressed

Read Isaiah 1:16–20

Cease to do evil, learn to do good; seek justice, rescue the oppressed, defend the orphan, plead for the widow … If you are willing and obedient, you shall eat the good of the land; but if you refuse and rebel, you shall be devoured by the sword.

(verses 17, 19–20)

In today's passage, we are challenged by the angry voice of God addressed to Israel's leaders when the temple was rebuilt, and many groups vied for positions of power. Within the Persian context, control of the temple equated to economic, political, social and religious power.

Isaiah 1:11–16 expresses anger against temple rituals and temple liturgy. God 'hates' religious festivals, sacrificial offerings, even the Sabbath, and pleads that leaders show regard for the most vulnerable members of their community (the oppressed, the widows and orphans), offering forgiveness if they allow themselves to be judged by the purpose of their liturgical lives. Social justice does not replace liturgy, but rather invites us to experience liturgy through the eyes of the oppressed, ignored or abandoned. What do our hymns sound like to someone who lives on the brink of destitution? Do our prayers evoke anger in the woman who can barely feed her children in the week between our services? Does the hope that we preach sound hollow to a child who does not feel safe in her home?

God speaks what we refuse to hear about our lack of activism for the relief of the oppressed. God's anger is the anger of those we fail to see. God tells us that if we allow ourselves to be judged and to recognise that we have not defended the vulnerable, then worship can become what it is meant to be: a place where our sins are washed away.

† God, may our worship draw us towards your presence and your word. Help us to hear your anger for what we are not doing, what we have left undone, and change us. Amen

For further thought

Whom does my church community ignore in our worship?

Saturday 3 June

Seek good and not evil

Read Amos 5:1–15

Seek me and live.

(verse 4b)

How beautifully simple is the repeated and central message of our reading today! Seek God: open the eyes of our hearts to see God's presence and work among us in all that is good, true and beautiful; hear God's heart beat for joy over creation and for sorrow over the suffering so many endure, and learn about the lives of others and their unmet needs.

Seek the Lord and live: respond to the call of God's love, in whose image we are created; let the mutual regard that Jesus shares with the Father and offers by the indwelling Spirit change the way we relate with others; offer to be part of the change that our communities, nations and world needs; and be God's hands and feet in the world today.

Amos called the people of Israel to 'Seek good and not evil, that you may live; and so the Lord, the God of hosts, will be with you, just as you have said. Hate evil and love good, and establish justice in the gate; it may be that the Lord, the God of hosts, will be gracious to the remnant of Joseph' (verses 14–15). Justice and mercy are to follow from seeking God's goodness for all God's creation. May it be so for me today. For God's glory in all the earth.

† Remind me, Lord, again and again, to begin by seeking you each day and in all my plans. May I be someone who seeks both your goodness and love as well as your justice and mercy in my life. Amen

For further thought

How do you start your day?

Social responsibilities and love in action

2 Maintain constant love for one another

Notes by **Helen Van Koevering**

For Helen's biography, see p. 148. Helen has used the NRSV for these notes.

Sunday 4 June

Joseph buries Jesus' body

Read John 19:38–42

Joseph of Arimathea, who was a disciple of Jesus, though a secret one because of his fear of the Jews, [and] Nicodemus… wrapped [the body] with the spices in linen cloths, according to the burial custom of the Jews. Now there was a garden in the place where he was crucified, and…there was a new tomb… And so, because it was the Jewish day of Preparation, and the tomb was nearby, they laid Jesus there.

(verses 38a, 39a, 40–42)

The details of Jesus' burial reveal the holiness of the day of Preparation and the Sabbath in the Jewish calendar. They also reveal the piety of tradition alongside a piety of expectation. The first holds respect, comfort, or even fear of change. The second is open to revelation of God acting in new ways for a new day, and embraces change. Concern for either piety is not to exceed our concern for human beings.

Joseph of Arimathea is a secret disciple. When it seems the movement has ended, he comes out of the closet of his fears to attend to respectable traditions. Fear is often like unproductive farmland, depleted of its nutrients by growing the same crop for too many years. Today our fears take many forms: ethnicity, socio-economic status, gender-based perspectives, human sexuality, political persuasion. Our fears keep us from living our faith.

Nicodemus represents the life of faith. He has changed since that night-time meeting in John 3, and he now speaks up for Jesus' fair treatment before his peers, and provides for the burial. By growing from inquirer, to advocate, to disciple, he models true faith for us all.

† Jesus, teach me to live in the knowledge that perfect love casts out fear. Show me how I might grow in my faith and point others towards you. Amen

For further thought

How have we, or people that we know well, changed as a result of encountering Jesus? Give thanks for the transformation he is bringing.

Monday 5 June

Dorcas

Read Acts 9:36–41

Now in Joppa there was a disciple … She was devoted to good works and acts of charity.

(verse 36)

Dorcas is described as a disciple. In the New Testament, a disciple, whether male or female, carried the expectation of being a role model for all those who follow, setting the pace and opening doors for future leaders. Dorcas' story comes to us because of her death. Too often we only value the good works and gifts of others after they have spent their lives and/or die.

Dorcas and Tabitha both mean 'gazelle'. The fact that the writer gives us both versions of her name, using one as an explanation of the other, suggests a significance that might otherwise be missed. Here was a woman who was perhaps beautiful and elegant on the outside appearance, but who was all the more beautiful on the inside. She made an example through good works and charity – despite her own wealth, she humbled herself to serve others.

On her death, the disciples in Joppa seek to honour her by preparing her body ahead of burial. They place it in an upper room, reminiscent of the rooms Elijah and Elisha visited in similar circumstances. Peter gladly comes, expecting to honour someone in her death. But what he is shown is the evidence of continued life – the spirit of Dorcas alive in her use of her privilege, her wealth, just acts and gifts, and prophetic speech, given for the benefit of the less privileged: the widows, indigent, the hungry, depressed, oppressed, marginalised and penalised. And the disciples learn that God's Spirit is active where acts of loving service to the needy happen.

† Holy Spirit, fall on us so we might recognise your presence in how the privileged use their power and in how the needy are cared for. Amen

For further thought

Think of those who have been examples to you of Spirit-filled concern and care for the needy.

Tuesday 6 June

Cornelius and his alms

Read Acts 10:1–8

In Caesarea there was a man named Cornelius, a centurion of the Italian Cohort ... a devout man who feared God with all his household; he gave alms generously to the people and prayed constantly to God.

(verses 1–2)

Cornelius, the Roman centurion, part of the military invading force that dominated Judea, made generous donations to the people, and God noticed his prayers. Like Dorcas, Cornelius understood, it seems, the flip side of privilege to be responsibility for those less privileged, including the colonised and marginalised.

A critical turning point for the early church happens when God calls Cornelius to go to Peter in Joppa, and, before he arrives there, Peter receives a vision from God. When they meet, Peter tells what he has learnt from his vision: 'I truly understand that God shows no partiality, but in every nation anyone who fears him and does what is right is acceptable to him' (Acts 10:34–35). And the Holy Spirit interrupts his preaching by falling on Cornelius and his household, proving God's intentions. No matter what barriers we might create around communities, God's Spirit is relentless and unrestrainable.

It all leads to the decisions of Acts 15 that reflect God's desire to welcome and draw together wildly diverse and widely inclusive communities. As the early church learnt, Gentiles and Greeks were already made clean by God, and the God of Israel redeems and saves Jew and Gentile alike. Fulfilling Acts' early call to be witnesses to the edges of the world necessarily required encountering the diversity of the ancient world as well as the expansiveness of the good news.

Peter, Cornelius and the community are profoundly transformed, converted by recognising the new way God was moving.

† Today, Lord, we hold the world church before you and ask you to bless us with new love, new understanding and new life. Amen

For further thought

How do you and your church show inclusiveness?

Wednesday 7 June

Lydia

Read Acts 16:12–15, 40

Lydia, a worshipper of God, was listening to us; she was from Thyatira and a dealer in purple cloth … When she and her household were baptized, she urged us, saying. 'If you have judged me to be faithful to the Lord, come and stay at my home.'

(verses 14–15)

Paul is on his way to Macedonia and his small team stop in Philippi, a leading regional city and a Roman colony. On a Sabbath day, they find a place of prayer in a gathering of women outside the gate by the river. Among them is Lydia, who is baptised, along with her household, after hearing Paul. Lydia invites Paul and his companions to stay at her home.

Although they meet in Philippi, Lydia is a businesswoman from Thyatira, a dealer in purple cloth. Her story points us to the truth that the growth of the church is a team effort that requires hospitality and generosity. Acts 16 includes the dramatic story of Paul and Silas in a prison break that brings the jailor and his family to baptism, before Paul and Silas are freed and return to Lydia's home for encouragement prior to moving on. Lydia serves as a bookend for Acts 16, and signifies the support that ministry needs in order for it to grow and thrive.

Throughout my ordained ministry and missionary life, I have seen the different ways that the visible individuals are seen as the missionaries and ministers: clergy, choir, readers, ushers. Mission and ministry are made possible by the many who are unseen, even unnamed. Acts 16 reminds us that it takes a team for mission and ministry to be effective. All are co-labourers in the growth of the church. And that hospitality is an encouraging gift of God.

† God, teach me how to be hospitable to your Spirit at work in others, that I might see how we all work together in your goodness and mercy. Amen

For further thought

How can you encourage someone with hospitality today?

Thursday 8 June

Grace gifts

Read Romans 12:6–21

We have gifts that differ according to the grace given to us: prophecy, in proportion to faith; ministry, in ministering; the teacher, in teaching; the exhorter, in exhortation; the giver, in generosity; the leader, in diligence; the compassionate, in cheerfulness.

(verses 6–8)

Following this wide and various list of gifts is a series of imperatives that focus on relationships and draw on the wisdom tradition. Together they emphasise that the gifts are God-given for blessing and social harmony, and focus on love as mutual service, hopeful perseverance and patient openness to others.

Just as Paul breaks out in poetic tribute to love in 1 Corinthians 13, after writing about spiritual gifts in 1 Corinthians 12, so he does in Romans 12. His poetry after 'let love be genuine' is about how love reaches for the common good in the church. He reminds us of Jesus' specific example – not just words, but behaviour for loving others. I've heard that distance runners don't just play general messages in their minds like 'Relax!' while running, but rather specific messages to keep their whole body relaxed, such as 'Keep my fingers loose!' Paul gives us specific ideas for authentic love in these verses that meet genuine needs, even of people who don't like us. Genuine love is the deepest theme in this section of Romans. It's not just about being nice to people, but having a moral orientation towards the good that moves folk towards God's goodness. So often we think Romans is all about doctrine, or justification by faith. Here, though, we see once again that the Christian life for Paul is about faith working through love (Galatians 5:6). Let love be genuine!

† Lord Jesus, show me again how my love is to be genuine. Remind me each day to live in genuine love for others. Amen

For further thought

Consider how you have known your faith works through love. What gift has God given you?

Friday 9 June

Love your enemies

Read Luke 6:27–36

I say to you that listen, Love your enemies, do good to those who hate you, bless those who curse you, pray for those who abuse you … Do to others as you would have them do to you.

(verses 27, 31)

Here is guidance in how the congregation can live and witness faithfully in its situation, considering the now and not yet of the kingdom, the realm of God. The community is to imitate its leader, Jesus, and seek to release people and circumstances from recrimination. Mercy is one of God's primary qualities, opening the possibility of repentance and turning towards the movement to the realm of God. Our experience of mercy deepens our experience of God's realm, and extends mercy as we model it for others. The realm calls for attitudes and actions that seek the good of the other, and goes beyond non-violence as non-retaliation towards promoting the welfare of those conflicting parties. The 'golden rule' of verse 31 is a reminder to relate to others according to the perspectives and actions of the realm. It might be stated this way: 'If you want to live in a world that has the qualities of the realm, then treat other people in realm-like ways.'

In being the change, the realm calls us also to imitate God's kindness – seek the best interest of the ungrateful and the wicked. The admonition to stop judging and condemning doesn't mean never make a moral judgement, but rather don't act as if we know the final verdict on those who oppose the realm of God. Our perception is finite, and God offers the opportunity to repent. In the security of the realm, forgiveness releases both the forgivers and the forgiven, the oppressors and the oppressed. The bottom line is that we and our communities are to live into the power of God's present-yet-coming realm.

† Thy kingdom come to earth, Father, as it is in heaven. May we live into your realm as Jesus showed us. Amen

For further thought

Who do you hate? Who are our enemies?

Saturday 10 June

A representative of God

Read 1 Peter 4:7–11

The end of all things is near; therefore be serious and discipline yourselves for the sake of your prayers. Above all, maintain constant love for one another, for love covers a multitude of sins. Be hospitable to one another without complaining. Like good stewards of the manifold grace of God, serve one another.

(verses 7–10a)

In the United States, the American Dream is often proclaimed as if it were gospel: anyone who works hard and makes good choices can be happy and successful. The First Letter of Peter understands it all. Don't be surprised at trials, make good choices, don't expect that doing good will make you healthy, wealthy and popular. Instead, rejoice as you share in the suffering of Jesus.

This isn't about why bad things happen to good people, but rather a pastoral word of hope and reassurance for people facing abuse, social rejection and public humiliation because they follow Jesus. They are being treated as they treated Jesus. And the effect of this suffering will be revealed in who we are. When, as we have explored this week, our actions are genuinely in accordance with God's will, do not be ashamed by this fellowship in Jesus' suffering and life in the Spirit. Whose opinion will count in the end?

Be confident in trusting God, our Creator and just Judge. Trusting God does not mean that we wait passively for the world to change. Like the one in whose footsteps we follow, we are called to action. We are called to do good in Christ's name, to the honour and glory of God.

† Jesus, be our companion wherever the road takes us. Be our example of all that is good, true and beautiful of God, so that we may grow in trust and confidence to always act in the way your love has been revealed to us. Amen

For further thought

Give thanks today for all God's blessing and goodness towards us.

Biblical library (3)

Apocalyptic

Notes by **Noel Irwin**

Noel is a Belfast boy and a Methodist minister. In 2000 he moved to Sheffield, first working for the Church of England as a community outreach worker, then as Superintendent of the Methodist Mission in the city centre. After working as Director of the Urban Theology Unit in Sheffield, he is now Tutor in Public Theology at Northern College Manchester and trains church-related community workers for the United Reformed Church there. In his spare time he enjoys running in the hills and Brazilian Jiu Jitsu. Noel has used the NRSVA for these notes.

Sunday 11 June

God's glory departs

Read Ezekiel 10:1–22

Their entire body, their rims, their spokes, their wings, and the wheels – the wheels of the four of them – were full of eyes all round.

(verse 12)

'Apocalypse' means an unveiling or a disclosure and typically relates to a huge, collective trauma. Perhaps the destruction of your land, exile, war, famine, environmental disaster, persecution, plague or pandemic. In the midst of such trauma, it is easy to lose sight of the bigger picture, hard to see God's hand or goodness, we become worn down and everything turns grey and confused. The authors of apocalyptic bring a different view: it may seem that good is struggling and losing the battle, but what is actually unveiled is the truth that there will be a judgement and evil will be destroyed and good will triumph.

Our reading focuses on 'eyes'; we may not see clearly, but the image reveals that God does. The national trauma that Ezekiel is responding to is the destruction of the temple and the taking of the Jewish people into exile (Ezekiel 1:1). The place where God dwelt has been destroyed and they have been removed from where he was. But Ezekiel stresses the continued presence and the mobility of God. The temple is gone, but God is not confined there and can still roam around the world. God is still with them.

† Pray about the 'apocalyptic' situations in our world today: exile, war, famine, environmental disaster, persecution, pandemic.

Monday 12 June

Daniel's vision of the beasts

Read Daniel 7:1–28

I was considering the horns, when another horn appeared, a little one coming up among them; to make room for it, three of the earlier horns were plucked up by the roots. There were eyes like human eyes in this horn, and a mouth speaking arrogantly.

(verse 8)

Hopefully last night you didn't have any nightmares about the chariot wheels with the eyes. Though we have got more eyes on the menu today! One of the important things to bear in mind in relation to apocalyptic writing is that, while some books in the Bible are designed to appeal to our reason, the way apocalyptic literature works is to engage our imaginations. Ezekiel yesterday and Daniel today give us impressive word pictures, which give an overall impression rather than a literal description. And this makes sense; people who are beset by traumatic, overwhelming events are generally not well placed to cope with closely argued reason, what they need is something that lifts them beyond the grim, current reality. Imagination can do this as it stirs our emotions and our spirits as well as stretching our minds.

Remembering this and that the purpose of apocalyptic writing is to reveal what God sees about a situation, what does today's passage reveal? As is often the case with apocalyptic writing, empires are at the centre of the action. Daniel has visions where beasts represent seemingly permanent and powerful empires. But then an 'Ancient One' judges the beasts and throws them into the fire. We're not given a minute timetable nor a detailed list of actions that will bring this about. But in dramatic picture language, our imaginations and our hearts are lit up. Despite the apparent strength of the great empires of the earth, heavenly forces are at work shaping the history of the earth for good. Ultimately there is justice; in the end, evil is defeated.

† Try and pray today focusing on your imagination and not your reason.

For further thought

As we go through this week, seek out artists' impressions of the apocalyptic word pictures in our texts. What do you think?

Tuesday 13 June
The beasts in Revelation

Read Revelation 13:1–18

They worshipped the dragon, for he had given his authority to the beast, and they worshipped the beast, saying, 'Who is like the beast, and who can fight against it?'

(verse 4)

While Daniel is important in and of itself, for Christians, it also gives us Jesus' favourite designation of himself: 'Son of Man'. Daniel also provides the book of Revelation with imagery to work with (compare the beasts in Revelation 13 with those in Daniel 7) and it is Revelation that we will focus on now.

Revelation can be a puzzling and difficult read for Christians. We either dismiss it as ridiculous and irrelevant or see it as a blueprint for the future and the end of the world. It is neither of these things. Of all the books in the Bible, it is so important to understand Revelation in its own historical context; that of the persecution of small Christian communities in Asia and the enforced worship of the Roman emperor. The passage is therefore all about the Roman Empire and we might well ask what that has to say to us. Well, it might not be emperors who think they are god-like and demand our worship, but there are modern-day 'empires' that oppress and impose their will on the poor and vulnerable; institutions and systems that thrive on domination and, as a by-product, destroy lives and even the planet. It's easy in the face of such overwhelming, seemingly undefeatable forces to ask, 'What can I do?' Easy to believe we can do nothing – 'Who can fight against it?', as those in our passage ask. Worshipping, submitting to the alive, dominant power might seem the only option, but John calls on his readers not to let themselves be deceived by passing power, but to worship the Lamb which is slaughtered and who will reign eternally.

Revelation calls us to be apocalyptic Christians – people of God who unveil or disclose that which devours in our world today.

† Pray through all that demands our allegiance (even our worship!) and how that relates to our worship and following of Christ.

For further thought

Watch or read the news wherever you are, then reread our passage and see if anything is unveiled or disclosed for you.

Wednesday 14 June

The King of Kings and Lord of Lords

Read Revelation 19:1–21

Come, gather for the great supper of God, to eat the flesh of kings, the flesh of captains, the flesh of the mighty, the flesh of horses and their riders – flesh of all, both free and slave, both small and great.

(verses 17b–18)

Sometimes when you read apocalyptic literature you feel there should be a 'Handle with care' warning! Because the style is designed to spur our imagination and engage our emotions, the language is often graphic and violent. But that is a reflection of the genre of writing, not the character of God. Without 'handling with care', extremists throughout the centuries have taken the imagery of passages like Revelation 19 and used it to justify themselves as holy warriors fighting their own cosmic battle, identifying themselves as good and their opponents as evil and demonic.

Because of this, there are many Christians who, being repelled by such imagery and the uses made of it, find it so unrelated to the world they live in that it does not bear any thought or consideration.

But handled with care, we can see something different. For the persecuted Christians first reading this, such images would have encouraged them in their apparently hopeless struggle against Roman might. It would have given them hope to endure and to be encouraged in their struggle to be faithful followers of Jesus, even in these most difficult of circumstances.

And even for us, where the horrors of two world wars and the use of nuclear weapons make us as believers more nervous of such imagery, if we handle with care, it can still speak to us. Against all the odds, God will come through. Despite the rampant injustice of our day, there will be justice; no matter how unlikely it may seem in difficult times, God will be victorious.

† God our judge, in our lives and communities help us to hold together both your love and your justice.

For further thought

Read through Matthew Bridges' hymn 'Crown him with many crowns', based on the image in Revelation 19:12. Does this hymn give you a different way of looking at the chapter?

Thursday 15 June

Judgement

Read Revelation 20:1–15

(The rest of the dead did not come to life until the thousand years were ended.) This is the first resurrection. Blessed and holy are those who share in the first resurrection.

(verses 5–6a)

If yesterday's passage has caused controversy over the centuries, it is nothing compared to the arguments about the millennium in this passage. Some Christians have divided into churches with pre-, post- and a-millennial theology. So strongly do some feel about their particular position that they have encouraged a nuclear conflagration or war in the Middle East in order to somehow fulfil the 'prophecy' they see in this passage! Yet the millennium is such a minor concept in the Bible, incredible that it should be lifted into such importance as to welcome the actual destruction the planet.

My mum used to speak about folk whom she thought were 'so heavenly bound, they were no earthly use'. Many Christians have a similar attitude to passages like this in Revelation: it's Star Wars rather than Poverty Wars and all about life after death, with nothing to say at all about life before death. Surely the focus should be on what John was actually trying to say to the Christians of his time? The clear thread through Revelation is a desire to give consolation, hope and encouragement, in the here and now, to tiny groups of Christians facing severe persecution.

If we want to be faithful today to what John was trying to do, by all means see the big-picture 'heavenly' message, but let's not neglect the earth. John pictures the conflict between light and darkness, using symbolism and figurative visions that we shouldn't attempt to apply to contemporary geo-politics.

† Pray for the persecuted church.

For further thought

What other 'minor' concepts in the Bible have become huge issues in the church? How can we avoid such distortions?

Friday 16 June

The one comes to resolve

Read Revelation 4:1–11

You are worthy, our Lord and God, to receive glory and honour and power, for you created all things, and by your will they existed and were created.

(verse 11)

If you were to ask many Christians for their overall impression of the book of Revelation, I am sure many would say things like 'chaos', violence', 'destruction', 'judgement'. Yet a careful searching for the focus of God in the book is perhaps surprisingly one of Creator. I am sure we know Revelation will end up with the creation of a new heaven and a new earth. This reading gives us a foretaste of how the book will finish. If you have grown up in church and sung its hymns, a phrase like 'holy, holy, holy' and then pictures of crowns being cast by the glassy sea of heaven will ring bells for us.

Being a Methodist I do love to sing, and the lack of communal singing was the thing I struggled with both in online worship and then when we returned initially to physical worship. One of the things which Revelation, particularly passages like this, has done for me over the years has been to disclose or unveil to me a wider, deeper, further reality to worship. This is especially true when I have been lifting my voice and heart in praise. There have been a few occasions in my life when I have been conducting worship and I have been overcome with a strong feeling that we are simply adding our voices to a praise that never ceases in heaven and throughout all of creation. This giving of glory to God in praise and by how we live our lives is a key part of who we are called to be.

† Concentrate your prayers today on giving praise to God.

For further thought

How today can we practically magnify who God is in the eyes of others?

Saturday 17 June

Worthy is the Lamb

Read Revelation 5:1–14

And I began to weep bitterly because no one was found worthy to open the scroll or to look into it.

(verse 4)

I keep saying John is writing to congregations who are experiencing persecution and difficulty. Do you think it might have been better for John to have given some nice clear advice, strategies, ideas, principles to help them? It's often our temptation, isn't it? To create a programme or a project ... Instead, John keeps pointing us to focus first on Jesus, to worship. In this passage, John sees the scroll of history and asks who can be trusted to unroll it in a way that is different from the current trajectory. Who can write a better ending than the one the current direction predicts? Tragically, he sees no one worthy and weeps, broken-hearted that the current direction is simply going to continue and get worse. Then the Lamb is revealed – there is one who can be trusted to do it, because he has already demonstrated his willingness and capacity. No wonder they rejoice, no wonder John's strategy to his congregations is to tell them to go and worship, to focus on the one who can write a better ending!

Remember apocalyptic is about unveiling and disclosure, and these scenes in chapters 4 and 5 in the heavenly throne room are disclosing, for John, the ultimate reality for the world around us. In the midst of struggle, of persecution, of a world gone wrong, here is the place of our greatest peace. Not in economic systems or material strength, or even in clever programmes, but in the Christ who is worthy of our trust in his ability to unroll history.

† Loving God, help us not to be seduced to worship those things which are not of you. May we give to you alone all of our worship and our lives.

For further thought

Perhaps the approach of John is not so ridiculous; he is reminding us how all of us worship something, which will eventually be revealed as not worthy of our worship, as only God is faithful, true, certain and worth us betting our lives on.

Who is my family?

Notes by **Alesana Fosi Pala'amo**

Alesana is Head of Department for Practical Theology at Malua Theological College in Samoa. An ordained minister of the Congregational Christian Church Samoa, his research interests include social ministries, Pacific research methodologies, theology and pastoral counselling. Alesana's PhD research through Massey University New Zealand explored pastoral counselling practices of Samoans. Alesana and his wife Lemau co-founded a pastoral counselling agency called Soul Talk Samoa Trust, and their sons Norman, Alex and Jayden attend college and primary school in Samoa. Alesana has used the NRSV for these notes.

Sunday 18 June

Doing the will of God

Read Mark 3:31–35

Whoever does the will of God is my brother and sister and mother.

(verse 35)

Understanding family from Western perspectives from places such as Australia and New Zealand may be different for someone from the Pacific region. The reason is that most Pacific nations value communal living and see family as a collective of extended family members rather than immediate family members that include a father, mother and their children. For Samoans, family (translated as *āiga*) is often understood in terms of the extended family, which includes grandparents, aunties and uncles, cousins, nieces and nephews.

This week I will present Christian traits for becoming members of the family of God, who all share the Spirit of God. A 'chiastic' structure is used: where corresponding days from the centre of the week share similar ideas. Reflections are thus framed around the centre of the week – Wednesday – which I propose as foundational to answer the question 'Who is my family?' For today's reading, anyone who does the will of God is a member of God's family and offers one answer to the question posed above. The challenge, however, becomes interpreting the will of God in our daily lives, above and beyond our own worldly desires for prosperity, power and status.

† Lord God, teach us to know your will within our daily lives, and give us courage so that we allow your will to be done. Amene

Monday 19 June

Led by the Spirit

Read Romans 8:12–17

For all who are led by the Spirit of God are children of God.

(verse 14)

On this day thirty-three years ago, I asked a similar question along the lines of 'Who is my family?' Growing up, my family and I moved around to rural places in Aotearoa New Zealand, such as Murupara and Taumarunui, to Vailoa Faleata in Samoa, and finally settled at Matraville in Sydney, Australia. My father was a church minister, which meant we moved around due to different callings and placements. As a teenager growing up in Sydney, I questioned God's plan when my mother suddenly passed away from a fatal asthma attack at home. That day I questioned why God would take our mother away from us, her five young children, even though my parents were God's servants who faithfully answered his calling around the Pacific. In addition, my youngest brother suffered from a rare condition known as Weaver-Smith Syndrome, where he could not talk, eat or walk, and required special care around the clock; our mother provided that care, and yet God took her away from us that day.

Today's reading reminds us that once we are led by the Spirit of God, we become adopted children of God. Upon reflection, I can confidently say that it is the Spirit of God that has answered all my doubts since then as an impressionable and confused teenager, to realise that God does not forsake his children carrying heavy and troubled hearts. Being led by the Spirit of God enables us to call upon God as 'Abba', Father, reminding us that God is love, who works miraculously in our lives during our times of need.

† Our powerful and supreme God, forgive us if we question your presence during our times of desperation. Encourage us, Abba, our Father, to seek you for strength and peace amid our moments of loneliness. Amene

For further thought

What drives us each day? Let the Spirit of God guide us to his love, so that we can lead others as well to God.

Tuesday 20 June

A child heir of God

Read Galatians 4:1–7

So you are no longer a slave but a child, and if a child then also an heir, through God.

(verse 7)

The Lands and Titles court of Samoa is a busy and vital component of the Samoan judiciary system. For several families where land is passed down from the preceding generations, there are times when the rightful ownership of land and *matai* titles, or chiefly titles for families, are questioned. Some of the underlying reasons behind such challenges include adoption issues and the gifting of family land out of prolonged and loyal service. Official adoption papers are at times overlooked, when children are adopted, or *vaetama*, from birth into their new families. Disputes arise when developments on family land and registering *matai* titles demand official documentation of entitlements for those making such claims. In some cases, family land and *matai* titles are gifted by leaders of families to those with no family ties, yet who had worked for the family over generations. These family workers attend to the plantations, livestock and other domestic household duties. When claims to the family land and *matai* titles are therefore raised, but with no biological family ties, challenges develop by surviving family members about the rightful owners of such heritage. Resolutions for such disputes within families are often sought in the Lands and Titles court.

Our passage today encourages us by saying that being a child of God gives us status as heir to God's family, where one is no longer slave to worldly disputes of rightful ownership to family property, status and heritage. As a rightful member of God's family, one acknowledges God as Abba, as Father, like a child dependent upon parents, relying upon God's Spirit to persevere through life's challenges.

† Abba, our Father, thank you for lifting our slave status to sin and worldly desires, allowing us membership to your divine family, through your Son and our Saviour Jesus Christ. Amene

For further thought

Are we still slaves to sin and worldly possessions, forgetting that God has freed us from such bondage? Let us rejoice in God's saving grace.

Wednesday 21 June

Born again child of God

Read John 19:25b–27

When Jesus saw his mother and the disciple whom he loved standing beside her, he said to his mother, 'Woman, here is your son.'

(verse 26)

Witnessing childbirth as a father is a special experience, one that is life-lasting and life-changing. I will never experience the pain all mothers endure at such a time, nor do I profess to know any parallel of such pain. What I can share, however, is the joy of bearing witness to God's miracle of life. When our eldest son Norman was born, the midwife echoed to me words similar to those of our text for today, to the effect, 'OK, Daddy, here is your son.' I cannot recall her exact words, as I stood in awe to see God's creation and majesty unfold before my eyes. What I do remember is crying out in joy, while my son cried out into this world, of how truly amazing God is! The event made me realise just how small and insignificant I am, and reminded me of God as our supreme Creator. I recall thinking that every person had been born into this world in such a way, regardless of wealth, status or nationality.

Today's reflection becomes the foundation to answering 'Who is my family?' It is only when someone is born again that one becomes a child of God. Yet not as an earthly rebirth, which is not possible, but born again through the Spirit of God. From the cross Jesus removed himself from his worldly birth, by calling his mother 'woman' and presenting his devoted follower John as her son. We too become a child of God and members of his family when we surpass our worldly origins, accept Christ as Lord, and are reborn in the Spirit of God.

† O God, thank you for your creation and humankind made in your image. May our hearts be receptive to being born again in your Spirit, revealing your likeness in all that we do. Amene

For further thought

Only when we are born again in the Spirit of God can we experience the fullness of life through our risen Lord.

Thursday 22 June

Becoming children of God

Read 1 John 3:1–14

Little children, let no one deceive you. Everyone who does what is right is righteous, just as he is righteous.

(verse 7)

Aligning with the chiastic structure used to understand readings for this week, today's passage is a plural reading of Tuesday's reflection, from a *child* heir of God, to becoming *children* of God. For most Samoan families, commonly there are many children, including siblings and their cousins. Within such settings, children play important and vital roles. These roles often include being care-givers and minders for their younger siblings and cousins. Other roles include running small errands for parents and grandparents around the house. For the older children, food preparation and cooking for the entire family are often part of daily chores. When our extended family gathered occasionally at Leauvaa in Samoa, several of us children at the time often stayed over for the weekends, including Sunday morning worship. We would get through our daily morning chores early on Saturday, swim in the sea, and gather around our large dining table that would fit up to twenty of us cousins and my siblings, eating porridge, bread and bananas.

Our reading today reminds us that we have all become God's children through Christ revealed to us as the Son of God. Just as our family children had our assigned roles to play at our family homestead, all God's children have roles to play within the family of God. Such roles include doing what is right in the eyes of God, loving one another and allowing God's love to dwell within. Becoming children of God means that we no longer are deceived by evil but live righteously, having Christ abide in us who himself is the completeness of righteousness.

† Lord God, thank you for Jesus Christ, our Lord and our Saviour, who has enabled us to become your children and granted our pathway to righteousness through his life, death and resurrection. Amene

For further thought

Do we try and live righteously without Christ dwelling within us? If so, then let us consider becoming children of God and love another.

Friday 23 June

Service to Christ

Read Romans 14:10–21

The one who thus serves Christ is acceptable to God and has human approval.

(verse 18)

Tautua, as the Samoan term for one's service to the family or village, is a practice and concept familiar to most Samoans. The reason is because *tautua* is one of the key features for Samoans, being a stepping stone towards leadership for families. The Samoan proverb, *o le ala i le pule o le tautua*, translated as the pathway to leadership is through service, captures the very essence and structure of Samoan families. Those who undertake the roles as *tautua* are assigned by *matai* or the chiefs and title-holders that lead families. Such roles are commonly assigned to the untitled young men of any family, who work the land and plantations, providing for the family and serve *matai*, who are often the elders and leaders of the family. Women and children also play their respective roles in service to the family. The harmonious living of Samoans therefore depends upon understanding these inherent and assigned roles, in terms of *tautua* or service to one's family. Service to Christ therefore is not a foreign concept to Samoans, as serving families and others is part and parcel of being Samoan.

Service to Christ involves being led by the Spirit of God at all times. Our reading today teaches us not to pass judgement on one another, but to strive for peace and harmony. The apostle Paul highlights the kingdom of God as not being concerned with physical sustenance through food and drink, but as being about spiritual well-being that upholds peace. Anyone who serves Christ wholeheartedly inherits the role of sharing God's peace with fellow members of God's family.

† O God, continue to teach us your ways so that all that we do through our service to Christ gives glory and honour to you, our gracious and loving God. Amene

For further thought

Who do we serve today – Christ as Lord, or someone else whom we value and to whom we extend the highest of respect? Who should we serve?

Saturday 24 June

Knowing Christ

Read Ephesians 3:14–19

... and to know the love of Christ that surpasses knowledge, so that you may be filled with all the fullness of God.

(verse 19)

I recall, when approaching the end of my most recent study towards further education, a close friend asked for a brief reflection about my journey. At the time, I was near the final submission of my work for examination. I responded that the journey had drawn me closer to God. At the beginning of my studies I was full of passion and drive to discover knowledge to fill a void that needed to be filled. Yet in the process I discovered just how challenging and demanding the search for further knowledge can become. Simply, it became a lonely place, with setbacks from receiving supervisory feedback and comments to the work submitted that required careful consideration to digest and comprehend. Extended family obligations and local parish commitments also needed to be balanced in the journey. I found however that spending time with my young sons and wife often paused study routines and became the much-needed self-care and time away from my desk. Upon reflection, therefore, the striving for further learning drew me closer to God for strength and direction and, through faith in him, ensured successful completion of the journey.

Knowing Christ involves understanding that must be shared, not kept hidden away. Such knowledge inspires one to share the love of God in all corners of the world – breadth, length, height and depth – with Christ who dwells in one's heart. Apart from the daily search for knowledge in different fields, knowing Christ governs our doing the will of God in our lives, united as members of God's family serving our Lord here on earth.

† Our loving God, thank you for the knowledge you have given us to understand you as Creator and loving Father. Encourage us to practise lives founded upon your love. Amene

For further thought

Let us live in the world today by sharing the love of God that embraces us, and know that God awaits us with love in eternity.

Readings in Amos

Notes by **Delroy Hall**

Delroy has over thirty years' experience in vocational ministry as well as being a psychotherapist, teacher and trainer. Delroy is committed to dealing with human pain while developing trust, so people can recover and thrive. He has lectured nationally and internationally. In September 2017 he was appointed as the chaplain for Sheffield United Football Club. Outside of his ministerial responsibilities, Delroy keeps fit by swimming, cycling and running. He is married to Paulette and has twin daughters, Saffron and Jordan. Delroy has used the NKJV for these notes.

Sunday 25 June

Judgement on the neighbours

Read Amos 1:1–2:3

For three transgressions of Damascus, and for four, I will not turn away its [punishment].

(verse 3)

What a graphic start to the book, like the opening scene in an action movie! There is no gentle introduction, no sweeping music with credits scrolling. Instead, we're straight into the action as Amos graphically describes the awful consequences poised to overwhelm the nations who have transgressed God's law of love.

Verse three is repeated five times in the first two chapters and in each case it makes the same point: God has been repeatedly 'turning away' the consequences of their wicked choices, so that they would have space to repent, but instead they have shown that their nature is now fixed. No matter how often God protects them from the full impact of their choices, they will never change. And therefore, his hand of restraint is about to be removed.

Paul tells us that ultimately we will 'reap what we sow' (Galatians 6:7) and they have been sowing havoc on human beings created in the image of God, casting off all pity (verse 11), ripping open the women with child (verse 13), and now the consequences will be fully felt.

As you lift your eyes from this page, perhaps you could ask, 'Are we not seeing the defenceless being abused today? Might not God be warning us too?'

† Father, may we be moved in our hearts to respond in prayer and action to the sights of dehumanisation we see in our world.

Monday 26 June

Judgement on Israel

Read Amos 2:10–3:12

Behold, I am weighed down by you, as a cart full of sheaves is weighed down.

(verse 2:13)

As you read this account you can feel the heavy heart, the disappointment and dismay in the heart of God. Like a betrayed lover, he recounts the wonderful times they spent together, the unique, intimate experiences. He lists the times he protected, rescued, nurtured and loved. And with a broken heart he tells of the unfaithfulness of their response and the consequences that must now follow.

This isn't the story of a passive-aggressive tyrant lashing out as a result of personal hurt. This is the pain of one who can no longer hold back the consequences of the unloving choices of the one he loves so profoundly.

As a shepherd must feel heartbroken after losing a sheep to a lion, recovering only the legs, or a piece of an ear, God is going to be just so with Israel. They are going to be devoured by a foe they are no longer equipped or strong enough to deal with and he can do no more.

Yesterday was all about the nations neighbouring Israel and Judah. It's always easier to see the faults in others, those outside our circle. So often, the church has found it easy to speak judgement on those outside. Yet the shocking part of today's reading is that God speaks the same message to Israel and Judah – and, by extension, to those who are called children of God.

There are consequences for us not following God's pattern of living. It is a constant theme in Amos. To live by God's principles brings life. When we do not, we expose ourselves to the errors and sins of our ways. There is no escape or short cut.

† Father, we can be so wrapped up in our ways of doing things. Help us to heed your warnings of turning back before we face a crisis because of our actions.

For further thought

Jesus encouraged us to 'take out the plank' in our own eye before the speck in others. What 'planks' do we need to remove?

Tuesday 27 June

Prepare to meet your God

Read Amos 4:1–13

'I blasted you with blight and mildew. When your gardens increased, your vineyards, your fig trees, and your olive trees, the locust devoured them; yet you have not returned to Me,' says the Lord.

(verse 9)

I read this portion of scripture with the voice of my Caribbean parent's dulcet tones ringing in my ears. If they warned me numerous times and I paid no attention, I would hear at some point, 'Delroy, if you do not hear, you will feel.'

The message of Amos is that there comes a point when we will not only be told what God is like, but we will personally experience who he is. In the words of the title for today, we will meet him – not just in eternity, but as his nature outworks in our lives, just as I would with my parents if I failed to respond to their words. Of course, being disciplined by your parents is not pleasant at the time and 'Prepare to meet your God' can sound like a doom-laden warning! In truth, though, the discipline of parents is a sign of their love, and meeting who God is should be a joyful and longed-for experience.

That's why these warnings are so stark – to shock people into an awareness of where their choices are leading before it is too late. A question I often ask when counselling is: 'On reflection, do you think you missed the tell-tale signs along the way when things in your life were drifting a little?' I ask it not to provoke guilt or shame, but to encourage honesty and the possibility of change. The answer, mostly, is 'Yes'. If only we responded to the word of God rather than waiting to meet him to discover the truth!

† Lord, teach us how to listen to you and our lives when we are beginning to drift from you. Teach us how to listen to your still, small voice to avoid unnecessary crises in our lives.

For further thought

If you paused for a while to listen to your life, would you find areas needing immediate attention to avert an unnecessary crisis?

Wednesday 28 June

Let justice flow down like a river

Read Amos 5:18–27

I hate, I despise … and I do not savor … I will not accept [your burnt offerings and your grain offerings] … I will not regard … Take away from Me the noise of your songs, for I will not hear …

But let justice run down like water, and righteousness like a mighty stream.

(part of verses 21–24)

Here we come to the heart of why God is acting now rather than continuing to turn back the consequences of their choices. Their sin is not just an offence against God, it is against those who have no power, no choice. In chapter 5 we see described in graphic detail the impact on the honest, on the vulnerable and the oppressed – injustice heaped on injustice.

The words I have highlighted above are a stark reminder that the mechanics of religion are a profanity against God unless they are motivated by the love of God expressed towards others. When we act unjustly towards others, to think that this will become acceptable to God provided that we jump through some religious hoops is to utterly misrepresent who God is. God despises and hates what the Israelites have done, but this is what he wants from them. He wants justice to flow as an unstoppable essence of life and godliness to invigorate and enliven the lives of all people.

God is making it clear that what he delights in is justice and righteousness, because they are the outworking of love, and God is love.

It was during the Civil Rights movement that Dr Martin Luther King used the words of Amos as a rallying cry to announce justice and righteousness not just for black people but for all humanity.[1] His challenge and that of Amos is still relevant today.

† The cry of your servant Amos is to 'let justice run down like water, and righteousness like a mighty stream'. Father, give us your grace that we may be vehicles of justice and righteousness right now in the present age.

For further thought

Ignatius encourages us to read the scriptures with all our senses. Try to read the passage again, empathically. As it stirs you and touches your soul, ask what God would have you do.

[1] William Robert Miller, *Martin Luther King, Jr.: His Life, Martyrdom and Meaning for the World* (New York: Weybright and Talley, 1968), p. 143.

Thursday 29 June

The plumb line is set

Read Amos 6:8–7:9

Behold, I am setting a plumb line. In the midst of My people Israel; I will not pass by them anymore. The high places of Isaac shall be desolate, and the sanctuaries of Israel shall be laid waste. I will rise with the sword against the house of Jeroboam.

(verses 7:9)

Anyone who has done any building work or even wallpapering will know the importance of a plumb line. My father was a builder's joiner who taught me that in wallpapering you had to set the first piece of wallpaper straight to ensure that all the others would hang accurately. Every time you started a new wall the plumb line was used again to ensure that all the other paper would hang correctly. This was imperative, especially if you had patterned wallpaper.

God had called the people to live together in such a way as to represent him to the nations so that all nations would receive the blessing of relationship with God. But, as we have seen, far from being a plumb line to the nations, showing what God was like by their just, merciful and loving actions, they had become like the other nations in their atrocious actions towards the poor and vulnerable. When the plumb line is no longer straight, God must set a new plumb line in their midst.

This is a message for today. What are the plumb lines we use in making our choices? What sort of plumb line do we present to the world? Is it the plumb line of God's character, or the plumb line of our own sophistication and technological achievements? Is it the plumb line of God's unchanging nature or a morality based on fashion and ease?

I recall, maybe a year or so ago, reading of some churches who said they were dispensing with the idea of discipleship as it was demanding and far too difficult. Really?

Jesus is our plumb line, there is no other.

† Lord, there are many standards in the world claiming our loyal attention. Let us not be distracted by the glitter of the world's plumb lines. Let us be enamoured by the challenge and beauty of who you are.

For further thought

The world faces many crises, from pandemics to climate change. But perhaps the biggest challenge comes when Jesus is no longer the plumb line. What do you think?

Friday 30 June

The time is right

Read Amos 8:1–14

I will make the sun go down at noon, and I will darken the earth in broad daylight; I will turn your feasts into mourning, and all your songs into lamentation; I will bring sackcloth on every waist … I will make it like mourning for an only son, and its end like a bitter day.

(verses 9b–10)

On Sunday, we saw the repeated phrase 'For three transgressions of …, and for four …'. God has watched patiently, given room for repentance and held back the consequences of their choices. But now, he has judged that, for the sake of the oppressed, and in light of their determined implacability, that time must end. It isn't arbitrary, it isn't passive-aggressive, it isn't done lightly. But with great reluctance and a broken heart, God declares that it is time.

This is not a side of God we often like to see. It is not a side of God we like to consider, but this is God acting in love. Love, as Paul says, 'does not seek its own' (1 Corinthians 13:5), it does not 'insist on its own way'. Love gives us the dignity of choice. But for choice to be real, it eventually has to lead to different outcomes. If all my choices lead to the same destination, it is no choice at all. If, irrespective of what I choose, God always intervenes to bring about the same outcome, he has removed my choice. At some point, when God judges the time to be right, we must receive the consequence of our choices. A God who is love, must also be a God who is just.

Israel and Judah came to believe that they were immune from the consequences of their choices. But 2 Chronicles records the fulfilment of Amos' prophecy. The people sinned until there was no remedy (2 Chronicles 36:16). As Christians, do we perhaps, fall into the same trap?

† Loving Father, as we read Amos, let us learn the lessons of your judgement in response to our behaviour with clarity. Teach us to heed your call for correction before it is too late.

For further thought

As parents or those in leadership, how do we judge that 'the time is right' to discipline? How do we do that with compassion and the right motivation?

Saturday 1 July

Destruction and hope

Read Amos 9:1–15

Behold, the days are coming ... The mountains shall drip with sweet wine, and all the hills shall flow with it ... I will bring back ... They shall build the waste cities ... They shall plant vineyards ... They shall also make gardens and eat fruit from them.

(part of verses 13–14)

Our readings for this week's devotional have been relentlessly dismal! Yet here, in these closing scenes, we see a glimpse of future hope. Yes, a God of love exercises judgement, allowing us to feel the consequences of our choices. But even in that there is mercy, the seeds of something better.

God, through the power of poetry, offers in the last few verses the potential of hope for a better future. But if we are to live in the reality of that hope we must go through the process of repentance, being renewed, and then being transformed. And sometimes the crisis that comes when we face the consequences of our choices can provide the impetus we need to initiate that process; it can bring life into focus and cause us to prioritise what really matters.

Sometimes a crisis may come as the result of our own choices, but all too often the crises we face are the result of choices made by those with the power to choose. Choices that demand justice on behalf of the poor and vulnerable.

Whichever it may be, Amos brings us hope – there will be justice, there is yet light, there is his presence. The justice of God includes the restoration of that which was lost.

Amos warns us to respond quickly, to act justly and, as we face crises, to live hopefully.

† Lord, as we call to you in prayer, let us remember, no matter how bleak or tough things become, you have not left us to suffer alone, and you have not left us without hope.

For further thought

To work through difficult times, we must face the immediacy of the situation while keeping an eye on the long game. What do you think?

The Gospel of Matthew (4)

1 Parables and controversies

Notes by **Ashley Barker**

Ash is a leadership developer, activist, communicator and church planter. He has intentionally lived and served in urban poor neighbourhoods from his native Melbourne to Bangkok and Birmingham, UK. Ash is passionate to see urban people and places grow into God's dream for fullness of life everywhere and founded Seedbeds (www.seedbeds.org) to help this happen. Ash has used the NIVUK for these notes.

Sunday 2 July

Ready for God's coming revolution?

Read Matthew 13:1–17

Blessed are your eyes because they see, and your ears because they hear. For truly I tell you, many prophets and righteous people longed to see what you see but did not see it, and to hear what you hear but did not hear it.

(verses 16–17)

Jesus' parables of God's incoming reign are subversive to the current powers. Not all will understand or join in with what God is doing. Indeed, growth into God's dream of shalom filling the earth as it fills heaven doesn't happen without subversion and struggle – something going underground.

We see this in today's reading. At a time when grain provided the staple diet that kept people alive, this farmer seems to be wasting one of their most valuable assets. Like many parables, Jesus is making a subversive point through compare and contrast. Just as they would expect the farmer to only scatter seeds on good ground, so the kingdom worker might choose to only work with those they think will respond. But while the farmer might be able to distinguish what will be fertile ground, we cannot, must not, presume. True, much-needed grain would eventually die if the seeds were thrown on hard paths or stones or among thorns and thistles; likewise not all hearts are ready to experience the seed of God's shalom in their lives. But those hearts and lives that are ready can multiply God's goodness in remarkable ways. Sowers must persevere.

† Lord, help us to hear and see what you're doing among us. Let us not be the ones clinging to present powers that we miss the coming revolution. Amen

Monday 3 July

Grit and fruitfulness

Read Matthew 13:18–43

The seed falling on good soil refers to someone who hears the word and understands it. This is the one who produces a crop, yielding a hundred, sixty or thirty times what was sown.

(verse 23)

Jesus explains the comparisons of the soils in subversive ways. Some we encounter won't have basic awareness and are like concrete. Others are like 'rocky ground', who initially have awareness and even joy about God's coming revolution, but not the roots to see it through. As we saw yesterday, we must expect to share our lives and God's love with all these diverse people; we don't know at the outset which will prove to be the 'good soil'.

Of course, the hard work doesn't stop once the seed is sown. Like the farmer growing grain, building the kingdom takes hard work and perseverance, it takes grit! But no amount of effort will produce fruit from concrete – doing the same thing over and over in that case is not perseverance but a kind of arrogance or selfishness.

In contrast, we can share life and God's dream with people who are ready. They are not shallow, have deep roots of awareness and keep growing. They can overcome even dramatic 'trouble' or 'persecution' because they have a fire deep in the belly for something much bigger than themselves that they see as worthwhile. I have had the honour of meeting such people all my life in the most unexpected places. There is a supernatural abundance of life that can flow from them if I am patient and gritty and hang in there with them. Sometimes, even we can be such 'good soil', 'fruitful' people.

† Lord, help us keep sowing the seeds we must. Enable us to have the awareness, grit and roots to be fruitful, to share in the fruitfulness of your dream coming true among us. Help us find and be fruitful people. Amen

For further thought

What does 'good soil' look like? What helps and hinders being fruitful?

Tuesday 4 July

Is giving all worth it?

Read Matthew 13:44–58

The kingdom of heaven is like treasure hidden in a field. When a man found it, he hid it again, and then in his joy went and sold all he had and bought that field.

(verse 44)

When we think of magic, we might think of spiritually aware or animistic cultures. In Bangkok, for example, we would often see neighbours making offerings to local spirits for protection each morning. However, make no mistake, the globalised, consumer-driven culture in the West has its own magic formulas. Consider the allure of most advertising campaigns: 'If you just drive this car or wear this perfume or have this house your life will be secure.'

There is a radical difference between faith and magic. Magic tries to manipulate the spiritual and physical with formulas to get what we want, but faith is about giving everything to God so that he can do through us what he wants done in the world. What it takes to resist the calculations of magic and to give all, like the one who gave everything for the treasure, is faith that the 'treasure' is genuinely valuable. Without that, it's too easy to succumb to magic formulas and miss out on real life.

On the other hand, if we give what we have in a situation, then we 'taste and see' that God is good. Like the prospector taking what he hopes is gold to the assayer and discovering its true worth, we learn that Jesus really is treasure, that we can let go and live deeply in a shallow world. This rebellion against magic is not about the superficialities of what clothes, music or body art we might choose, but is a whole-of-life surrender to discerning the will and heartbeat of our Lord together and responding faithfully.

Even to taste such life has no equal. It's worth giving all we have to pursue it.

† Lord, help us give up all control and manipulation. Free us to give all for your kingdom come. Amen

For further thought

What holds you back from giving all for God's dream coming true in the world? How can you start to let go and invest in what matters most?

Wednesday 5 July

Moving from scarcity to satisfaction

Read Matthew 14:1–21

Jesus replied, 'They do not need to go away. You give them something to eat.' 'We have here only five loaves of bread and two fish,' they answered.

(verses 16–17)

The disciples don't feel the same as Jesus about the hungry multitudes in a wilderness. It is getting late in the day and the disciples start to display what Parker Palmer calls 'the scarcity assumption'.[1] The disciples see the needs and problems around them, but also the limited resources that they have to feed them.

Jesus' question 'What do you have in your hands?' challenges those instincts and this story flows in a new direction. Jesus had an 'abundance' approach to life. When we look at urban people and communities we serve we can, like the disciples, get resentful, fearful or overwhelmed by unmet needs. However, we can also join Jesus in taking an inventory of strengths and what can be offered. As asset-based community developers would say, 'Use what's strong to fix what's wrong.' Jesus never did anything for anyone that they could do for themselves and never created dependencies. Indeed, his miracles only happened within the context of co-operation, empowerment and the dignity of the most vulnerable. In the hands of Jesus, their combined loaves and fish are abundantly enough.

As the panic buying and hoarding in the recent Covid-19 pandemic shows us, the scarcity assumption is alive and well. People were scared to give up their own little 'loaves and fish' in case they missed out. Hoarding, however, diminishes us all and creates an environment of fear, mistrust and instability. Faith moves in the other direction. If we can release what we have in faith, miracles are possible. We might need to move slowly at first, at the 'speed of trust',[2] but it's possible with Jesus. Moving from scarcity to appreciating what we have in our hands together for abundance, is one of the most needed shifts for us to learn today.

† Lord, we give you what we have in our hands. Bless it, and may it be enough for us today. Amen

For further thought

What can stop us sharing what God has given us with others?

[1] Parker Palmer, *The Active Life: A Spirituality of Work, Creativity, and Caring* (New York: Jossey Bass, 1999), p. 122.

[2] Stephen M. R. Covey, *The Speed of Trust: The One Thing that Changes Everything* (New York: Free Press, 2008).

Thursday 6 July

Stepping out of the boat in storms

Read Matthew 14:22–36

Then Peter got down out of the boat, walked on the water and came toward Jesus. But when he saw the wind, he was afraid and, beginning to sink, cried out, 'Lord, save me!' Immediately Jesus reached out his hand and caught him. 'You of little faith,' he said, 'why did you doubt?'

(verses 30–31)

Matthew's Gospel often shows the disciples getting into trouble without Jesus. Here, they have left Jesus on the shore and go out in a small boat, just as it's starting to get dark. When the night is at its darkest, a severe storm crashes over them. This was frightening physically and spiritually; open water and darkness were considered the domain of evil; serious trouble on every level!

I can be tempted to be a 'functional atheist' at times, trying to live as if God doesn't exist, limiting any risks, seeing faith as an add-on when it's safe to do so. Yet, in this story God's intervention is needed and Jesus literally walks on stormy water to reach the disciples. 'Take courage. I'm here.'

Peter doesn't recognise Jesus and thinks he's an underworld figure, come to take him under, so he comes up with a test: 'Let me come to you and walk on water too.' Jesus agrees and Peter gets out of the boat and starts to walk on water. However, he loses his nerve as he looks around at the crashing waves. Peter cried out for Jesus' help. Jesus quickly grabbed Peter, got in the boat with him and calmed the storm for all.

I can relate to Peter. I can lose my nerve. I can focus on troubles. I can fail to recognise Jesus' help in storms. However, Jesus doesn't lose nerve, focus or awareness. Jesus can grab us, enter our situation and calm storms beyond our control. Sometimes, even a little faith and co-operation with Jesus can make the biggest difference.

† Lord, help us step out in faith and trust you with our lives. Amen

For further thought

What could co-operation with Jesus look like today?

Friday 7 July

Moving to why?

Read Matthew 15:1–20

Then some Pharisees and teachers of the law came to Jesus from Jerusalem and asked, 'Why do your disciples break the tradition of the elders? They don't wash their hands before they eat!'

(verses 1–2)

Why we choose to keep certain traditions, methods and policies and not others is important. So often we get caught up in maintaining methods that no longer work or, worse, cause harm. What might start out as helpful can, in different circumstances, become a hindrance to God's mission.

The same was true in Jesus' day; the Pharisees and Sadducees were deeply concerned with continuity and the fidelity of Israel's life together and are furious at Jesus' blatant disregard of the traditions that they saw as upholding these. Jesus, however, quickly identifies their hypocrisy and goes to the heart of the matter: are you faithful to the traditions themselves, or to the reasons why these traditions exist?

Like Jesus, we must seek the heart of why methods were chosen in the first place. Where those still resonate with Jesus, then we can be loyal to them in whatever way possible. On the other hand, if we prioritise practices above the reasons why they exist, we will no longer be faithful to the original intent or relevant to current needs, even if we continue with the same practices.

At the centre of God's mission is the 'why' of hope, a hope rooted in the promise of God that all things will be reconciled in Jesus and that the world will be put right one day. This is God's redeeming mission with Abraham and is why the Christian church exists today. As Lesslie Newbigin says, 'The church is sign, instrument and foretaste of God's reign for that place.'[1] To be faithful to this promise, we must continually find new methods to do this.

† Lord, help us find deeper meaning and purpose. We are grateful for all those faithful ones who have gone before us. Free us to be your people in the world for this day at this time. Amen

For further thoughts

What methods are we using that are missing the point of God's dream coming true today. How could we try something new?

[1] Lesslie Newbigin, 'On Being the Church in the World', in G. Ecclestone (ed.), *The Parish Church?* (Oxford: Mowbray, 1988), p. 31.

Saturday 8 July

Crumbs and abundance

Read Matthew 15:21–39

'Then Jesus said to her, 'Woman, you have great faith! Your request is granted.' And her daughter was healed at that moment.

(verse 28)

In today's reading two stories are shown, side by side. A common theme is that it can take initiative to see the abundance of God released.

In the first story we see a desperate woman ask Jesus to heal her daughter. She is Canaanite, not from Israel, and Jesus pushes back. Overcoming ethnic and gender power structures, the woman makes her case for God's mercy and will not take no for an answer. Jesus seems to change his mind, heals the daughter and commends the woman for her great faith. God's mercy can stretch far and wide enough after all.

The disciples are soon in a 'remote place' with Jesus and a crowd, seeing miracles happen, but multitudes have not eaten for three days. We have seen this scene before at the start of our week's reading. The disciples should know the drill. Give what they have to Jesus and all will be well. Will the disciples step up and show some initiative like the Canaanite woman? No, they don't. Jesus has to ask them, 'How many loaves do you have?' Eventually they give up their seven loaves and fish, and in the hands of Jesus the crowds are satisfied and there is abundance again.

Both Jesus and the Canaanite woman needed to persevere to see God's mercy and abundance flow. Neither tried to take short cuts or take responsibility for what others can do. That thoughtful resilience proved to be the difference between abundance and scarcity in both stories.

† Lord, help us not to give up in the face of overwhelming need. Let us share what is in our hands, but not more; knowing that, in your hands, abundance is possible. Amen

For further thought

What is in your hands to give today? What steps of faithfulness can you take to see God's abundance flow?

The Gospel of Matthew (4)

2 Son of Man, Son of God

Notes by **John Birch**

For John's biography, see p. 127. John has used the NIVUK for these notes.

Sunday 9 July

Looking for signs

Read Matthew 16:1–12

He replied, 'When evening comes, you say, "It will be fair weather, for the sky is red," and in the morning, "Today it will be stormy, for the sky is red and overcast." You know how to interpret the appearance of the sky, but you cannot interpret the signs of the times.'

(verses 2–3)

I'm reminded of the saying, 'Red sky at night, shepherd's delight; red sky in the morning, shepherd's warning'. I always thought this was ancient folklore, but its roots are here in the words of Jesus, and scientifically correct! So, it seems I too can reliably predict tomorrow's weather. But as for 'signs of the times', if all I'm looking at is the political landscape of this world and seeking truth within it, then I'll have the same problem as the Pharisees and Sadducees.

These two groups were not close politically or socially, but there was unity in their desire to eliminate Jesus. There had to be a sign heralding in a genuine prophet or leader, and so far they had seen nothing. Which is why Jesus hints at blindness because the sign had already appeared through Jonah. Not just the whale, the sign was the whole story: repentance, mercy, healing for Jonah – a revelation of the character of God.

Here's your sign, the last word from God, implies Jesus, and yet you cannot see the truth even when it is standing before you. And if you cannot see God in me, then nothing will convince you.

† Oh, that the eyes of a seeking world might be opened, to see the love and light of Christ in our lives. And seeing, believe. Amen

Monday 10 July

Who do you say I am?

Read Matthew 16:13–28

'But what about you?' he asked. 'Who do you say I am?'

(verse 15)

I'm not a fan of giving people fancy titles such as 'Lord' or 'Lady', as politicians can hand them out in response to favours given, rather than deeds done. However, some people rightly deserve recognition for all they have done in life, and that's fine with me.

But what name or title best fits Jesus?

Some who saw and heard Jesus said he was John the Baptist returned from the dead, others suggested Elijah or Jeremiah, both expected to herald in God's Anointed One. And people were genuinely paying Jesus a compliment by comparing him to the greats of their faith. If one of those prophets reappeared suddenly, then the kingdom of God would be close!

But Jesus didn't want to hear that when he asked his disciples, 'Who do you say I am?' I wonder if there was a pause while they gathered their thoughts – about his teaching, authority and power. What did that say about Jesus? Was he teacher, prophet or more? It falls upon Peter to call him 'the Messiah, the Son of the living God', and at that moment Jesus knew that all would be well because here was someone who understood.

I like the idea that the disciples were told not to spread the word that Jesus was the Messiah. There were political reasons, of course, but all believers should really answer that question themselves, because faith is a journey of discovery, of not just learning about Jesus, but knowing Jesus for who he is, and what that means for us all.

† Help us on our journeying with you, dear Lord, to know you more deeply, follow you more closely and allow your love to be at the centre of all we do and say. Amen

For further thought

Set time aside to read one Gospel in its entirety with the help of a commentary, such as the resources of Bible Gateway. Let it enlarge your understanding of who Jesus is.

Tuesday 11 July
Son of God

Read Matthew 17:1–13

Peter said to Jesus, 'Lord, it is good for us to be here. If you wish, I will put up three shelters – one for you, one for Moses and one for Elijah.' While he was still speaking, a bright cloud covered them, and a voice from the cloud said, 'This is my Son, whom I love; with him I am well pleased. Listen to him!'

(verses 4–5)

I am an avid reader of detective fiction, and the more complex a case being investigated the better, when only in the closing pages does the gathering evidence make sense, reaching a point where the detective reveals not only who did it but why and how.

This is not fiction. Jesus was hoping his disciples wouldn't need him to make the big reveal, but just open their eyes and examine the evidence before them, realising who he was and what that ultimately meant for them. There had been lots of discussion, with Peter recently calling Jesus 'Messiah!' The pieces are coming together, so Jesus leads his close team of Peter, James and John to an experience they will never forget, on the slopes of Mount Hermon. Here they see, in the radiant light illuminating Jesus, something of God's glory, and beside him stand Moses and Elijah, a picture of the Law and Prophets of the Old Testament being fulfilled in Jesus.

Peter offers to build three shelters, or tabernacles, for them. But the message from God goes far beyond the traditions of the Old Testament: 'This is my Son, so listen to him!' When the disciples look again, there is only Jesus standing there, explaining what must happen next. Here is their friend, their Messiah, the Son of God, and the Suffering Servant of Isaiah 42:1, telling them that no one must know what they've seen, until he has risen from the dead. That's quite a big ask of anyone, but now they understood, and anything is possible!

† May the lives we live and the words we speak say so much about you, our Saviour, Lord and friend. Amen

For further thought

What is it about the stories about Jesus in the New Testament that, when looked at as a whole, provide you with the bigger picture of God's love and grace?

Wednesday 12 July
Having faith

Read Matthew 17:14–27

Truly I tell you, if you have faith as small as a mustard seed, you can say to this mountain, 'Move from here to there,' and it will move. Nothing will be impossible for you.

(verse 20b)

Jesus and the three disciples come down from the mountain where God's heavenly glory was so discernible, straight into an earthly problem, a distressed father and his epileptic son, whom the other disciples had failed to heal. The frustration Jesus felt at that moment is striking. Earlier he gave his disciples authority over demons and to heal every disease and illness, and yet, when it mattered so much, they had been found wanting. The only good news is that the father had faith in Jesus, and his son was healed.

The problem, says Jesus, is that their faith is seemingly not up to the task. Perhaps they were thinking it was magic, this power conferred upon them, and they were forgetting its source. But it always troubles me when I read those words, because I know what Jesus is saying. When my faith was young, it was like me as a child, unafraid to do anything despite all the bruises and twisted ankles. I heard that a young friend had cancer and my first reaction was to ask God to heal him. And it happened!

Now, older, and apparently wiser, I am sometimes less confident when faced with situations such as that. It is then I am reminded of Jesus' words to the disciples, that a mustard seed is all it takes to move a mountain or overcome great difficulties. And I remember those same disciples sowed the seeds of the church of which I am a part. As Jesus said, 'Nothing will be impossible for you.'

† Grant us, dear Lord, a faith that is strong enough to move every mountain that prevents us from doing your work. Amen

For further thought

If someone asked you about your belief in miracles, is there a situation in your life where you can remember feeling certain that the power of God was discernible?

Thursday 13 July

Who is the greatest?

Read Matthew 18:1–9

He called a little child to him, and placed the child among them. And he said: 'Truly I tell you, unless you change and become like little children, you will never enter the kingdom of heaven.'

(verses 2–3)

There is a well-used literary device involving someone entering a building and shouting, 'OK, who's in charge round here?' You may well have tried it yourself to sort out issues that might otherwise have to be referred upwards to 'management'. Human beings like structure, and a management hierarchy can be a source of comfort, knowing our place within the bigger picture. But how does that work in God's kingdom? That was the thought going through the disciples' minds after so much discussion about who Jesus was, why he had to die, and what the implications were for them. Where did they as individuals fit into this kingdom, and who might be the greatest?

God often turns the constructs of human minds upside down, and certainly when we are talking about greatness and power. Life in the kingdom bears little resemblance to the operation of big business or politics, and Jesus singles out a child as his example. In most families, a small child is not at all concerned with scales of greatness, simply content to belong, dependent on those who love and care for them, trusting their daily needs will be met.

This, says Jesus, is the pattern of life in the kingdom of heaven, one of humility and trust, one which is not concerned with social status, and in humility and love greets as equals all who are a part of God's family. The welcome you give to others, says Jesus, says much about the welcome you give to me in your lives.

† May there always be a welcome in our hearts for others, for we are all God's children, equally deserving of love. Amen

For further thought

Have you given any thought to volunteer opportunities within your local community and how your own skills and talents might be put to good use?

Friday 14 July

The good shepherd

Read Matthew 18:10–20

What do you think? If a man owns a hundred sheep, and one of them wanders away, will he not leave the ninety-nine on the hills and go to look for the one that wandered off? And if he finds it, truly I tell you, he is happier about that one sheep than about the ninety-nine that did not wander off.

(verses 12–13)

We have a man across the road who owns around a hundred sheep, and it's interesting to follow the highs and lows of Graham's shepherding year, and reference them in sermons, of course! Graham is not a hill shepherd, so his sheep are unlikely to wander too far, but it's his attention to detail which is so relevant to Jesus' parable. This year, the damp weather brought plenty of foot problems, and he has spent a lot of time giving attention to any sheep limping across the fields. This individual care extends through lambing and ensuring there is always fresh pasture to take them to. It is obvious to anyone passing that Graham loves his sheep.

The story Jesus uses teaches us a lot about God's nature, and he relates it to the little ones of yesterday's passage, the ordinary and sometimes vulnerable followers of Jesus. It tells us that God's love is an individual love, for each sheep is precious. Sheep are certainly prone to wander, but also very time-consuming, and God's love is patient and forgiving of individual demands, not waiting for the wanderer to return but actively seeking it. And God's love is a rejoicing love, every wandering sheep brought joyfully back into the fold.

This sense of individual love should overflow into our churches and the relationships that exist within them, with a willingness to work together, humbly and patiently, through the highs and lows of each year for the benefit of the entire community of believers.

† For your individual love for all who count themselves as part of your flock, we thank you, loving God. Amen

For further thought

Are there individuals known to you who are struggling with daily life? Even if it is difficult to become involved personally, could you bring them regularly to God in prayer?

Saturday 15 July

The debt cancelled

Read Matthew 18:21–35

Then Peter came to Jesus and asked, 'Lord, how many times shall I forgive my brother or sister who sins against me? Up to seven times?' Jesus answered, 'I tell you, not seven times, but seventy-seven times.'

(verses 21–22)

Numbers in the Bible often have several meanings. Rabbinic teaching was that forgiveness was possible for a sin repeated up to three times, but at the fourth there would be no forgiveness. So, Peter might have expected a thumbs-up from Jesus for suggesting a maximum of seven times, but Jesus' response is that you cannot put such limits on forgiveness.

For many who have been hurt in life, mentally or physically, forgiveness is often difficult, and the scars from words or actions become burdens carried for many years. Forgiveness can bring release, but there is also an element of sacrifice, of letting go, and that can be a hard thing to do. Jesus' parable speaks into this.

The king's servant faces enslavement for the whole of his family after finding himself unable to repay a massive debt. The king shows mercy, cancelling the entire debt, but then the servant refuses to do the same for a colleague over a much smaller amount. He is called to account by the king and punished for his actions. It is an uncomfortable story, but one with a simple message. Those who receive forgiveness must become forgiving people. It was human sin that resulted in the death of God's own Son. This is the scale of our own massive debt. As we accept God's saving grace in our hearts, this debt is cancelled, and a relationship restored. Our willingness to forgive others can bring restoration to our own broken relationships, as well as removing the self-imposed burdens we allow ourselves to carry.

† May we become a forgiving people, remembering all you have done for us, willing to let go and become the people you would have us be, ever-loving God. Amen

For further thought

How easy do you find it to forgive? Are there strained relationships that might be eased with prayer and input from yourself?

Faithfulness

1 God's faithfulness to us

Notes by **Kate Hughes**

Kate worked for the Anglican Church in Southern Africa for fourteen years. Since her return to the UK she has worked as a freelance book editor, mainly specialising in theology. She lives in a small council estate in Coventry with Gypsy, her Cavalier King Charles Spaniel, is involved in her local community and preaches regularly at her local Anglican church. Kate has used the NRSV for these notes.

Sunday 16 July

Steadfast love

Read Psalm 33

All his work is done in faithfulness.

(part of verse 4)

In his book *What St Paul Really Said*,[1] the New Testament scholar Tom Wright says that for St Paul God's righteousness is his faithfulness. God has committed himself to human beings, in particular to the people of Israel, and his love shown in that commitment is unshakeable. The composer of the psalms was saying the same thing. God is not just concerned with nations and world affairs. He may have created the heavens and the earth, but his loving care extends to every single human being. And while our capacity to see or receive the outworking of his love can be affected by our response, his love is always there, even through the trials and dangers of life. The truth is that we can never stop God loving us! Even if we turn away from him or reject his love, he still loves us. We might not always experience that love because of our choices or the choices of others, but we can expect that God's love will take care of us, even if it is in ways that we could not have predicted (or, sometimes, even wanted!)

I hope that this week's readings will make you more sure than ever of how much God loves you – with unshakeable faithfulness.

† Lord, your love and care for your creation is amazing, and you are always faithful to it. Thank you.

[1] Tom Wright, *What St Paul Really Said* (Oxford: Lion, 2001).

Monday 17 July

Kindness

Read Psalm 145:13b–21

The Lord is just in all his ways, and kind in all his doings.

(verse 17)

One theme that will run through this week is that God's righteousness or justice is his faithfulness to his covenant not only with Israel but with everyone and everything he has created. Today's psalm also speaks of the kindness of God. I know that my neighbours on the small estate of social housing where I live look out for me because I am elderly, live alone and have no family nearby. People generally are kind because I am old: they stop their cars to enable me to cross the road safely, they give me their seats on buses, offer to carry my shopping. And one small way that I can be kind to them is to remember to smile and thank them for their kindness to me. I think that kindness is looking out for ways to build up other people; it is not always being nice to them – it may be kind to tell someone that they are behaving badly. And in order to be kind we need to notice other people and see their needs, however small.

Today's psalm tells us that God is kind in the same way. 'The Lord watches over all who love him' (verse 20). The Lord is always looking out for us and doing things that will build us up and help us to become the people that he has created us to be. The wicked don't want God's kindness and they refuse to be kind to others; their unkindness destroys others and finally destroys themselves.

† Thank you Lord that you look out for us in order to show us kindness and that your Spirit shows us ways in which we also can be kind to others.

For further thought

Look back over last week: how did you experience the kindness of God and of other people? How did you return that kindness?

Tuesday 18 July

The sign of God's faithfulness

Read Isaiah 42:1–9

I have called you in righteousness, I have taken you by the hand and kept you; I have given you as a covenant to the people, a light to the nations.

(verse 6)

Who is Isaiah talking about here? Who is this servant of God? The people of Israel, whom God calls to be a light for the nations, to share their covenant relationship with God with the world – and so often failed to do so? Or is Isaiah foreseeing an individual, a unique prophet who will live out the special relationship that God wants to have with everyone he has created? Christians, of course, see this prophecy fulfilled in Jesus. This passage seems to perfectly describe the life and ministry of Jesus – bringing sight to those who cannot see clearly the life to which God calls them, releasing those who live in darkness, in captivity to fear or suffering or sin. This servant has been called by God in righteousness (verse 6) – he is a sign of God's faithfulness to his creation and his covenant. Nothing can stop Jesus – 'he will not grow faint or be crushed' (verse 4); not even the agonising death of crucifixion can stop him steadfastly loving God's people. Every representation of the cross says to us, 'This is how much God loves us, this is how far the faithfulness of God will go.' 'I am convinced that neither death, nor life ... nor anything else in all creation, will be able to separate us from the love of God in Christ Jesus our Lord' (Romans 8:38–39). And we are called to share in the work of showing that love to others.

† O God, make me as one of your servants, that like Jesus I may bring your faithful love to others.

For further thought

Spend some time this week looking at a cross and thinking about what it says about the love of God.

Wednesday 19 July

Falling away and returning

Read Lamentations 3:22–33

Although he causes grief, he will have compassion according to the abundance of his steadfast love.

(verse 32)

It is almost certain that the book of Lamentations was written at the time of one of Jerusalem's greatest calamities, its successful siege and defeat by the Babylonians, which led to many of its citizens, including the king, being taken into exile in Babylon around the year 597 BC. The calamity is seen as having been both avoidable and deserved. The people of Israel had not kept their side of their covenant with God; they had been behaving like other nations, wheeling and dealing with the great powers that surrounded them and not listening to what God was saying to them. Chapter 3 is an acknowledgement that God has allowed the terrible things that have descended upon Jerusalem – but also an acknowledgement that this is the result of God's loving faithfulness to his covenant with his people. Israel is at its best when it is living out its side of the covenant relationship with God. When it fails as spectacularly as it has done, God's love will not let them get away with it. But at the same time he is waiting for the moment when his people turn to him again, in order to show mercy and compassion and to help them walk in the right way.

So often we suffer because we make wrong choices that separate us from God. But God's faithfulness never fails. If we turn to him he will help us to see where we have failed and give us his love and strength to do better. 'The steadfast love of the LORD never ceases' (verse 22).

† Thank you, Lord, that when I stumble and fall through my wrong choices you are always waiting to help me up and set me on the right way again.

For further thought

Can you remember a time when you failed God but he helped you to move forward? What did you do, and what did God do?

Thursday 20 July

Called into fellowship

Read 1 Corinthians 1:4–9

God is faithful; by him you were called into the fellowship of his Son, Jesus Christ our Lord.

(verse 9)

God is faithful to his covenant with his creation – but this does not mean that he is going to bully us, force us to keep our side of the bargain. God knows from the inside what it is like to be human: Jesus experienced temptation and knew only too well what it was like to face the horror of crucifixion. But God does not expect us to struggle on our own. Part of being human is to interact with other people: to accept the help of others and to help others in our turn. God calls us to discover the possibilities of being truly human, and that means fellowship. Fellowship with Jesus the human being as we learn to live as he lived; and fellowship with others in the group of people that he gathered round him to continue his work. In his life, death and resurrection Jesus steadfastly lived out the faithfulness of God, showing that nothing can stop God loving his creation. And in spite of failure, wrong turnings, the human passion for imposing rules and regulations and trying to domesticate God, that is what the church, the fellowship of Jesus Christ, is still called to do. When people look at the church, both as a worldwide institution and the gathering of a few in the local congregation, that is what they should see: the love of God given freely and faithfully to everything and everyone he has created. In order to do that, we need the love and support of the fellowship.

† Thank you, Lord, for our fellowship with Jesus and with each other. Help us to be faithful to them as you are faithful to us.

For further thought

What does it mean to you to be 'called into the fellowship of … Jesus Christ'?

Friday 21 July

God being God

Read 2 Timothy 2:11–13

He remains faithful – for he cannot deny himself.

(verse 13b)

Although we may not be aware of it, we all have something, some part of our character, that makes us who we are. For some people it may be a love of music. For others a love of their family. It can also be something that pushes us to do wrong, like a desire for wealth. Whatever it is, it dictates how we act and the decisions we make. Today's reading reminds us that being faithful is an unshakeable part of God being God. If we try to respond by being faithful in our dealings with God, he will make us part of his plan for his creation. We shall be citizens of the kingdom of God, working with him, being faithful with him, dying to our faithless selves so that we know the real life for which he has created us, enduring the troubles of this world in order to be part, now and in the future, of the alternative reality that is God's eternal plan for his world. We have the freedom to deny God, to reject the life he offers us, and he will not force us to respond to his faithfulness. But he will still remain faithful, still love us, still show us his vision of what life could be like for us if we should choose to go along with him. If God stopped being faithful to his plan for his creation, he would stop being God.

† Thank you, Lord, that nothing can stop you being the kind of God that you are, a God of love and faithfulness.

For further thought

What does being a citizen of the kingdom of God mean to you?

Saturday 22 July

He will do this

Read 1 Thessalonians 5:23–24

The one who calls you is faithful, and he will do this.

(verse 24)

When I get on a bus I try to sit in the front seat downstairs because it has plenty of room for my long legs. This seat is often next to the space for babies and toddlers in buggies and I find it interesting to watch the interaction between (usually) mother (but occasionally father) and child. Sometimes an older child is trying to talk to his or her mother but she is absorbed in her phone and doesn't listen to them. Sometimes the child has a phone to look at, which gives its mother a few moments to do nothing, just gaze out of the bus window. At other times, though, the child is tired and scratchy, whining and demanding, and the mother is driven to the last resort of harassed parents: 'If you don't stop whining, I won't buy you an ice cream/take you to McDonald's/(or the ultimate threat) love you any more.' And sometimes parent and child enjoy the bus ride, talking and playing games together.

Thankfully, God is not like an all-too-human parent. We don't have to earn his love by being good and doing what we are told. Co-operating with him is a response to his faithful, unshakeable love, given to us before we even knew he existed. God will never say to us, 'If you don't do what I want, I will stop loving you.' Instead, he calls us into fellowship with him and will enable us to respond if we are prepared to change and learn his ways. He is faithful and he will do it.

† O love that will not let me go, faithful love that is your gift to me – thank you.

For further thought

How difficult do you find it to let God love you and not feel that he will only love you if you are good?

Faithfulness

2 Faithful people, faithful living

Notes by **John Proctor**

For John's biography, see p. 43. John has used the NRSVA for these notes.

Sunday 23 July

Faithful waiting

Luke 2:26-38

Anna … lived with her husband for seven years after her marriage, then as a widow to the age of eighty-four … At that moment she came, and began to praise God and to speak about the child to all who were looking for the redemption of Jerusalem.

(part of verses 36–38)

Our focus last week was God's faithfulness. The theme now is human response – our faithfulness to God. How does trust in God lead people into lives of integrity and service? Today we look at Anna, and at faithful waiting.

Old age may teach a person many virtues – patience, wisdom, realism, calm. But it is not always a hopeful season. The years allow us to look back, but it may be harder to look positively forward. Yet Anna and Simeon were clearly people of hope. They longed for the 'the consolation of Israel' (verse 25), 'the Lord's Messiah' (verse 26) and 'the redemption of Jerusalem' (verse 38). They expected God to touch the world with fresh goodness, and they waited, trusted and prayed with that in mind. From among their people, in answer to their prayers, light and promise would dawn.

Anna had known a lot of solitude – about sixty years on her own. Yet she found sustenance and strength in God. Her spirit did not wither with the years, but blossomed and reached for the light. When she saw the child Messiah, her heart leapt with praise and delight. She wanted to tell everyone that God was stirring. Here, in person, was the fulfilment of God's promise and of Anna's hopes.

Anna reminds us that time waiting need not be time wasted. God is in the slow places, and grace is always peeping over the horizon. Most of us will pass through times when we need to remember this.

† Remember people who are waiting – for news, for opportunity, in solitude, in sorrow. May God give them a sense of hope and purpose.

Monday 24 July
Faithful dealing

Read Luke 16:10–13

Whoever is faithful in a very little is faithful also in much … If then you have not been faithful with the dishonest wealth, who will entrust to you the true riches? … No slave can serve two masters … You cannot serve God and wealth.

(part of verses 10, 11, 13)

The unjust steward (Luke 16:1–9) is surely the most perplexing of Jesus' parables. Like a blob of mercury in your palm, you can never pin it down. But mercury is certainly useful for taking a person's temperature. Today's verses follow the parable. They suggest that stewardship of money is itself a kind of thermometer, a measure of the health and well-being of a person's spiritual life.

Verse 10 starts with trust. A person who deals uprightly and carefully with small matters can be trusted with something bigger. And vice versa, of course. Here the 'small matter' is money. Do we use the wealth that passes through our hands in ways that honour its true owner, God? Will we spend responsibly, share gladly, give generously and deal honestly? If we can, we shall discover treasure far greater than any material goods.

The mention of 'dishonest wealth' (verse 11) recalls that money is strangely deceptive. It often promises more than it delivers. Cheap credit, safe investment, special offer, easy instalments – the slogans seem so attractive. Yet they do not always mean what they say.

The word translated 'wealth' (verses 11 and 13) is unusual. It is 'mammon' – almost a name, as if money had a personality of its own. In its original Hebrew, 'mammon' probably meant 'what people trust'. And that's part of the deceit. Money seems so dependable, but if we do rely on it, our love and loyalty are misplaced. God and mammon often pull in opposite directions. Wealth rightly used may serve God and neighbour. But only God deserves our commitment and trust.

† May God be in our pockets and our purses, our purchasing and our planning. May God guide what we do with what we have, because it all belongs to God. In Jesus' name.

For further thought

Stewards in Jesus' world were trusted, but they were accountable too. Do you find it helpful to think of yourself as a steward for God?

Tuesday 25 July

Faithful representatives

Read 2 Corinthians 5:17–6:10

So we are ambassadors for Christ, since God is making his appeal through us ... We are treated as impostors, and yet are true ... as dying, and see – we are alive ... as sorrowful, yet always rejoicing; as poor, yet making many rich; as having nothing, and yet possessing everything.

(part of verses 5:20 and 6:8–10)

'Ambassadors for Christ' (verse 5:20). An ambassador in the ancient world usually had a specific mission to fulfil – a place to visit, people to address, a message to convey. The task mattered; so did the tone. People would judge the sender by the servant. So it was important to be authentic. The way you spoke and acted could help hearers make sense of the message and take it seriously.

Christians are ambassadors. We speak for Christ in a world that has quite a patchy knowledge of his love and good news. So it matters to represent him well. Can others see the kind of person he is, by looking at the kind of people we are? How do you represent a crucified and risen Lord?

Today's verses suggest that cross and resurrection, suffering and strength, will go together when we do the work of Christ. Neighbours may both resent and respect what we stand for. We may find ourselves sharing the strain in other people's lives, yet be able to pass on confidence and courage in ways we had not expected. If success and fortune pass us by, opportunities for service and kindness will not; there will still be plenty we can give.

All of this is surely what ambassadors should expect, from the Lord of Good Friday and Easter. This is authentic representation – life and death plaited together, hope coming out of hollow and hurting places, and promise emerging from difficulty and distress. Living this way is a privilege; it reflects and reveals the life of Jesus.

† Teach us, good Lord, to serve you as you deserve ... to labour and not to ask for any reward, save that of knowing that we do your will (Ignatius Loyola, 1548).

For further thought

Do you think of the Christian life as a demand or as a gift – as costly commitment or as abundant fulfilment? Or is it both?

Wednesday 26 July

Faithful suffering

Read Revelation 7:13–17

These ... have come out of the great ordeal; they have washed their robes and made them white in the blood of the Lamb. For this reason they are before the throne of God ... the Lamb ... will be their shepherd ... and God will wipe away every tear from their eyes.

(part of verses 14, 15, 17)

For many Christians in the world, persecution is a fact of life. Even if pressure lifts for a while, the memory remains, as does the awareness that it could happen again. Resilience gets passed on across the generations. Martyrs are remembered with honour. For many of our sisters and brothers in Christ, this is part of what it means to be church.

Revelation was written in an atmosphere of this kind. John's readers needed to reckon with suffering. Christians were a minority, a suspect people. Liberty, and even life, could well come under threat. As ever when persecution is afoot, you never knew quite when or whom it would strike. It might not be everyone; but it could be anyone.

So the vision of today's verses portrays the whole multinational church as a martyr people. Persecution is a 'great ordeal' that they share together. As a fellowship they have been made clean by 'the blood of the Lamb': they are a people defined by the cross of Jesus. He suffered for their sake, and they must be ready to suffer in his name.

Yet Christians are people of hope. The Christ of the cross is the Lord of Easter, the good shepherd, who sets fears and tears to rest. If he leads his people into darkness, he will lead them on into light. If he asks us to share his sorrows, he will not leave us to weep. In time and in eternity, he is able to offer healing, wholeness and joy.

† Remember some of the lands where it is hard to be a Christian, and pray for the people who love Jesus in these places. Ask God to give them courage, confidence, wisdom and patience.

For further thought

Reflect on the thought that the church is described as a martyr people. Might God be asking you to deepen your commitment to Jesus?

Thursday 27 July

Faithful prophets

Read Acts 21:7–14

When we had finished the voyage from Tyre, we arrived at Ptolemais … The next day we left and came to Caesarea; and we went into the house of Philip the evangelist, one of the seven, and stayed with him. He had four unmarried daughters who had the gift of prophecy.

(verses 7–9)

Caesarea was a smart and imposing city on the coast of the Holy Land. It had been extensively rebuilt by Herod the Great, a few years before Christ. By the time of our reading, in the AD 50s, Judea's Roman governors lived there, with a sizeable military depot. The main religious building in town was a Roman temple. Caesarea faced outwards to Rome, not only as a port but also in matters of power and worship. This was not the most obvious place to nurture Christian faith.

Yet Philip the evangelist had settled here. To judge from Acts 8, Philip had the gift of sharing the gospel across cultural and racial barriers. Now we find him, twenty years later, passing on faith and Christian formation to a new generation, to 'four unmarried daughters who had the gift of prophecy'. These young women were serving Christ in a place that was not especially sympathetic. They were walking an uphill journey as disciples. They would surely develop spiritual energy and backbone, for any changes or challenges ahead.

According to the historian Eusebius, these women went on to make quite an impact. They migrated to the land we call Turkey, where their tombs were honoured and visited by Christians for many decades after their death. Evidently their experience at Caesarea had equipped them to live effective Christian lives amid new surroundings, and to carry respect and responsibility in the church. Even though Caesarea had turned its face away from Israel's God, Christians there were able to invest in the next generation. That investment bore fruit, for a long time to come.

† Pray for Christian young people you know, whose Christian journey may confront them with challenges that their parents and grandparents have not had to face. Ask God to give them wisdom and stamina.

For further thought

What is your church doing, and what could it do, to invest in the Christian formation, gifting and growth of young people?

Friday 28 July

Faithful and fruitful

Read Galatians 5:13–23

You were called to freedom … Live by the Spirit, I say, and do not gratify the desires of the flesh. For what the flesh desires is opposed to the Spirit … By contrast, the fruit of the Spirit is love, joy, peace, patience, kindness, generosity, faithfulness, gentleness, and self-control.

(part of verses 13, 16, 17, 22, 23)

Freedom, flesh and fruit – all of them factors in faithful living. Freedom, in Galatians, means that Gentile Christians are free to be Gentiles. Jesus meets them and walks with them amid the culture and customs they know. They do not need to take on the external habits of Jewish law. But freedom involves responsibility too, to make good choices about behaviour and lifestyle.

For a Christian it is a conflict zone, between flesh and Spirit. We are liable to be pulled in two directions. 'Flesh', in this connection, is the human life we can see and no more – gifts and desires, relationships and plans – with no deeper source, no wider horizon and no place for Christ. If this set of realities calls all the shots, we shall surely make some perverse choices in the course of the years, and grow some quite selfish habits. That's what our text means by 'works of the flesh'.

By contrast, the Holy Spirit is keen to prompt us from within, and to lead us in the footsteps of Jesus. Then fruit will grow – 'fruit of the Spirit' (verse 22) – gradually, steadily and persistently. These qualities are attractive. They nourish other people. They build trust. They come from God; we cannot manufacture them. But, as with fruit-growing of any kind, it helps if we create good conditions for their growth. Which brings us back to making choices, and living as a conflict zone. When there is a tussle, a decision, a clash of values, which way do I go – flesh or Spirit; desires or fruit; self or Christ?

† Lord Jesus Christ, please help me to trust your Spirit, to follow the Spirit's leading, to walk in step with the Spirit, and to grow the Spirit's fruit.

For further thought

How would you explain to a new Christian what the Holy Spirit's involvement in your life means to you?

Saturday 29 July

Faithful community

Read 1 Thessalonians 1

We always give thanks to God for all of you and mention you in our prayers, constantly remembering before our God and Father your work of faith and labour of love and steadfastness of hope in our Lord Jesus Christ.

(verses 2–3)

This letter was sent to a group of new Christians, from the people who had helped them come to faith. It is full of warm affection and love, as well as of careful teaching. The very start of the letter sets the tone: 'always ... all of you ... constantly' (verse 2). The words are intense and emphatic, underlining the writers' concern. They had put a lot of effort into their pastoral and missionary work, and their commitment came from the heart. They cared deeply for the well-being of their friends.

The Thessalonian church too had shown that same combination of heart and effort, of inner belief and visible Christian output. The letter speaks of their 'faith, hope and love' (verse 3). Faith looks upward, to Jesus crucified and risen. Love looks outward, to the needs of neighbour. Hope looks forward, to the full completion of God's work in the world. And all three of them stir and shape a person's life.

For each of these words is paired with a busy, active word. 'Work of faith' – trusting Jesus is an energetic quality; it shows in character and behaviour. 'Labour of love' – the word speaks of sleeves rolled up, of taking trouble to help other people. 'Steadfastness of hope' – this suggests endurance, consistency and firmness under pressure. Here is good news that makes a difference in practice, attitudes expressed in deeds, heart and hands working as one. This new community was rooted in basic Christian values, and growing in lively Christian practice. Thessalonica is a good place to conclude our week on faithfulness.

† Could you pray for three people you know: for someone who is finding faith a struggle; for a person to whom love does not come easily; and for one who is running out of hope?

For further thought

Is your local church strong in faith, love and hope? Could you pray and work for growth in one of these areas?

Fresh from The Word 2024

Thinking ahead, now is the right time to order *Fresh from The Word 2024*.

Order now:

- direct from IBRA web shop (see below)
- from your local IBRA rep
- from the SPCK website: www.spck.org.uk
- in selected Christian bookshops
- from online retailers such as Amazon, Eden and others

To order your copy from IBRA

- Website: **shop.christianeducation.org.uk**
- Email: **ibra.sales@christianeducation.org.uk**
- Call: **0121 458 3313**
- Post: **using the order form at the back of this book**

E-versions of *Fresh from The Word* are available through online retailers such as Kindle, Kobo and Eden.

How are you finding this year?

Let us know how you are finding this year's daily Bible reading notes. If you are on Facebook or Twitter, we would love to hear your thoughts, as little or as often as you like! You never know, it may also encourage others to investigate The Word and form a deeper connection with our fellow readers.

 **www.facebook.com/freshfromtheword**

 **www.twitter.com/IBRAbibleread**

Would you consider leaving your own legacy to help spread the Good News?

IBRA and *Fresh from The Word* are only possible through you, the readers, and your donations. At this moment, when the world is changing rapidly, we need your help. A gift in your will to IBRA's International Fund will help continue its Bible reading legacy of 141 years. Every penny of your donation goes directly towards enabling hundreds of thousands of people around the world to access the living Word of God.

> ***So then, brothers and sisters, stand firm and hold fast to the teachings we passed on to you.***
>
> **2 Thessalonians 2:15a (NIV)**

It was the vision of Charles Waters to empower people in Britain and overseas to benefit from the Word of God through the experiences and insights of biblical scholars from around the world. The goal was to strengthen and encourage people in their homes and situations, wherever they were. His legacy lives on today, in you, as a reader, and in the IBRA team, across the globe.

Our work at IBRA is supported by sales of our books, and since 1882 we continue to ensure that 100% of donations to the IBRA International Fund go to benefit our local and international readers. We are blessed every year by those who leave a legacy in their will – ensuring that their hopes are carried on and fulfilled by IBRA, when they have risen into eternal life with our Lord. To continue this important work, would you consider leaving a legacy in your will?

To find out more please contact our Finance Manager on 0121 458 3313, email ibra@christianeducation.org.uk or write to International Bible Reading Association, 5–6 Imperial Court, 12 Sovereign Road, Birmingham, B30 3FH.

- To read more about the history of IBRA go to the inside back page.
- To find out more about the work of the IBRA International Fund go to page 369.

Faithfulness

3 People of faith

Notes by **Shirlyn Toppin**

Shirlyn is a presbyter in the Methodist Church. She believes passionately in the preaching of the word of God without compromise and exercising a pastoral ministry of grace. She enjoys various forms of leisure, reading and shopping. Shirlyn has used the NRSVA for these notes.

Sunday 30 July

Joseph, entrusted with great power

Read Genesis 41:33–46

Now therefore let Pharaoh select a man who is discerning and wise, and set him over the land of Egypt.

(verse 33)

Excluded, abandoned, trafficked, accused and imprisoned would not be experiences that engender faithfulness in God. A sense of hopelessness is a seemingly dominant factor, which can render a person to doubt and even question their frame of mind. No one reading Joseph's story would be critical if he displayed a lack of faith in God, given his traumatic experiences. Yet, the opportunity to interpret Pharaoh's vision was an exercise of faith, not in himself but in God to reveal the answers to the vision. God's promise was fulfilled perhaps just at the point of Joseph accepting the unknown. God remained faithful even if Joseph's faith may have waned, because God's faithfulness is not contingent on one's faithfulness to him.

Joseph's faith in God and faithfulness to him took him from the prison to the palace; serving to be served; lack of power to great power. When God reveals his vision for your life it would be humanly impossible to achieve it. But faithfulness to God despite inevitable difficulties remains key for him to direct us in the most fulfilling paths for our lives. Are you willing to trust your faithfulness to God? Let this week's notes be reminiscent of how faithfulness in God can be varying, challenging and miraculous.

† Thank you, Father, for all the beautiful surprises you are planning for my life. Help me to see your faithfulness at work in my life. Amen

Monday 31 July

Peter and John, faithful in danger

Read Acts 4:13–20

Whether it is right in God's sight to listen to you rather than to God you must judge; for we cannot keep from speaking about what we have seen and heard.

(verses 19b–20)

Peter and John's faith could be summarised as having a bold trust in God, with an awareness and certainty in God's word and promises. Such confidence and knowledge equated to risking their lives, by remaining faithful even in the presence of danger. Empowered by the Holy Spirit, their words conveyed a boldness that's beyond physical courage and more probably linked to being integral witnesses. For that reason, it was impossible to separate their experiences from their words, which became an opportunity to display fearlessness, despite what was expected of them in their given context.

Some people who feel that their opinions are suppressed because they are not agreeable to public sentiments may admire Peter and John's defiance. Anti-racism protestors, climate change activists and other campaigners for worthy causes may be inclined to align themselves to the standpoint of the apostles. They would be prepared to risk their lives for what they considered to be humanly and morally unjust. Overt demonstration would not appeal to all; however, what is crucial is that the outcome influences action and inspires change.

Faithfulness in danger, though a bold act, was necessary to maintain duty to God instead of civic obligation. The choice was quite clear, bearing similarities to the plot against Daniel whose life was placed at risked in the lion's den. A choice between life and death; a choice of being faithful to God or to human authority.

† Lord, I pray that my faith in you will be expressed in my life through boldness and truth. Give me courage to risk something of myself for you. Amen

For further thought

Have you ever denied your faith in Christ for approval from others? Will you risk your life for the gospel?

Tuesday 1 August

Phoebe, a generous benefactor

Read Romans 16:1–2

I commend to you our sister Phoebe … so that you may welcome her in the Lord as is fitting for the saints, and help her in whatever she may require … for she has been a benefactor of many and of myself as well.

(verses 1–2)

If these words were a recommendation for a job application, it's likely that more would be expected to be said of the candidate for a successful outcome. Paul's introduction and recommendation of Phoebe to the churches in Rome, though simple in its formality, denoted a carefully worded statement that addressed more than her ministerial responsibility as a deacon. Paul spoke of her generosity to himself and others, which may suggest that she was a wealthy woman who gave financial and social support to her former church in Corinth.

Was Phoebe commended because she was a generous benefactor? Is this an acceptable measure for validating someone for a role in the church or elsewhere? Is this symptomatic of the political and elitist domain, be it for support or gaining a peerage? Ironically, prominence and material wealth, often used as significant attributes for welcoming others into the 'inner circle', also find their way into the church, resulting in many people being overlooked for certain roles.

Paul's recommendation of Phoebe was based more on the faithful manner in which she served than on her financial sustenance. She gave generously of her time and leadership skills. She was generous in her response to the social needs around her, exercising her faith and love in actions. She was a generous benefactor who did not try to over-compensate because of her gender, or focus on her own needs, wants and comfort. Phoebe's character has a lot to teach us today, in the way we seek to minister in the church and society. Could you be recommended for any Christian virtues?

† Gracious God, thank you for the opportunities to give generously of my time and gifts so others may be enriched. Amen

For further thought

Actions speak louder than words! Are you able to implement that principle in your life?

Wednesday 2 August

Silas, a faithful companion

Read Acts 16:19–31

About midnight Paul and Silas were praying and singing hymns to God, and the prisoners were listening to them.

(verse 25)

Paul and Silas' extensive missional journey around Europe, though challenging, did not dissuade them from responding to Paul's call in a vision to go to Macedonia, a commitment that ultimately landed them in prison, victims of the Roman judicial system. Was this what Silas signed up for when he embarked on this journey with Paul? Possibly not. However, Silas' attitude demonstrated that he was totally committed and in solidarity with Paul, despite the risk.

Persecuted Christians may be able to identify with some aspects of the inhumane treatment the disciples suffered for the gospel. Missionaries imprisoned for their faith can probably testify and feel akin to the trailblazers. What could have been a terrifying situation for many, turned out to be a worshipping moment for the two friends. Their ability to remain faithful to God, instead of drowning in self-pity or giving in to fear and incrimination, triggered an unprecedented earthquake, followed by the miraculous unfastening of the chains that held them shackled. Silas may not have foreseen that he would face this level of persecution, but the ensuing chapter 17 showed that he continued, focused and resilient, as Paul's faithful companion.

It may seem easy to give up when obstacles appear that will derail your purpose, take you off course and disable your goals. Accepting 'your portion' may even be a tempting option. Yet, the fact that God's presence showed up for Paul and Silas in a seemingly helpless situation should remind us that God can do what is humanly impossible, as faith is exercised in genuine fellowship with him.

† Loving Father, thank you for the challenges in my life that will make me grow stronger in faith and draw closer to you. Amen

For further thought

Reflect on Psalm 139:7–12.

Thursday 3 August

Martha, an unshakeable faith

Read John 11:1–7, 17–27

Martha said to Jesus, 'Lord, if you had been here, my brother would not have died. But even now I know that God will give you whatever you ask of him.'

(verses 21–22)

No one is exempted or immune from death. Shocking, painful and sometimes hard to come to terms with. The sense of loss can be so profound that it may manifest itself in feelings of anger, guilt and blame. Yet, grief is present and real. It was real for Lazarus' sisters and heard in Martha's cry of anguish in confronting Jesus. What took you so long to come? Why did you not come sooner to heal my brother? Although her words are laced with anger and criticism, like many in the grieving process her mood changed from accusation to a faith so unshakeable that it belied her earlier statement. It appeared that she needed to voice her hurt, before acknowledging a depth of faith that moved her beyond grief to a place of hope or wishful expectation.

I have conducted many funerals where the family members showed great depth of sorrow in the church, yet an unexpected calmness and even elements of joy at the cemetery or crematorium. What was the reason for the change in their disposition? Is it finally accepting the loss? Is it realising that it is finished? Maybe it is recognition that if a miracle were to happen it was too late. Martha was similar in her attitude and changed from sadness to a resigned hope that her brother will rise on the day of resurrection. And yet, I feel that voicing her faith that God would do whatever Jesus asked of him was in fact an appeal for a miracle that would fortify her faith even more.

† Lord God, help me to trust in your promises now and in the future. Open my eyes to your comforting presence. Amen

For further thought

Who do you turn to in times of bereavement? Is Jesus your place of refuge and strength?

Friday 4 August

Epaphras, a faithful prayer warrior

Read Colossians 4:12–13

Epaphras, who is one of you, a servant of Christ Jesus, greets you. He is always wrestling in his prayers on your behalf, so that you may stand mature and fully assured in everything that God wills.

(verses 12–13)

Wrestling in prayers! The imagery that comes to mind is that of amateur or professional wrestlers fighting in a ring, often in agony, trying to overcome an opponent. Wrestling in prayer does evoke aspects of the sport, with a sense of being alert, agonising and determined to be victorious. When Paul said that Epaphras was 'always wrestling in his prayers' for the church in Colossae, it showed a man faithfully interceding, filled with agonising moments, yet unwilling to accept defeat. He was a faithful prayer warrior.

What was the purpose behind Epaphras' unrelenting prayers to God? He wanted the church to excel in their relationship with God, by standing firm in the will of God. However, standing firm in God's will does not come easy, as revealed in Jesus' agonising prayer in the Gethsemane experience. For when the ultimate prayer struggle centres in the will of God, then it can become a battle and only a warrior-like approach will prevail.

Is the idea of a prayer warrior an archaic discipline in our society? I have experienced prayer meetings that felt like battle cries to God, persistent, vigorous, reviving, yet tiring. The process of wrestling in prayer is patiently unrelenting and demanding all or nothing. Do you give up too easily in your prayer life? God is still looking for people who will adopt a mindset of a warrior, sacrificial of time and commitment. He is seeking those who are willing to bring the burdens of others before him in agony. He is still looking for those like Epaphras.

† Lord, help me to be steadfast in my prayer life, focused even in the midst of struggle and agony. Amen

For further thought

Are there any situations that require you to develop an Epaphras-like approach?

Saturday 5 August

Mary, a faithful follower

Read John 20:11–18

Jesus said to her, 'Woman, why are you weeping? For whom are you looking?' Supposing him to be the gardener, she said to him, 'Sir, if you have carried him away, tell me where you have laid him, and I will take him away.'

(verse 15)

Today's reading climaxes this week's theme of faithfulness: people of faith, with Mary's commitment to remain a faithful follower of Jesus in his death, as she was in his earthly life. So dedicated, she sought him out by going to his tomb. Was this a step too far in faithful discipleship? Luke and Mark's account of the resurrection points out the significance of the women visiting the tomb (they took spices); John and Matthew record them only visiting. Irrespective of the differing details, visiting the tomb/cemetery was a traditional practice then as now. Cultural practices vary, seemingly like a futile exercise for some people, but for others a measure of comfort and maybe unknowingly an ongoing act of administering care to their dearly departed. Therefore, visiting the grave of a loved one, replacing the flowers weekly and cleaning the tombstone, are interpreted as signs of love and dedication.

Mary's anguished response when questioned by the supposed gardener verified her desire to remain a faithful follower even in death. She simply wanted to find Jesus' body, hold on to his body and grieve over his body. Her faithfulness was contributory in her recognition and encountering of Jesus in his miraculous resurrection. Unexpectedly, Mary's faith, like that of Martha's in Thursday's readings, increased significantly; where it may have been shattered or 'dead', perhaps, it was renewed and given new life. However, being a faithful follower may not be miracle-revealing, as in Mary's scenario, but miracles can happen. Will you be able to recognise them?

† Lord Jesus, strengthen me as I faithfully follow you. Give me a discerning heart and mind to recognise your miraculous power. Amen

For further thought

Is your discipleship exemplary or misleading?

Biblical library (4)

Prophecy

Notes by **David Painting**

You can read David's biography on p. 120. David has used the NRSVA and NLT for these notes.

Sunday 6 August

The God who will

Read Genesis 3:1–15

I will put enmity between you and the woman, and between your offspring and hers; he will strike your head, and you will strike his heel.

(verse 15, NRSVA)

As we look this week at prophetic literature in the Bible, we begin in the beginning. The context for the prophecy in verse 15 is the tricking of Eve into eating the forbidden fruit. For the serpent, and for Adam and Eve, there are immediate consequences to their actions, but those consequences will spill out geographically across the earth and ripple on across history. God succinctly explains that those consequences will include ecological disaster, death in all its forms, enmity between men and women, between humankind and God and between humanity and the cosmos. It is an unremittingly stark future.

Yet, into that desperate picture, God shines this glimmer of light. Awful though the consequences for humankind and for himself will be, they are not the full story, nor its end. God promises to sovereignly weave the free choices and their consequences into this outcome – that a descendant of Eve will one day contend with the serpent and, even though it will cause harm, that descendant will prevail and the serpent will be defeated.

It isn't a detailed prophecy that they could look at and count off the days to its fulfilment. Its aim, as with so much prophecy, is not to make minute predictions but to point to the character of God and the encouragement knowing him brings.

† O Lord, thank you that even when the future is uncertain, even when it looks bleak, the knowledge of your goodness and mercy sustains and encourages.

Monday 7 August

The God who won't

Read Jonah 3:1–10

Jonah began to go into the city, going a day's walk. And he cried out, 'Forty days more, and Nineveh shall be overthrown!'

(verse 4, NRSVA)

Divided into the kingdoms of Judah and Israel, Jonah 'works' as a prophet in Samaria, the capital of Israel (2 Kings 14). We know the story – God calls him to go and exercise his prophetic gift in Nineveh – the capital of the hated Assyrian empire. Hated because of what they had done to the nations they had conquered, including Israel. They were brutal, razing cities with fire, deporting families and abusing the women. Having witnessed this and certainly knowing of it in detail, Jonah wanted justice for his friends, his family and perhaps himself. So, the message God gives him should thrill his heart: 'Forty days more and Nineveh shall be overthrown' – finally, they will get what they deserve. But Jonah understands that some prophecy is not a statement of a fixed future, but a warning of what will happen based on the character of God unless the choices of the people change. Prophecy isn't always about an inevitable future, but one which will happen unless … and Jonah knows this. The reason Jonah had refused to go to Nineveh was not out of a fear that he would die, but out of a fear that the people wouldn't.

And so it transpired: Jonah finally goes and preaches, the people repent and God does not do what he had said he would do. Jonah is distraught because in his heart, unlike in God's, mercy does not outweigh judgement. Yet, while God points this out to Jonah, he is not harsh with him. Jonah exhibits many of the symptoms found in trauma survivors, and God graciously works for his healing even while Jonah fulfils his calling.

† O Lord, thank you that your mercy has flowed to me. Help me to be merciful to those who have offended me.

For further thought

There are many in the Bible who seem to have mental health issues. Observe how God deals with them. What can we learn as church?

Tuesday 8 August

God has

Read Isaiah 9:2–7

For all the boots of the tramping warriors and all the garments rolled in blood shall be burned as fuel for the fire. For a child has been born for us, a son given to us; authority rests upon his shoulders; and he is named Wonderful Counsellor, Mighty God, Everlasting Father, Prince of Peace.

(verses 5–6, NRSVA)

So far this week, we've seen a prophecy that God has unilaterally declared will happen and one where the outcome was contingent on people's response. Today we see one that has multiple fulfilments. First, it is seen as a prophecy by Isaiah to King Ahaz of Judah that a son would be born to him who would restore Godly worship and the fortunes of the nation and thus become the greatest of the kings of Judah (as described in 2 Kings 18 about Hezekiah). This served as a warning to Ahaz to change his ways and also as an encouragement to the people that God was still active on their behalf. And when it came to pass, the people would have pointed to the prophecy and seen in Hezekiah its fulfilment and given thanks to God.

Of course, we see an even greater fulfilment in exactly these same words, pointing not to Hezekiah, the greatest king of Judah, but to the King of Kings – the one who would in the end fulfil our first prophecy this week as he indeed strikes the head of the serpent.

It should be no surprise to us that God is creative enough to use one prophecy for multiple purposes; the fact that it has already been fulfilled should not preclude us seeing the bigger picture that it also points to. Whenever we read or hear something presented as prophetic, we should first test whether it resonates with what we know of Jesus and then what type of prophecy it is – unilateral, contingent or multiple. Asking the Holy Spirit to lead us into all truth is a great first step!

† O Lord, we are so grateful for the prophetic signposts you have given in scripture; help us always to be discerning as we give or receive prophecy.

For further thought

Are there any other prophecies in the Bible that might have dual fulfilments?

Wednesday 9 August

Oh, that was a prophecy!

Read Psalm 22:1–18

My God, my God, why have you forsaken me? Why are you so far from helping me, from the words of my groaning? O my God, I cry by day, but you do not answer; and by night, but find no rest.

(verses 1–2, NRSVA)

I preached at a church I'd never been to before and rehearsed the sermon with my daughter on the journey there. She liked the made-up story of a couple whom God called into missions who kept putting it off for various reasons, but suggested I give names to the characters to make it more dramatic. So, when I got to that point in the sermon, I did, and it seemed to go very well. I was feeling pleased with myself when the vicar came over to speak to us: 'You may have noticed it went quiet during the illustration you used. Let me introduce the couple who are giving you lunch …' You've guessed how this ends – our hosts were the couple I'd 'made up' – the same names, the same story about missions. It made for an awkward lunch, though there was a happy ending – but it made me realise that we sometimes speak words of knowledge or the prophetic without realising it.

It's the same with this psalm. David was lamenting to God about what he was going through while trying to hold on to the promises God had made. He feels he is on his own, he feels encircled by those who had betrayed him, he feels poured out, dried up, disjointed, abandoned by God. And when it is over, he writes it down and sets it to music so that others can use it and know they are not alone, that others have experienced it and lived.

It never dawns on him that there will come one who will use it, who is God himself.

† Thank you, Lord, that you can use our experiences, our words, to bless others. Even when we do not know it. Thank you that we can even bless you.

For further thought

What experiences from your life might God use as a prophetic witness and encouragement to others?

Thursday 10 August
Handling prophecy

Read Joel 2:28–32

Then afterwards I will pour out my spirit on all flesh; your sons and your daughters shall prophesy, your old men shall dream dreams, and your young men shall see visions. Even on the male and female slaves, in those days, I will pour out my spirit.

(verses 28–29, NRSVA)

In Acts 2, Peter uses this passage to explain to the crowds that what they are witnessing is a fulfilment of prophecy. As such, we have a worked example of how we can safely use prophecy too.

What I notice when I lay out the passage in Joel next to the one spoken by Peter is that they are not quite the same. The order is slightly different (old men and young men are transposed), wording is changed (great and terrible becomes great and glorious) and Peter adds a statement (slaves will prophesy – Acts 2:18). What Peter appears to do is to take the words of Joel and, while he does his best to quote him accurately, he understands that the message is in the spirit behind the words, not in the precision of the words. He understands that Joel isn't trying to make distinctions between old and young, male and female, slave or free – he agrees with Paul that the whole point is that in Christ there are now no such distinctions. He knows that Joel isn't seeking to set out rules about who can receive what and in what manner, but rather is poetically seeking to put words to an indescribably wonderful truth, that in this new kingdom God can speak through everyone.

In 1 Corinthians 14:32, Paul explains this – that the spirits of the prophet are under the control of the prophet. Of course, the Spirit of God is inspiring, but it is inspiration not dictation; the words the prophet speaks or writes are under their control, using their vocabulary through the lens of their experience and personality! This is clear, the Holy Spirit-inspired scripture written by Peter is distinctive, different from that written by Paul or Mark or Luke.

† O Lord, help us to understand what is the heart behind the words, rather than seek to dissect them or the speaker.

For further thought

How do we interpret prophecy, whether from scripture or modern individuals? How do we discern what the Spirit is seeking to communicate through what is being presented?

Friday 11 August

Not all prophecy is directive

Read Acts 21:4, 30–36

We went ashore, found the local believers, and stayed with them a week. These believers prophesied through the Holy Spirit that Paul should not go on to Jerusalem.

(verse 4, NLT)

I sometimes hear prophecy being spoken about as if it were simply a prediction of the future. But what would be the point of that? If what was going to happen was inevitable and bad, being told about it with no possibility of changing it would seem unkind. On the other hand, if it was going to be something good that was guaranteed, well, I could just put my feet up and wait for it to happen.

We saw from our reading in Jonah that prophecy is often given in order to warn people of what will happen unless they act differently. It is less a statement about an immutable future and more about the character of God: 'I am just and look out for the oppressed – judgement will come on those who oppress the vulnerable.'

The other misconception is that prophecy is always a directive from God. Do this, or do that, 'This is the way, walk ye in it!' In today's passage, Paul receives prophecy from local believers, independently confirmed by a reputable prophet from out of town – Agabus. Both messages agree, if Paul goes to Jerusalem, bad things will happen to him. The result? Paul goes anyway and bad things happen to him! The prophecies were true, but Paul understood what the bringers did not – that sometimes the prophetic is for information, not direction. Knowing what would happen was not intended to stop Paul from going, but to prepare him for what would happen when he went. 'Why all this weeping? … I am ready not only to be jailed at Jerusalem but even to die' (verse 13).

† O Lord, help us to be strengthened by prophecy to face what you call us to do.

For further thought

Are there other examples of prophecy being intended to prepare rather than direct?

Saturday 12 August

The end

Read Mark 13:2–13

Many will come in my name and say, 'I am he!' and they will lead many astray.

(verse 6, NRSVA)

I wonder how much time, energy and money has been spent on books, movies and TV shows about the 'end-times'? Of course, the aim of prophecies about the end are there to encourage us to be prepared – just as Paul was prepared for what he was about to face in our last reading.

But because of that, they have to work equally well in every generation. If 'end-times' prophecies only became credible in the moments before the actual end, all the generations preceding that could happily ignore them! For that reason, the prophecies are deliberately designed to fit every generation. In every decade since Jesus spoke there have been 'wars and rumours of wars', there have been famines, floods, droughts and earthquakes. And with them, the possibility that tomorrow could be the day; we must therefore live today prepared for that real possibility.

Spending time analysing the precise words to fit against specific events, trying to determine exactly where we are on the roadmap to the end, trying to identify this politician or that celebrity with characters from the apocalypse may be entertaining, but it is to miss the point. The message is simple and clear. Be ready, live now as if tomorrow is the end. Keep clear accounts, be fully present, love one another.

So, the warning in today's verse is apposite: whatever the prophecy, be discerning. What is the Spirit saying to the church, to the world, to you? Don't be distracted or dismayed, be encouraged, be ready.

† O Lord, help me to live my life today in the light of eternity, encouraged by your presence and promise.

For further thought

How can we live prepared? What prophetic words does God want to give to you or give through you?

Peaceful sleep

Notes by **Ian Fosten**

Ian has ministered within the United Reformed Church in Norfolk, Suffolk and on Holy Island (Lindisfarne). He is director of a community theatre in Lowestoft where he lives with his wife and two youngest children. He runs open-mic poetry readings and has a particular interest in landscape and spirituality. Ian has used the NIVUK for these notes.

Sunday 13 August
Adam's deep sleep

Read Genesis 2:21–25

So the Lord God caused the man to fall into a deep sleep … he took one of the man's ribs and … made a woman from the rib… That is why a man leaves his father and mother and is united to his wife, and they become one flesh.

(verses 21, 22, 24)

Given that it is how we spend one-third of our lives, sleep is something to which we give little thought – until, that is, it is withheld for some reason and then it swiftly becomes a preoccupation. This week we will consider aspects of sleep as it features in a wide selection of Bible readings.

Beginning at the beginning with Genesis, we have the story of woman being created out of Adam as he was anaesthetised by sleep. Throughout history some people (men, usually) have cited this story as evidence for male superiority – created first, and all that. A fine counterpoint to this suspect view is the old joke which runs along the lines of: having created man, God reviewed his handiwork and spotted flaws and deficiencies, so God had another go and this time made a far better job of it!

Actually, both opinions miss the point of the story – the Creator's intention for men and women is not to live in competition but mutuality. Their intrinsic oneness sets out God's intention for all relationships, whereby any differences of gender, race or ability are never to determine status or value. Humanity's marvellous equality is the only value that matters to God.

† God of unity and love, challenge my inclination to rank people by importance. Instead, let me delight in the marvellous equality you have given to all people. Amen

Monday 14 August

Awake in safety

Read Psalm 3:1–8

But you, Lord, are a shield around me, my glory, the One who lifts my head high … I lie down and sleep; I wake again, because the Lord sustains me.

(verses 3, 5)

For most of us, most of the time, climbing into bed and cosying down is a time for delightful, restful withdrawal from the activities of the day. At other times, lying down to rest serves only to make us aware of our vulnerability – for refugees on the move or rough sleepers in shop doorways, sleep means a loss of vigilance and openness to robbery and attack. Even for those in bed within the physical security of their home, attempts to sleep can be gate-crashed by past regrets and mistakes, and populated by exaggerated versions of people who make some claim upon us. For many, the night hours can be a fearful and exhausting place.

What help can the psalmist offer at such times? Honesty, for a start, about life's circumstances – the writer makes no bones about the trials faced daily at the hands of folk around them. But the writer also speaks of a tried and tested experience of God's presence by both day and by night.

Such faith is not necessarily a cure for insomnia, but what it does is provide the security of companionship even when sleep is elusive or dreams are disturbing. I certainly find that on those occasions when my night-time brain is hyperactive and I come down to a cold kitchen to make a cup of tea, as I sip my drink and let troublesome thoughts subside, I know that I am not alone – far from it. The Lord who steers me through my daytime muddles often seems closer still in the unwelcome, wakeful hours of the night.

† Constant God, thank you for your companionship at all times – especially in those night-time hours when sleep is disturbed by bleak and tiresome thoughts. Amen

For further thought

Who or what populates your dreams? Why not spend a few minutes in prayer before going to bed, asking God to settle your thoughts and guard your needs until the morning.

Tuesday 15 August

Sound sleep

Read Proverbs 3:21–26

My son, do not let wisdom and understanding out of your sight … When you lie down, you will not be afraid; when you lie down, your sleep will be sweet.

(verses 21a, 24)

You may be familiar with the expression, `You are what you eat.' To anyone who, like me, could benefit from losing a few kilos, it is a chilling indictment. Today's reading from Proverbs has a similar though broader intention. We might summarise it as, 'We sleep how we live' or, less snappily, 'The quality of our sleep is directly related to whatever has filled our minds (and bodies) during the day.'

The qualities of wisdom and understanding to which Proverbs points us can seem to be in short supply today. The media, both formal and social, is awash with information (some reliable, plenty not), opinions, criticism and blame. It seems to thrive on conflict and tragedy and has little space for stories which feature kindness and generosity. Many of us who like to 'just catch up on the news' before bedtime are probably doing to our subconscious what a supper of rich and spicy food might do to our stomach.

I don't believe that Proverbs directs us to ignore the sadness and need of our broken world but what it does do is remind us that our world also has much that is beautiful, honest, hopeful and bears witness to God's intention in Creation. Wisdom is shown when we choose this more balanced and complete understanding of how our world is. Wisdom is exercised when we make space for the stories of violence, failure and aching need in our daytime prayers, but allow stories of goodness and beauty to fill the day's final waking moments.

† Today, dear God, I will acknowledge the news stories which have moved, alarmed and disturbed me – and I pray for those caught up in them. Tonight, dear God, I will acknowledge news stories, memories, encounters which have reminded me of goodness, graciousness, delight and love. Amen

For further thought

Notice, critically, the (im)balance of positive and negative stories in the reported news.

Wednesday 16 August

Little more sleep, slumber

Read Proverbs 24:30–34

I went past the field of a sluggard, past the vineyard of someone who has no sense … A little sleep, a little slumber, a little folding of the hands to rest – and poverty will come on you like a thief and scarcity like an armed man.

(verses 30, 33–34)

For a few months after leaving school, I worked nights as the operator of a bread roll machine in a commercial bakery. A green light came on and the machine delivered eighty rolls into a plastic tray. Then a red light came on to indicate a brief pause to allow the operator to stack the loaded tray on to a trolley and replace it with an empty one. Then the light turned green again and the next eighty rolls were delivered. All was fine until the night after a day when I skipped sleep and went to a reunion instead. Standing at the machine that night my eyes grew heavier and heavier until, although I was dimly aware of changing lights, no trays were stacked. The angry shouts of supervisors woke me to witness a dreadful scene of bread rolls cascading over the side of the machine and on to the floor.

Thus, it is with some humility that I consider the slumbering fool and his neglected vineyard!

If making the most of the opportunities God gives us in work, relationships and using our gifts and talents is important, then rest and sleep have a vital role to play. We must be alert, 'on task' and never be found asleep on the job if we are to give of our best. But we can only do that if we have previously taken sensible rest whenever that needs to be.

† Help me, dear God, to regard sleep not as a waste of precious time or guilty pleasure, but as a delightful gift to be received and enjoyed gratefully. Amen

For further thought

When we are busy or distracted, sleep can be regarded as a dispensable element in our life. Do you value sleep as much as you ought?

Thursday 17 August

Asleep in the boat

Read Mark 4:35–41

A furious squall came up, and the waves broke over the boat, so that it was nearly swamped. Jesus was in the stern, sleeping on a cushion. The disciples woke him and said to him, 'Teacher, don't you care if we drown?'

(verses 37–38)

The story of Jesus calming a storm and rescuing a wave-tossed boat and her terrified crew can be read as evidence of two miracles taking place. Jesus can override even the most severe weather in order to bring calm and safety – he can also sleep through a tempest which even experienced fishermen could not handle.

While I have no doubt that the God we know in Jesus performed many miracles, reading this passage afresh I am struck by something less exceptional and more readily transferable into our own experience. I wonder if Jesus was able to sleep through the tumult not because he was superhuman but because he was exhausted. Anyone who has cared enough and given their all, in order to connect with the needs of other people, has probably also known times when they were utterly depleted as a consequence. Think about how often we read of Jesus not only teaching but also responding to unplanned interactions with sick and desperate people. The gospel stories speak of Jesus feeling 'power going out of him'; they also tell of occasions when Jesus takes himself off alone, despite the crowds clamouring for healing, because he needs to be restored before he can have anything more to give.

For Jesus, and for you and me too, proper restorative sleep is not an interruption of the kingdom's work but, along with prayer and knowing the scriptures, is one of its foundations.

† Loving Father, tonight and every night may I be blessed with deep and refreshing sleep that each morning I may wake refreshed and ready to serve you. Amen

For further thought

Our society prizes endurance and stamina. Maybe we should give equal approval to those who recognise that they are spent out and need to rest.

Friday 18 August

Not dead but asleep

Read Mark 5:35–43

When they came to the home of the synagogue leader, Jesus saw a commotion, with people crying and wailing loudly. He went in and said to them, 'Why all this commotion and wailing? The child is not dead but asleep.' But they laughed at him.

(verses 38–40a)

The raising of Jairus' daughter is a very beautiful story, I love it, but on reading it I cannot but link it to one of the most challenging and hard-to-resolve incidents in my ministry. The husband of a church member asked me to accompany him to view the body of his nephew, not yet ten years of age, in a funeral director's chapel of rest. I had met the boy when still alive and knew that he had an incurable condition, and now his uncle and I looked into the child-sized coffin and tearfully said our goodbyes. The brutal fact was that this little boy was not asleep – in this life, at any rate, he would never again wake up and return to the life of his family.

However, the apparent hopelessness of this recollection begins to weaken when, in the story of Jairus' daughter, Jesus confronts the professional wailers and mourners. Their trade was to declare an end to life and hope – Jesus, by contrast, shows himself to be the source of life and unimagined possibilities.

Given that Jesus is never facile or trite but deals with the deepest realities of life, I hear in this story an invitation to step back a pace or two from the open coffin of a child, and also from the stories of unbearable sadness brought to us daily by news on the TV and elsewhere, and hear him say, 'This is not the last word, for within the Father's love there is a better word spoken – hope and healing and peace for all eternity.'

† Dear Lord, sometimes I have questions that tear my mind apart. Give me peace in knowing that all things, ultimately, are held within the loving purposes of God. Amen

For further thought

When hard, honest questions arise, it is better to allow them to stand unresolved than to tidy them up with unsatisfactory answers.

Saturday 19 August

We shall not all sleep

Read 1 Corinthians 15:51–58

Listen, I tell you a mystery: we will not all sleep, but we will all be changed – in a flash, in the twinkling of an eye, at the last trumpet. For the trumpet will sound, the dead will be raised imperishable, and we will be changed.

(verses 51–52)

I once overheard a conversation between an enthusiastic Christian man and an elderly church member. 'My dear,' he said, 'when you get to heaven you will be sixteen and a beautiful young woman once again!' The woman thought for a moment or two and then said, 'But I won't have met my husband or had my children ...'

Likewise, when St Paul strays into territory which, from our human perspective, is unknowable, he too runs the risk of unhelpful speculation. Why trumpets? Why instantaneous transformation? In truth no one really knows, and, in any case, maybe that kind of speculative detail is unnecessary and even unhelpful. Maybe the mystery of eternity within the love of God is best left unopened because it doesn't need our futile attempts to describe the unknowable. Maybe it is enough to have known the closeness of God through all the vagaries of this life and to find in that sufficient faith that such closeness will not be interrupted by the apparent finality of death?

In Luke's story of the resurrection two messengers pose the question, 'Why seek the living among the dead?' They remind us that Jesus' concern was to open up life in all its fullness to people who were, to all intents and purposes, socially, racially, spiritually and sometimes physically 'dead'.

So, let's delight in the promise of eternity with God, but then let's get on with enabling the people we meet today to live as fully as they can.

† Help me today, dear God, to be a life-opener, a life-fulfiller and a life-affirmer with everyone I meet. Amen

For further thought

Living faithfully within a 'margin of mystery' sometimes may be more useful than trying to describe in detail what, in this life, is unknowable.

Readings in 2 Corinthians

1 The God of all comfort and mercy

Notes by **Joshua Taylor**

Joshua is an Anglican priest in New Zealand, currently working on his PhD in practical theology. He's married to Jo, with three daughters (Phoebe, Esther and Eve), and together they've been exploring what it means to be a family following the way of Jesus. In his spare time, he loves to spend his days off being mocked by fish while holding a fishing rod or playing in his pottery studio. Joshua has used the NRSV for these notes.

Sunday 20 August

Feeling overwhelmed?

Read 2 Corinthians 1:1–14

Blessed be the God and Father of our Lord Jesus Christ, the Father of mercies and the God of all consolation, who consoles us in all our affliction, so that we may be able to console those who are in any affliction with the consolation with which we ourselves are consoled by God.

(verses 3–4)

The Second Letter to the Corinthians is a powerful letter for this present moment. In a world full of suffering and trouble it's easy to feel overwhelmed. In the face of suffering, this letter paints a picture of what resilient Christian faith looks like. The early Christian community in the Roman world experienced much persecution for being followers of Jesus. Paul reminds them that they are sharing in the sufferings of Christ, and that they also share in the comfort of Christ.

Paul calls the community to patiently endure their suffering for the sake of the gospel. He doesn't just preach this; Paul lives this out. We see a catalogue of his own suffering and weakness on display in this letter. Paul has been hassled for his suffering, as if it invalidates his faith. However, Paul argues just the opposite. Paul points out that weakness and suffering for Christ doesn't mean Christians are on the wrong track. In fact, it is a mark of their Jesus-shaped lives. What we find as we explore this letter is that Paul keeps coming back to the cross of Christ. This is the place where God's merciful character is revealed to a world in desperate need. God's mercy is on display through the cross of Christ. God comforts us in our afflictions by entering them and sharing them with us.

† God of all comfort, when we feel overwhelmed by troubles, lift our eyes to the cross to see your mercy in sharing our sufferings through Jesus Christ our Lord. Amen

Monday 21 August

Genuine Christian ministry

Read 2 Corinthians 1:15–2:11

I wanted to visit you on my way to Macedonia, and to come back to you from Macedonia and have you send me on to Judea. Was I vacillating when I wanted to do this? Do I make my plans according to ordinary human standards, ready to say 'Yes, yes' and 'No, no' at the same time?

(verses 16–17)

Have you got one of those friends who often cancels or pulls out from a social occasion at the last moment? Or one who hits the 'maybe' buttons on Facebook events? There's always that flaky friend who keeps their social options open until the very last minute in case something comes up that is better. In today's reading Paul is accused of being that flaky friend. In fact, Paul is defending himself from charges of being a flaky pastor. The Corinthians are upset with him for planning a visit to them and then changing his plans.

This led some of the Corinthians to conclude that Paul was dishonest, and that he had mixed motives in his ministry. Paul defends himself by laying out an argument for his ministry. We see him sketch several elements of what genuine Christian ministry looks like, five of which I want to highlight here:

1. Genuine Christian ministry doesn't boast in self but in God. (1:12–14)
2. Genuine Christian ministry is not about the strengths and talent of the minister but God working in and through us. (1:12–14)
3. Genuine Christian ministry is theocentric. It focuses on what God is doing. (1:19–20)
4. Genuine Christian ministry is Christocentric, it focuses on Jesus. (1:19–20)
5. Genuine Christian ministry is led and empowered by the Holy Spirit. (1:21–22)

When we consider our own ministries and the ministries of others around us, these five points are worth considering. Are we measuring what counts?

† Lord, help me to serve you genuinely and honestly for the sake of your glory and not my own. Amen

For further thought

Paul is willing to stand his ground, even when he is accused of getting it wrong because he knows who he serves and why. Could we say the same?

Tuesday 22 August

Do you smell like Jesus?

Read 2 Corinthians 2:12–3:18

But thanks be to God, who in Christ always leads us in triumphal procession, and through us spreads in every place the fragrance that comes from knowing him.

(verse 2:14)

One of my favourite aromas is the smell of freshly brewed coffee. I associate it with the joy of a new day or the ritual of meeting a friend to connect and catch up at a local cafe. The sense of smell is closely linked with memory, and certain smells can evoke moments in our lives – the smell of birthday candles blown out, the briny sea air, or freshly cut grass. Paul here speaks of the fragrance or aroma of Christ. It's an interesting idea that he develops to talk about the gospel and our response to it.

The image is used within the context of a 'triumphal procession', which refers to the victory parades that the Romans celebrated after winning battles. Using similar imagery in 1 Corinthians 4, Paul speaks about being at the end of the procession as a spectacle, like the prisoners who were brought in at the very end of the procession in humiliation and defeat. This is a powerful image of the sufferings Paul has faced for Christ.

Often at these victory parades, incense would be spread abundantly in celebration. I wonder if this is why Paul uses this particular language of aroma? To those who are perishing, who can't understand or see it, this suffering looks foolish. It is a bad smell. However, others see the suffering for the gospel in a different light. In the light of Christ, it is a beautiful aroma, pointing to the love of God expressed in Jesus' suffering and death for the sake of the world.

† Lord, thank you for your love expressed on the cross as you suffered and died for me. When I encounter suffering for you, help me to bear it in such a way that others are drawn to your sacrificial love. Amen

For further thought

Do you smell like Jesus? Funny question, I know! However, it's worth thinking about. Does our life attract others to Christ or repel them? Good smell or bad?

Wednesday 23 August
Clay jars

Read 2 Corinthians 4:1–15

But we have this treasure in clay jars, so that it may be made clear that this extraordinary power belongs to God and does not come from us.

(verse 7)

Paul begins this section with a metaphor. He says: 'We have this treasure in jars of clay.' The treasure is the gospel – the message of Jesus saving and redeeming this broken world through his life, death and resurrection. The clay jars are the carriers of the gospel.

The image of clay jars doesn't refer to grand Grecian art pieces or fine pieces of pottery. Rather, here Paul is talking about a cheap and humble pot. Paul might even be referring to night-time oil lamps that were manufactured and sold in Corinth. These were thin and delicate so light would shine through them but because of this were also very easy to break.

Paul is highlighting the clay jar as cheap, humble and simple. This metaphor isn't to denigrate the messengers of the gospel. It isn't saying they don't count for anything. Rather it is to accentuate the treasure of the gospel.

A celebrity preacher draws attention to the cheap pot, which is not the point. The point is the treasure, which is the good news of Jesus. This is the point Paul makes. The clay jar is a good image for Paul's ministry, as the jar is a humble instrument which carries the true treasure. This is food for thought for us in a world in which Christian celebrities are not only possible but even prolific, and in which we, like the Corinthians, might be tempted to gaze at the jar itself rather than the treasure.

† Heavenly Father, thank you that you use ordinary people like me to share the glorious news of Jesus. Amen

For further thought

Can you think of someone who exemplifies this 'clay jar' way of ministry? What characteristics exemplify it?

Thursday 24 August

Life after death

Read 2 Corinthians 4:16–5:13

For while we are still in this tent, we groan under our burden, because we wish not to be unclothed but to be further clothed, so that what is mortal may be swallowed up by life.

(verse 4)

What happens when we die? This is one of the big questions that all humans ask – across cultures and throughout history. Some religious traditions believe in reincarnation; some philosophies believe that our lives are merely a simulation (like a really complex video game or the film *The Matrix*); some believe that there is no such thing as an afterlife (this has been popularised by the maxim YOLO – teen speak for 'you only live once'). Or in a recent TV show about life after death called *The Good Place*, life after death is presented as a custom-made heaven full of frozen yoghurt and whatever other delights your mind can conjure up.

In 2 Corinthians 5 Paul gets into the topic of life, death and beyond. In this passage we don't get an exhaustive Christian view of life after death, but we do get a robust theology of resurrection hope.

Paul uses three central images to contrast life in the present age and life in the age to come:

1 an eternal building (in place of a tent)
2 being 'clothed over' (instead of being naked)
3 what is mortal being swallowed up by life.

Paul uses these three images to refer to the transformation of the body in resurrection life. Death is a source of anxiety and concern for all people. We live with its reality casting a shadow over our days. Yet for Christians, we are reminded by Paul that death is not the end and that we can have confidence in the hope of resurrection.

† Jesus, we give you thanks and praise that you conquered the grave. Through faith in you we can share in your resurrection. Thank you for this wonderful hope. Amen

For further thought

How can hope in life after death shape our present life and the way we face challenges?

Friday 25 August
Reconciliation

Read 2 Corinthians 5:14–21

All this is from God, who reconciled us to himself through Christ, and has given us the ministry of reconciliation.

(verse 18)

The Second Letter to the Corinthians is a book that tells the story of Paul's conflict as a leader with the Corinthians, as well as conflict in the church. Earlier in this letter Paul speaks of anguish, pain and tears. There is a very raw pain that we encounter when we come into conflict with those whom we love. Any of us who have been through a conflict with a family member, a loved one or close friends knows the deep grief associated with breakdown in relationship. Songs are composed about it, books written, entire films scripted around the hurt of broken relationships.

In chapter 5, we find arguably the centre of Paul's argument – and at the very heart stands Jesus Christ who died and was raised for us. The one who knew no sin took it upon himself so that we might be reconciled to God. At the heart of the Christian faith is the reality that, through Christ, God has brought forgiveness, reconciliation and healing to humanity. Sin is a relational term which describes the breakdown of relationship as we turn from God and go our own way (we see this in the Genesis story). Jesus took the consequences of this sin upon himself and forged a new way forward for us to be reconciled to God. This is the beautiful news of the gospel, and it changes everything. This means that in Christian community we are called to be reconciled to one another, and we are called to be agents of reconciliation in the world.

† Lord, where there is division and broken relationships in my life, help me to look to your reconciling love, and may your Holy Spirit empower me to be an agent of reconciliation. Amen

For further thought

How might being a follower of Jesus shape your approach to conflict resolution?

Saturday 26 August

Eyes to see

Read 2 Corinthians 6:1–7:1

See, now is the acceptable time; see, now is the day of salvation!

(verse 2b)

I remember going to see my first three-dimensional film. It was a whole new experience and I felt so immersed as all the characters leaped out of the screen towards me. At one point I thought I would take my special 3D glasses off to see what it would look like. Turns out it just looks like a blurry mess. The glasses are essential to making the whole thing work. They are the lens through which the 3D film makes sense.

In a similar sense, today's reading from 2 Corinthians invites us to see through a certain lens. On one level, Paul's ministry can look like a list of failures, but through the lens of the cross it is the story of God's servants walking in the way of Jesus.

In this chapter Paul appeals to the Corinthians to keep their focus on Jesus and the cross. Paul quotes from Isaiah 49:8, saying, 'At an acceptable time I have listened to you, and on a day of salvation I have helped you.'

Paul is doing a couple of important things here. First, as he quotes Isaiah, Paul sees himself like Isaiah as a servant called by God to proclaim God's grace to the nations. The second thing Paul is doing as he quotes Isaiah is that he draws attention to the importance of responding to the message. Now is the day, he says, now is the moment of salvation. Jesus has died on the cross to reconcile us to God. Paul invites his audience 'to see'. The Corinthians are invited to respond, and so are we.

† Lord, give us eyes to see what you have done through Jesus and what you are doing in our lives, even in the mess and muddle. Amen

For further thought

What practices in our lives help draw our focus and attention back to Jesus regularly?

Readings in 2 Corinthians

2 Living by God's grace

Notes by **Dafne Plou**

Dafne is a retired social communicator, a women's rights activist who participates in the women's movement in her country. She's a member of the Methodist Church in Argentina. In her local church, in the suburbs of Buenos Aires, she works in the area of 'community building and fellowship in liturgy'. She has a big family and loves spending time with her ten grandchildren. Dafne has used the NIVUK for these notes.

Sunday 27 August

Godly sorrow

Read 2 Corinthians 7:2–16

See what this godly sorrow has produced in you: what earnestness, what eagerness to clear yourselves, what indignation, what alarm, what longing, what concern, what readiness to see justice done.

(verse 11)

Being the daughter of a Methodist minister (who was appointed to a new church every four years), I have seen/heard of difficult personal confrontations, tough theological or doctrinal controversies, power clashes in leadership, harmful moral criticism, and the aggressive rejection of unorthodox novelties, like the introduction of guitars and drums in the service, which almost broke congregations and made parishioners feel upset, confused and ready to walk away. How hard to restore dialogue, heal wounds and accept the need for repentance and sincere change!

In this reading Paul is utterly open. He's deeply concerned for the faithful in Corinth. He knows he has reprimanded them harshly, but he can't just let things go astray. In his pastoral suffering, he wants this congregation to get back to Jesus' teachings. He has sent a mediator, Titus, trusting he would tell him truly what the real situation was. But he just can't wait still for him, he's anxious and travels from Troas to Macedonia to meet Titus and hear the news.

What a relief to learn that Corinth's faithful had answered God's call in godly sorrow. God's love and grace at work to renew their lives.

† Grant us, Jesus, the openness to unfold mistakes and transgressions in our church life and seek godly repentance to walk again your way.

Monday 28 August

Overflowing joy and generosity

Read 2 Corinthians 8:1–9:2

In the midst of a very severe trial, their overflowing joy and their extreme poverty welled up in rich generosity.

(verse 8:2)

He rang the bell in a hurry and begged for food. It was the country's third month in tight lockdown because of the Covid-19 pandemic and I had lost track of him, a well-known street seller in the neighbourhood. 'I was locked with my family in fear and police was not allowed to work in the streets. I went down 20 pounds and we're all hungry at home.' His case was one in too many and though money and resources were scarce in every home, members of this suburban congregation did not turn their backs on him and his people.

What should be done? Who would help? The street seller told us there were many families in his area going through the same situation and even sickness was haunting them. Thanks to cell phones and communications technologies, the congregation got organised in a heartbeat! An unusual collection took place in church: groceries, nappies, bleach, hand sanitisers, everything was offered with joy and enthusiasm. After so many weeks in lockdown, sometimes feeling scared and depressed, it was incredibly inspiring for the faithful to answer this call to action and confirm the 'grace of giving' (verse 7) with sincerity and love.

In his call to generosity, Paul does not dictate to the Corinthians how much to give, but says lucidly 'your plenty will supply what they need, so that in turn their plenty will supply what you need' (verse 14). The congregation was awakened by God's love and the assurance that the 'goal is equality'.

† Help us, Lord, to embrace your grace and understanding when we commit ourselves to help others in times of darkness and difficulties. Let your Spirit awaken us!

For further thought

Paul says 'your plenty will supply what they need'. In this consumer society, do we ever have enough? Let's discuss how generosity is challenged today.

Tuesday 29 August

Cheerful givers

Read 2 Corinthians 9:3–15

Each of you should give what you have decided in your heart to give, not reluctantly or under compulsion, for God loves a cheerful giver.

(verse 7)

In times of crowdfunding and online donations via apps, bank transfers or credit card, it is engaging to read the different arguments Paul draws on to make his case and convince Corinthian Christians to assist the church in Jerusalem. Nowadays, just a short description with a photo or short video showing what donations are needed for is enough to appeal and convince unknown donors all over. People are willing to donate to philanthropic organisations, NGOs, social activists and even families who have to face expensive treatments or surgeries for their dear ones. Is it that in some way we have learned from Paul's early call to generosity and solidarity?

In truth, I like Paul's arguments in this reading. He's not shy at all when asking for a donation. He confirms from the very beginning that he expects a 'generous gift'. The words 'generous' and 'generosity' are repeated and emphasised several times. No amount is mentioned, but surely the Corinthians had heard of hard times in Jerusalem and felt challenged and convinced by the apostle's insistence. They trusted their gift was God's will.

In church we usually sing bright songs during offering time. We praise God for his blessings and care for us, we promise to open our hands and share the gifts received from him and to help others with heart and soul. Paul teaches us that offering should result in thanksgiving to God and that cheerful giving enriches us in every way.

† Jesus, open our hearts and hands so that generosity and solidarity come first when giving witness of your call in difficult economic and social situations.

For further thought

Have you ever tried crowdfunding for your church programmes? You could be surprised by unexpected generosity.

Wednesday 30 August

Confronting untruth

Read 2 Corinthians 10:1–18

For it is not the one who commends himself who is approved, but the one whom the Lord commends.

(verse 18)

In times of social networks, instant messaging and many apps for direct contact between individuals or in groups and communities, we have learned a lot about online dissent that can turn aggressive and even violent because of 'haters', trolls, cyberbullying and more. Church leaders, religious persons, theologians, pious activists and believers can easily become targets of faithless fanatics or, worse, other religious fundamentalists with contending perspectives or beliefs. But this is not new. As the Christian community was growing and expanding, we are told that the apostle Paul had to bear gossiping, talk behind his back and harsh judgements and reproval for his teachings and behaviour. No cell phones or internet at that time but papyrus rolls and feather pens helped him to write severe, tough words to his detractors, like the ones we read in this section of the epistle.

Paul readily rebukes his critics and builds solid arguments that become weapons to 'demolish strongholds', those positions and perspectives that don't allow the faithful to look beyond and focus on new challenges and territories where the gospel should be preached. They keep them selfishly concentrated in their own self-centred achievements and mistakenly 'measure themselves by themselves and compare themselves with themselves'. In social networks, we see a lot of this, don't we?

Wisely, Paul surprises us. Though knowing his reprimand was surely hard to bear, he requests the Corinthian faithful to receive him again with open arms 'by the humility and gentleness of Christ'. In his love, all is possible.

† Open our eyes, Lord, to see clearly what you expect from us and our faith communities in a time when individualism and self-righteousness hinder us from giving witness to your mandates and truth.

For further thought

If your community were the target of any anti-religious attack, would you be able to respond in a way that builds the kingdom? How?

Thursday 31 August

Do we need 'super-apostles'?

Read 2 Corinthians 11:1–15

I do not think I am in the least inferior to those 'super-apostles'. I may indeed be untrained as a speaker, but I do have knowledge.

(verses 5–6a)

In this reading Paul sounds truly upset and expresses his annoyance with hard words and bitter criticism. Scripture commentators consider that 2 Corinthians 10–13 belong to the severe letter the apostle sent to the Corinthians earlier and that he explains in the first part of this epistle.

Why is Paul alarmed? Historians tell us that in times of the early church, teachers and philosophers were expected to charge for their lessons and lectures. Some Greek cities had even established that such teachers and philosophers were free from paying taxes. So, the trained preachers Paul refers to were just doing their own business, disguising themselves as apostles to hide their ambitions. Perhaps they put Paul down by saying that he did not charge for his preaching because he was just an apprentice. Believers in Corinth seemed not to be aware of this dishonesty and were happy to welcome and listen to those Paul describes as 'false apostles, deceitful workers, masquerading as apostles of Christ' (verse 13).

In the late 1980s and early 1990s Latin America was 'invaded' by all sorts of 'super-preachers' coming from abroad, with costly shows and pompous sermons. They were soon imitated by local emulators. Did they all have the knowledge, the commitment, the strength to build up fellowship and care for new faithful? Many of them faded away, leaving behind dismayed followers. 'Each tree is recognised by its own fruit', affirms Jesus in his teachings (Luke 6:44). Paul unveils the situation in this tough letter.

† Inspire us with your Spirit to be consistent and true in our church work, dear Jesus, knowing that credibility, care and love for others come first.

For further thought

How do we build strong fellowship in our congregations or church groups today? How should we start?

Friday 1 September

Grace and weaknesses

Read 2 Corinthians 11:16–12:13

But he said to me, 'My grace is sufficient for you, for my power is made perfect in weakness.' Therefore I will boast all the more gladly about my weaknesses, so that Christ's power may rest on me.

(verse 12:9)

The congregation was glad to see their dear retired minister back in Sunday service. She had gone through a risky surgery and had been hospitalised for several weeks. Everyone welcomed her back with affection and care and there were prayers of gratitude for her recovery. In response, she stood up and walked down the aisle to the altar saying in a loud voice: 'Even though I walked through the darkest valley, I feared no evil, for the Lord was with me; his rod and his staff, comforted me' (Psalm 23:4). And she added, quoting Paul, 'His grace was sufficient for me and his power held me up.'

This is a difficult time to admit our weaknesses, isn't it? Would we ever dare to say we feel weak, helpless, without hope? We think people around us wouldn't take it. Perhaps we fear they would criticise us, look down on us, belittle our efforts. People are supposed to be strong, daring, successful. No one seems to be ready to show his or her concerns, frights or pains openly. This retired minister was bold enough to do so. And the congregation was strengthened by her words and attitude towards sickness and insecurity.

Paul took a courageous step when he decided to talk about the real body pains he suffered, his prayers to be free from them and God's answer. Are we ready to accept our weaknesses and by doing so give evidence of God's power? Let's open our hearts and trust him!

† Jesus, keep us away from discouragement in difficult times and from arrogance when we achieve success. Bless us and strengthen our hope.

For further thought

Have you ever shared your fears and doubts with your church group? Have you ever listened to others with the same concerns? What keeps us from doing so? Be honest!

Saturday 2 September

Testing ourselves

Read 2 Corinthians 12:14–13:14

Examine yourselves to see whether you are in the faith; test yourselves. Do you not realise that Christ Jesus is in you – unless, of course, you fail the test?

(verse 13:5)

For several years I worked for a non-governmental organisation that had an interesting and stressful evaluation method: every year each employee had to fill in a spreadsheet with his or her self-appraisal, including performance, leadership/co-ordination skills, project and programme development and management, role in team building, etc., etc., each item according to a given score. Then, a meeting with management followed. What marks did I deserve? It was daring to keep a cool head and calmly analyse each answer. Was I being sincere and fair? What would others think of my work and the outcomes achieved?

'Test yourselves', commands Paul. Should we also fill in a spreadsheet and score our Christian faith and witness? Paul demands the Corinthians, and us, to consider if we are truly firm in our faith and in full confidence of the gospel. This challenge includes examining if our religiosity is genuine and if we feel certain that God's fidelity and grace sustain us. We should be able to find out if we truly live in Christ and are honest members of his community. Are we afraid of failing the test? In his call to self-assessment, Paul wants to build us up and not tear us down (verse 10).

Paul's final salutation gives us a hint of some outcomes we should achieve as communities of faith. He calls the Corinthians to recover their fellowship: 'Strive for full restoration, encourage one another, be of one mind, live in peace' (verse 11). Are we on the right track?

† Uphold us, Jesus, as we try to walk in your way and discern the challenges and demands of being your true disciples.

For further thought

The Corinthians are invited to rejoice in fellowship. Does your congregation do it often? Plan a joyful thanksgiving initiative with your church group.

Fasting

Notes by **Erice Fairbrother**

Erice lives in Napier, Aotearoa, New Zealand, where she assists as an Anglican priest at the cathedral and in the surrounding community. She is an established writer whose liturgies, meditations and poetry have been published and used widely both within and beyond the church. Latterly, Erice offers retreats, quiet days and ministry support through spiritual companioning and mentoring. As an Oblate of the Order of the Holy Cross, Erice supports others seeking to follow Christ in the Benedictine tradition. Erice has used the NRSVA for these notes.

Sunday 3 September

What is an acceptable fast?

Read Isaiah 58:3–11

Is not this the fast that I choose: to loose the bonds of injustice, to undo the thongs of the yoke, to let the oppressed go free …? If you offer your food to the hungry and satisfy the needs of the afflicted, then your light will rise in the darkness and your gloom be like the noonday.

(verses 6a, 10)

What makes a good fast? Isaiah posed the question to God's people millennia ago, yet it has a strangely contemporary ring. What good are our spiritual practices? Is there a place for fasting in 2023? Here in New Zealand questions have arisen in discussions about what good we can hope for in the face of an evolving pandemic, along with social and workplace changes that are developing as it progresses. What possible help can ancient practices such as fasting be at this time? What good can it do, and can it be truly life-giving when hope is fragile?

Our readings this week focus on that question, suggesting fasting is a form of prayer; prayer that is about leaning into God, seeking God's will in the space we make when we set aside our own will. Making room for others by choosing to see with God's eyes what is truly needed rather than what we might imagine. Isaiah sets the scene, outlining God's expectations for the work of fasting; namely, that it has demonstrable impacts for change where there is oppression, injustice, homelessness and hunger. Our acceptable fast? Making space to work with God, to heal his world.

† Pray that you will rediscover the effect of fasting time, to be with God over this week. Notice the renewal and delight it brings.

Monday 4 September

Good fasts take time

Read 1 Samuel 14:24–30

Now Saul committed a very rash act on that day. He had laid an oath on the troops, saying, 'Cursed be anyone who eats food before it is evening, and I have been avenged of my enemies.' So none of the troops tasted food.

(verse 24)

Having heard a stirring sermon on feeding the hungry, during which the preacher called his congregation to do what Jesus would do when they met anyone who was needy, a couple spontaneously invited a street person begging for money to come home with them for dinner. Which he did. However, he kept returning and the couple began to feel overwhelmed. Eventually they contacted their minister and shared with him a sense of shame for their growing fear of the needy person, their increasing feelings of great personal distress and a sense of being used. The preacher had made, albeit in good faith, a 'rash' call which left the couple themselves in need and vulnerable.

Saul spoke rashly when he called for his troops to fast. The consequences of his rash oath were to create a vulnerable army, who were, as we read later, 'faint'. Jonathan saw that their ability to defeat the enemy was less than had been hoped for. Like the preacher in the story above, Saul hadn't stopped to consider the wider consequences of his call.

Christian outreach develops through prayerful consideration. Similarly, fasting is an intentional prayerful act, a time of stepping back and waiting on God. In that space we learn how we can respond to needs around us in love, along with prayerful community support. Similarly, in our own daily decision-making, how important it is to take time to prayerfully ensure that the impact of what we decide won't diminish or lessen the ability of those around us to function as well as they can.

† God of love, help me to step back and wait on you as I face making decisions that might affect the lives of others.

For further thought

Make a list of everyday things you need to do. Notice how even the simplest might impact on someone else.

Tuesday 5 September

Fasting – a strong foundation

Read Daniel 1:3–17

Let us be given vegetables to eat and water to drink ... At the end of ten days it was observed that they appeared better and fatter than all the young men who had been eating the royal rations ... To [the] four young men God gave knowledge and skill.

(verses 12b, 15, 17a)

A few years ago, while chaplain at a church boarding school, I was interested to observe how personal phones and devices were managed by staff. Students only had access to their phones from the end of school until after supper, at which time they were handed back into the office until the same time next day. Similarly, use of laptops was limited. More than a routine, it was a practice that established a work–life balance which St Benedict would have understood. Through that practice, students developed the capacity to delay self-gratification, the ability to adapt to normative social constraints and explore alternative ways of relating. It was a form of fasting, laying faith foundations of spiritual resilience, and the ability to step back and to reflect; foundations that would support them well in the future.

Daniel, Shadrach, Meshach and Abednego are examples of how resilient faith can sustain us in the most challenging of situations. Finding themselves held by a foreign regime where their own cultural heritage was colonised (even to the changing of their names), these four young men were able to draw on previous learnings and routines they knew would sustain them physically and spiritually. Risking all, they resisted eating the rich royal rations, choosing instead to remain faithful to what they believed was their source of strength and wellness.

The students were learning the strengthening mental practice of fasting from devices, just as the four young men had already learned the strengthening physical practice of a disciplined healthy lifestyle, which later enabled their survival, both physically and spiritually, under duress.

† Pray for friends and teachers who instilled in you the spiritual foundations and experiences that sustain you in difficult times. Give thanks for their part in your life.

For further thought

Think of a time when your faith was tested. What earlier learnings and practices sustained you? Diary, or share your experience with another person.

Wednesday 6 September

Humility and repentance

Read 1 Kings 21:20–29

He fasted, lay in the sackcloth, and went about dejectedly. Then the word of the LORD came to Elijah the Tishbite: 'Have you seen how Ahab has humbled himself before me? Because he has humbled himself before me, I will not bring the disaster in his days.'

(verses 27b–29a)

It's never easy to confront someone with their mistakes or poor behaviour. Perhaps, however, it's much harder when we are confronted with our own failings. No matter what positive spin we might put on it, the latter carries a sense of being judged and found wanting. Our responses can vary from wanting to justify our actions to feeling utterly crushed.

As a child, the story of Ahab was taught to us as a cautionary tale; if you act badly and offend God you will be judged with terrible consequences. It wasn't until later that I became aware of how the judgement delivered by Elijah actually ended for Ahab. How I wished the end of the story had been equally emphasised, because there is something very powerful in Ahab's response. He hears the truth, and yet, crushing as it is, it is what he does with it that's important. He turns to the ancient practice of repentant fasting, revealing how faith that has been held in the past can be re-found even in times of deepest despair.

In New Zealand the Māori word for humility is *whakaiti*, meaning to diminish oneself completely. Ahab's fast is an example of *whakaiti* as he strips off everything that signified his evil life. The word 'dejection' powerfully describes the depths of hopelessness he reached. He becomes physically and spiritually naked; no excuses, no arguing back. As Ahab humbles himself, God recognises true repentance, responding with divine compassion; reminding us that none of us are ever beyond God's forgiveness and love. A fast of humble repentance will lead us there.

† Pray that God will lead you to a place where you can let old memories, worries or shame be absorbed into his all-embracing loving forgiveness. Give thanks for the peace that follows.

For further thought

Is there someone who needs your loving forgiveness that you can offer to them at this time?

Thursday 7 September

Intercession – fasting for others

Read Nehemiah 1:1–2:5

The survivors there in the province who escaped captivity are in great trouble and shame; the wall of Jerusalem is broken down, and its gates have been destroyed by fire. When I heard these words, I sat down and wept, and mourned for days, fasting and praying before the God of heaven.

(verses 3–4)

Faced with the enormity of global issues of injustice and conflict, it is hard to imagine how we can respond. I recall the agony of watching as refugees, plucked from their sinking boat in the Pacific, had to wait on the *Tampa*, the tanker that had saved them, to hear which country would take them in. Images of people with nothing, living on an open deck in hot sun, with little food, and in fear of being returned to places they had fled. Governments argued over them, communities protested against having them be settled anywhere near them. During the stand-off, many Christians kept a vigil of hope, taking time out from usual routines to pray for the refugees; prayers that included petitioning our Prime Minister to make a compassionate response.

Becoming aware of the plight of his people, Nehemiah took time apart with God in prayer; prayer that included petitioning his ruler, and a fast that revealed a God who hears his people. Twenty years later, while taking a taxi across the city, I learned my driver was the son of a refugee. His father, it turned out, had been one of the refugees saved by the *Tampa*. He is proud to be a New Zealander, he told me. We were the only ones who took them in.

As I left the taxi, I thought of all those who had prayed in faith over many days. They too had been part of revealing a God who hears and responds to our prayers for others.

† God of justice and mercy, help me to pray faithfully for your world and its suffering, trusting that you hear my prayers and that your justice and peace will be revealed here on earth.

For further thought

As a fast, set aside a particular time to pray for others whose lives are at the mercy of others.

Friday 8 September

Community fasts

Read Ezra 8:21–23

So we fasted ...

(verse 23)

In New Zealand, Māori understand community as being inclusive of all members, including the *whenua* or earth on which they live. Whether there is joy or sorrow, the effect is shared among them all, usually by gathering together. If the community is vulnerable to outside threat, all who belong to that community are affected; a truth borne out in the history of colonisation in this country. For example, when preparing to fight to retain Māori land at Gate Pa, Māori leader Henare Taratoa required his warriors and his community to embrace gospel values. It was a call to fast from vengeance and indiscriminate destruction during, and following, the impending battle. As a result, the Battle of Gate Pa has become famous for the actions of a woman warrior who, hearing an enemy soldier cry out that he was thirsty as he lay dying, risked her own life to take water to him and others.

At the time of writing, the global community has just met in Scotland to address the vulnerability of our earth. The meeting ended with calls for an inclusive world community response; to 'fast' from practices that are having a destructive impact on our planet. There are many other vulnerable situations and many vulnerable peoples across the world who are 'calling' out for intentional fasts of action. What kind of fast can we make? Perhaps stepping aside to discern our community's responses will become the most important fast of our time. To pray that God's will be done on earth, the most important entreaty of all.

† Pray for discernment to know what you are called to fast from at this time. What is the Spirit calling you to pray for?

For further thought

Look for local opportunities to share in helping make the world a more sustainable place.

Saturday 9 September

God is with us

Read Acts 13:1–3

While they were worshipping the Lord and fasting, the Holy Spirit said, 'Set apart for me Barnabas and Saul for the work to which I have called them.'

(verse 2)

Is there a relationship between worship and fasting? Is there an added value the apostles knew about? I remember a woman who shared her difficulty with the care of her ageing mother. She talked about the care consuming her, how her prayers were reduced to quick short pleas for God to care for her mother. Her anxieties were keeping her awake at night. We talked about stepping back from making immediate responses. How would it be, we wondered, if she stopped for a moment to call to mind that God was with her; giving thanks that he was caring for her, as she cared for her mother. It changed her sense of burden as she developed a practice of fasting from anxiety and taking time to give thanks to God.

Our readings this week have explored the place of fasts in the lives of individuals, leaders and communities. We have meditated on fasts of repentance, fasts that have become a source of strength, discernment fasts, thoughtless fasts, community fasts. In every instance each fast was met by a God who was already there for them; listening, hearing and responding. We have encountered a God who is ready to give full attention to anyone who seeks it. God, it seems, fasts with us. Even Ahab, who had gone as far away from God as humanly possible, finds the God whom he had abandoned had not abandoned him.

Fasting leads us to God. Worship is formed as we respond with thanks, becoming the source of renewed strength, hope and faith.

† O Lord, help us to be thankful and, as we fast, to receive renewed hope and strength.

For further thought

Which of our meditations this week have resonated most for you?

The Gospel of Matthew (5)

1 He who comes in the name of the Lord

Notes by **Stella Wiseman**

Stella is a newly ordained minister in the Church of England, working in a parish in the south-east of England. She came to ministry late, after a career in journalism, and alongside her ordained ministry, works in parish administration and communications, which has given her good insight into how the church operates. She also writes fiction for children and young people. She has three adult children, a husband and ten cats. Stella has used the NRSVA for these notes.

Sunday 10 September

Tough law and proper love

Read Matthew 19:1–15

'"For this reason a man shall leave his father and mother and be joined to his wife, and the two shall become one flesh." So they are no longer two, but one flesh. Therefore what God has joined together, let no one separate.'

(verses 5–6)

This week we follow Jesus on his last journey to Jerusalem and the fate that awaited him at the hands of those who wanted him dead. Tensions are heightening and Jesus is at his most provocative – challenging those who lived by the letter of the law but who didn't see the spirit behind it. It's a challenging read too but points us to a greater reality beyond the words.

The question of marriage is a good example. The law Moses gave said that a man could divorce his wife, simply by giving her written notice, which was particularly tough on women – they were property and could be cast off. The Pharisees were looking to trap Jesus into denying the law, but Jesus looks past their question to their motivation and points them past the law to the love that underpins it. He points them to the truth that there is something much better than the law – the way of God which involves us opening ourselves to God's love.

Our reading begins with Jesus being confronted by those who, through their own cleverness, thought they knew God. It ends with little children who, in their innocence, are able to receive him.

† Loving God, may we be open to your spirit as we seek to live in the modern world.

Monday 11 September

Threading the camel

Read Matthew 19:16–30

Truly I tell you, it will be hard for a rich person to enter the kingdom of heaven. Again I tell you, it is easier for a camel to go through the eye of a needle than for someone who is rich to enter the kingdom of God.

(verses 23–24)

For those of us who have material possessions, and maybe a little more than we need, this must be one of the most challenging passages in the New Testament. Are we barred from the kingdom of God, or do we turn away from entering it by relying on dead things such as wealth and possessions rather than on the one who is the source of life? What does it really mean when he talked about the camel and the needle?

There are several ideas about this – was the 'Eye of the Needle' the narrow city gate through which a camel would have a hard time squeezing or was Jesus talking about threading a darning needle with a ship's cable? (The Greek the story was written in sounds similar.)

It could be either but, whichever it is, the picture it paints is both amusing and alarming! If we are rich, it is all too easy to use those riches to protect us from the vagaries of the world, or to distract us from them – in which case we miss out on seeing the love of God in action on our behalf. And if we don't know the love of God in our life, we are unlikely to have compassion and love for others. That's what the kingdom of God is all about – living the life God offers us. But Jesus goes on to say that it is not impossible for the rich to enter the kingdom and have this full life – after all, 'for God all things are possible'.

† Loving God, may our priority be to follow you and find the life you have to offer us – life in all its fullness.

For further thought

Wealth inequality is not just about money, food and housing but about access to opportunities that might make a difference in the future, even down to whether you can get vaccines and other medicines.

Tuesday 12 September

A fair wage

Read Matthew 20:1–16

Take what belongs to you and go; I choose to give to this last the same as I give to you. Am I not allowed to do what I choose with what belongs to me? Or are you envious because I am generous?

(verses 14–15)

In this passage Jesus says God's kingdom is like a vineyard owner who decides to pay everyone the same – a standard day's wage – regardless of how many hours they have worked during the day. This makes the workers who have been there the longest and toiled hard in the hot sun cross and jealous. They'd agreed to a wage but now they wanted to be given more. How dare someone give everyone an equal wage? Hadn't they worked harder and longer than these other wastrels who'd turned up late? If more money was on offer shouldn't *they* have it?

At first glance they might seem to have a point. After all, we like justice and fairness. But think again. They had received what they had agreed was a fair and just wage for the work they had done. It is an act of generosity, not unfairness, to give the later workers the same amount. Why shouldn't he be generous? Surely, it is up to him. Maybe there were good reasons why everyone could not be there at first light; we aren't told. And if we think of the vineyard owner as God – which Jesus asks us to do – then this is just an example of God's exuberant, abundant love, poured out for us, not because we deserve it or can work hard enough for it, but because God wants to give. Sounds like a great deal!

† Thank you, loving God, for the generosity of your love which we don't need to work for – it is just given to us, whoever we are.

For further thought

If we have been a Christian a long time we can think we are superior and fail to listen to the insight of new believers.

Wednesday 13 September

The upending of expectations

Read Matthew 20:17–34

Whoever wishes to be great among you must be your servant, and whoever wishes to be first among you must be your slave; just as the Son of Man came not to be served but to serve, and to give his life a ransom for many.

(verses 26b–28)

Jesus is going up to Jerusalem where he will face the agony of betrayal, injustice, physical torture and the cruellest of deaths. He knows this and has repeatedly told his disciples this before. Surely, they'd be devastated, or perhaps they were still in denial – most of us would be, wouldn't we, if we were in their place? How could this extraordinary person who had healed people, spoken with wisdom and grace, exuded the spirit of God, be going to meet such a terrible end? That would be the end of all their hopes and dreams.

In that context, tensions were continuing to run high and perhaps that is why the mother of Zebedee's children – probably Mary's sister Salome – asks the really rather presumptuous question about her sons James and John, and the other disciples are angry. Everything was feeling uncertain, upside down, and they wanted to know it would all be OK. It's a very human reaction, but Jesus responds with something that upends all their expectations yet again – the idea that greatness lies in service.

Sometimes, of course, this can be used to make people feel that they must not care for themselves and must allow others to walk all over them, but if we look at Jesus' life that isn't the example he gives. He challenged wrongdoing and injustice but found his place among the despised and unloved, dying as one of them. That was not the end, as the resurrection showed, and in the resurrection we find the ultimate upending of expectations.

† Lord Jesus, may we follow your path of loving service, for we know that in serving others we serve you.

For further thought

Sometimes we do understand that true greatness lies in service – think of the respect given to health-workers caring for people in the pandemic.

Thursday 14 September
Hosanna – set us free!

Read Matthew 21:1–11

A very large crowd spread their cloaks on the road, and others cut branches from the trees and spread them on the road ... shouting, 'Hosanna to the Son of David! Blessed is the one who comes in the name of the Lord! Hosanna in the highest heaven!'

(verses 8–9)

This is such a familiar, celebratory passage. At last, Jesus is getting the recognition that he deserves – riding into Jerusalem like a king on a donkey. You might expect it to have been a horse, but a donkey was viewed as a noble beast in the Middle East, and a king riding one showed that he came in peace.

He also came at a time when the city was heaving with thousands of, perhaps even as many as 2.5 million, people who were there for the annual festival of Passover. It was a time of great religious excitement and the crowds seemed ready for him, waving and spreading palm branches on the road, which echoes what happened when the temple was restored in 164 BC (see 2 Maccabees 10). They also spread their cloaks, which was an ancient way of recognising a new king who was usurping an old one. And their shouts of 'Hosanna to the Son of David' were provocative to the authorities – for generations the Jewish people had been praying for a king like David to come to save them. 'Hosanna' actually comes from a word meaning 'Save us!'

The crowd recognised that this was someone they needed, someone who could set them free, only they didn't realise what sort of freedom that meant. No wonder, though, that the religious and the secular authorities decided to clamp down on him. He appeared to be inciting rebellion, something that would disturb the uneasy peace between those authorities. The stage was set for a confrontation.

† Lord Jesus, may we recognise that you can set us free, not from the rulers in the world but in our hearts.

For further thought

Jesus riding into Jerusalem like this required real courage in the face of what was to come.

Friday 15 September

Temple dealings

Read Matthew 21:12–27

He said to them, 'It is written, "My house shall be called a house of prayer"; but you are making it a den of robbers.' The blind and the lame came to him in the temple, and he cured them.

(verses 13–14)

The tension ramps up even further today with Jesus throwing people out of the temple and turning over tables and chairs. It seems surprising that he could do this single-handedly and perhaps he had help, which would have made the authorities even more certain that he had come to incite rebellion.

The background to this is that it was perfectly legal to change money, in fact required. All Jews had to pay a temple tax, which had to be paid in certain high-grade currencies, so people had to change their own currency into acceptable ones. And dove-selling was legitimate too. The sacrifice of doves was necessary for certain acts of purification and it was all set down in the law – Mary and Joseph offered doves when Jesus was presented at the temple in Luke 2:24. But the cost of doves sold in the temple was often far higher than those outside and sometimes ones bought outside were rejected as having blemishes, so not good enough for sacrifice. People were making a profit on the backs of others, especially the poor, and this again was against the spirit of the law. Not only that, but the outer courts that they had turned into a marketplace were the only part of the temple in which women and foreigners were allowed to worship. The presence of the traders meant these marginalised groups were excluded.

Once again Jesus was on the side of the poor and powerless, and, when he had driven out the exploiters, he turned to the marginalised – the poor and the lame – and healed them.

† Loving God, give us insight to see where established practices are open to exploitation and give us courage and wisdom to know how to challenge them.

For further thought

There are often echoes of other passages in the Bible. The welcoming of the blind and lame here echoes their rejection in 2 Samuel 5:6–10.

Saturday 16 September

It's not always easy to see the truth

Read Matthew 21:28–46

Truly I tell you, the tax-collectors and the prostitutes are going into the kingdom of God ahead of you.

(verse 31b)

At the end of this passage, the chief priests and the Pharisees are longing to seize Jesus but they are afraid. He still has the crowd on his side, and they are also afraid that maybe, just maybe, he could be the Messiah. After all, in yesterday's reading he had taken control of at least one of the outer courts of the temple, and certainly the ordinary people seemed to think he was something special.

In the first parable here, Jesus is saying that the despised people are the ones who will enter the kingdom of God first as they are following the way of righteousness, even though their lives don't seem particularly righteous, and he is full-on attacking the religious leaders. In the second parable, he goes even further, by suggesting that the Pharisees and chief priests are wicked tenants who want control of the vineyard, that is, God's kingdom.

Looking back now, knowing who Jesus is, it is easy to judge the religious leaders. They were part of a great tradition and had an uneasy alliance with the Romans, allowing them to continue the practice of Judaism. Jesus seemed to be an upstart who threatened them and their ways – and could they be sure that he was actually the Messiah? Some of the threat was to their privileged position and power, but some of it was to the continuation of Judaism. It took a bold leader to side with Jesus.

† Loving God, may we be blessed with the wisdom to know when you are showing us the way of truth.

For further thought

Would we have recognised Jesus for who he was at the time?

The Gospel of Matthew (5)

2 Confrontations

Notes by **Andy Fisher, Paul Cavill and Tom Hartman**

Andy, Paul and Tom are three friends who meet for fellowship and lunch as often as their timetables permit, which is quite infrequent and not made any easier with a pandemic. Andy is a philosopher with a special interest in ethics and education. Paul is an author and specialist on English place names and the faith of ancient peoples. Tom is a zoologist who has specialised in evolutionary genetics. It is an unlikely group, but it seems to work. Andy, Paul and Tom have used the NIVUK for these notes.

Sunday 17 September

There is such a thing as a free lunch

Read Matthew 22:1–14

'Tell those who have been invited that I have prepared my dinner' … But they paid no attention and went off – one to his field, another to his business.

(part of verses 4–5)

As students, a few of us spent time in Israel-Palestine. On one occasion, wandering in Ramallah desperate for respite from the heat and needing a cooling drink, we were approached by a man who, in broken English, invited us to his brother's cafe where he would buy us all lunch. In that one moment we were confronted by a painful fact: we were prejudiced. Here, on the face of it, was an amazing offer, one which would meet our immediate needs and leave us better off. Yet, surely a man living here could only have dangerous intentions? There must be a catch; there is, after all, no such thing as a free lunch. Thankfully we took him up on his offer, had a wonderful time, and were all taught something very special about hospitality, grace and ourselves.

Hearing the word 'confrontation', our minds might turn to road rage, church splits and housemates. Yet often it is the confrontation within us which means we miss out. At these points we can either pay no attention and go off to our field or business, or focus on the King and face the fact there is really such a thing as a free lunch.

† Pray you have the courage to confront those things in your life which make your fields and businesses more attractive than the King's amazing banquet.

Rights and duties

Read Matthew 22:15–22

'Tell us then, what is your opinion? Is it right to pay the poll-tax to Caesar or not?' Then he said to them, 'So give back to Caesar what is Caesar's, and to God what is God's.'

(verses 17, 21)

The people in this passage were trying to trap Jesus by asking a tricky question. But though Jesus saw through the motive, he used the opportunity to teach them. These people were disciples – students – used to asking questions and debating answers, but they recognised the profound wisdom of Jesus' words and realised that they needed to think hard about them.

The question itself is an important one: who has the right to our obedience? Jesus makes it clear that it was a duty to obey Caesar in paying taxes. But the radical part of his answer was that Jesus made it even clearer that Caesar was not God, despite the Roman imperial cult which worshipped him. Caesar had the right to certain duties, but the one true God has the right to our love and obedience.

Jesus welcomes and frequently asks questions in the Gospels; and he always listens to the answers. This passage leaves us with questions we need to ask ourselves. All kinds of claims are made today on our time, attention, loyalty and money. It is often a struggle to know where our duty lies and which of the competing claims comes first. We may need to confront pressures from others or within ourselves to ensure that we give our first obedience to God.

† Think about the responsibilities you have in the world, and pray that you will be able to put God first in your life.

For further thought

Questions can often have different 'right' answers. Jesus welcomed questions and understood genuine answers. Our answers to difficult questions like that in today's reading may change over time.

Tuesday 19 September

Be an answer to the person not the question

Read Matthew 22:23–46

'At the resurrection, whose wife will she be of the seven, since all of them were married to her?' Jesus replied, 'You are in error because you do not know the Scriptures or the power of God. At the resurrection people will neither marry nor be given in marriage.'

(verses 28–30a)

I am a philosopher, which means I can say with some authority that philosophers are an odd bunch. What makes us odd is that our questioning is unbounded, we question things which others don't. The historian might question certain primary sources, the biologist the possible extinction of a species, the scholar of literature various interpretations of a text. Whereas the philosopher might ask if the historian has a mind, why we should worry about extinction in the first place, and what, if anything, is the meaning of 'meaning'. As philosophers we often confront others not about the details of certain disciplinary disputes but rather about the assumptions behind the disputes themselves.

In today's passage we see Jesus the philosopher. Here is someone who in a confrontation doesn't accept the terms and conditions he is being asked to accept. The Sadducees' question doesn't lead anywhere because Jesus changes the perspective – 'At the resurrection people will neither marry nor be given in marriage.' As Christians we too should not simply accept the parameters of a confrontation. We should ask ourselves what it is that we are being asked to buy into. What reasons do they really have for asking this question? This requires patience, a supernatural perspective, a knowledge of scripture, a boldness to challenge others, and a vulnerability to be challenged. But being a reflective Christian in this way means we can be Christ-like and ultimately provide an answer to the person and not the questions they ask.

† Pray that Jesus may shine a light on the things we are not seeing in our lives, the assumptions and biases, the values and priorities handed to us by the world, so that we can become more like him.

For further thought

Next time you are confronted about your faith ask how you can be an answer to the person rather than the questions they are asking.

Wednesday 20 September

Jesus stirs up trouble

Read Matthew 23:1–12

But do not do what they do, for they do not practise what they preach. They tie up heavy, cumbersome loads and put them on other people's shoulders, but they themselves are not willing to lift a finger to move them.

(verses 3b–4)

We have many words that we use to describe Jesus: Jesus the Saviour, Jesus the Messiah, Jesus the man of sorrows, Jesus the Son of Man, even Jesus, firstborn from the dead, but rarely do we associate him with stirring up trouble – Jesus the troublemaker. Yet in so many stories in the Gospels he is provoking those in authority and challenging them. How often did he clash with either the religious authorities or the military rulers from Rome?

That was not the whole story, of course. Jesus had many supporters among the establishment and at the end of Mark's Gospel the person who recognised him for who he was, at the crucifixion, was a soldier of the occupying army.

It seems to be a part of the human condition that we take something that is supposed to make us free and start imposing restraints. We cordon off part of the experience. Everyone has to fall into line. Jesus, here, makes a bold claim. Religious leaders are not there to delegate the heavy burdens (at my church it sometimes seems that there is a committee for everyone) and leave people to it. Check out the rest of the passage: Jesus calls for servanthood to be the core of our faith; looking out for the best for everyone and supporting one another. When you look at how that strikes to the very core of society, it is surprising that Jesus lasted as long as he did.

† Who are the oppressed that you know? Pray for those who struggle with heavy burdens with no one to help them. Pray for your church to be enabled to support them and proclaim freedom for the oppressed.

For further thought

It is so easy to add to the 'cumbersome load' rather than reduce it. How can your fellowship support those who are struggling?

Thursday 21 September

Keeping up appearances

Read Matthew 23:13–28

You give a tenth of your spices ... But you have neglected the more important matters of the law – justice, mercy and faithfulness. You should have practised the latter, without neglecting the former. ... You appear to people as righteous but on the inside you are full of hypocrisy and wickedness.

(verses 23, 28)

Oscar Wilde famously defined a cynic as someone who knows the cost of everything but the value of nothing (from his play *Lady Windermere's Fan*). Jesus saw the teachers of the law and the Pharisees as cynics: they calculated minutely the things that had to be done to fulfil the law, and then they thought that those things made them righteous. They were in fact concerned with appearances rather than heartfelt obedience to God. They valued the rules rather than the Ruler.

The Pharisees were much respected and admired in Jesus' day. They were the people who kept Judaism pure in the face of secularising powers and social laxity. They aimed to please God and set a standard of behaviour. But Jesus accuses them of superficiality and judgementalism. They thought God would be satisfied with the precise dutiful details. But God loves justice, mercy and faithfulness. Attention to detail is not the problem, but lack of attention to God's character of love makes detail meaningless and, ultimately, cynical. They knew the cost but not the value of their practices.

Christians sometimes fall into the trap of overvaluing outward appearances. We sometimes do things to impress others rather than to honour God. We are sometimes more concerned to be right than to love God and our neighbour. Jesus invites us to examine ourselves so that our lives are focused on the more important things rather than just ticking boxes.

† Take a moment or two to think about the things that you do as a Christian. Are the little things designed to impress or to build a character rooted in God's grace? Pray through your conclusions.

For further thought

How can we model God's generosity to others?

Friday 22 September
Parental love

Read Matthew 23:29–39

Jerusalem, Jerusalem … how often I have longed to gather your children together, as a hen gathers her chicks under her wings, and you were not willing … you will not see me again until you say, 'Blessed is he who comes in the name of the Lord.'

(verses 37, 39)

Jesus often used the idiom of the Old Testament prophets in his preaching. This passage comes at the end of a series of terrible denunciations of the religious leaders, using 'Woe to you', echoing Isaiah 5. It contrasts sharply with Jesus' announcement of the kingdom of God using 'Blessed', in the beatitudes of Matthew 5. Jesus preaches like a prophet, knowing well how prophets have been treated in Jerusalem.

But fierce anger turns quickly to deep compassion. Jesus speaks of his love for the people of Jerusalem as a mother's love, gathering together her children, just as Isaiah spoke of God's love for his people: 'As a mother comforts her child, so I will comfort you' (Isaiah 66:13). Being a parent is one of the most challenging experiences we can have: children can sometimes cause grief and anger as well as pride and joy. But the key factor in parenthood is always love for the child, love that 'bears all things, believes all things, hopes all things, endures all things' (1 Corinthians 13: 7, ESV). This is the love Jesus has for us.

Love has the last word in this passage. Jesus has shown profound indignation at the teachers of the law and the Pharisees, and at the indifference of the people of Jerusalem. But in contrast to his pronouncing of 'Woe', he finishes this discourse with the joyful, hopeful declaration of blessing from Psalm 118: 26, 'Blessed is he who comes in the name of the Lord.' He looks forward to his return and, in blessing him, Jerusalem will be blessed.

† Pray for parents, especially for any whose children cause them grief. If you are a parent, rest in the knowledge that you are a child of God, loved and blessed by him.

For further thought

Love has the last word. Jesus was angry about some things, but his love was inextinguishable. It's okay to be angry about some things, but let it be rooted in love.

Saturday 23 September

Good news for the unsure

Read Matthew 28:1–20

Then the eleven disciples went to Galilee, to the mountain where Jesus had told them to go. When they saw him, they worshipped him; but some doubted. Then Jesus came to them and said, 'All authority in heaven and on earth has been given to me.'

(verses 16–18)

In every Bible that I've looked through, the heading that introduces this verse is 'The Great Commission'. When it is preached on it is common to hear the clear call to spread the word about the good news of Jesus Christ and the forgiveness of sins. Our focus is so often on Jesus Christ that we forget that the eleven disciples who were gathered on the mount were, as it is often commented upon in the Gospels, not of one mind and often confused. Here they were on the very cusp of the events that were to reverberate through history, and while they worshipped, we are told that some still had doubts. Seriously? At this point, when Jesus was still present among them, there was room for uncertainty?

Within the church there has to be room for people at all stages of faith and doubt. It is there for those who are seeking and those who have been found, those who are looking for answers and those who have come with questions. Whether people are paused in their journey or rushing forward, a church needs to offer places to rest and recuperate as well as challenge and encourage. Jesus didn't require all his disciples to be of one mind, but he did ask them to follow him and know that within him was all authority.

† Father, for all those who have heard you call and found themselves beset with doubts and fears, may your Spirit rest on them and supply them with whatever they need. Equip your church with patience.

For further thought

How can you best support those people beset with doubts without making them feel worse or unwanted? Is there a place for confronting them?

Sowing and reaping

Notes by **Simei Monteiro**

Simei Monteiro is a Brazilian poet and composer. She has worked as Worship Consultant at the World Council of Churches in Geneva, Switzerland. She is interested in worship and the arts, and her book, *The Song of Life* (ASTE/IEPG, 1991), explores the relationship between hymns and theology. As a retired missionary from the United Methodist Church, USA, she lives in Curitiba, Brazil, with her husband the Revd Jairo Monteiro. They have two daughters and three grandchildren. Simei has used the NRSVA for these notes.

Sunday 24 September

God's provision

Read Psalm 65:9–13

You visit the earth and water it, you greatly enrich it; the river of God is full of water; you provide the people with grain, for so you have prepared it. You water its furrows abundantly, settling its ridges, softening it with showers, and blessing its growth.

(verses 9–10)

In one of the Portuguese versions, verse 9 says: *God's streams overflow so that the wheat never runs out, for thus thou hast ordained.*[1] Yes! We can remember that our daily bread is blessed and must be guaranteed for all humanity.

Living in the south of Brazil, I am also very proud of our Iguaçu Falls. These days, the falls are not flowing in all their usual glory but look as if they were dripping from a broken tap. It is an upsetting sight to see the *iguaçu* (in Tupi language, 'larger river') transformed into an *imirim* ('small river').

The recent rainy season was the driest of the past twenty years and water reserves are suffering greatly. Families have been asked to reduce their consumption of water and electricity, which even has to be rationed. In addition to the changes in the scenario and the effects on people's daily lives, the drought imposes losses in important areas of the state's economy.

We know that there is no life without water and that is why we give thanks every day for the blessed water we still have.

† O Holy River, have mercy on us; save our planet threatened by environmental disasters. Come, visit us, and send us your healing waters!

[1] Nova Versão Internacional (NVI).

Monday 25 September

Celebrate the harvest

Read Deuteronomy 16:13–15

Rejoice during your festival, you and your sons and your daughters, your male and female slaves, as well as the Levites, the strangers, the orphans, and the widows resident in your towns … for the Lord *your God will bless you in all your produce and in all your undertakings.*

(verses 14, 15b)

What is a people's festival? It is a time to celebrate something very meaningful; to enjoy being in the community in remembrance of an event.

During the festival of Sukkoth, the Israelites gave up the comfort of their home to commemorate God's salvation – a national feast because it belongs to the whole community and not just a part of it. Even the slaves were invited to be part of the festival!

It is described as a time of jubilation and thanksgiving for God's continued provision in the wilderness for forty years. It could be tempting for the Israelites to sit in their houses after a great harvest and say, 'Look at what we did and how we have profited.' Therefore, living in booths for a week reminded them that their success in Canaan was wholly on account of the Lord's grace.

More and more, we have so many displaced people around the world. Living now in a strange land, they cannot feel really part of a community. As long as we still have marginalised people around us, festivals cannot be fully enjoyed. It is a shame if people are starving when others are feasting and consuming; if some have a house to live in and others live on the streets.

'Enlarge the site of your tent, and let the curtains of your habitations be stretched out' (Isaiah 54:2a). On account of God's grace, let us dare to do good and enlarge our tents! Then, maybe we can celebrate together what is meaningful and what can bring us hope.

† Dear God, help us to understand that the best place in this world is the shelter of your presence. Help us to surrender our greed and the comfort of non-essential things and just celebrate your salvation!

For further thought

Imagine you are living for a while in a tent in the wilderness without any comfort. What would you celebrate there?

Tuesday 26 September

The right to land is the right to life!

Read Nehemiah 5:1–12

Let us stop this taking of interest. Restore to them, this very day, their fields, their vineyards, their olive orchards, and their houses, and the interest on money, grain, wine, and oil that you have been exacting from them.

(verses 10b–11)

There is a big issue being discussed in Brazil: the demarcation of indigenous lands. Due to the complexity of the problem, each time the theme comes to the Congress it is postponed!

The indigenous want recognition for the land where they have being living since a long time ago. Now the indigenous population and their land are reduced significantly and it seems that the question is no longer a priority.

The government proposal, led by agribusiness, aims to limit the number of claims to land by indigenous people by requiring them to prove that they occupied the land at the time of Brazil's 1988 constitution. This is not right since it will deny many their rights to land.

By contrast, it is amazing to see that the Bible proposes a restorative justice which goes far beyond the common justice practised in that time. It brings light to the kind of justice God wants!

If we analyse the colonial process in our world and the worldwide claim for a 'restorative justice', we must accept the fact that what the Bible proposes is much more radical, as we read in the books of Leviticus and Numbers.

God's justice is fundamentally a restoring and renewing justice. For most offences, justice was secured through recognition, repentance, restitution and reconciliation – things that served to repair relationships and restore community.

This concept of justice requires us to cross over into a different social and political world from our own. Therefore, if another world is possible, we must consider this theme urgently. Peace and justice for our world!

† Dear God! The Earth is yours and all that is in it! We are your children; we must serve our neighbours equally. Help us, to promote your justice and your peace!

For further thought

Look on the internet for people and ethnic groups not yet recognised geopolitically. Where are they? Which language do they speak?

Wednesday 27 September

Sharing with those in need

Read Ruth 2:2–8

'Let me go to the field and glean among the ears of grain, behind someone in whose sight I may find favour.' ... Then Boaz said to Ruth, 'Now listen, my daughter, do not go to glean in another field or leave this one.'

(verses 2, 8)

The book of Ruth takes seriously the pastoral concern for refugees, migrants and their families. It points out practices that can help humanity to build up a society in solidarity, kindness and peace. Boaz is an exemplary model of generosity and kindness but we must remember that all this solidarity trend starts with the gesture from Ruth towards Naomi. Her decision to stand beside Naomi demonstrates the kind of value which can create a hopeful future for families and communities. Naomi's role in bringing Ruth and Boaz together shows prudence and a sense of responsibility for shaping the common good.

In Brazil, we are getting into a serious economic crisis not only because of the pandemic but for other reasons also. Consequently, we see more and more people in the streets asking for money and food. Supermarkets have responded to the problem by selling, or giving free, bones that have a little meat on them.

Many churches and social organisations are trying to help those who are being affected, but none of these efforts seems to be enough. While such organisations are doing what they can, it is hard to do so much relying on volunteers.

One thing we have noticed is that the poor are often the most involved in helping others. Significant work is being led by *Centrais de Favelas* (organized groups in the slums). What they are able to do is incredible! Working without ceasing, they can make step-by-step progress, mobilising people to provide food and goods for those in need.

† O Holy Healer! We pray for countries where poverty increases so much. Please, help us to overcome all these difficulties through solidarity and love.

For further thought

What can we do in our communities to help the poor and to promote equality?

Thursday 28 September
Reaping what others have sown

Read John 4:35–38

But I tell you, look around you, and see how the fields are ripe for harvesting. The reaper is already receiving wages and is gathering fruit for eternal life, so that sower and reaper may rejoice together … I sent you to reap that for which you did not labour.

(verses 35b–36, 38a)

Being missionaries in Geneva and working with Latin American immigrants, my husband and I were amazed to see the diversity in our small community. The parishioners, coming from different Christian denominations, including Roman Catholics, were from an average of sixteen countries. All these people were considered by us a harvest from other churches and pastors.

Worshipping in such an environment, in the French-speaking part of Switzerland, in a church building still called Evangelisch-Methodistische Kirche, built by Methodists from the German part of Switzerland, we formed a multicultural congregation. We worshipped in three languages with several accents and many mistakes. It was also a floating congregation since people appear and disappear constantly. The majority had no legal status to live and work in Switzerland and had to return to their home country. Others remained to wait to get permission. Many women worked as house cleaners and stayed in the family houses for a long time. We also had students of the French language coming from other countries for a brief time.

Back in Brazil, after twelve years, we got some good news from other pastors and Christian leaders now helping this community. Those who stayed there frequently sent us greetings and messages.

We celebrate the fruits of our missionary work. I believe we can say: 'I planted, Apollos watered, but God gave the growth. So neither the one who plants nor the one who waters is anything, but only God who gives the growth' (1 Corinthians 3:6–7).

Thanks be to God!

† Let us pray for all the missionaries in the world and churches that support missionaries. May God bless all the churches receiving displaced people!

For further thought

Have you ever experienced starting a work that was finished by someone else? How did you feel about this? If possible, make a list of missionary agencies in the world. What about sending them a letter?

Friday 29 September

Reaping what you sow

Read Galatians 6:7–10

So let us not grow weary in doing what is right, for we will reap at harvest time, if we do not give up. So then, whenever we have an opportunity, let us work for the good of all, and especially for those of the family of faith.

(verses 9–10)

The word in Portuguese for to sow is *cultivar*, to cultivate. It means to prepare land and grow crops on it. The particular connotation in it is that it describes the process and relationship between the sower and the soil. It is related to the way a sower touches the ground. Consequently, there must be an ethical dimension in here not always considered. A Brazilian song describes this relationship: 'To caress the earth, get to know the desire of the earth and forge in the wheat the miracle of bread.'[1]

The plain near the river is more suitable for herding cattle or growing wheat; the slopes, for vines or forestry. Each soil has its own characteristic and we need to know it to get a good agricultural result. The destruction of Amazon forest is interfering in the climate not only in Brazil but also in the world. It seems we are violating its natural 'desire' to be an earth lung. We are so focused on producing more food that we are paying little attention to how we produce that food. The soil is not given to us just to be exploited, exhausted and devastated but to be caressed, cared for and respected.

Despite our promise to take care of our earth, sometimes we finish by violating the 'natural potential' of the earth and destroy it. 'So let us not grow weary in doing what is right, for we will reap at harvest time.'

† Dear God, help us to be resilient and never give up our Christian commitment towards our earth; strengthen our confidence in your mercy and grace while we insist on doing what is right.

For further thought

Are you a resilient person? Have you ever grown weary in doing what is right?

[1] 'Cio da Terra' by Chico Buarque and Milton Nascimento (1977); author's own English translation.

Saturday 30 September

God gives a body to the seed

Read 1 Corinthians 15:35–44

What is sown is perishable, what is raised is imperishable. It is sown in dishonour, it is raised in glory. It is sown in weakness, it is raised in power. It is sown a physical body, it is raised a spiritual body.

(verses 42b–44)

Seeds can be stored, some for a long time, some for a shorter time, but it is necessary to sow them in order to make them sprout. In our Christian life we cannot just be a stored seed, protected and infertile, waiting for our final destiny or resurrection. Even when our physical body seems unproductive, disabled or old, the transformative power of resurrection and new life is kept intact in it!

Why does the text mention those bodies 'sown' in dishonour and weakness? What does that mean?

We can remember Jesus' dishonoured crucifixion and death; how his body was 'sown' without any glory. We can remember too our Christian martyrs in the past and nowadays!

There is a Latin American saying: 'They tried to bury us, they did not know we were seeds.' Those who have suffered immensely might help bear the fruits of justice later on. We can remember what Jesus said: 'Blessed are you when people revile you and persecute you and utter all kinds of evil against you falsely on my account' (Matthew 5:11).

During difficult times, such as in the early community of Christians, the metaphor of seeds holds particular emotional sway. The more Christians were, and still are, oppressed, the more they will just continue to spring back up again; they will come back stronger and larger than ever before.

Our spiritual power can be hidden during our earthly life. We can be persecuted and despised, but the eternal life is ready to sprout out and the fruits of our labour will remain!

† Dear God, help us not be afraid of persecution and even a death. We are witnesses of your love. Give us the power to be seeds of hope in this world!

For further thought

Read some martyrs' histories. What can you learn from them? Which one inspired you most?

Biblical library (5)

Narrative

Notes by **Ellie Hart**

Ellie is a Bible teacher, writer, artist and the author of *Postcards of Hope* (BRF, 2018). She is passionate about reading the Bible in community, about understanding it well and allowing it to change our hearts and lives. She is especially enthusiastic about helping people to read and reflect on narrative in scripture. After ten years in overseas missions, she now lives in Derby, England, with her husband Andrew, three children and a disobedient but loveable brown dog. Ellie has used the NRSVA and the NIVUK for these notes.

Sunday 1 October

To the ends of the earth

Read Acts 1:1–11

They asked him, 'Lord, is this the time when you will restore the kingdom to Israel?' He replied ' … you will receive power when the Holy Spirit has come upon you; and you will be my witnesses in Jerusalem, in all Judea and Samaria, and to the ends of the earth.'

(part of verses 6–8, NRSVA)

This week we're going to look at how to read biblical narrative well, starting here with this crucial hinge piece between the Gospel of Luke and the story of the newborn church in Acts. Our first task when reading biblical narrative is to ask 'Who?' and then 'Where?' In this scene we find the disciples, ordinary people who have ridden the extraordinary rollercoaster of life with Jesus, tasted the despair of his death and been blown away by his resurrection. And they are here, with the risen Jesus, in Jerusalem, the centre of the Jewish world. The next chapter of the story of God and his people is about to begin. 'Jesus is back,' they think to themselves, 'now it's time to restore Israel to glory!' For them that is obviously what happens next. But once again, Jesus surprises them, telling them instead that *they* will be his witnesses, not just here in Israel's home, to their own people, but also to the wayward cousins they hate and then on and on to the ends of the earth. This story was never just about Israel. And then, just when the disciples are utterly baffled Jesus drops the microphone and walks away.

† Lord, help me to cope with life's surprises, and to trust you deeply as you unfold your story in my life.

Monday 2 October

Stopped in his tracks

Read Acts 10:9–47

The voice spoke to him a second time, 'Do not call anything impure that God has made clean.' This happened three times.

(verses 15–16, NIVUK)

We start today with the words of Jesus still ringing in our ears: 'be my witnesses in Jerusalem, in all Judea and Samaria, and to the ends of the earth'. As we read, let's ask ourselves again about *people*, *places* and *plot* and see what they can tell us. 'Peter the Rock' is a much braver man than the one who trembled as he denied Jesus. He has seen many healed and thousands turn to Jesus. He has defied the powerful Sanhedrin and 'filled Jerusalem' with the good news. We find him now in Joppa, a coastal town some sixty kilometres north-west of Jerusalem. He has travelled out through Judea and is on the borders of Samaria. And it's his turn to be stopped in his tracks. Luke tells us that Peter is on the road when he feels the need to stop and pray – there's a barrier God needs to deal with before Peter can go any further. It's a barrier that needs to fall before the gospel can continue its journey too.

As he prays (and his stomach rumbles), Peter has a vision. And it's clear that it's not just about abandoning traditional food laws about unclean food, but about accepting *people*.

Cornelius' invitation takes Peter north, deep into Samaria, and onward on his adventure. Arriving in Caesarea, he steps out of the traditional laws that kept Jews from speaking to Gentiles, preaches the gospel to a large crowd and sees many of them saved. The unfolding of the gospel from Jerusalem to the ends of the earth is underway.

† Lord, make me a person of courage. Help me to become someone who will cross over boundaries and break down barriers to take the good news of salvation to the ends of the earth.

For further thought

Have you ever been stopped in your tracks by Jesus as Peter is here? What can we learn from how Peter responded?

Tuesday 3 October

God at work on the edges

Read Acts 11:1–30

'If God gave them the same gift he gave us who believed in the Lord Jesus Christ, who was I to think that I could stand in God's way?' When they heard this, they had no further objections and praised God.

(verses 17–18, NIVUK)

In today's reading we get to see two scenes from the story. The first is set back in the centre of the Jewish world, the second, 500 kilometres away in Antioch! Again, Luke is challenging us to think about where God is at work, in the centre and right out on the edges of the spreading kingdom. Reports are getting back to the church in Jerusalem about what happened in Caesarea – and they're not sure that they like what they're hearing!

I notice here that Peter is being a witness once again, this time to the concerned believers at the centre! He's telling them about what God has been doing way out on the edges among the Gentiles. They are cautious at first but when they hear the full story they come to the place where they can give praise to God. It's easy for us to underestimate what a massive turning point this is for them, what an upheaval of everything they've learned so far. But somehow they measure what's happening by its fruit and not by whether it fits inside their understanding of how God should behave.

Just as we see the home church open their hearts to the idea that God could accept Gentiles into the new kingdom, another shock arrives on their doorstep. News from Antioch, right out on the edge. A 'great number' of people have turned to Jesus there. Even with Jesus' warning that this gospel was on the move, the acceleration is taking them by surprise. But God is turning the kingdom inside out and this is just the beginning!

† Lord, help me to be someone who listens to stories of what you are doing and rejoices. May I be flexible when I need to bend and be strong when I need to stand.

For further thought

I'm amazed at how gracious this church is – listening and even rejoicing in what God is doing even though it blows their worldview apart. Inspiring!

Wednesday 4 October

The big story: bringing salvation to the earth

Read Acts 13:13–52

I have made you a light for the Gentiles, that you may bring salvation to the earth.

(verse 47b, NIVUK)

Are you getting the hang of the pattern: People? Places? Plot? Today I'm going to add in another question: how does this scene fit into the whole story? For us, that's the story of the gospel and its journey to the ends of the earth, and also the wider story of God's plan to bless the world through his people.

In Acts 13 we're with Paul in Pisidian Antioch, deep in modern-day Turkey, more than 800 kilometres away from where we started. We're a *long* way from Jerusalem! But you might remember Paul's description of himself in Philippians – the Hebrew of Hebrews. He's like Jerusalem on legs! God is taking the centre right out to the edges. In this scene, the first place Paul and Barnabas go is (still) to the Jews. So, Paul shows up in the local synagogue and magnificently does exactly what we should do when we read biblical narrative – he takes the story of Jesus and places it in the context of the whole history of Israel. He connects Jesus into the great stories of Moses the rescuer-prophet and David the glorious king and shows how Jesus is part of the same story and yet greater than both of them. And when the Jews reject him? He goes to the Gentiles. It might look like a break in the story, as though God were giving up and starting again. But Luke wants us to know that this gospel-for-the-Gentiles is part of the Israel story. Paul's words, taken from the prophet Isaiah, declare the truth: this was always meant to be the next chapter.

† Lord, help me to see how I fit into your 'big story' of bringing salvation to the earth.

For further thought

'Salvation to the earth' sounds so big. What would it look like where you are? In your street? In your family?

Thursday 5 October

Where have we seen this before?

Read Acts 15:1–29

[God] did not discriminate between us and them, for he purified their hearts by faith ... No! We believe it is through the grace of our Lord Jesus that we are saved, just as they are.

(verses 9, 11, NIVUK)

Today we are right back at where it all began. A lot of the action in the book of Acts is at the edges, but the centre hasn't lost its value – this is the place Paul comes to check out his doctrine. It seems that some people are teaching that male Gentile believers should be circumcised, that is, they should become Jews, in order to be saved and admitted to the family. In terms of our wider story, this is a stumbling block for the Gentiles, and therefore for the gospel. Paul, the Jew with the mission to the Gentiles, is concerned enough to travel all the way back here to speak with those whose opinion counts.

After the scene is set, some new characters pop up: the Pharisees. Today's new question is: where have we seen this (or them) before? If we leaf back through his Gospel, we see Luke has told us about the Pharisees already, the ones who grasp at a sense of self-importance through 'getting it right'; the ones who despise those who struggle, making their burdens heavier, but refuse to help. These are our first 'Pharisee Christians', but we know what to expect of them, and sure enough here they are, insisting on stricter rules for the Gentiles. The challenge I hear in this story is that, once again, God doesn't discriminate. To love is more important than to be right, to invite in is more important than to guard the gate, and to do the right thing more important than to be seen to do the right thing.

† Lord, help me to care more about following you than about my own importance. May my need to be right never be a barrier to the spreading of the good news.

For further thought

Are you shocked by the idea of 'Pharisee Christians'? Do you know some? What do you think Jesus would say to them today?

Friday 6 October

Bowing to pressure

Read Galatians 2:1–14

When Cephas came to Antioch, I opposed him to his face ... For before certain men came from James, he used to eat with the Gentiles. But when they arrived, he began to.... separate himself from the Gentiles because he was afraid.

(verses 11–12, NIVUK)

Today the spread of the gospel comes under pressure again. This time in a conflict between two of its loudest voices. Paul and Peter (Cephas) both love Jesus. They're both driven to take the gospel to the ends of the earth. And they've both had a revelation from God that the gospel is for Gentiles as well as for Jews. They've separated into their own lanes: Peter taking the good news to the Jews and Paul preaching to the Gentiles. But in Peter's world, the old traditions of religion, even though they were set aside by the church in Jerusalem, are still asserting themselves. Many voices are still insisting that, in order to follow Jesus, a Gentile has to become a Jew and it seems that Peter is beginning to bow under the pressure. Jewish believers are refusing to share a meal with their Gentile brothers and sisters, silently declaring them 'less than' or 'unclean', and Peter, in spite of God's direct revelation, is starting to shrink back from doing so himself.

Even after all he's experienced, Peter is still human. He's still prone to being swept about by fear and the desire to be accepted, even after Jesus' gentle grace in his threefold 'Do you love me?' and then in his rather pointed threefold instruction to accept the Gentiles as clean. As a result, Peter and Paul have a very public falling out. But in the end the gospel isn't hindered, even by Peter's weakness in this moment. Paul carries on being a witness for Jesus among the Gentiles, and the kingdom continues to grow.

† Lord, help me to walk in grace and love, even when the pressures of the world are strong. Let me not be controlled by fear but led by you.

For further thought

What part do you think this scene plays in the overall story of the journey of the good news? Do you think Paul handled the situation well?

Saturday 7 October

Looking back and looking forward

Read 2 Peter 3:1–16

Bear in mind that our Lord's patience means salvation, just as our dear brother Paul also wrote to you.

(verse 15, NIVUK)

There are times when, as on a long walk in the hills, it's good to stop, sit down and reflect back on where the Lord has brought you. It appears that this is what our writer is doing today, remembering, perhaps, Jesus' promise to Peter and the other disciples that they would be his witnesses at the centre and at the edges of the kingdom of God, and his commission to them to carry the gospel into the world. He looks back over the words of the prophets to Israel, over the life of Christ and the teaching of the apostles and sees that they are all part of the same story. A story that isn't finished yet. We see that Peter has made his peace with Paul, recognising that his letters, while sometimes difficult to understand, have themselves become scriptures. And then he turns and looks ahead to the certainty of Jesus' return and to a restored heaven and earth. And although he will not walk much further himself, he writes to the churches, and to us, with advice for the path ahead: pay attention to the scriptures, he says, being careful that no one twists them. Be patient and live well while you wait. The lost are still the priority. The church has never been on the fringes of the world. It started at the centre and moved out. Just as Peter and Paul wrote their lives into the great story of the gospel's journey to the ends of the earth, so we too get to take our place in that ongoing story.

† Lord, as I listen to the story of what you've done, and what you're still doing, may my heart always fill with praise. Show me every day how I can be part of that story.

For further thought

Place? People? Plot? Where have I seen this before? How does it fit into the big story? Keep asking these questions, may they bring biblical narrative alive!

All one in Christ

Notes by **Kristina Andréasson**

Kristina was ordained as a priest in the Church of Sweden in 2007, where she worked before moving to the Swedish Church in London in 2014. In 2019 she started serving the Church of England as Associate Vicar of St John's Wood Church in London. She truly believes that God is there for everyone, no matter who we are or where we're from. She reflects on how, and in what way, God is there for us, and how we are all united. Kristina has used the NRSVA for these notes.

Sunday 8 October

Blessings to all of us through God's creation

Read Genesis 1:26–28

God blessed them, and said to them, 'Be fruitful and multiply, and fill the earth and subdue it; and have dominion over the fish of the sea and over the birds of the air and over every living thing that moves upon the earth.'

(verse 28)

It was a day when you could feel God's grace. It was sudden warm sunshine, and blue sky in September, after days of rain and grey weather. The day had to be treasured! I love animals, so London Zoo felt like a great idea. On a weekday it was peaceful there, and the sunshine, together with the excitement of seeing the animals, made it feel like a complete break from everything else. Penguins always make me smile, the sloth is really charming, and the tiny otters surprised me with how very cute they were, with their little paws and adorable squeaky sound. People looked at each other smiling, while the animals held us fascinated with their own, sometimes peculiar, ways.

We easily talk about God's presence in nature, among birds and fish. But the dog, the cat, even a squeaky otter, are God's creation too, and just as holy. We have responsibility for God's creation, but God's blessing can also reach us through nature and animals around us.

A little otter makes a cute sound. Tiny little paws have the power to bring us people together. Tiny little paws can carry the traces of God's blessing on all of us.

† God of life, thank you for the world that you've given us. Help us day by day to see the blessings around us. Amen

Monday 9 October

Words from God to you, and me, and everyone

Read Psalm 139:13–16

I praise you, for I am fearfully and wonderfully made. Wonderful are your works; that I know very well.

(verse 14)

Shortly after pandemic restrictions had eased I went with two friends for a hike in Sweden. From the top of a cliff we watched the waves on a big lake going away to I don't know where, and we saw how the wind kept moving in the trees around. It all seemed to capture something about taking a new breath after a lot of pandemic restrictions. A new breath, but not being quite sure where things are heading. We came to speak about Psalm 139, how it is so beautiful. 'And to think', my friend said, 'that those words are meant for you, yourself.'

Later that year, I had a couple of busy weeks affected by the uncertainty about the pandemic. Constantly during this time, Psalm 139 kept reappearing. People wished for it to be read during different services, people referred to it, it came up as the psalm of the day when we safely gathered for Morning Prayer on Zoom. I thought, then, that I could write here about how the psalm always seems to fit, whether you are celebrating life, or going through struggles, or even when this life comes to an end.

But now, when I look back, something else becomes clear. The reappearing of the psalm feels like a message about God's constant presence, how we are somehow carried by God, when life is filled with waves out into the unknown. And I hear my friend's reminder to think about how the words are meant for you and me, ourselves. You are fearfully and wonderfully made, and God's presence is there for us, all of us.

† God of life, you have searched me and known me. Be close with your presence when waves go stormy out into the unknown. Let me know that even then your hand shall lead me. Amen

For further thought

Can you look back and see how God was close in difficult times in life? What does that say about God's presence right now?

Tuesday 10 October

The Samaritan woman and our true colours

Read John 4:1–14

Jesus said to her, 'Everyone who drinks of this water will be thirsty again, but those who drink of the water that I will give them will never be thirsty. The water that I will give will become in them a spring of water gushing up to eternal life.'

(verses 13–14)

If there should be a song for Jesus' meeting with the Samaritan woman, I think it should be 'True Colours' by Cyndi Lauper, as a message from Jesus to the woman, and as a message from God to us.

Their conversation is the longest conversation that Jesus has with anyone in the Bible. Yet, there has been a lot of focus on just a few verses, regarding men in her life. But the five 'husbands' that are mentioned could easily also be translated as 'five lords', and the Samaritan people worshipped five gods. But whatever we choose to think about that, the Samaritan woman could probably tell us about the experience of not being seen for everything that you are, being labelled or judged on the surface. And whoever we are, I think we can recognise that feeling: being labelled, or misinterpreted because of prejudices and assumptions, making us want to correct things, or show how we are so much more.

Jesus sits down, meets her for who she is. They talk about faith, and there are layers and layers in their conversation, making it deeper than the well itself. And when we, just like Jesus, try to really meet the Samaritan woman, I think like a fresh spring of water we are reminded about God in our lives. And it's the same with other people when we dare to venture past the surface. True colours can appear and God comes close. The God who sees us for who we really are is there, where our true colours are allowed to shine through.

† God of life, you embrace us wholly. Help us to make our true colours shine through, and to see them in people we meet, so we can be blessings for each other. Amen

For further thought

Have you ever felt God's presence in the meeting with another person? What was it that made that meeting so special?

Wednesday 11 October
God's love for all of us

Read Acts 17:24–28

Indeed he is not far from each one of us. For, 'In him we live and move and have our being.'

(verses 27–28)

Sometimes we are pushed to question words from the Bible. I read in the news about another brutal attack on the streets of London. When the news revealed details about the evil action, the innocence of the victim, the barbaric brutality, I was forced to question if God is always close to each one of us. Are there Godforsaken places or moments in this world? Where was God when that young woman never made it home? Is God with some but not with others?

We don't get an answer when evil makes us ask the painful question, 'Why?' But we do get to hear that God is with *each one of us*. God has created us all, and is with us all. The thought of God being everywhere, however, does not save us from hurt and pain. This world is not perfect, and it can for sure feel like God is far away sometimes. But in evil, heartbreaking moments, the words about God's presence make me see the crucified God with arms wide open. And when we cry out our 'Why?', we don't get an answer, but our cry is captured by the crucified God who also cries, 'Why have you forsaken me?' And in that cry, I sense a love that would never cause us any harm, and looks with sorrow on what is evil.

God is not far from each one of us, in the sense that God's love is never completely quenched. It is for us to search and hold on to that love, and spread it to one another, and show with love that we do not tolerate evil.

† God of life, help us to believe and trust in the power of your love. When the world is a scary and unfair place, help us conquer evil with love. Amen

For further thought

Has life ever made you question God's presence? Could it be down to us to make God's love more visible?

Thursday 12 October

God as all things to all people

Read 1 Corinthians 9:19–23

To the weak I became weak, so that I might win the weak. I have become all things to all people, so that I might by any means save some. I do it all for the sake of the gospel, so that I may share in its blessings.

(verses 22–23)

A school is connected to the church where I currently serve. I think the youngest are about 3–4 years old. One time, a little boy stood alone in the church hall, while all the others were already outside playing. He looked at me with a sad and worried look. I knelt down and asked what was up. He was too shy to talk, but he waved with his blue jacket. I realised he couldn't figure out how to put it on himself. I gently took his jacket and held it up carefully so as not to scare him. The second it was on, he quickly ran out to play.

I think it is easy to think that weakness, being sad or shy, is best comforted with strength. But when it really matters, when meeting someone who is weak or small, we become gentle and sometimes even almost mimic their sad expression to show compassion.

To the weak, Paul became weak. Could that also be saying something about God? We tend to talk about God as strong and almighty, but maybe God comforts in the same way we do?

The little boy with his jacket warmed my heart. And I felt how some things that were fragile within me received a healing touch from that very meeting.

What if God knows exactly how it is to be a little toddler who just started school and can't put his jacket on himself? To me, it becomes like a gospel, an image of God, that shows how God can truly be there for us all, also in times of weakness.

† God of life, thank you for speaking to us in different ways at different times. Rejoice with us when we are glad, cry with us until our tears have dried. Amen

For further thought

Does your image of God change depending on what's going on in your life? Could it be helpful to have many images of God?

Friday 13 October

All unique, but also one in Christ Jesus

Read Galatians 3:26–29

There is no longer Jew or Greek, there is no longer slave or free, there is no longer male and female; for all of you are one in Christ Jesus.

(verse 28)

For the dinner table in my home, I've collected different second-hand chairs and then painted them all in the same colours. So, they are all unique, but still look like they belong together.

It's an interesting balance to think of: our own unique identity and a feeling of belonging. I think we need both somehow. We are all one in Christ. We all belong. I love these words from Galatians. But in what way do we belong? My chairs got repainted. Do we all have to change who we are in order to belong, to be one in Christ?

The words from Galatians say nothing about the need to change. It says 'through faith'. A lot in this world is like my chairs – we might feel that we have to reshape or change in order to fit in and belong.

But God who embraces us wholly calls us for who we are, and when we simply believe and trust that, we belong. Rather than a door that may or may not be open for us, we are invited. It is an invitation, which promises unity whoever we are. I'm sure such a loving invitation affects and shapes us – into the one we truly are, rather than into something else.

We can look around us, knowing that we are all invited. And if I were to imagine a God's dinner table for us all, I imagine it would be with all sorts of chairs, so very different, but somehow all still seeming to fit and belong.

† God of life, remind us that every one of us is unique and loved for who they are. But when you invite us to your table, let it speak about one humanity. Amen

For further thought

Where or when do you most feel a sense of belonging? Can you connect it with your faith?

Saturday 14 October

Every tribe and nation together as one

Read Revelation 7:9–12

After this I looked, and there was a great multitude that no one could count, from every nation, from all tribes and peoples and languages, standing before the throne and before the Lamb, robed in white, with palm branches in their hands.

(verse 9)

The words are beautiful, especially if we let it be an image of the time that one day shall come. People from everywhere, talking all sorts of languages. They might all be robed in white, but they are not all the same, and that is the very beauty of it, I think.

I remember a couple of summer days in London shortly after some of the many pandemic restrictions had eased. There were quite a lot of people filling the city and the streets again. Some took their masks off, as it wasn't required any more. Not sure myself how to feel about the sudden freedom, it was still so lovely to see the smiles on people's faces again. Cautiously taking off my own mask where it felt safe to do so, I could smell the mix of scents you get when you're among people from everywhere. I remembered thinking that it had been such a long time since I'd felt that. I'm not sure about other times, but there and then it just made me happy. Outdoors at a pub, someone shouted, 'We're allowed to hug again, let's do group hug!' Hugging strangers suddenly felt like the best thing ever. I think of those summer days sometimes, when we didn't react or did what we normally would not have done, because of the joy and hope that filled the air. Differences didn't seem to matter, when people looked at each other with excitement and relief, when strangers felt connected. Did I get a tiny glimpse of the day that one day shall come? I do treasure those days as such.

† God of life, thank you for glimpses of your kingdom already here on earth. Help us treasure those moments and make them fruitful for the future of our earth and the people in our world. Amen

For further thought

When have you felt the beauty and joy in diversity? Was God close?

Approaching Leviticus

Notes by **Christopher Took**

Chris is an Anglican from an open evangelical tradition. Currently living near the top of a tower block in inner London, he has lived in the English Midlands, Durham Castle and Co Dublin. He runs a website for Irish election results, had some early success in the Sermon of the Year competition and chairs a residents' group on fire safety for his local council. Find more resources at his website, www.biball.org. Chris has used the NIV for these notes.

Sunday 15 October

Ritual and obedience: glimpsing God

Read Luke 2:21–35, 39

When the parents brought in the child Jesus to do for him what the custom of the Law required, Simeon took him in his arms and praised God.

(verses 27b–28)

In all honesty, I can't say I'm a creature of habit. While there's some freedom in not having set times for meals or laundry, I probably waste time making decisions about when to do these basics. Or worse, find the day is almost over with certain urgent and important things undone. Mary and Joseph had been brought up in a tradition of ritual and ceremony going back centuries. They knew what to do and when for many common tasks as well as for major life events. There was no question but that Jesus would be circumcised on the eighth day. That's what the law required. Later, Mary would have to be cleansed after childbirth, Jesus would need to be dedicated and a sacrifice offered. These laws might seem rigid (even controlling) but they encouraged a habit of obedience, and lent an order to life and society.

There is, of course, a danger of ritual and habit becoming empty and meaningless. God never intended obedience to the law to be an end in itself, but a way of making relationship with him easier. Simeon's habit of obedience over many years allowed him to glimpse God's incredible purpose for this baby boy.

† Father, encourage me to develop habits that will help me to know you better and respond to your call on my life.

Monday 16 October

Making us holy to serve

Read Leviticus 4:1–35

In this way the priest will make atonement for them for the sin they have committed, and they will be forgiven.

(verse 35b)

Today's passage is a challenging one, not least for vegetarians or those who faint at the sight of blood! What are we to make of these rituals which haven't been practised even in Judaism since the destruction of the temple in AD 70? Note that all this ceremony was required for *unintentional* transgressions. Because God is holy, all those who seek to serve him must also be counted as holy.

Sin is sin, whether accidental or deliberate, regardless of whether it arises from what we do or through what we *don't* do. Sin separates us from God. It has to be dealt with; ultimately, we need to be forgiven. From our reading we would be right to conclude sin is a messy business with serious consequences. Putting it right is complicated: it involves a distasteful and unpleasant process, requiring an intermediary to act on our behalf; the substitution of an innocent in our place, and the shedding of blood in sacrifice.

The writer to the Hebrews draws several parallels between Leviticus 4 and what Jesus did on the cross. We are reminded Jesus is both priest *and* sacrifice (Hebrews 10:12). He offered himself as the perfect sacrifice and shed his blood on the cross for us. The blood of Jesus accomplishes once and for all what the blood of goats and bulls tried repeatedly to do.

Where today's passage ends with the reassuring promise to God's people that 'they will be forgiven', Hebrews 9:13 reminds us wonderfully that the shedding of Jesus' blood is also 'so that we may serve the living God'.

† Thank you, Lord, that through your blood shed on the cross, I can be forgiven and made holy in order to serve you, the living God.

For further thought

How is the living God calling you to serve him? What might be getting in the way of serving him wholeheartedly?

Tuesday 17 October

What's the point?

Read Leviticus 9:1–24

Fire came out from the presence of the Lord and consumed the burnt offering and the fat portions on the altar. And when all the people saw it, they shouted for joy and fell face down.

(verse 24)

After a week for their ordination, Aaron and his sons emerged on the eighth day – Sunday for us, the day after the Jewish Sabbath. Was this a foreshadowing of the shift to the first day of the week for Christian worship in commemoration of Jesus' resurrection? This is just one of many questions this chapter raises.

Nowhere else in the Bible is a bull-calf required for sacrifice. Often this word occurs referring to the idolatrous golden calf of Exodus 32. Is this to remind Aaron of his sin? Could the ram allude to the sacrifice God provided for Abraham in place of his son Isaac in Genesis 22? The detail provided for carrying out animal sacrifices can only underline how tedious, repetitive and unpleasant they were. The text raises the questions: was it worth the effort? What's the point? The answer comes in the last verse when God's presence erupts in fire, and the people shout for joy and fall prostrate in worship. Yes, it was worth the effort!

Aaron begins his priestly ministry by offering a sacrifice for his own sin. Only then is he able to offer a sacrifice on behalf of the people. Whatever ministry God has called you to, it has to start with your own relationship with God. Daily, or more frequently, seeking forgiveness for our failings may be tedious, repetitive and unpleasant for us. However, once our sin is forgiven and forgotten, we are freed to experience fully God's presence with us and his love for us, empowering us to serve. That's the point!

† Lord, help me to seek and accept your forgiveness for myself, so I am free to live my life by serving you and others.

For further thought

Do we take for granted what Jesus did on the cross? Think about the lengths to which God has gone to forgive and save you!

Wednesday 18 October

Cleanliness next to godliness?

Read Leviticus 13:1–45

The priest is to examine them, and if the sores have turned white, the priest shall pronounce the affected person clean; then they will be clean.

(verse 17)

As I write, the world is waiting to see how serious the Omicron variant of Covid-19 is going to be. This is probably the first time in generations when everyone reading Leviticus 13 shares a common idea of the consequences of self-isolation and quarantine. Modern concepts of medical treatments and pharmaceuticals didn't exist for the Israelites, although we might have done well to follow the laws on ritual cleanliness in the centuries before hygiene was rediscovered by people like Mary Seacole and Joseph Lister.

Our bodies matter to God, so they should matter to us. Our inclusion in God's people and our living for the kingdom isn't something that happens when we die, but when we are made clean through what Jesus accomplished on the cross. As well as investing in a right spirit, we need to do what we can to care for our bodies.

As someone who suffers with chronic illness, I know that good physical and mental health aren't guaranteed. Sickness and disability don't exclude us from the kingdom; rather we need to make every effort to include those who suffer more than we do. It's a tragedy when exclusion comes not from God but from those who should be behaving like brothers and sisters.

Hebrews 9:13–14 reminds us that if the blood of animal sacrifice could lead to outward cleanliness, how much more the blood of Jesus makes us clean before God! There may be good public health reasons why sometimes self-isolation and quarantine are necessary, but we can be confident nothing will separate us from the love of God in Jesus (Romans 8:37–39).

† Lord Jesus, may I have the strength to welcome all those whom you welcome into your kingdom; may I be an example of how your love is with your children for ever.

For further thought

How can you live authentically despite obstacles and challenges? How can you witness to God's love and forgiveness in the face of sickness and suffering?

Thursday 19 October

Atonement: our sins lifted and carried off

Read Leviticus 16:1–34

The goat will carry on itself all their sins to a remote place; and the man shall release it in the wilderness.

(verse 22)

One of the basic meanings of the Hebrew verb *nasa'* is 'lift' or 'carry off'. The same word is then used in the sense of 'forgive'. In today's reading we have a vivid image of the scapegoat 'carrying off' the sins of Israel to a remote place, and verse 22 contains a neat pun in the Hebrew with 'carry off' also suggesting 'forgive'.

How remote a place? The psalmist declares, 'as far as the east is from the west, so far has he removed our transgressions from us'. The preceding verse reminds us, 'so great is his love for those who fear him' (Psalm 103:11–12).

The context of our sin always ends up as the greatness of God's love. In verse 16, perhaps God is revealing his disappointment and frustration with his people: '*whatever* their sins have been'. Their sin is a given – there's no point in thinking otherwise or mentioning just a few major transgressions. But God's response to our sin is never 'whatever'! A serious problem requires a serious response.

It's God's great love that makes our sin so terrible and unacceptable. But it's God's great love that provides a remedy for that sin and makes us acceptable to God – a holy people set apart for him.

From a Christian perspective, Isaiah 53:4 speaks of Jesus: 'Surely he took up (*nasa'*) our pain and bore our suffering.' What the scapegoats did every year at the Day of Atonement, Jesus has done once and for all. He has lifted our sin from us and carried it far away for ever.

† Saviour of the world, thank you for taking up my sin and carrying it far away; help me to live in the knowledge of your love and serve in the freedom forgiveness brings.

For further thought

Psalm 103 is a song of praise about forgiveness and the blessings forgiveness brings. What does this psalm say about God's love for you?

Friday 20 October

Living distinctly and radically

Read Leviticus 25:1–17

Do not take advantage of each other, but fear your God. I am the Lord *your God.*

(verse 17)

Verse 17 is a version of the 'golden rule' from the Sermon on the Mount when Jesus said, 'in everything, do to others what you would have them do to you, for this sums up the Law and the Prophets' (Matthew 7:12).

In the Hebrew, 'fear your God', 'your' is singular, but in 'I am the Lord your God', 'your' is plural. The force of this is each of us is accountable through our individual relationship with God to the whole community that is the people of God.

We might feel proclaiming Sabbath and jubilee years is beyond any power we have! However, we should note the pattern for Sabbath years follows the pattern for the week in the Ten Commandments (Exodus 20:8–11). The Sabbath or day of rest was made for our benefit (Mark 2:27), and a pattern of six days' work and one day's rest is good for our physical and mental health. But there's another reason we're commanded to keep it: it's about being holy, a distinct people set aside *by* God, *for* God.

The notion of resting every seventh and fiftieth year may seem wildly unrealistic because of modern career patterns or the practicality of daily survival. But even if that exact pattern of radical living is beyond us, we're still called to live differently from those around us. The most important consideration is we don't take advantage of others – often difficult when what we consume may involve unknown people in distant places. We still have the responsibility to do the best we can for our planet and all its inhabitants.

† Creator God, show me how to live in a way that is distinct and radical; may I be an example of your loving care for both people and planet.

For further thought

What might it mean to be accountable to the people of God? What responsibility do we have to the whole of God's creation?

Saturday 21 October

Love not law

Read Leviticus 27:1–34

The Lord *said to Moses, 'Speak to the Israelites and say to them: "If anyone makes a special vow ..."'*

(verses 1–2a)

Special vows are always voluntary in the Bible. While they are acceptable, they aren't exactly encouraged. The danger of a vow made rashly is illustrated in the story of Jephthah and his daughter (Judges 11). There is sound advice in Ecclesiastes 5:5 : 'It is better not to make a vow than to make one and not fulfil it.'

In Leviticus 27 we have a pattern of dedication followed by redemption. If someone wants to recall a person, an animal or property offered by vow, there are means of *redemption* (in other words, 'buying back'). Our experience is the reverse. God has redeemed us first – bought us back through the blood of Jesus on the cross. Our dedication to God flows from this. While there are situations where vows are useful – think of marriage, baptism, ordination – even better is where we respond out of our love for God. Weak and inadequate though our efforts may be, it's that authentic response that God delights in and that all the Law (and the Prophets) aimed to produce.

If we think back to Simeon (see p. 290), we can see how love and relationship grew alongside dedication and obedience. It was through Mary and Joseph doing 'what the custom of the law required' that God's vow was fulfilled: Simeon had waited patiently to see the Lord's Messiah – the person through whom God would redeem his people once and for all.

It's always *relationship* that's important, not *rules*. Love, not law.

† Holy God, help me to understand the real intention of your laws so I can develop habits of obedience and holiness; help me deepen my relationship with you, to serve you in love and freedom.

For further thought

While Leviticus contains *rules* for God's people to be holy, Psalm 51:16 reminds us these are there to help develop our personal *relationship* with God.

Readings in Esther

Notes by **Eve Parker**

Eve is a Research Associate at Durham University, focusing on inclusion and diversity in theological education. She is the author of *Theologising with the 'Sacred' Prostitutes of South India* (Brill, 2021). She has previously worked for the Council for World Mission and the United Reformed Church, and is passionate about intercultural ministries and liberationist theologies. She is married to James, and they have three children. Eve has used the NRVSA for these notes.

Sunday 22 October

A woman resists

Read Esther 1:1–22

For this deed of the queen will be made known to all women, causing them to look with contempt on their husbands, since they will say, 'King Ahasuerus commanded Queen Vashti to be brought before him, and she did not come.'

(verse 17)

Here in the book of Esther we read of a tale of domestic violence against a queen. King Ahasuerus, a powerful ruler, is showing off his wealth and drinking copious amounts of alcohol (1:7). Under the influence, he commands seven of his eunuchs to bring his wife, Queen Vashti, before him 'wearing the royal crown, in order to show the people and the officials her beauty' (1:11). He objectifies her and expects her to obey his command, yet she refuses – she is a woman, not an object to be used, judged and violated. The king, like many violent men who expect to be obeyed by their wife, gets enraged in the face of resistance against his misogyny. He consults other men, who are scared about what the queen's resistance will mean for other women who may be inspired to resist their oppressive husbands. Queen Vashti became conscious of her oppression, the male elites feared other women would also become conscious and say 'no' to violence against women.

Violence against women is apparent in all societies throughout the world – such violence includes 'honour' killings, rape, infanticide, enforced prostitution and domestic violence, which affects one in four women in the UK in their lifetime.

† God of resistance,
We have heard the cries of beaten and bruised wives,
We say 'no' to violence against women,
Hear our prayer. Amen

Monday 23 October

A woman replaced

Read Esther 2:1–23

Let the king appoint commissioners in all the provinces of his kingdom to gather all the beautiful young virgins to the harem in the citadel of Susa under custody of Hegai, the king's eunuch, who is in charge of the women; let their cosmetic treatments be given them.

(verse 3)

Queen Vashti is punished and silenced for resisting the patriarchal system that sought to objectify her and, in order to prevent further resistance, the servants of the king seek to 'put women in their place', by gathering women 'virgins' to display before the king. The women in this text are for the most part, with the exception of Esther, without name and voice, they are reduced to objects of beauty to be watched under the patriarchal gaze. The intention here is to restore patriarchal order and make it clear that women exist to serve men as sexual objects that are replaceable. The story is one of male violence, male fantasy and the commodification of women, where the men who hold the power reduce women to sexual parts, items of 'beauty' and instruments of lust, and in the process, women are separated from their personhood and identity. The commodification of women is a form of violence against women that is apparent today in the form of gender inequality, the devaluation of women's bodies, the portrayal of women as passive, domesticated objects, and the very fact that women do not feel safe to walk down a street without the threat of being violated, harassed or abused. It is in a world of such fear that King Ahasuerus sets his sights on Esther – who struggles in a context that oppresses her not only for her gender but also her ethnicity, as a Jewish woman in hiding.

† God of love, when you made Eve, Hagar, Ruth, Vashti, Esther, Rahab and all other women, you numbered the hairs on their heads, you created them whole, in personhood, and in love. Amen

For further thought

What actions can we take in our communities to prevent violence against women?

Tuesday 24 October

The threat of annihilation

Read Esther 3:1–15

Letters were sent by couriers to all the king's provinces, giving orders to destroy, to kill, and to annihilate all Jews, young and old, women and children, in one day, the thirteenth day of the twelfth month, which is the month of Adar, and to plunder their goods.

(verse 13)

Esther has won the king's favour, but she is not safe and nor are her people. Her uncle Mordecai has refused to bow to Haman, who is one of the king's most powerful men. In doing so, Mordecai has enraged Haman, who decides to punish all of the Jewish people. In this narrative, we witness the dangers of aggressive masculinity intertwined with xenophobia. Haman has been publicly humiliated by Mordecai, after Mordecai has refused to submit to his demands. Haman seeks to punish those who have offended and humiliated him. When the powerful elite feel that their authority is under threat, they often respond with violence in order to instil fear in the people so that they do not rebel. They seek to prevent solidarity in resistance and so they create environments of separation, where people are terrorised, isolated and live in a state of discomfort and fear. Such systems of power are apparent throughout the world today in contexts where people are persecuted for their ethnicity, sexuality, gender, caste and class. The question is, what role do we play in such contexts – are we the persecuted, are we the oppressors, or are we indifferent to threat of violence against the *other*?

† We confess our failures to speak out against injustice. We confess those times when, as individuals and as churches, we have witnessed the fracturing of humanity along ethnic grounds and yet have remained silent. Amen

For further thought

Why is leadership like that of King Ahasuerus and Haman dangerous?

Wednesday 25 October

For such a time as this

Read Esther 4:1–17

For if you keep silence at such a time as this, relief and deliverance will rise for the Jews from another quarter, but you and your father's family will perish. Who knows? Perhaps you have come to royal dignity for just such a time as this.

(verse 14)

The passage highlights the situation of the Jews who were in exile in Persia. They were vulnerable and persecuted to the extent that Esther had been forced to hide her ethnicity. Her uncle Mordecai had publicly lamented upon finding out about an edict to murder the Jewish people and, having just heard that the lives of her people were in danger, Esther must now decide what actions she must take.

Esther is in an exceptionally difficult position. She has the privilege of enjoying the king's hospitality and is in a temporary state of safety. However, her people are at risk and she knows that she could also be put to death if the king discovers her identity. Mordecai responds to her fears by highlighting the injustice of keeping silence during times of suffering and suggests that this is her opportunity to show real leadership for her people at 'such a time as this'. Esther acknowledges the need to resist the oppressor, she gathers her people, and is willing to risk her life for them, stating, 'If I perish, I perish.'

Esther's bravery is immense, she has witnessed the struggles of the oppressed, she has the choice to stay silent, yet she chooses to risk her life for the Jewish people. This is a woman showing a model of leadership shaped by sacrificial love – where she takes the side of the marginalised and is willing to give up her own privileges and power to do so.

† Holy God, Creator, and Reconciler, send your Spirit at such a time as this, so that we may be true witnesses to the struggles of the oppressed. Amen

For further thought

If I remain silent when God's people suffer, who will rise up? If I close my eyes when God's people suffer, who will see the injustice?

Thursday 26 October

If I perish, I perish

Read Esther 5:1–6:14

As soon as the king saw Queen Esther standing in the court, she won his favour and he held out to her the golden sceptre that was in his hand. Then Esther approached and touched the top of the sceptre.

(verse 5:2)

In this text, we read of a tale of exile, diaspora, empowerment, assassination attempts, banquets and ethnic cleansings. Esther has come to recognise her responsibility to the Jewish people and align herself with her community so they may all find liberation. She could not remain silent and watch her people's persecution from the safety of the palace and so she takes action. She uses her beauty in order to get the king to do what she needs, to stop Haman from killing her people.

Esther displays immense bravery as she risks her own safety for that of the Jewish people. We learn from the book of Esther about how terrifying it can be for people who are forced to hide who they are because of their religion and ethnicity. It brings to mind the kind of bravery displayed by the Nobel Peace Prize winner Maria Ressa, a Filipino journalist willing to take great risks to speak truth to power in order to protect the freedom of expression in contexts where such freedoms are at risk.

Despite Esther's story being one of fear and hostility, it also gives us hope as we discover that the rulers on earth who deny people of their freedoms shall not reign eternal. Today around the world many people continue to be denied freedom of religion and expression, it takes bravery to stand up for such freedoms and the freedoms of others.

† Let us rejoice in those who have risked their safety for the freedom of others. Let those in exile, the refugees and asylum seekers, shine light on the injustices of the nations. Amen

For further thought

What are some of the ways in which personal freedoms are denied around the world?

Friday 27 October

Learning from Esther

Read Esther 7:1–8:17

In every province and in every city, wherever the king's command and his edict came, there was gladness and joy among the Jews, a festival and a holiday. Furthermore, many of the peoples of the country professed to be Jews, because the fear of the Jews had fallen upon them.

(verse 8:17)

King Ahasuerus has destroyed Haman at the will of Esther, who sought to prevent her people from being killed. She has also convinced the king to call for an end to an edict against all the Jewish people, so that they may no longer be persecuted. The text describes her uncle Mordecai's liberated social positioning, as he is now free to wear 'royal robes of blue and white, with a great golden crown and a mantle of fine linen and purple' (8:15). However, what we do not read about is Esther's liberation – is she free to wear what she wants and to walk about the city without the fear of being violated? Or has she freed her people at the expense of her own body, where she is trapped in a loveless marriage to a man who has objectified her, and knows what will happen when he tires of her?

One of the most important campaigns, which I hope more Christians around the world will join, is the World Council of Churches' 'Thursdays in Black'. The campaign is simple: wear black on Thursdays. In doing so, you make a statement that you are part of a global movement resisting attitudes and practices that permit violence against women. One of the greatest things about being part of the global ecumenical church is the knowledge that together we are stronger, and in solidarity amazing things can happen. We can all learn from Esther and take a stand against injustice and violence.

† O God, Esther did not name you, but in the acts of solidarity, in the resistance to oppression, in the calls to assemble, in the cries of lament, you were made known. Amen

For further thought

We learn from the book of Esther that, in order to change the world, we have to act as though it is possible for it to be radically changed.

Saturday 28 October

Let us not forget

Read Esther 9:1–10:3

Now the other Jews who were in the king's provinces also gathered to defend their lives, and gained relief from their enemies, and killed seventy-five thousand of those who hated them; but they laid no hands on the plunder.

(verse 16)

In the final chapter of the book of Esther, the story has gone from one of the struggle of a marginalised people, to one in which the oppressed people gain access to wealth and splendour and seek revenge and violence on their enemy. It is difficult to read this text and not be saddened that a story of resistance can end in the killing of thousands of people. Yet the reality is that fear and persecution often leads to violence from both the oppressed and the oppressor. However, the story ends calling for peace and security to all the Jews, with 'orders that these days of Purim should be observed at their appointed seasons'. In the Jewish faith, the celebration of Purim takes place in honour of Esther, who liberated the Jews during a period of immense struggle. Purim is a time of joy, celebration and remembering. During the festival of Purim, there are parades and people wear fancy dress, often dressing as characters from the story of Esther. There is also a feast, where alcohol is consumed. The Shabbat before Purim is called Shabbat *Zachor*, the shabbat of remembering. Remembering and witnessing are so vital in understanding our role and purpose as people of faith – if we are to prevent atrocities against communities and individuals we must remember all who have suffered throughout history and we must never be indifferent in the face of such suffering.

† Praise God, the unifier
Praise God in solidarity
Praise God for such a time as this
Praise God. Amen

For further thought

What actions of solidarity can we take to resist the emperors of our age who seek to impose unjust orders of oppression?

Healthy humility

1 Walk humbly with God

Notes by **Andy Heald**

Andy is a professional communications, marketing and fundraising consultant, and has led fruitful young adult and small group ministries. He is an active pilgrim exploring how to introduce a fatherless generation to their heavenly Father. In 2019 he sold his home in Sussex and, with his wife and three young daughters, began travelling Europe in a motorhome, to explore God's principles of faith, freedom and family and to live a different way. Andy has used the NRSVA for these notes.

Sunday 29 October

Here I am: let it be

Read Luke 1:26–38

'And now, you will conceive in your womb and bear a son, and you will name him Jesus.' … Then Mary said, 'Here am I, the servant of the Lord; let it be with me according to your word.'

(verses 31, 38a)

I don't know what is more astonishing about this event: Mary conceiving without a biological father, becoming the mother of God's Son, or the ease by which she accepts this life-changing news.

A few years ago, my wife and I, as a response to following Jesus, defined some family values and 'repentant humility' (putting God and others before ourselves) is one of them. Sometimes living it is straightforward, but more often I can only dream of having Mary's humility. The news she'd received could destroy her engagement to Joseph and her life. She knows that events are out of her control but is reassured by God's presence. Mary knows who she is in relation to God, his servant, so she responds by serving, putting him first with apparently peaceful conviction and contentment. Let it be.

Her astonishing response, giving permission, reveals a deep level of trust in God, understanding that his will and plans are good. I believe we can take comfort in this – because we too can trust him and his goodness. When we receive life-changing news, outside our control, we have it within us to humble ourselves before his will, trust him and simply let it be.

† Lord, help us know who we are in relation to you. Help us respond to you with humility, saying, 'Here I am, let it be.'

Monday 30 October

Hope in the Lord

Read Psalm 131

I do not occupy myself with things too great and too marvellous for me. But I have calmed and quieted my soul, like a weaned child with its mother.

(verses 1b–2a)

Do you feel the peace and hope that overflow from the psalmist? Attributed to King David, anointed by God, a 'man after his own heart' (1 Samuel 13:14), wealthy and powerful. Yet here he knows his place; that there are things beyond him, things he doesn't need to concern himself with, and so he writes from a place of contentment.

How often do we spend our time on things that are outside our control or remit, hoping (perhaps futilely) that we can deal with them? Frequently, the time and mental energy we devote to these cause us worry, fear and distress. David encourages us that we don't need to live like this; instead, we can recognise that there are things beyond our knowledge and control. Acceptance of this is humility and accompanying peace.

He demonstrates that we have a part to play in choosing this state of being. When I'm unsettled, dwelling on something that I can't do anything about, I often ask God to give me peace. But David states that he calmed himself, not that God did.

In Jewish tradition, the whole community celebrated when a child was weaned, able to feed itself, signifying a step in the child's maturity. By learning to place more trust in God than ourselves, we too can mature in our faith and reap the benefits.

Stepping away from things that don't concern us frees us to see God working there instead. Hope in ourselves is replaced by hope in the Lord – we can experience peace, contentment, and confidently expect what he has promised.

† Lord God, please teach us how not to occupy ourselves with things beyond us, but instead learn to quiet our souls and fill them with hope in you.

For further thought

How do you fill your time? Are there things you don't need to concern yourself with? What might happen if you let them go?

Tuesday 31 October

God's faithfulness

Read Psalm 146

Do not put your trust in princes, in mortals, in whom there is no help … Happy are those whose help is the God of Jacob, whose hope is in the Lord *their God … who keeps faith for ever.*

(verses 3, 5, 6b)

I was once challenged by these comments: 'What does one do when you no longer trust the police, politicians, the media, the experts, the science, the commentators, the reality. Seriously. Where does one turn?'

From birth to death, we have to live by trusting others; for food, water, clothing, shelter, identity and love. We have innate needs for nourishment, safety and belonging, often turning to people (including ourselves), places and material things to meet them. The trouble is, they will all let us down; crops fail, rivers run dry, buildings fall into ruin, and people 'return to the earth', their plans failing.

But God offers us all we need. He feeds, frees and delivers justice. He loves the righteous and is the champion for the oppressed, lonely and rejected. Knowing this, the psalmist shares his warnings and wisdom with us. People and their plans will pass away, there isn't any help there. Hope, help and happiness are to be found in the God of Jacob – who keeps faith for ever.

I think this reveals a deep-seated humility in the psalmist, his recognition of God's everlasting faithfulness to his people (himself included) leads to his trust in God surpassing all else, pouring out of him in lifelong praise. This song expresses that; it's a glorification of God, an anthem of worship for who God is and all that he does. The happiness of the writer is evident for all to see.

The psalmist's message is simple, powerful and joyful. Think of God more highly than all else and turn to him. He is faithful for ever.

† Thank you, Lord God, that you promise to provide for all our needs and that you keep your promises for ever. Please help us to be humble, knowing you and trusting you above all others.

For further thought

The Bible helps us know God and his promises. Read Isaiah 40, think about who God is and what that might mean to you.

Wednesday 1 November

God dwells with the humble

Read Isaiah 57:14–16

For thus says the high and lofty one who inhabits eternity, whose name is Holy: I dwell in the high and holy place, and also with those who are contrite and humble in spirit, to revive the spirit of the humble, and to revive the heart of the contrite.

(verse 15)

There are some days when God seems very far away from me. I don't want a relationship with a distant God, I want my heavenly Father to be close by. I want – need – to be in his presence, where I am known and loved.

I'm sad to say that in my late teens I pushed my parents away. Despite the love and care they gave me, I moved out to live as I thought best, choosing to do what I wanted. Both consciously and not, I said and did things that were hurtful and kept myself at a distance.

My relationship with God can be the same. When I think I know best, echoing Adam and Eve's sin, I think I'm god and, intentionally or not, I communicate to God that I don't need him or want him around.

While pushing God away isn't the only reason he might feel distant, he does have an encouraging message for us. He dwells with those who consider themselves less than him. As we've read this week, Jesus' mother, King David and a psalmist all know this, their stories make humility look astonishingly easy – when for me (and others perhaps) it's not.

Thankfully, both my parents and God are forgiving, and I've dwelt with them again. That's the power of God's mercy and Jesus' death on the cross, which removes the obstructions and makes the way. When I think about this, it humbles me and I can, as the apostle James says, 'draw near to God', where he will dwell with me again and revive my spirit.

† Father God, thank you that you want us, your children, to be in your presence. Help us make choices that humble ourselves before you, so you will dwell with us, and we will know you.

For further thought

Does God ever feel distant to you? Do you think you ever push God away? What does living humbly mean to you?

Thursday 2 November

Walk humbly

Read Micah 6:6–8

He has told you, O mortal, what is good; and what does the LORD require of you but to do justice, and to love kindness, and to walk humbly with your God?

(verse 8)

Do you ever ask yourself what it is God wants from you or how you can honour him? I do, frequently. In the years I've followed Jesus, I've sometimes found myself lost in what worship really is, or what it means when people say that God wants a relationship with me, or even how I can serve him. I struggle to know my place in relation to him.

I sympathise with Micah as he too tries to figure this out, wondering what kind of offering will please God, and I've concluded that we are over-complicating the issue. I think that the biggest revelation in God's requirement of us is that God wants to spend time with us; our place is to move around with him.

But to walk humbly means we must walk a certain way. My country's culture is so fast-paced that people are often busy, running around. God's requirement is that we slow to walking pace – 'the pace of grace' my friend calls it. We are to emulate his character of goodness; being just, kind and thinking less of ourselves than him and others. Like the first disciples that learned from Jesus by following him around, walking with him, we must walk in such a way that we follow his lead and not our own.

We must 'deny ourselves' (Luke 9:23), to follow God and walk humbly with him. And when we do, our place becomes clear; we serve him (John 12:26) and have the light of life (John 8:12).

† Jesus, help me recognise you as my God, and follow your lead wherever it is that you want to go, acting justly, being kind and knowing what is good.

For further thought

Go for a walk with God somewhere, either physically or in your mind, as you pray. See where he leads you.

Friday 3 November

'Words fail me!'

Read Job 42:1–6

I had heard of you by the hearing of the ear, but now my eye sees you; therefore I despise myself, and repent in dust and ashes.

(verses 5–6)

I find Job's story unsettling. In God's own words, Job is 'a blameless and upright man who fears God and turns away from evil' (Job 1:8b), so how is it that all the bad things happen to him? Our material comfort and well-being is separate from our right standing with God, 'bad things' are consequential to the fall of God's creation. Satan accuses God of blessing Job so he would fear and honour him, effectively 'removing' his free will. But God knows Job, stating that, even with blessings removed, Job would still choose rightly, thus proclaiming him righteous.

Initially, Job's understanding of God was based on what he had heard, not direct experience. This can cause a misunderstanding of God, and can, if unintentionally, direct us to think of him in our own terms, limiting our relationship.

Job's experience of God radically changes when he encounters him – as does ours. We stop framing God with our own measurements and are humbled in response to who God really is, a being we cannot fully comprehend. Yet the wonderful truth about being humbled before God is that we don't have to be. When Job meets his maker, God's revealed greatness and relationship to Job is awe-inspiring – no wonder he's lost for words! Words fail us because words don't exist that fully communicate who God is – but that's OK, because in our humility before him we don't need them. This humility removes the limits we place on God, freeing us. And, despite our failings, as he demonstrates to Job, we experience his sufficient grace (2 Corinthians 12:9).

† Thank you, Creator God, that your power is made perfect in our weakness. Help us encounter you to experience the freedom of humility in your presence and the sufficiency of your grace.

For further thought

Read Job's whole story. Can you relate to his understanding of God in the beginning and God's revelation of who he is at the end?

Saturday 4 November

The servant king

Read John 13:12–20

So if I, your Lord and Teacher, have washed your feet, you also ought to wash one another's feet. For I have set you an example, that you also should do as I have done to you.

(verses 14–15)

As we walk humbly with our God, and grow in our faith in him, we move beyond our own standards. Jesus shows us what humility really means. His disciples had watched him amaze great crowds, perform healings and other miracles, dwell with sinners and challenge the authorities. He had revealed truth to them, and they had come to their own conclusions that he is their Messiah, God's Son, their long-awaited King and Saviour.

For him to wash their dirty, stinking feet – a job for only the lowliest of servants – must have been shocking. Once again, he turns their world upside down. He reveals the nature of his kingship – servant-heartedness, placing his subjects before himself. What's more, he affirms their place as citizens of his kingdom, by commanding them to follow his example and adopt his character; to humbly serve one another.

They continue to walk with him to his crowning moment, at the cross, and watch him express the deepest act of humility the world has ever seen. He's falsely accused, judged unjustly, mocked, beaten, bruised and killed as he puts the lives of those he loves – us – before his own. He is the servant King.

By not thinking of ourselves more highly than we ought (Romans 12:3), and by laying our own lives down for him, we can place ourselves under his authority, obediently serving and pleasing him – a true act of worship (Romans 12:2). In our humility, we too can receive our royal inheritance and take our places as citizens of his kingdom.

† King Jesus, thank you that you humbled yourself and died for our sins. Help us to be like you, servant-heartedly loving others, sacrificially placing them before ourselves.

For further thought

Think of a dirty task that you don't like doing. Imagine how you would feel if a king offered to do it for you.

Healthy humility

2 'Let the same mind be in you'

Notes by **Stephen Willey**

Stephen is a Methodist minister who has been involved in mission to the economic world through industrial chaplaincies and work against human trafficking. Much of his ministry has been in areas of multiple deprivation. He is currently based at a city-centre church in Coventry, England, where he has encouraged the use of the arts to develop spirituality and address issues of mental health, inside and beyond the church, especially for people who are young or vulnerable. Stephen has used the NRSVA for these notes.

Sunday 5 November

'I must decrease'

Read John 3:28–31

The friend of the bridegroom, who stands and hears him, rejoices greatly at the bridegroom's voice. For this reason my joy has been fulfilled. He must increase, but I must decrease.

(verses 29b–30)

There was a moment during my daughter's degree ceremony when we applauded those graduating. Suddenly, to my surprise, those receiving degrees started applauding us, for our support. I looked towards my daughter and nodded my head, a resounding 'Yes' in my heart, as now her formal education was going beyond mine. She was going to do more study, whereas I had stopped at the point she was. My nod of assent was a bit of a surprise – I was proud of her and excited for her, but I also realised that this was something that changed my relationship to her. Now she was going beyond me – I was going to decrease in relation to her. She would increase – and I wanted to cheer!

I believe that John the Baptist is cheering at this moment in John's Gospel – he is rejoicing not for himself but for Christ, the Lamb of God who is going to increase as he decreases. John rejoices at this moment of recognition, his eyes not on himself, growing less, but directed towards the Christ who is going beyond him; his friend, Jesus, the Christ, who will forgive sins and bring salvation.

† Christ, Lamb of God, you bring joy to the world and you cheer our hearts. We rejoice in you!

Monday 6 November

Humble or exalted?

Read Luke 14:7–14

When your host comes, he may say to you, 'Friend, move up higher'; then you will be honoured in the presence of all who sit at the table with you. For all who exalt themselves will be humbled, and those who humble themselves will be exalted.

(verses 10b–11)

As chaplain to a large commercial organisation, somehow I'd managed to end up on the top table at a special dinner sitting alongside radio and TV stars – there was even a prince in the room! My job was to say grace before we began to eat. The IT technicians had decided to display, on a large screen, the order of the speeches. As the event progressed, they replaced the name of a previous speaker with the name of the next. When it was time to eat, my grace made me the last speaker for forty minutes, meaning my name was on the screen throughout the meal. I felt embarrassed and yet slightly pleased that my name was on the screen longer than the prince's!

By contrast, later, I was talking with a security guard who asked me what I did. I explained about chaplaincy and offering a listening presence, but he didn't appear to be listening, instead he proceeded to talk about his complicated life and relationships. After an hour I was tired out. Active listening can be hard work. I was surprised and honoured at his trust in me to share such things. Then he asked me again, 'So what do you do?'

Jesus alerts his listeners to the dangers of thinking of ourselves as greater than others and suggests that it is in our humility that we are blessed. There may be moments of surprise when we are put on the 'top table' but we should not attempt to be highly regarded by placing ourselves in places of honour.

† Generous God, you have given your love to the whole of humanity in Christ, forgive us for the times when we have desired earthly glory rather than the joy of serving you.

For further thought

Have I felt the seeming importance of being at the 'top table'? How might hidden places of service hold the fullness of the kingdom?

Tuesday 7 November

Don't be like the Pharisee

Read Luke 18:9–14

The Pharisee ... was praying thus, 'God, I thank you that I am not like other people ... like this tax-collector.' But the tax-collector ... was beating his breast and saying, 'God, be merciful to me, a sinner!' I tell you, this man went down to his home justified rather than the other.

(part of verses 11, 13–14a)

My Canadian niece, aged 9, was in the back of our car while on holiday with us in England. I had put some chocolate in a bag in the back of the car for later on, but, about forty-five minutes into our journey I smelled chocolate. Turning round I saw her lips covered in the stuff! 'I'm disappointed in you,' I said, before I could stop myself, not reflecting that she was on holiday and a long way from home, and her parents were in the car in front. My niece dissolved into tears and sobbed until we stopped and she got back into her parents' car.

Who has not stolen some chocolate or something sweet in their lives? I certainly have! My response, to my 9-year-old niece, although seemingly morally correct, was, on reflection, really self-righteous. I wonder now why I approached the situation with a condemning heart rather than a forgiving one.

The challenge of this parable is not for my niece but for me – the self-righteous one. Like the Pharisee in Jesus' story, I remained in my sins; my niece, distraught, sorry and in tears, knew remorse – she knew she had done something wrong and she sought a safe haven and acceptance in the company of her parents.

† Holy God, you offer your forgiveness even when we are undeserving. Help us to know you better so that we may not condemn others but treat them with the compassion we see in you.

For further thought

Do I trust that God will have a forgiving, generous heart towards me, and if so, how does that change my response to others?

Wednesday 8 November

Don't despise others

Read 1 Corinthians 11:17–22

When the time comes to eat, each of you goes ahead with your own supper, and one goes hungry and another becomes drunk. What! Do you not have homes to eat and drink in? Or do you show contempt for the church of God and humiliate those who have nothing?

(verses 21–22a)

The writer of 1 Corinthians wanted to avoid the humiliation of those who have nothing, in the celebration of communion. The solution he suggested was to make the meal more symbolic and to eat at home. This seems to be a long way from the early church where everyone held everything in common, shared according to need and broke bread at home (Acts 2:44–46). However, here, a serious concern about division is being caused by the distribution of food among the people as they share communion; the union of communion is in danger of being lost because of the unequal sharing of food.

The number of food banks, giving out donated food, has increased in the UK as demand for food has increased. This is true in Coventry, where many people struggle to provide enough food for their families. Here, mothers sometimes do without food in order to make sure their children are adequately fed. At our harvest festival we send food to the food bank. These gifts are distributed to local people, and our local food bank sends food parcels overseas. At the same time, food is often wasted in more affluent homes. Access to food is a cause of division and conflict in our world.

In 1 Corinthians, readers are invited to re-examine their relationship with the food they eat so they can share communion with their sisters and brothers. What is true for the people of Corinth is also true for the people of Coventry and the wider world.

† May our communion truly be communion with our brothers and sisters throughout the world. May we learn to share our bread as you shared your body for us on the cross.

For further thought

Does our communion with one another relate to the degree to which all are fed?

Thursday 9 November
A servant leader

Read Luke 22:24–27

[Jesus] said to them, 'The kings of the Gentiles lord it over them; and those in authority over them are called benefactors. But not so with you; rather the greatest among you must become like the youngest, and the leader like one who serves.

(verses 24b–26)

I was having a pastoral conversation in the home of a very wealthy and widely respected elderly couple, looking out at the wonderful view of their garden and the hills beyond. When I was handed a cake tin, I took a piece of parkin (a kind of cake) not realising it was covered in green mould! I politely ate the cake and decided that, if offered the same cake tin in the future, I would politely say no.

This experience contrasts with the experience of the welcome I have often received at the homes of people who have very little but share what they have with great generosity. I think of the single parent living in a small basement flat with her two teenage daughters. She insisted I ate fresh rice and curry with them before we started to talk about their recent bereavement.

Jesus challenges me, in this story from Luke's Gospel, to think again about generosity and greatness. It is hard not to be impressed by the comfortable homes and status of the wealthy, but Jesus is clear with his disciples that it is not affluence or social standing that make a person truly great. No, it is their humility, their vulnerability and their willingness to serve. Jesus brings this generosity of spirit to the table at the Last Supper when he generously offers his life as food for the disciples. Despite his teaching, it is still hard for them to understand his greatness as he serves them and washes their feet.

† Lord, may I always be ready to share what I have with those who are around me. May my welcome, my generosity, be renewed by your love each day.

For further thought

How can my generosity be relevant and new each day, so all may know your blessing through my kindness?

Friday 10 November

Who do you think you are?

Read Romans 14:1–6

Those who observe the day, observe it in honour of the Lord. Also those who eat, eat in honour of the Lord, since they give thanks to God; while those who abstain, abstain in honour of the Lord and give thanks to God.

(verse 6)

My Zimbabwean friend came to England and started to compliment larger people on their weight – 'You look so rounded and healthy,' she would say. She soon discovered that on this matter UK culture contrasts with Zimbabwean culture. In the UK, people may spend thousands of pounds a year to look thinner (a major problem for some who suffer from eating disorders, which can lead to death). Her compliment, in the UK, might be felt as an insult! My friend soon stopped making comments about people's weight.

The writer to the Romans understands the importance of changing how we behave in relation to the situation we find ourselves in. We live in a world where it is not always clear what it is best to do, how best to serve God. A compliment here may be an insult elsewhere, and it is not always obvious why or when. Nevertheless, as the letter to the Romans points out, it is still tempting to judge others who are not doing as we are. We are encouraged to be discerning! If what I am doing is causing problems for others then I should consider stopping it and trying another approach, but also, more importantly, we should not assume that the behaviour of others, which is directed towards God's honour, is any less than our own behaviour, even when they differ.

† Dear God, as your followers we often live differently from one another. As we come to understand our mission in relation to you better, keep us close to your heart of love and one another.

For further thought

Can I honour God without judging those around me who do things differently? When should I challenge another person's behaviour?

Saturday 11 November

Turning the world upside down

Read Luke 1:45–55

And Mary said, 'My soul magnifies the Lord, and my spirit rejoices in God my Saviour, for he has looked with favour on the lowliness of his servant. Surely, from now on all generations will call me blessed; for the Mighty One has done great things for me.'

(verses 46–49a)

Mary's song reflects her own situation. Mary (who would have thought it?) becomes the one who is lifted up while others, proud and powerful, fall. Her prophetic song comes true, as the young woman, Mary, is today honoured much more than any of the powerful of her day. From those of her time, it was only her son, Jesus, humble and crowned with thorns, who became revered more highly.

Young women can have a hard time, which Mary knows all too well. 'Georgia' and 'Nadia', whom I came to know through my work, told me stories of their oppression and domination by men who manipulated their lives for their own ends. Having lived in cultures which seemed to say that it was OK to treat a woman in such a way, both found, in the Gospels, new hope and a new determination to resist the pressures placed upon them. Their lives were turned upside down as a result.

God's action in Mary, God's words in Mary's mouth, reveal that domination is never something God desires! In Mary's time and in our own time the humblest young women can reveal that, while there is oppression in the world, there is no better place to look for humility, new hope and new life than the woman who rises from the ashes of oppression and domination.

† Lord, you pay attention to marginalised, poor and seemingly insignificant people. Grant that we may see with your eyes, discovering in our hearts the love you feel for each one.

For further thought

Who do I know who is facing oppression and domination? What words can I use which might offer encouragement and help turn things around?

Human fragilities and follies

Notes by **Carla Grosch-Miller**

Carla is a practical theologian with specialisms in trauma and in sexuality, and a poet. Her books include *Trauma and Pastoral Care: A ministry handbook* (Canterbury, 2021) and *Lifelines: Wrestling the Word, gathering up grace* (Canterbury, 2020). She lives in Northumberland, England, where she enjoys walking and sea swimming. She is very human and has many fragilities and follies! Carla has used the NRSV for these notes.

Sunday 12 November

Grey-tinted glasses

Read Mark 8:14–21

They said to one another, 'It is because we have no bread.'

(verse 16)

That's a bald lie. They did have bread; they had one loaf. Yes, they had forgotten to bring more, but they did not have 'no bread'.

Scarcity thinking. We all do it. If we are lucky, our children hang on the open refrigerator door and say, 'There is nothing to eat in here!' when that is a patent falsehood. We see the world through grey-tinted glasses, counting up what we don't have, exaggerating our need.

Jesus says, 'Beware the yeast of the Pharisees and the yeast of Herod.' The yeast is the seed of always wanting more: more power, more things, more status, even more righteousness. That yeast drives Western economies – cultivating longing, leaving us hungry and wanting, no matter how much we have.

Which begs the question: what is enough? More to the point, am I enough? The good news is that the answer to the latter question is 'Yes'. We are enough. As slow to understand as we are, we are more than enough. We are beloved. There is an abundance at our fingertips – an abundance of love, of life, of being. Take off the grey glasses. See baskets filled with bread broken, remnants of sharing.

† Let me know that, by your grace, I am enough. Meet my deep hunger with the bread of life.

Monday 13 November

Fear can make us stupid

Read Exodus 32:1–6, 15–24

So I said to them, 'Whoever has gold, take it off'; so they gave it to me, and I threw it into the fire, and out came this calf!

(verse 24)

You threw it into the fire and out came this calf? Another less-than-half-truth.

Aaron demonstrates two human follies here: he doesn't own up to his own agency in crafting the calf by hand, and he appears to have bowed quickly to the crowd's pressure to provide the darn thing in the first place! In fact, he didn't just make it, he built an altar before it and proclaimed a festival day to honour it. He was all in.

In my study of trauma I learned that we are literally made for each other. Our nervous systems read those of the people around us, asking 'Am I safe? Do I belong?' We co-regulate each other's emotions. My anxiety may well kick-start yours; my calmness is also infectious. That is why leaders can offer the best of themselves when they take care of themselves and are able to draw on needed resources in times of pressure.

The people were anxious. Their leader was gone too long. They fell back on what they knew from others: graven images of gods. Aaron being sucked into that was not surprising. It's a human thing.

When strong emotions overcome us – anxiety, fear, anger, hatred – we lose access to our thinking brains. We flip our lids and do or say dumb things, things that can be hurtful.

What could Aaron have done differently? He could have taken a deep breath or three, calmed himself, and reminded himself and the people that although Moses was late in returning, God remained present and faithful. No golden calf was necessary. Just simple trust.

† When I fall prey to my worst fears, call me back to the breath that is the gift of life. Breathe in and through me so that I may walk forward in faith and hope.

For further thought

What actions of yours are driven by anxiety? What actions of your church or community are? How can you inject calm into situations?

Tuesday 14 November

From the donkey's mouth

Read Numbers 22:21–35

Then the Lord *opened the mouth of the donkey, and it said to Balaam, 'What have I done to you, that you have struck me these three times?'*

(verse 28)

Who doesn't love a talking animal? I grew up in 1960s' America with television's Mr Ed. I still gravitate to talking animals: dogs who sing on adverts, Pluto 'addressing the internets' on YouTube.

The prophet Balaam, though, did not love his donkey's vocalisation. This little folk story is a weird and contradicting insertion into a general narrative in which Balaam is doing exactly as God asked. In it, Balaam's folly is his refusal to accept what is, and his insistence on shooting (beating) the messenger.

How often – when things are not going as we expect or desire – do we refuse to acknowledge that our best-laid plans are rubbish? How quickly do we lambast the critic, shout 'fake news' and generally ignore that we are on the wrong track or have the wrong end of the stick?

Who is the real donkey when we do that? Brazen (bray-zen?) blindness, indignation, rage ... all to no good effect. In the story, God opens Balaam's eyes so that he can see what is really happening.

What is, is. Wanting it to be some other way can't make it so. Stating a lie as if it is fact serves no one, especially not God. When a donkey talks back, think of it as a gift horse delivering a reality check.

† When things are not as I wish, desire or expect, open my ears to those who would speak the truth and my eyes to the reality before me. Help me to do the right thing.

For further thought

Where are you bumping uncomfortably against something you do not accept? Is it time to take down your guard and think again?

Wednesday 15 November

There is only us

Read Judges 12:4–6

They said to him, 'Then say Shibboleth,' and he said 'Sibboleth,' for he could not pronounce it right. Then they seized him and killed him at the fords of the Jordan. Forty-two thousand of the Ephraimites fell at that time.

(verse 6)

War, enmity, discrimination, exploitation … them versus us. These are great follies in human life. At their root is a failure to recognise and respect the full humanity of each person – to see them as made in the image of God with the right to life and dignity, to see them as us.

This story begins with wounded pride: the Ephraimites were offended that Jephthah had not made an alliance with them to fight the Ammonites. It became a declaration of war. It did not end well for them.

Margaret Silf shares the story of a rabbi who asked how we can tell when night has ended and day has dawned.[1] The students offered different answers: it is when you can tell that the animal in the distance is a sheep, not a dog; or that the fruit tree at the bottom of the garden is a fig, not a peach. To each answer offered, the rabbi shook his head, 'No'. Finally, after they clamoured for the true answer, the old rabbi, eyes gazing off into the distance, said that we will know that night has ended and day has dawned when each woman and each man can look into the face of a stranger and there see the face of a sister and the face of a brother.

There is no them. There is only us.

† When my fear turns to anger or hatred, call me back to the truth. May my words and my actions, my choices and my intentions be part of the dawn of a new day.

For further thought

Who do you think of as your enemy? What is that about? Imagine them as someone's son or daughter, someone worthy of love.

[1] Margaret Silf, *One Hundred Wisdom Stories from Around the World* (Oxford: Lion Publishing, 2003), p. 86.

Thursday 16 November

Hope in times of catastrophe

Read Ezekiel 37:1–14

Then he said to me, 'Mortal, these bones are the whole house of Israel. They say, "Our bones are dried up, and our hope is lost; we are cut off completely."'

(verse 11)

I think of hopelessness not as a human fragility but as a human phenomenon best approached tenderly. Terrible things happen in people's lives, things that dry out bones and pull the rug from beneath us. Things that make hope itself seem a folly.

I can't respond to hopelessness with cheery commands or facile reassurance. I know how bad it can get and how despair becomes an overcoat that seems necessary given the weather.

The prophets knew that when the hard times come, when people are dried up and cut off, the word to be spoken is one of comfort. One that acknowledged how unfair things really are. 'Comfort, O comfort, my people' (Isaiah 40:1).

Many of us are living through hard times – economic, environmental, personal, political. There is much happening that drains hope from our hearts. The Old Testament scholar Walter Brueggemann says that when times are really hard, our prophetic (and I think pastoral) task is to face reality head on, name and grieve the losses, and nurture hope.[1] Not the 'don't worry, God's in charge, everything will be all right' kind of hope. But biblical hope, which is about the fact that God is and that God calls and equips fragile, fallible people into the great divine–human project of the flourishing of life and the redeeming of the times.

'Prophesy to the bones,' the Lord says to Ezekiel. Share a life-giving, hope-building word.

† When I despair about the state of the world or the state of my soul, when I feel dried up and cut off, breathe your Spirit into me that I may stand and live.

For further thought

What gives you hope? Hold fast to it.

[1] Walter Brueggemann, *Reality, Grief and Hope: Three Urgent Prophetic Tasks* (Cambridge, MA: Eerdmans, 2014).

Friday 17 November

Taking advantage

Read 1 Samuel 24:3–7, 11–15

He came to the sheepfolds beside the road, where there was a cave; and Saul went in to relieve himself ... Then David went and stealthily cut off a corner of Saul's cloak.

(verses 3, 4b)

This may be the only time in the whole Bible we read about someone needing a wee (the King James Version speaks of Saul going to the cave to 'cover his feet'. Ha!). Makes me smile. Yes, we all wee. And when we do, we are uniquely vulnerable. In the bathroom, as in the bedroom, we are momentarily naked and defenceless.

David takes advantage of this vulnerability to sneak up and cut a corner of Saul's cloak – an act that is meant to remind Saul of his vulnerability and of David's wiliness and restraint. He could have killed Saul (who was hunting David), but he didn't.

Vulnerability comes from the Latin *vulnus*, meaning wound. To be vulnerable is to be able to be wounded. Sometimes our vulnerability makes us feel ashamed. We think we should be strong, invulnerable – but that would be inhuman.

Sometimes people use our vulnerability against us. Yet, often, sharing vulnerability is what makes for intimacy. Showing our soft side, taking a risk, speaking of need or want – these things are what make connection and love possible.

David's conscience was cut to the quick that he had cut the corner of Saul's cloak. He knew it was wrong. He wasn't expecting to make a friend of Saul – he knew that he would take his place. But he understood that, as God's anointed king, Saul was deserving of respect.

Vulnerability is a tricky thing, requiring us to tread gently. An inner compass set towards respect serves us well.

† When I feel exposed or ashamed, remind me that I am human and help me to protect or express my vulnerability as may be appropriate. May I never take advantage of the vulnerability of another.

For further thought

When and where do I feel vulnerable? How comfortable am I with my own vulnerability and the vulnerability of others?

Saturday 18 November

We do go on a bit

Read Acts 20:7–12

A young man named Eutychus, who was sitting in the window, began to sink off into a deep sleep while Paul talked still longer. Overcome by sleep, he fell to the ground three floors below and was picked up dead.

(verse 9)

Now I know the origin of the phrase 'bored to death'. Paul talked until midnight, only stopping long enough to resuscitate Eutychus. Then he went on until dawn.

Confession: I can go on a bit. I started teaching with a team a few years ago after many years of solo teaching. I discovered that I taught a bit differently from my co-teachers. They often stopped and asked or solicited questions. Their teaching had breathing space in it, space for engagement and integration. I do a bit of that, but sometimes in my passion to share I cram too much into the allotted time. And I know that if I was given a longer period, I would find more essential things to say!

There is no doubt that Paul was convinced that what he had to share was utterly life-giving. I'm encouraged that in verse 11 it says that Paul 'conversed' with them until dawn. I hope this means he listened as well as spoke.

Sometimes Christians are so passionate about the answers we have found, we don't stop to find out what questions or ideas others have. Real conversations are two-way, give and take. We need to check our intentions and cultivate the humility to enter into the kind of space that allows all parties to grow in understanding. No one person knows it all. All of us are works in progress.

† When I think that what I have to say is essential, remind me that listening is just as, and sometimes more, important. Unsettle my assumptions and make the space clear for real conversation.

For further thought

Notice who is talking and who is not talking when you are in a group of people. How can you facilitate more inclusive participation?

Biblical library (6)

Law

Notes by **Lucy Rycroft**

Lucy is the founder of The Hope-Filled Family (www.thehopefilledfamily.com), a blog encouraging Christian parents and adopters. She also offers support on Instagram (@thehopefilledfamily). A former teacher and lecturer, Lucy now focuses on full-time blogging and writing, and is the author of *Redeeming Advent* (Gilead Books, 2019) and the Mighty Girl Mighty God series for children (Onwards and Upwards Publishers). Lucy lives in York, UK, with her husband, four children and a crazy Cockapoo called Monty. Lucy has used the NIVUK for these notes.

Sunday 19 November

Moral law – the law displays God's perfection

Read Deuteronomy 5:1–33

The Lord our God has shown us his glory and his majesty, and we have heard his voice from the fire … Go near and listen to all that the Lord our God says. Then tell us whatever the Lord our God tells you. We will listen and obey.

(verses 24a, 27)

Welcome to our week in the law! Wait – don't go! Where are you going? Come back!

I realise that the prospect of studying the law hardly feels like a party. But over the next seven days, I hope you'll get excited as we consider how to better understand the law and its relevance to us today.

Today's passage kicks us off well: the ten commandments are, after all, a very good place to start. Here, they are being recalled forty years after God gave them to Moses at Sinai. They are the basis of Israel's relationship with God, and the centre of the judicial system of much of the world today. We know they make sense – yet we also know we regularly break them. As hard as we might try, we are unable to keep God's commandments.

But the law's purpose is not to beat us into perfection. It gives good moral advice, but a life of high morality is not sufficient to enter God's presence. No! The law shows us the perfection of God. In order to come to him, we need a perfect Saviour who is able to fulfil the law on our behalf. Praise God for sending Jesus!

† Thank you Jesus for coming and dealing with all the consequences of sin. It is such a relief to walk free! Hallelujah! Amen

Monday 20 November

Ceremonial law – the smell of forgiveness

Read Leviticus 1:1–17

It is a burnt offering, a food offering, an aroma pleasing to the L*ORD.*

(verse 9b)

Yesterday we read about the moral law, God's perfect standard, and our inability to keep it. Today we examine ceremonial law – what to do when we break the moral law.

When we read of this time-consuming process of bringing burnt offerings before the Lord, it can seem rather ritualistic to us who live in the post-resurrection era of God's grace. But sin is serious, and God is holy, and the only way we could ever have a relationship with him was by offering something that had not succumbed to sin.

For the Israelites, animals without defect were the best option. The person bringing the offering had to lay his hand upon the head of the animal to indicate solidarity (verse 4); this animal's death would be acceptable to God in place of the person coming before God. Most people would offer a sheep or goat (verse 10), but instructions were also given for bulls (verse 3), which the wealthy would be able to afford, and birds (verse 14), which were cheaper and could be offered by the poor. No one was exempt, rich or poor: all needed to be made right with God.

The aroma of the burnt animal was 'pleasing to the LORD' (verse 9). However, it was not a long-term solution. One day, God would send the ultimate sacrifice – his only Son, Jesus. And he would be described as a 'fragrant offering' (Ephesians 5:2). We cannot atone for our own wrongdoing, but God is pleased to accept a sweet-smelling offering from the one who fulfilled the law on our behalf.

† Lord, thank you for accepting Jesus' sacrifice in place of mine. Please do not let me take this for granted, but be empowered to live in the grace of your wonderful gift. Amen

For further thought

Although the days of burnt offerings are gone, there's still a cost to discipleship (Matthew 16:24). What is it costing you today?

Tuesday 21 November

Judicial law – guidance for the grey areas

Read Exodus 21:1–36

'These are the laws you are to set before them.'

(verse 1)

Reading about slavery and violence is always going to be hard for our twenty-first-century ears. It's a part of the Bible we wish didn't exist – it doesn't seem to align with who God is or how he designed us to live.

But God has given us free will, and the Israelites had developed a culture which included both these things – just as our own culture has also developed ungodly practices. God is not condoning these practices but giving laws to protect the vulnerable within these situations. We call this judicial law – principles to help those in charge to make fair, just decisions. It is the outworking of the moral law we observe in the ten commandments.

For example, God clarifies the fact that Hebrews should not remain slaves for ever (verse 2), establishes the difference between murder and manslaughter (verse 13), and protects pregnant mothers and unborn children (verses 22–23). The famous 'eye for eye, tooth for tooth' law (verse 24; see Matthew 5:38) is not intended to encourage retaliation, but to limit it. You only need witness my children's heated arguments to realise that, when we are wronged, our nature is to give the other person more suffering than they have inflicted on us.

The Israelites were fortunate to receive these clarifications, helping them interpret the ten commandments wisely. Today we are faced with numerous ethical decisions for which no biblical blueprint is given. Our job is to use the principles God has set forth in his word to discern the right action. How can we most glorify God within the situations we face?

† Father, thank you for the guidance you've laid out for us in the Bible, and give us daily as we ask. Please help us with the decisions we're facing right now. Amen

For further thought

Whether you're facing a big decision right now or several smaller ones, commit to seeking God's will for your life through regular prayer.

Wednesday 22 November

The law explained – how can we become righteous?

Read Matthew 5:17–22

Do not think that I have come to abolish the Law or the Prophets; I have not come to abolish them but to fulfil them.

(verse 17)

My boys love playing spies. One of the items in their toolkit is invisible ink. Despite requests to limit this to paper, they enjoy writing on the walls, thinking they'll get away with it. But on the other end of the pen is a UV light – shine it on the wall, and the invisible ink shows up: the boys are found out!

The law is like this light – showing up the sin in our lives. We cannot read it without becoming aware of our faults, including those invisible to others. Jesus did not come to abolish it, because it didn't need abolishing: the law is rooted in who God is – love. It represents to us how holy God is, and how holy we aren't – and, as such, it is uncomfortable, but it is also helpful. It will only become defunct once 'everything is accomplished' (verse 18) – in other words, when Jesus returns and sin is abolished for ever. But for now it remains, revealing our own lack of righteousness.

If we are so lacking, how is our righteousness supposed to 'surpass that of the Pharisees and the teachers of the law' (verse 20)? Jesus had no time for outward religiosity – it was irrelevant because it would never make us as righteous as we needed to be. The Pharisees – and we – need a Saviour, someone to do what we can't. Only Jesus, being righteous before God, could live in perfect obedience to the law and, thus, die for our disobedience. This is how he fulfils the law for us. What a gift!

† Jesus, I am so grateful for your sacrifice because I know how much I need it. Thank you for loving me so much to give your life for mine. Amen

For further thought

Other belief systems involve working towards your own salvation. What a relief to know that we can't – and, because of Christ, don't need to!

Thursday 23 November

Where the law is powerless, the Spirit has power

Read Romans 8:1–11

The mind governed by the flesh is death, but the mind governed by the Spirit is life and peace.

(verse 6)

We have seen that the law is helpful: it sets God's standard, reflects his holiness and shines a light on our own lives, showing us where we are dishonouring God. But the law cannot do everything. It is powerless (verse 3) to overcome sin. It cannot make us righteous. It does not, in itself, draw us closer to God – it only tells us of our distance from him.

There is good news, however; God sent Jesus 'in the likeness of sinful flesh to be a sin offering' (verse 3) to overcome sin for us. This has enabled the Spirit of life to set us 'free from the law of sin and death' (verse 2). Does this mean we no longer sin? No – verse 10 confirms that our bodies will still die because of sin. We cannot avoid physical decay and eventual death. But this is not the end of the story; because of the righteousness Jesus has won for us, our spirits are alive now (verse 10) – and our bodies will be resurrected (verse 11) to live for ever with God in heaven!

We don't have to wait till then, though: living in the power of the Holy Spirit right now brings life and peace (verse 6). We sin less because we are living by the Spirit rather than according to our old sinful nature (verse 9). And as we submit more and more to the Spirit's leading, our desire to honour God increases.

† Holy Spirit, fill me with life and peace. Give me more desire to honour God with my thoughts, words and actions. Please bring to mind an area I need to submit to your loving ways. Amen

For further thought

What might it mean to fully receive the overcoming power of the Holy Spirit in your life?

Friday 24 November

Written on our hearts – the law in our hearts

Read Jeremiah 31:23–34

This is the covenant that I will make … I will put my law in their minds and write it on their hearts. I will be their God, and they will be my people.

(verse 33)

When I'm attempting to sort out an altercation between my children, the guilty party (unsurprisingly) is usually evasive. 'Did you really hit your brother?' 'Yes, but he threw a book at me!' 'She turned the TV off in the middle of my programme!' 'He was being really annoying!' And on it goes.

It's not just children who don't like to own up to their wrongdoings – adults aren't very good at it either. We would much rather point the blame at others than acknowledge our own flaws. We're more inclined to blame our parents, our colleagues, our children's school and the government, before we're willing to examine our own hearts. The Israelites were in a terrible state – Babylonian invasion, terrible kings and many people exiled – yet they'd misinterpreted God's law in a way that blamed the sins of their ancestors for this turn of events, rather than looking inward to see if they themselves had sinned against God.

It has been said that God has no grandchildren. You cannot live your life of faith through your parents – or, in fact, anyone else. We are each responsible for our own response to God. Jeremiah told his people, 'everyone will die for their own sin' (verse 30). It's what we deserve. But Jeremiah prophesies of a time when God will put his law in our minds and our hearts (verse 33). We have the privilege of knowing how this is achieved: through the death of Jesus and the indwelling of the Holy Spirit. By this, God forgives and even forgets every single act of disobedience (verse 34).

† Lord God, I want to know you more each day. Please put your law in my mind and write it on my heart. May my life overflow with the generosity you have shown me. Amen

For further thought

Is your faith truly your own? Or do you ride on the faith of your Christian friends, your church group, the Christian conferences you attend?

Saturday 25 November

A new commandment – let there be love

Read John 13:31–35

A new command I give you: Love one another. As I have loved you, so you must love one another. By this everyone will know that you are my disciples, if you love one another.

(verses 34–35)

We've spent this week thinking about how the law sets God's perfect standard and shows up our own sin. We've been reminded of the amazing truth of his love for us in sending Jesus to keep the law for us and implanting his Holy Spirit into our hearts to overcome sin.

Today we look at Jesus' words concerning a new commandment: love one another. It is not really 'new', because all of the ten commandments have love at their heart. If you love others, you won't want to murder them, steal from them, cheat on them, lie to them, or anything else the commandments may cover. But there are two key elements to this commandment.

First, the basis for this love is that Jesus has first loved us (verse 34). When God first started to challenge me about adoption, we already had two birth children. I cried out to God, 'I don't think I could love adopted kids! I don't have that much love!' His response was simple: 'But I do.' We are not asked simply to imagine what love is like, drawing reserves from an empty pot. In Jesus, we see the true love of God and experience it in our hearts. It is this love that Jesus is asking us to draw on to fulfil his commandment to love one another.

Second, the outcome of this commandment is that others will know we follow Christ. Unity, forgiveness, grace, kindness – extended to non-believers: love is our present to the world. And there is no greater witness.

† Jesus, you loved like no other. Please fill me with your love today, so that how I treat those around me may be a witness to the world. Amen

For further thought

Satan loves it when Christians bicker; it is the worst possible witness. Are there any situations you could diffuse or improve right now?

Hidden heroes and heroines

Notes by **Jan Sutch Pickard**

Jan is a poet and former Warden of the Abbey in Iona. Earlier, she edited publications (*Now*, *Connect*, the *Methodist Prayer Handbook*) for the Methodist Connexion, and is a 'Local' (lay) Preacher. Having served twice on the WCC (World Council of Churches) Ecumenical Accompaniment Programme in Palestine and Israel, Jan continues to support such peace monitoring there, praying for justice and peace. With the Iona Community she shares this commitment and works on liturgy that reflects ordinary life as well as God's goodness. Jan has used the NRSVA for these notes.

Sunday 26 November

A force of nature (Shiphrah and Puah)

Read Exodus 1:15–21

The king of Egypt said to the Hebrew midwives, one of whom was named Shiphrah and the other Puah … 'if it is a boy, kill him; but if it is a girl, she shall live'. But the midwives feared God; they did not do as the king of Egypt commanded them, but they let the boys live.

(verses 15–17)

It's good to know the names of these two subversive midwives. Shiphrah and Puah, God-fearing women, with good reason to fear the king of Egypt too. Why would he let them stand in the way of his plans? Yet they found a way to let children live and their community thrive; he could be deceived because he didn't understand the culture of the people he wanted to destroy. Told to do wrong, but called to do right, they just got on with it!

The story of these Hebrew women reminds me of a local heroine in Wales: Betty Campbell (1934–2017), Britain's first woman of colour to become a head teacher. With a Welsh mother and Jamaican father she met prejudice early, loving learning but told by teachers she could never become a head teacher. Through an outstanding teaching career, she pioneered awareness of Black History, and encouraged each child. A statue to her, recently unveiled in Cardiff, celebrates her determination, aspiration and inspiration: a positive role model.

She enriched the lives of the children she taught, like those midwives who brought both boys and girls safely into the world. Like birth itself, such women are 'a force of nature'.

† Strong, life-giving Spirit, you bring us into being and you nurture us: thank you for those – women and men – who share this labour of love.

Monday 27 November

Where there's a will (Mahlah, Noah, Hoglah, Milcah, Tirzah)

Read Numbers 27:1–11

They stood before Moses, Eleazar the priest, the leaders, and all the congregation, at the entrance of the tent of meeting, and they said, 'Our father died in the wilderness … Why should the name of our father be taken away from his clan because he had no son?'

(verses 2–4)

In a man's world, surrounded by a male group of leaders, what were these women doing? Five sisters, daughters of Zelophehad, confronted an entrenched tradition in their community. Believing they could see a better way and standing in solidarity with each other, they found the courage to speak out. They remind me of women's groups in many places today, 'sisters' who know that they are stronger when they stand together.

In some African societies, women have united to challenge traditional practices like 'cutting' (female genital mutilation). Like Zelophehad's daughters, they claim equality and economic justice. 'Wise Women', a small group in Zambia, applied for help from Lendwithcare, a microfinance scheme. Where men are seen as heads of households, they'd long been dependent on their husbands for their families' basic needs. Each put their share of a group loan of £2,000 to work: setting up stalls to sell produce and household basics. Money earned paid rent on homes, schooled children and restocked the stalls. Standing together, the Wise Women quickly repaid the loan.

In Malawi, members of Makande Women's Group lost their homes – sometimes everything – in Cyclone Idai. Together they started a project to make juice from the fruit of the giant baobab trees. Christian Aid helped provide solar power for refrigeration. Now they're no longer dependent on the decisions of the men in their lives, or the belief that women can't take initiatives. They're like the daughters of Zelophehad, whose stand was affirmed by God. Did those sisters – outside the 'tent of meeting' long ago – also sing and dance to celebrate?

† God of love, we are all your children. Free us from traditions and prejudices that deny the full humanity of other people. Help us to support each other in love, to stand together for justice.

For further thought

Buy something fairly traded – fruit juice, trail mix, chocolate. Share and enjoy it.

Tuesday 28 November

Discerning what's right (the men of Issachar)

Read 1 Chronicles 12:32

Of Issachar, those who had understanding of the times, to know what Israel ought to do, two hundred chiefs, and all their kindred under their command.

(verse 32)

We know their tribe, but that's not the same as knowing their names! Yesterday the names of just five sisters (Mahlah, Noah, Hoglah, Milcah, Tirzah) were sung out in praise of a small act of witness which God, we're told, approved. Here, there's a cast of thousands, a roll-call of military leaders and tribes, all men, coming to support David against Saul. Rank upon rank, like ocean waves. How can we tell them apart?

What was distinctive about the men of Issachar, these two hundred chiefs and their kindred, appears to have been their 'super-power', their ability to discern the signs of the times, 'to know what Israel ought to do'. Whereas some of those who gathered to support David were just spoiling for a fight!

Have we seen this happen much closer to home? Supporting a cause, we may develop tunnel vision. Our Patient Participation Group, trying to raise urgent issues with the local medical practice, found those in charge very defensive. The temperature rose, as some members wanted to respond aggressively. Others looked at the context: the practice was understaffed, the budget was overstretched, an immunisation programme was just beginning ... So, we responded politely to the managers' brusque response, remembering that we were there to support them, aiming for the common good, not to score points. Improving communication between our group, fellow patients and the staff of the practice needed to begin with respectful listening.

Just as listening to the Holy Spirit, and taking careful note of the signs of the times, may help us to act with discernment.

† God, who calls each of us by name, too often we divide the world into 'us' and 'them'; open our eyes to what's real, our minds to other lives, to signs of our times. Amen

For further thought

Awareness of the climate crisis is a sign of the times. How can we heed it? What meaningful action can we take?

Wednesday 29 November

Keeping faith beyond death (Rizpah)

Read 2 Samuel 21:1–14

Rizpah the daughter of Aiah took sackcloth, and spread it on a rock for herself, from the beginning of harvest until rain fell on them from the heavens; she did not allow the birds of the air to come on the bodies by day, or the wild animals by night.

(verse 10)

This heart-rending image, of a woman keeping watch over the unburied bodies of her kin, appears elsewhere in myth (in Greek legend, Antigone disobeyed a royal decree that her brother should neither be buried nor mourned). And it recurs in real life. The story of Rizpah reminds me of the Madres de Plaza de Mayo, the Mothers of the Disappeared in Argentina and Chile – women steadfast in bearing witness to missing sons and daughters, believed killed by government forces. Demonstrating year after year, with quiet dignity, holding up pictures of their children, they've challenged those in power. Rizpah's vigil, in the end, shamed King David into giving decent burial to Saul and others in whose deaths he had a hand.

Now I can see another example, much closer, of folk keeping faith with those they've loved and lost. Opposite the Houses of Parliament, in London, there's a wall along the riverbank. Once just a length of concrete, now it has become the National Covid Memorial Wall, covered with more than 150,000 painted red hearts, each representing a life lost to Covid-19. People have written the names of a family member or friend. A group meets weekly to care for it, painstakingly refreshing the paint, ensuring the names can still be read. 'There are people who would like to see it fade,' said one widow. 'We are not going to let that happen.' Sadly, they also have the task of adding more hearts, more names. Confronting Parliament as it does, it makes a powerful statement. Like Rizpah's vigil, it cannot be ignored.

† Just and compassionate God, you are present when people protest and cry out in pain, understanding our distress. The names of those we've loved and lost are written on your heart; and so are ours.

For further thought

Kat Armas explores what women on the margins teach us about wisdom, persistence and strength in her book *Abuelita Faith*[1] – why not have a read and be inspired!

[1] Kat Armas, *Abuelita Faith* (Grand Rapids, MI: Brazos Press, 2021).

Thursday 30 November

Putting oneself in God's hands (Jabez)

Read 1 Chronicles 4:9–10

Jabez was honoured more than his brothers; and his mother named him Jabez, saying, 'Because I bore him in pain.' Jabez called on the God of Israel, saying, 'Oh that you would bless me and enlarge my border, and that your hand might be with me, and that you would keep me from hurt and harm!' And God granted what he asked.

(verses 9–10)

What is this man doing here? I asked myself. In the 'social media' of Chronicles he appears briefly amid chapters of name-checking, in which many people are mentioned very briefly. What's memorable about them? And why does this week's scriptural thread nominate him as a hero? Baffled, I reflected on this verse. Jabez isn't noted for his heroic actions – in fact, the thing that's mentioned twice is suffering. His mother said, 'I bore him in pain.' Pain is in his very name. So, not surprisingly, his prayer to God was about being spared from hurt and harm. A hope that's only human.

He also prayed for God to take his side. Eagerness for our borders to be enlarged can mean expanding our territory at the expense of others, the exercise of power even when (or perhaps because) we feel small, weak, unsure. That's what the playground bully does, the colonist, the army of occupation. It's a dangerous human trait; there's nothing heroic about it. But on the other hand perhaps we need to notice – and respect – Jabez because he is an ordinary vulnerable human being, and admits it. I can relate to that.

So as I read these words, with the brief baffling appearance of Jabez, I'm reminded of human beings like myself, frail, often afraid, flawed, yet not quite managing to hide the image of God in which we are made.

† Loving God, in you each of us can find our home: no one needs a second one. Sharing a world, we don't need more territory – but wider horizons.

For further thought

On a world map, in a newspaper, find the names of places where border disputes – or land-grabs – displace people. Pray for them.

Friday 1 December

Steady support, wise words (Priscilla and Aquila)

Read Acts 18

[In Corinth] Paul stayed with Aquila with his wife Priscilla and they worked together – by trade they were tentmakers ... [In Ephesus] Apollos began to speak boldly in the synagogue; but when Priscilla and Aquila heard him, they took him aside and explained the Way of God to him more accurately.

(paraphrase of part of verses 1–3 and 26)

Yesterday just one Bible verse gave a thumbnail sketch of one man. Today a whole chapter feels like a fast-moving documentary. Here's Paul, like someone you might see on a screen, travelling the world, meeting local people, working with them, preaching in that place and having an impact on the wider community ... he moves on ... now we glimpse those who met him, finding their own different and complementary forms of ministry.

Aquila and Priscilla, man and wife, remind me of laypeople I've met in many places, over the years. Often their names are linked in the minds of those who meet them (partners I name now are Cliff and Ruth, Maggie and Cathy, Joy and Ian, Ian and Stephen). Some, though bereaved like my friend Sally, continue with a calling (formerly shared with a companion) of hospitality and care for others. Maybe they see themselves as supporters, not key figures in ministry and mission, yet they have their own unique role.

Sally, welcoming asylum seekers to her home, enjoyed finding the common ground. Priscilla and Aquila did the same: I imagine Paul, sitting in the sunshine in Corinth with his hosts, together plying their down-to-earth skills of tent-making. Today it's more likely to be working in a community garden, or helping out in a food bank or kitchen, where ministers learn by volunteering side by side with local laypeople.

And when, in their enthusiasm, incomers let their words and actions run away with them (like Apollos), wise folk who know the situation better can take them on one side, suggesting a different approach.

† Thank you God, for those who offer a warm welcome, wise listening, good advice. Give us the grace to do the same.

For further thought

Write down the names of those who have offered you this ministry, and speak them aloud. This could be a good time to get in touch, thank them.

Saturday 2 December

Messengers and meanings (Epaphroditus)

Read Philippians 2:25–30

I ... send to you Epaphroditus – my brother and co-worker and fellow-soldier, your messenger and minister to my need; for he has been longing for all of you, and has been distressed because you heard that he was ill ... He came close to death for the work of Christ.

(part of verses 25–26, 30)

Epaphroditus is a bit-player, and an interesting person.

He's a messenger – having been sent by the Christians in Philippi with their gift to Paul in prison: practical support and a sign of solidarity. Rome (or maybe Ephesus) is a long way from Philippi. An elder in that congregation – Paul calls him a 'co-worker' – entrusted to make the journey, he is now returning with Paul's message. In between, he has been ill, and this short extract from Paul's letter gives a sense of mutual care – Epaphroditus worried about his colleagues back home worrying about him, and Paul concerned for all of them. So far, so human. They all live with risk: travelling in small boats, facing illness, risking arrest, so the overall message of this letter – about standing firm – makes sense.

Epaphroditus means 'Dedicated to Aphrodite'. It's a reminder of the pagan community surrounding the Christians of Philippi. Here's someone who hasn't changed the name his parents gave him, but his commitment is different now – Paul calls him a 'soldier of Christ', and he stands firm in that identity.

In the UK, reasons for given names may be family tradition or current fashion. People don't always know the meanings of their names. We began our family in Yoruba-land, in Western Nigeria, so our three children's several names include Omotayo ('a child brings joy'), Ore-ofe ('God's grace') and Olusola ('honour of God'). We've travelled far since then, but those names were gifts to them from a Christian community that cared for us. Names with meaning, as I hope our lives have meaning.

† Stand, O stand firm and see what the Lord can do: O my brothers/O my sisters, stand very firm ... Stand, O stand firm and see what the Lord can do.[1]

For further thought

Find out the simple, joyful tune of this call-and-response song. Sing it! Or look up what your name means. Write it down. Or reflect on the names for the Messiah in Isaiah 9:6.

[1] From a traditional song from Cameroon.

Ephesians plus

1 No longer strangers

Notes by **Liz Carter**

Liz is an author and poet, writing about finding God's treasure in the midst of pain and brokenness, living with long-term illness. She lives in Shropshire, UK, with her husband Tim, a church leader, and their two children. Her first book, *Catching Contentment* (IVP, 2018) explores how we can find peace when life doesn't work out as we would hope, and her second book, *Treasure in Dark Places* (Capstone House, 2020) is a collection of poetry and re-imaginings of encounters with Jesus. Liz has used the NIVUK for these notes.

Sunday 3 December
Part of a bigger story

Read Ephesians 1:1–10

For he chose us in him before the creation of the world to be holy and blameless in his sight. In love he predestined us for adoption to sonship through Jesus Christ, in accordance with his pleasure and will.

(verses 4–5)

When our lives are weighed down with struggle, it's easy to forget the bigger picture and get caught in the details. Paul begins his letter to the Ephesians with a reminder and a promise all wrapped up in a glorious overarching story. He is so caught up in it that the first fourteen verses of this book are one ongoing sentence; an outpouring of worship, a summing up of the gospel.

Worship is the foundation of his teaching, and, in this case, it is written out of his own pain – he wrote it from prison. Paul gives us an example of what it is to be courageous within our brokenness, and he does that by reminding us of the bigger story: God's love, lavished on us. Paul shows that this story, God's promise to bring all things in heaven and earth to unity, and our status as chosen people, are all connected. They are all a part of a bigger whole, a mystery that was once shrouded by the law, now freely made known to us through Jesus' saving work on the cross. Over the next few days, we will explore what it means to be included in that story.

† Father, I praise you that I am chosen to be part of your great story. Please open my eyes to your bigger picture.

Monday 4 December

Marked with a seal

Read Ephesians 1:11–14

When you believed, you were marked in him with a seal, the promised Holy Spirit, who is a deposit guaranteeing our inheritance until the redemption of those who are God's possession — to the praise of his glory.

(verses 13b–14)

A local church was trying to buy some property in order to turn it into a community house and house of prayer. They were in a bidding war, and stress was mounting. The day they were finally able to put their deposit down, they were thrilled and excited: at last, they could begin to imagine what was to come, to rejoice in the certainty of a promised future.

In this passage, Paul is talking about a deposit, too, but one that is even better than for a property, and a million times more worthy of trust than a monetary transaction. Having laid out this story of the gospel, Paul is telling us that we are already included in this story – we already have this 'down payment'. We are marked with a seal: the Holy Spirit.

The Holy Spirit is much more than a deposit as we would see it, though. A financial deposit might give us assurance and hope for something in the future, but the Spirit gives us abundant life in the present, a taste of what will be in the now. We are already living within the promise, and claiming our inheritance.

The incredible truth is that this inheritance is for everyone. When Paul says 'and you, also', he is talking to Gentiles, gathering them into the great story of the Israelites he has just recounted.

You are included in this promise, too, because you have believed, and now you have this seal of hope – both a window on your future and peace beyond understanding in your present.

† Holy Spirit, thank you that you are my assurance. Thank you that you have called me and chosen me, and that I can stand firm on your guarantee of my inheritance, now and in eternity.

For further thought

In what areas in your life do you feel you are lacking assurance and hope? Ask the Spirit to seal the promise in your heart.

Tuesday 5 December

Called into upside-down power

Read Ephesians 1:15–23

That power is the same as the mighty strength he exerted when he raised Christ from the dead and seated him at his right hand in the heavenly realms, far above all rule, authority, power and dominion, and every name that is invoked.

(verses 19b–21a)

In Paul's time, Ephesus was a major centre of influence, a place where authority, power and dominion were all evident in the political and religious spheres. Paul knew this when he wrote so passionately about the incomparable power of Christ. For Paul, the power that raised Jesus from the dead set him well apart from any earthly powers; he stood starkly against cultural expectations and notions of power.

And it's not only that this power was made manifest in Christ's resurrection – it lives in us, too.

Sometimes, though, we wonder where that power is. We feel weak and helpless, far from the potency of the words in this passage. For me, living with long-term lung disease, I often feel as though any power drains far too quickly. But thankfully, this power isn't dependent on us and what we do. It originates in the riches of God, and is given to us as loved, chosen children. It's a power born in suffering, so often finding its fullness in more suffering.

In Ephesus, the culture was one of the powerful, stamping on the weak. But Paul reminds us of God's upside-down priorities here; we are Christ's body, and in Paul's picture of the body every member is honoured, unlike pictures of the body in the contemporary politics of his time, where weaker members didn't matter as much as those who were stronger. God turns power structures on their head, and we can be encouraged that, however weak we feel, the same power that raised Christ from the dead lives in us.

† Thank you, Lord, that you overturn cultural expectations, exalt the weak, and that your upside-down power is incomparable to any other. Thank you that we are called to be part of your glorious hope.

For further thought

Think about your church culture. Are there any power structures set up in opposition to the profound power found in the gospel?

Wednesday 6 December

Saved by scandalous grace

Read Ephesians 2:1–10

For it is by grace you have been saved, through faith — and this is not from yourselves, it is the gift of God — not by works, so that no one can boast. For we are God's handiwork, created in Christ Jesus to do good works.

(verses 8–10)

One of my favourite musicals is *Les Misérables.* When the main character, Jean Valjean – released after nineteen years in a chain gang – steals some silver from a church, he expects punishment and even execution when he is caught, used to the harshness of his culture. Instead, the bishop tells the police that the silver was a gift, and, on top of that, he gives Valjean some valuable silver candlesticks. Instead of condemnation, Valjean experiences grace – abundant, wild grace – and it transforms him.

As Paul says in this powerful passage, we've messed up, too. We are all steeped in the nature of sin and the world around us. But instead of wrath, we are lavished with grace – Paul is so excited by this that he says it in several different ways! We are not saved by our own actions – we have nothing to boast about – but we are saved by a grace that is so unusual it is scandalous. And, just as Valjean was transformed, so are we.

These are more words of inclusion. These words are for those who don't think they can be saved, or those who don't know why they should be, or those who think they don't deserve it. Here, again, is the overwhelming kindness of God, reaching out to us, gathering us in – whoever we are. Grace is free and undeserved, it is untamed and beautiful, it is gentle and powerful, and, most of all, it is transformative. Today, allow the words of this passage to gather you in, too, to remind you of your place, not earned but freely given.

† Lord, thank you for your grace. Thank you that you, rich in mercy, brought me into your story. Refresh me anew today with this incredible truth, and assure me that I, too, am included.

For further thought

Who do you know who needs to experience the same kind of grace as the bishop showed to Valjean? How could you help?

Thursday 7 December

Everyone's included

Read Acts 11:1–18

Then I remembered what the Lord had said: 'John baptised with water, but you will be baptised with the Holy Spirit.' So if God gave them the same gift he gave us who believed in the Lord Jesus Christ, who was I to think I could stand in God's way?

(verses 16–17)

During the lockdown, I had to shield because I am vulnerable to Covid-19. I felt daunted and saddened by the possibility of being excluded from the church community. As it was, church went into lockdown too, and most churches began to explore ways in which they could still be present in their communities, offering online worship. For me, and for many others who are disabled and long-term ill, we were finally fully included, able to be a part of worship every week, valued enough to be welcome. I am so thankful that many churches will continue this online ministry.

Peter's vision was one of unlikely inclusion, too, and also led to a revolution; people who had been traditionally excluded from the community were now welcomed in. The Holy Spirit revealed to Peter that Jesus had broken down the barriers between Jews and Gentiles, and that he was to include them with fullness of heart. For Peter, it was a big shift. Before, God had been for 'his people', for those included in the old covenant. But now, Peter needed to see that God had always planned to reach out to everyone, that his story was not restricted, that salvation was for everyone.

For us, it's important to remind ourselves that everyone is included, not just people like us or people who we feel comfortable with. God's story is most beautiful in its radical, grace-filled embrace of any person who responds, whatever their background, whatever their sin, whatever their knowledge: who are we, to think we can stand in God's way?

† Dear Lord, I am amazed at the way you lavish your love on all who ask. Thank you that you are a God who includes. Help me to reach out to others – whoever they are.

For further thought

Are there people in your church and community who are excluded because of race, disability, or anything else? How can you help change the culture?

Friday 8 December

Welcomed into the family

Read Ephesians 2:11–22

Consequently, you are no longer foreigners and strangers, but fellow citizens with God's people and also members of his household ... In him, the whole building is joined together and rises to become a holy temple in the Lord.

(verses 19, 21)

Some friends of mine are amazing adoptive parents. They spend a large amount of time grounding the children into the family, wrapping them in love and acceptance, challenging the narrative that each child carries as part of their past. Children who are taken into care so often feel groundless and without hope, and people like my friends don't just take them into the home but bring them into the family: they make them fellow citizens of that family. These children do not become members of the family through following rules, but through the love lavished on them by their mum and dad. And it is a joy to see.

Paul's words here bring pictures like this to mind because of the language of love and transformation he uses, the gentle and potent grace of God at work, bringing lost children into his family and giving them equal status. It's not only that we are included in God's family, but we are also part of a community, joined together with one purpose. In Judaism, the temple was an important religious and political building, but Paul gives us a new understanding of what the temple is – a place where we, as fellow citizens, are joined together. We are no longer strangers, no longer outsiders, but we are right in the midst. So, when Paul wrote this, he was envisaging a new community, not Jews and Gentiles alongside one another, careful to keep the boundaries so entrenched in their society, but both groups becoming one, forming family together – just like my friends with their children.

† Lord, I praise you that I'm not an outsider in your glorious kingdom. I thank you that you welcome me in, and that I am joined with other believers in a family that transcends barriers.

For further thought

How is your church divided? What racial and cultural barriers do you have to overcome if you want to be built into this temple?

Saturday 9 December
Heirs of the promise

Read Ephesians 3:1–6

This mystery is that through the gospel the Gentiles are heirs together with Israel, members together of one body, and sharers together in the promise of Christ Jesus.

(verse 6)

Recently, I watched a TV drama about an inheritance. The father who died had split his money equally between his three children – but what they didn't know was that there was a fourth, illegitimate, child and he too had an equal portion. The three children were not happy and fought against the inheritance of this stranger in their midst.

We, as Christians, having experienced the beauty of grace, mustn't reject those who are heirs alongside us – even the unexpected ones. For Peter, in the passage we explored the other day, it was a bit of a learning curve to accept that Gentiles were included, and it must have been for many Jews in the early church. The beauty of Paul's teaching is that he shatters all these barriers, leaving no room for any bickering: everyone is an heir to the promise, everyone is welcome.

We started off this week thinking about the greater story, and we end back in that place, too. From the beginning, God had crafted this story, hinting at the truth in secret through the prophets, and then fully revealing it in Christ. God had always intended to bring Jews and Gentiles together as his family, and still intends to bring us together, with every member equal and honoured. The big story of the gospel is one of sheer grace and lavish kindness, of drawing us all into a place where we can sit on our Father's lap and say that we are no longer strangers; we are heirs, together with Israel, of the promise in Christ Jesus.

† Jesus, as I reflect this advent on how you came to break down the barriers between us, I am so grateful. Thank you that I am an heir of the promise, in your great story.

For further thought

As the Christmas season brings busyness, joy and sorrow, think about ways in which you can remind yourself – and others – of the greater story.

Ephesians plus

2 A life worthy of your calling

Notes by **Bola Iduoze**

Bola is an entrepreneur, author, conference speaker and mentor. She specialises in helping people grow through practical application of spiritual principles. Bola began her career as an accountant over twenty years ago and her entrepreneurial journey in 2000. Since then, she has trained, coached and mentored over seven hundred home business owners around the world. In addition to her stint in the marketplace, Bola co-pastors Gateway Chapel alongside her husband Eddie. They have two children, Asher and Bethel. Bola has used the NIVUK and the NKJV for these notes.

Sunday 10 December

God can use anyone to preach his word

Read Ephesians 3:7–13

I became a servant of this gospel by the gift of God's grace given me through the working of his power. Although I am less than the least of all the Lord's people, this grace was given me: to preach to the Gentiles the boundless riches of Christ.

(verses 7–8, NIVUK)

Paul's recognition of the assignment he was given from God despite his lack of qualification, to be the one chosen to preach the gospel to the Gentiles, is worthy of note. Paul received an uncommon revelation and had to go and deliver the same to the Gentiles.

This experience of Paul reminded me of a situation from my early teen years. My local Baptist church in Ibadan, Nigeria, had a home mission week when members were chosen to go and preach Christ to a neighbouring village. Few congregants would usually be willing to go because the village was not easy to get to and people were unsure if the gospel message would be received by the hearers.

I considered myself to be one of the least qualified in all ways to be a missionary preacher on this trip, but discovered I was chosen. At that point it was obvious to me that the message is always bigger than the messenger.

God can use anyone he deems available to deliver his message to his world. The call is for us all to make ourselves available for the message God wants to use us to deliver to our generation.

† Lord, help me to be available any time you want to use me to deliver your valuable message to your valuable people.

Monday 11 December

Understanding the depth of the love of Christ

Read Ephesians 3:14–21

... so that Christ may dwell in your hearts through faith. And I pray that you, being rooted and established in love, may have power, together with all the Lord's holy people, to grasp how wide and long and high and deep is the love of Christ.

(verses 17–18, NIVUK)

One of the key messages Paul was tasked with delivering to the Ephesian church was the message of the depth of the love of Jesus to the Gentiles. He established the fact that it takes a lot to grasp the depth of God's love towards us in Christ Jesus.

As I was meditating on these verses, I remembered an incident in my first year in university when I discovered that I had failed my examination and was advised to withdraw from that university. This was a dark time for me, but knowing the depth of my earthly father's love for me took me through this difficult period.

My dad went above and beyond to let me know how much he loved me as a daughter despite my failure. He then went straight into action in helping me secure another university place the following year. I cannot but appreciate my father's love and action in this most difficult time of my life. His action taught me a little bit more about the depth of God's love towards me.

God loves us unconditionally, whether we consider ourselves a failure or a success. Never underestimate the level of his love for you even if you do not understand it.

† Father, I thank you for your love for me. There are times I will not totally understand it, but I will choose to rest in you and your provisions for me in word. Thank you, Lord!

For further thought

We may never understand the depth of our father's love, but we can get to know more of him by acquainting ourselves with his word.

Tuesday 12 December

No separation from the love of God

Read Romans 8:37–39

For I am convinced that neither death nor life, neither angels nor demons, neither the present nor the future, nor any powers, neither height nor depth, nor anything else in all creation, will be able to separate us from the love of God that is in Christ Jesus our Lord.

(verses 38–39, NIVUK)

I was privileged to speak with a young woman recently who mentioned how she felt as if she had to do things to deserve God's love. According to her, every time she does something she thinks God is not happy with, she feels as if God moves away from her. Her thought was that her behaviour could separate her from the love of God.

It was obvious to me that, just like this young woman, many of us compare God the Father to our earthly schoolmaster or even tough fathers. We think we can earn his love by being good. It is however not being good that gave us the reconciliation with God in the first instance, so being good is surely not what will sustain us.

This scripture once more shows us the opportunity to learn that the love of God in Christ Jesus is not worked for nor earned by us. It is dependent on what Jesus Christ has done for us on the cross of Calvary. God is not like a person who comes close when we are good and moves away when we are bad. Nothing can separate you from the love of God which is in Christ Jesus.

† Father, please give me the depth of understanding of the truth of your love for me. Let me see daily that your love for me is not dependent on me.

For further thought

Nothing can separate us from the love of God. It is a provision God has made from the very beginning, so we can depend on him.

Wednesday 13 December

Make every effort to keep the bond of peace

Read Ephesians 4:1–6

I, therefore, the prisoner of the Lord, beseech you to walk worthy of the calling with which you were called, with all lowliness and gentleness, with longsuffering, bearing with one another in love, endeavouring to keep the unity of the Spirit in the bond of peace.

(verses 1–3, NKJV)

Paul was addressing an issue that looks so easy, yet can be quite tough to live out daily. He mentioned that we as believers should be patient with others and deal with others in love. He then added that a believer should make every effort to keep the unity of peace in the bond of the Spirit.

Living with others when you cannot control their behaviour or reactions to things, yet have to ensure you keep the bond of peace within the community, is a tricky but necessary instruction to follow.

As a young mother I had to take time out to teach each of my two children this simple instruction, and at various times they struggled with the instruction. One would say, 'What if I want to pursue peace and the other is not interested in living peacefully? Should I still take responsibility for that?'

This could be a difficult situation to navigate, where you know that you are trying to keep the bond of peace, but the other parties are either not at that stage of understanding yet or they are not interested in keeping the bond of peace. What do you and I do in such circumstances? The Bible says, 'As much as lies in you, live at peace with all men' (Romans 12:18). The question to ask oneself repeatedly is, 'Have I made every effort? Have I done as much as lies within me?' If your answer is a yes, then what is left is to pray for the other party. Pray that the Lord may touch their hearts.

We have the task as believers always to make every effort to keep the bond of peace.

† Father, in the name of Jesus, grant me the grace to continually live in peace even when I find myself with other people who are not open to being at peace with others.

For further thought

We are expected to make every effort to keep the unity of Spirit in the bond of peace. It will require effort, but it is doable.

Thursday 14 December

Growing to become the mature body of Christ

Read Ephesians 4:7–16

Instead, speaking the truth in love, we will grow to become in every respect the mature body of him who is the head, that is, Christ. From him the whole body, joined and held together by every supporting ligament, grows and builds itself up in love, as each part does its work.

(verses 15–16, NIVUK)

Every time I see a new baby, I marvel at the creation of God in how he has made this little body complete. Yet the body requires maturity to be able to fulfil all the functions it's been created for. The life in the little baby is all the life it needs, but time and nourishment and a few other factors like environment and knowledge then shape how the baby turns out as an adult. The baby's full potential is therefore dependent on the maturity of this baby over time.

The same goes for the body of Christ. He has redeemed us, and it is now our turn to grow to become the mature body that will represent the head correctly and nicely fit into all the functions the head has prepared for us as the body. Time and nourishment are therefore very important to our fulfilment of our parts in the body of Christ.

Another amazing thing to note about this scripture is that we as Christians are part of the whole body but cannot fulfil our function fully in isolation. We are called to function fully within the body and supply our bit to ensure the proper function of the whole body. What a privilege we have, knowing that we have a part to supply in supporting the fullness of the body.

We therefore need to take seriously our parts in growing to become a mature Christian to ensure the body functions well.

† Father, thank you for counting me worthy of being part of the body of Christ. Help me be faithful in my role so the body can be effective.

For further thought

I have a part to play in the body of Christ and must grow to fulfil my function for the effective function of the whole body.

Friday 15 December

Take off the old to put on the new

Read Ephesians 4:17–24

You were taught, with regard to your former way of life, to put off your old self, which is being corrupted by its deceitful desires; to be made new in the attitude of your minds; and to put on the new self, created to be like God in true righteousness and holiness.

(verses 22–24, NIVUK)

The very first wedding in my family in Africa was that of my first cousin, whom my father had the responsibility of leading to the altar. The wedding preparation and procession was done from my home, and I was part of the wedding train. We had been given beautiful traditional dresses that were going to mark out the special members of the train. I was excitedly looking forward to this day and wearing the dress.

The wedding morning came, and we all got into the special car taking the bride and train to the church; I noticed that my beautiful green traditional wear had some red clothing showing under it. First I was puzzled and later I realised that in all the excitement, I had forgotten to remove my older dress before putting on my beautiful new bridal train clothes. I seemed to have no way of changing, so I tried adjusting my appearance. I thought it was all sorted, only to realise when the official pictures of the wedding were released that my beautiful traditional wear had some red materials showing through it. It was not a pretty sight at all; but this situation taught me the lesson on how we must put off the old to be able to put on the new effectively.

Our new life in Christ is a beautiful life, but the beauty cannot be appreciated if we do not take off our old garment, nature, character and influences. Then put on the new.

† Lord Jesus, thank you for giving me a new life in you. I pray that you will help me to identify the old nature I need to get rid of and to put on the new person effectively.

For further thought

Our new nature will not be appreciated unless we allow God to show us what to take off in our old nature so the new nature can shine forth.

Saturday 16 December

Your words can be helpful in building others

Read Ephesians 4:25–32

Do not let any unwholesome talk come out of your mouths, but only what is helpful for building others up according to their needs, that it may benefit those who listen. And do not grieve the Holy Spirit of God, with whom you were sealed for the day of redemption.

(verses 29–30, NIVUK)

When it comes to becoming all that God has planned for us here on earth, we must understand the power of our mouth and the words we speak. Our words matter and we can use them to build the lives of the people around us or otherwise. The Bible made us understand that life and death are in the power of the tongue (Proverbs 18:21); this means that what we speak can affect how the life events around us can be shaped. What we say can build up if we are careful to know the types of words we speak daily.

Paul said to the Ephesian Christians, as well as to us, that we should not let unwholesome talk come out of our mouths, but that which is helpful for building up. So, we have control over what we allow to come out of our mouths. If that is the case, let us choose always to speak words that can build other people.

We have a tool that we have control over and are admonished to become destiny builders with this tool of ours. We should therefore consciously choose words that do not just build others but words that will also benefit and bless others.

† Father, please give me the grace to watch out for the words of my mouth and always speak words that will bless and build the people around me in Jesus' name.

For further thought

Your words matter. So, mind the mouth. Always ask yourself if your words will bless, benefit and build before uttering them.

Ephesians plus

3 Living in the light

Notes by **Mandy Briggs**

Mandy is a Methodist minister who lives in Bristol. She is currently working as the Education Officer at John Wesley's New Room, the oldest Methodist building in the world (www.newroombristol.org.uk), Twitter: @NewRoomBristol @mandbristol. Mandy has used the NIVUK for these notes.

Sunday 17 December
Living in the light

Read Ephesians 5:1–14

For you were once darkness, but now you are light in the Lord. Live as children of light.

(verse 8)

Do you light candles in Advent?

At home, we light a numbered candle every day and watch it gradually burn down through December, date by date, until we celebrate the birth of Jesus on Christmas Day.

Each Sunday in Advent, many churches around the world also focus on an Advent ring – lighting one candle, then two, then three and more – as part of their retelling of the Christian story, the anticipation of the coming of Emmanuel, God with us.

This week's theme is 'Living in the light'. Together, we are being asked to explore what Paul is saying to the followers of Jesus in Ephesus about holy living, about what that phrase means in their context. The call comes – 'Live as children of light' – let people see Jesus in you.

As we read and reflect this week, our own calling to 'Live in the light' also has an extra overlay. For as we read, we cannot ignore the fact that we are also immersed in another story – the story which leads us to a stable in Bethlehem, a story of angels and shepherds, animals and kings.

How could these two stories intertwine? Let's go on a journey and find out.

† God of light and love, help us to explore what living in the light meant for the Ephesians then and what it means for us now.

Monday 18 December

Overcoming hate

Read 1 John 2:7–11

Anyone who claims to be in the light but hates a brother or sister is still in the darkness.

(verse 9)

Today's reading takes a swerve into 1 John (don't worry, we'll be back in Ephesians tomorrow). It's a swerve which makes sense. For as we continue the theme of living in the light, today's verses are important.

In a season where we naturally light candles, today's reading talks about the absence of light and the absence of love. The suggestion in these verses is that the light of Christ in us enables us to love one another. Those who show hate are 'without light' and there is a clear encouragement to turn away from hatred and live in the way of light and love.

Fifteen years ago I visited the Auschwitz-Birkenau Memorial and Museum, the site of the notorious concentration and extermination camp run by Nazi Germany in occupied Poland during the Second World War.

It is difficult to walk into such a place and not feel a chill: it was the site where thousands and thousands of people lost their lives, a place where it was said that even the birds stopped singing.

As a guide led us around the site, small things brought comfort. In particularly difficult places, such as the now defunct gas chambers and the wall used by the firing squad, flowers had been placed, often accompanied by a lit candle.

The candles, as symbols of light, had been deliberately placed as a focus for remembrance, but they also seemed to me to be small symbols to counter the hatred which had once reigned in that place. Light was used effectively to communicate a different message – love and hope are still possible.

† Jesus, Light of the World, there is nowhere that your light cannot shine. We name places where hatred seems to have the upper hand, praying that love and light may become evident and bring hope and change.

For further thought

You can find out more about the Auschwitz-Birkenau Memorial and Museum at www.auschwitz.org/en/ (English version of the original website).

Tuesday 19 December

Advice from John Wesley

Read Ephesians 5:15–21

Do not get drunk on wine, which leads to debauchery. Instead, be filled with the Spirit.

(verse 18)

We return to Ephesians today, looking at what on the surface appears to be a rather stern command to avoid drunkenness and debauched behaviour. We're in the season of Christmas parties, so again, how do we see these verses through the lens of the festive season?

I work at John Wesley's New Room, the oldest Methodist building in the world. A widely held belief about Methodists is that we are teetotal – and to be fair, in Victorian times, teetotalism and 'taking the pledge' were very popular in Methodist circles.

John Wesley, however, was not teetotal. He would often drink a 'small beer' (it was sometimes healthier than drinking water in Georgian times!). What he did disapprove of and speak out against was the overconsumption of strong spirits like gin.

This was not a drink presented in a pretty bottle with a garnish and ice; it was harsh and lethal stuff. Wesley could see the damage that alcohol addiction caused, not just to the individual but in the knock-on effects on whole families.

These verses from Ephesians do not insist that we should all become teetotal (and, indeed, only some Methodists are these days). But they do encourage us to make wise decisions and to seek fulfilment and joy through the power of the Holy Spirit instead of looking for it in the wrong places.

† God of Wisdom, help me to make wise decisions through the festive season, especially when there is the opportunity to eat or drink to excess.

For further thought

There is hope and help available if you want to discuss issues surrounding alcohol addiction and its effect on individuals and families. Alcoholics Anonymous (www. alcoholics-anonymous.org. uk) and Al-Anon (www.al-anonuk.org.uk) can help.

Wednesday 20 December

On the way to Bethlehem

Read Ephesians 5:22–33

However, each one of you also must love his wife as he loves himself, and the wife must respect her husband.

(verse 33)

I confess that as we carry on journeying through Ephesians, the verses set for today made me think of another very significant journey.

In the run-up to Christmas Day we remember the story of Mary and Joseph travelling to Bethlehem. Joseph is from the house and line of David and has to go back to the town to register in the census. Mary goes with him because, as the Gospel of Luke tells us in chapter 2, she was 'pledged to be married to him and was expecting a child'.

Another way of understanding 'pledged to be married' is betrothal. This was a formal contract between families and was as legally binding as marriage itself. This is why, in Matthew 1, Joseph considers divorcing Mary quietly when he hears she is pregnant. They were legally bound to each other even though a marriage ceremony had not yet taken place.

What was that journey like? Were there times of mutual support and care – words of encouragement to each other, rest stops and maybe a backrub or two for the expectant mother? Were there grumpy moments, sharp words, moments of impatience or frustration as the inconvenience of making a major trip while heavily pregnant took its toll?

We don't know much about Mary and Joseph's journey. But after both having powerful spiritual experiences and difficult conversations back home, here they are, together on a long journey, preparing for an imminent birth while also trying to be faithful to the law and to each other.

I have no doubt that the journey they took and the experiences they had must have powerfully shaped their relationship at a time when they were both still learning how to be a couple.

† God of relationships, we thank you for the people who support us, and pray that we may also be a source of support to them.

For further thought

Visit the website of the Methodist Modern Art Collection: www.methodist.org.uk/our-faith/reflecting-on-faith/the-methodist-modern-art-collection/. Look for the picture *Rest on the Flight to Egypt* by Nicholas Mynheer. How does this image speak to you?

Thursday 21 December

Different worlds

Read Ephesians 6:1–9

And masters, treat your slaves in the same way. Do not threaten them, since you know that he who is both their Master and yours is in heaven, and there is no favouritism with him.

(verse 9)

It is difficult to read these verses without having to look the language of 'masters and slaves' squarely in the face. These instructions from Paul should be understood in context; household slaves were common in his world and in his overall list of 'instructions for household members' – wives, husbands, children – he is trying to encourage right relationships between 'masters and servants' in an attempt to include everyone in the house.

I think that this is Paul's attempt to work within the limits of his world. He is calling for right relationships between all people – whatever their position in society. We would probably prefer him to call out the evils of slavery, and indeed we now live in a world where slavery in all its abhorrent forms is something to be challenged and eradicated.

In 1788, John Wesley stood in the pulpit at the New Room in Bristol and spoke about his support for the abolition of the transatlantic slave trade. His last letter, written just before he died in 1791, was to MP William Wilberforce, supporting his campaign to bring in official legislation which would deem slavery illegal.

The question remains – where does that leave us? People are still enslaved in our world, in our context, but all too often we do not see or hear. It's time to change that, and acknowledge the reality of slavery now.

† Please pray today for freedom for children, women and men who are enslaved, trafficked, abused and exploited in today's world.

For further thought

Find out more about the fight against modern slavery by visiting www.antislavery.org.

Friday 22 December

Going into battle?

Read Ephesians 6:10–17

Therefore put on the full armour of God, so that when the day of evil comes, you may be able to stand your ground, and after you have done everything, to stand.

(verse 13)

Contrary to popular belief, today's verses have nothing to do with last-minute shopping and battling your way through a busy shopping centre or supermarket with hundreds of other consumers desperately elbowing each other to get to eleventh-hour gifts!

The predominant image in these verses is of a soldier going to war, arming themselves ready for a fight against evil. It's a powerful image, which has informed much of the language that we have used in the Christian church down the centuries. But what do we do if the images of war and battle do not feel comfortable, or even appropriate now? How do we understand the metaphors and the context in which they were written? How can we still gain encouragement from these verses while moving away from the idea of engaging in 'holy war'?

I found it useful to look at the core instructions that the Ephesians are being given. Be truthful. Get right with God. Be ready to share the gospel of peace. Hold your faith close in your head and your heart. Treasure the Bible and be open to what it says within its pages.

This is not to downplay the need to work against evil, to pray in all circumstances and to believe passionately in justice, righteousness and the power of God's love in Christ and through the Holy Spirit. However, we live in a violent world; should the images we use to talk about faith mirror that violence, or provide an alternative to it?

† God, help me to find a still moment today. Help me to take a breath today. Help me to give thanks today. Help me to share your love today.

For further thought

Discover how a national group of churches are working for justice and peace in today's world by visiting www.jointpublicissues.org.uk.

Saturday 23 December

Being fearless

Read Ephesians 6:18–24

Pray also for me, that whenever I speak, words may be given me so that I will fearlessly make known the mystery of the gospel.

(verse 19)

December is a time for giving and receiving cards and festive greetings. Some people also take time to write Christmas letters, full of news about their experiences over the past year. In today's reading, Paul is signing off his letter to the Ephesians. Some theologians believe that Ephesians is more of a 'circular newsletter', a missive that was also sent to other followers as well as those in Ephesus. It includes a lot of the major ideas in Paul's teaching and particularly focuses on unity.

What I love about Paul's closing words is the practical encouragement to keep on going. There is a commitment to prayer and a clear sense that Paul wants to be brave and fearless in sharing the gospel message, even though he is probably in prison at this point.

Paul speaks about making known the mystery of the gospel, and at this time of year we are encouraged to pause and really take some time to consider the mystery and power of the incarnation. This is much more than a story of a baby in a manger. It is much more than a newsletter. It is the story of God revealed in a tiny, helpless child, who would go on to change the world and demonstrate the power of love over death and evil.

Give thanks for Paul's faithfulness – and give thanks for this season of greetings and encouragement.

† Thank you, God, for the power of communication and the many ways that we can greet each other and share love and encouragement.

For further thought

Who can you send a last-minute greeting to?

Christmas with John

Notes by **Emma Wagner**

Emma spent thirteen years in missions, leading and pioneering teams and initiatives to reach out and share God's love. Now in her mid-30s, Emma lives in Scotland with her husband, three children, and her sourdough starter, Doris. Under pen name Emma Browne, she writes books for 9–12-year-olds and writes contemporary Christian romance novels. Emma has used the NIVUK for these notes.

Sunday 24 December

In the beginning was the Word

Read John 1:1–9

In the beginning was the Word, and the Word was with God, and the Word was God.

(verse 1)

Writing with a Jewish audience in mind, Matthew begins his Gospel by tracing Jesus' genealogy through David and back to Abraham. In doing this, he emphasises Jesus as King and the fulfilment of the Abrahamic covenant in which God would bless all nations through his people. Luke, writing to a Roman audience, goes even further, tracing Jesus all the way back to Adam, emphasising Jesus' humanity, but also that he comes from God as a 'second Adam'.

John, writing to all people, moves the story even further back, echoing the opening of Genesis and placing Jesus at the start of creation. John isn't as interested in Jesus' ancestry: John wants to explain what Jesus is *like*. And John chooses to describe Jesus as the Word – *Logos* in Greek. Looking up the word *Logos*, one finds that it can be translated into 'word', 'sentence', 'message', 'conversation', and so on. It's a word that encompasses *communication*. So, in describing Jesus as *Logos*, John tells us to listen up: God has something to say.

And this time, he's not sending us a message on a couple of stone tablets, like he did with the ten commandments. This time, he's coming himself. This time, he's coming to *be* the message, and to invite us into conversation with him. Tomorrow will be Christmas Day, Immanuel, God with us!

† Jesus, help me to listen as you communicate your good news to me and to the rest of the world.

Monday 25 December

Light has come into the world

Read John 3:16–21

For God did not send his Son into the world to condemn the world, but to save the world through him.

(verse 17)

Happy Christmas! One thing I love about Jesus is that his light, and his truth, is available not just to those of us who are already in his family, but to *everyone*. Which means that my Christmas greeting isn't just nice words, it's a real possibility, but one that requires us to choose.

When his light shines on darkness, brokenness, we all have a choice to make. We can retreat into the darkness, to lick our wounds and hide, or we can choose to let the light expose the ugly truth of it all and begin a journey of healing. Retreating into darkness is perhaps our first instinct – we don't like looking at our own brokenness, and the idea of anyone else seeing it can fill us with shame. And that shame can take us further into darkness, leading to more hiding and more shame. However, if we dare let the light shine on our darkness, if we dare agree with Jesus as he tells us the truth about our brokenness, we can be saved and healed from it.

Letting the light expose the truth about us can be terrifying, but Jesus doesn't shine his light to shame us, or to condemn us. He doesn't come to expose our brokenness and all the places where we need to make better choices, and then leave us stuck in that broken place. No, he shines his light so that we truthfully can be saved from the darkness. He is light and truth, so that he can be our loving Saviour and healer.

† Jesus, thank you for bringing light into the world. Help me to allow your truthful light to shine on me fully. And help me to rely on you as my Saviour.

For further thought

We *all* get two choices: to stay in darkness and shame, or dare to let Jesus shine his light, tell the truth and bring healing. On this Christmas Day, which will you choose?

Tuesday 26 December
The Word became flesh

Read John 1:10–14

The Word became flesh and made his dwelling among us. We have seen his glory, the glory of the one and only Son, who came from the Father, full of grace and truth.

(verse 14)

Though people had been looking for the Messiah for a long, long time, they didn't recognise him when he finally came. They didn't recognise the source of all life, the one through whom we are all made. Why? Because Jesus was nothing like what they expected him to be like, in part because people had failed to represent God accurately. Maybe they expected him to come as a king? To come in power and show his strength? Maybe they expected him to come and take control of the political situation?

Instead, John tells of a Jesus who is God but chooses to leave heaven and all its glories behind. He comes not to force anything on us, and he doesn't come with violence to establish himself as Lord. No, Jesus comes as a vulnerable baby, and goes on to live out his message of love in relationship with us – because that's what love is like. That's what *God* is like. Jesus isn't controlling and he doesn't insist on his own way. He doesn't insist on being ruler or showing his power. Instead, he moves in next door; sets up a tent in our camping ground; becomes a neighbour and friend to us. And the world didn't recognise him because Jesus is so altogether different from whatever we expect God to be like.

Mathew and Luke tell us Jesus is King, he is the blessing for all people, and he is God's Son. But John goes further. He tells us that Jesus is the message of love that has moved into our area to show us a better way to live – a loving way.

† Jesus, show me where I believe lies about you and help me recognise you as you really are.

For further thought

How have you seen God communicate his message of love to the world recently?

Wednesday 27 December

God's Chosen One

Read John 1:29–34

I myself did not know him, but the reason I came baptising with water was that he might be revealed to Israel.

(verse 31)

John the Baptist was a strange man. He had left civilisation to live in the desert and he knew he was there to prepare people for the coming Messiah. He had his own followers and would call on the people to turn away from wickedness and confess their sins so that they might be forgiven. He baptised people and invited them to live a lifestyle of sharing their belongings and living righteously. He challenged the religious and the political elite and so stood by his convictions that he ended up beheaded. And still, by his own admission, he did not recognise Jesus as Messiah when he first saw him coming towards him. Perhaps he didn't expect the Messiah to be his second cousin. Or maybe he too was hoping the Messiah would come in power and sort out the oppressive systems the people lived under. And yet, he knew God's ways *enough* that when he heard God point Jesus out as 'God's Chosen One', he trusted this to be the truth. At least at first. Later on, John sends his followers to ask Jesus if he really got it right – was Jesus *really* God's Chosen One? And Jesus tells them to look at how people were healed and restored, and to report back to John.

It is possible to know God's call to righteousness deeply and truly in our hearts, and still not recognise Jesus as God's Chosen One. It is possible to be zealous in our conviction for truth and righteousness – to be good people – and still not know Jesus.

† Jesus, help me know and recognise you for who you are – wherever you are.

For further thought

Where are my ideas about God and righteousness keeping me from truly knowing and recognising Jesus?

Thursday 28 December

The Son of God

Read John 1:43–51

Then Nathanael declared, 'Rabbi, you are the Son of God; you are the king of Israel.'

(verse 49)

As we've seen in previous days, Matthew and Luke in their genealogies emphasise Jesus' status. They reveal Jesus as King, and that he's God's Son. And some of the disciples are impressed when the respected Nicodemus comes to meet with Jesus, while James and John want to be seated at his right and left in the kingdom. And when Nathanael makes his declaration, setting Jesus' status higher than ever, Jesus tells him that he will see even greater things. Status seemed to be a big deal!

And the same applies today. For some people, status is still very important: what family do you come from? What does your bank account say about who you are? How powerful are you in society? People spend an awful lot of time trying to prove that they're important, significant people.

But John portrays Jesus as unconcerned with his own status. The important thing isn't that he's powerful, or that he could flex his muscles and cause the Roman Empire to come crashing down. 'Greater things than these', Jesus says, pointing not to higher status but to a picture of angels ascending and descending on him. It reminds us of the story of Jacob's dream pathway of angels coming to earth from heaven and going to heaven from earth.

This greater thing is not to do with status but to do with who Jesus is: the one who brings heaven to earth and earth to heaven, who makes a pathway for us.

† Jesus, you are my King. But I would like to know who you are – beyond your status. Please would you show me?

For further thought

How would my life be different if I placed less value on status and more value on the things that matter to Jesus?

Friday 29 December

The light of the world

Read John 8:12–19

When Jesus spoke again to the people, he said, 'I am the light of the world. Whoever follows me will never walk in darkness, but will have the light of life.'

(verse 12)

I grew up in Scandinavia, and at this time of the year everyone in Scandinavia is well acquainted with darkness. I lived far enough south that we still got a few precious hours of daylight each day, but mostly it was just dark. Still, it is when the darkness is the thickest that the smallest light makes the biggest difference.

In a few days we'll celebrate Epiphany and remember how the wise men followed the bright star to find Jesus. And though today we might not search the stars for guidance, it is true that as we seek to follow the light, it will lead us to Jesus. To Jesus who wants to show us a new way to live. Not in darkness but in his light.

As we said on Monday, one of the purposes of light is to reveal the things that are broken so that they can be seen and therefore healed – a good thing, even if the process can be uncomfortable or even painful. But light doesn't just shine on the darkness of brokenness. Light also brings clarity to that which was muddled or confused, allowing us to see what is true. It takes us from fumbling around in darkness to being able to see beauty. It helps us find a way when we're lost. His light brings life in all its fullness. It takes us out of our mess and helps us see that which truly is important. It takes us from a state of sleep to being awake and alert. It sets our hearts on fire for him and allows us to enjoy life as it was meant to be enjoyed.

† Jesus, shine your light on me. Show me beauty and truth. Help me to truly see. Show me your solutions. Awaken me to your life.

For further thought

How is your life different because of Jesus' light?

Saturday 30 December

Life through the Son

Read John 5:16–27

Very truly I tell you, whoever hears my word and believes him who sent me has eternal life and will not be judged but has crossed over from death to life.

(verse 24)

The Pharisees were people who had spent years of their lives trying to live according to God's law. They were 'good people' and they thought they knew and understood God. But they had spent so much time studying the law and coming up with all kinds of fine print that it had become impossible to follow. In doing so, they had disconnected God from the commandments, making the law their god instead. And their 'god' was a very strict judge, far more interested in rules than people, a 'god' devoid of love and compassion.

Jesus dramatically seeks to shine light on their shadowy understanding. He tells them they've got it all upside down! He does miracles on the Sabbath and asks them how it would be possible for him to do them unless God approved? Did they truly not recognise God's work as God's work, just because it was done on the wrong day of the week? How had they got so stuck in the detail of the law that it had become impossible for them to recognise the Spirit behind the law?

And then he goes even further and says that whoever recognises God in Jesus will not be judged but have eternal life. The law isn't God. The law was meant to point to God, but it isn't God.

It's easy for us to be astonished at the Pharisees, yet, I wonder, aren't we sometimes the same? Our legalistic interpretation of scripture, the rules we invent, the traditions we can't change? The people who remain unhealed, unsaved, unloved because we remade God in our image?

† Jesus, show me where I'm stuck in the details of the law and where I don't recognise who you truly are.

For further thought

What is truly important to Jesus?

Sunday 31 December

The way and the truth and the life

Read John 14:6–14

If you really know me, you will know my Father as well. From now on, you do know him and have seen him.

(verse 7)

The Law and the Prophets found their fulfilment in Jesus; they ultimately pointed to him and who he is. And Jesus points us to the Father; he is the full revelation of God. As Paul puts it, all before were shadowy pointers, but now that which was unclear has been made clear.

You cannot know God without knowing Jesus. God is fully revealed in Jesus. God has always been and will always be like Jesus. John has shown us that Jesus is not concerned with status or with the letter of the law. He didn't come to overthrow an empire or to take up a political cause. He didn't come to force us to change, or to control us. And, radically, John is saying that God is like that too. If Jesus was not the Messiah the Pharisees were expecting, how much more shocking when John shows them, and us, that *God* is different from what we think he is like.

So, what then is Jesus like, what is God like? Jesus is the way, the truth and the life. He is the one who becomes like us, moves in next door. He is the one who comes to be the message, and who invites us into conversation with him. He is the light of the world, who comes to save and to heal. He comes to show us beauty and truth, and he comes to show us a different way to live. A way that is kind and gentle and patient and caring. And he invites us to walk alongside him and talk to him about it all, and to live like he lives, fully immersed in his love.

† Jesus, thank you for showing us what God is really like.

For further thought

What are three ways in which your understanding of what God is like changes how you live your life?

IBRA scheme of readings 2024

Hope for a new year

The Gospel of Mark (1)
1 Preparing the way
2 Sowing the seed

Calling
1 Biblical figures are called
2 God calls us

Big Story: Bible framework
Following the thread of God's Word

Rebuilding in Nehemiah

The Gospel of Mark (2)
1 Authority over evil
2 Holy Week with Mark

Reconciliation
1 Stories of reconciliation
2 Taking steps to reconciliation

Arts in the Bible (1): Song – the power of song

Letters to Timothy

Camels
Marking 2024 as the United Nations International Year of Camelids with a celebration of the role of camels in the Bible

Leaders in the early church
Bringing good news and building Christian communities

The Gospel of Mark (3)
1 Who is this miracle worker?
2 Getting the message

Readings in I Chronicles

Civil rights
1 Rights and responsibility
2 Justice

Arts in the Bible (2): Dance

Letter to the Philippians

Readings in Nahum and Obadiah

Creation
1 Our environment
2 Climate justice

Travelling
1 People on the move
2 God's travel directions

Gospel of Mark (4)
1 Not to be served, but to serve
2 Approaching the kingdom

Eat of the bread and drink of the cup
1 Bread
2 Wine

Questions

Words of the beloved: Song of Solomon

Parts of the body
1 Gifts from God
2 What to do with them

False gods

Remembering and remembrance

Arts in the Bible (3): Handicraft

God of surprises

Hope at Advent
1 Watching and waiting
2 The prophets
3 John the Baptist

Christmas with Luke
1 Mary's gift
2 Luke continues the Christmas story

IBRA International Fund

IBRA brings together readers from across the globe, and it is your donations and support that make it possible for our international partners to translate, print, publish and distribute the notes to over a hundred thousand people. Thank you.

Are you able to make a donation today?

How your donations make a difference:

£5 can send an English copy of *Fresh from The Word* to any of our international partners

£10 can print 12 copies of *Fresh from The Word* in India

£25 provides 20 copies of *Fresh from The Word* in Nigeria

£50 could fund 1,000 IBRA reading lists for a country that does not currently receive IBRA materials

Our partners are based in ten countries, but the benefit flows over borders to at least thirty-two countries all over the world. Partners work tirelessly to organise the translation, printing and distribution of IBRA Bible study notes and lists in many different languages, from Ewe, Yoruba and Twi to Portuguese, Samoan and Telugu!

Did you know that we print and sell 4,000 copies of *Fresh from The Word* here in the UK, but our overseas partners produce another 42,000 copies in English and then translate the book you are reading to produce a further 31,000 copies in various local languages? With the reading list also being translated into French and Spanish, then distributed, IBRA currently reaches over 700,000 Christians globally.

Faithfully following the same principles developed in 1882, we continue to guarantee that your donations to the International Fund will support our international brothers and sisters in Christ.

If you would like to make a donation, please use the envelope inserted in this book to send a cheque to International Bible Reading Association, 5–6 Imperial Court, 12 Sovereign Road, Birmingham, B30 3FH or go online to ibraglobal.org and click the 'Donate' button at the top of the page.

Global community

Our overseas distribution and international partners enable IBRA readings to be enjoyed all over the world from Spain to Samoa, New Zealand to Cameroon. Each day when you read your copy of *Fresh from The Word* you are joining a global community of people who are also reading the same passages. The coronavirus pandemic has impacted on international communications as well as worship gatherings since 2020 but our readings continue to offer support to people worldwide:

Ghana

Our partners in Ghana report:

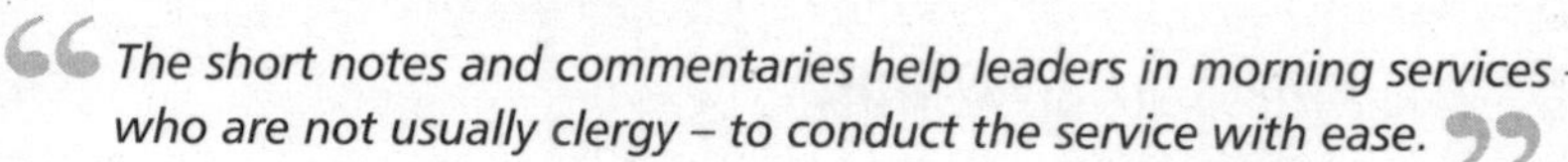

> *The short notes and commentaries help leaders in morning services – who are not usually clergy – to conduct the service with ease.*

New Zealand

A pastor in Auckland tells us:

> *It really helped during younger days back home [with] Sunday school and youth groups ... I'm now still using it and sharing it with church members.*

Nigeria

Fresh from The Word is read by Nigerians in many states including Lagos, Ogun, Abuja, Kano, Oyum Kaduna, Eno, Ondu Osun and Taraba. IBRA Nigeria's National President Segun Okubadejo observes:

> *It makes the Bible become more relevant to their everyday situation and is aiding the development of their spiritual stamina.*

India

The Fellowship of Professional Workers in India value the shared experience of following *Fresh from The Word*'s daily readings with a world community:

> *The uniqueness of the Bible reading is that the entire readership is focusing on a common theme for each day, which is an expression of oneness of the faithful, irrespective of countries and cultures.*

Samoa

Samoan readers know *Fresh from The Word* with the title *Tusi Faitau Aso*. A reverend in Samoa tells us of the readers' experience:

> FfTW *is an outstanding text/book. It shares a great amount of spiritual insights and teachings throughout the whole year. It brought comforting messages to their sorrows and sufferings, as well as inner joy in times of many challenges of faith they faced.*

A global community following God's Word

Readers have kindly shared how IBRA's *Fresh from The Word* reading scheme and notes support their Christian journey:

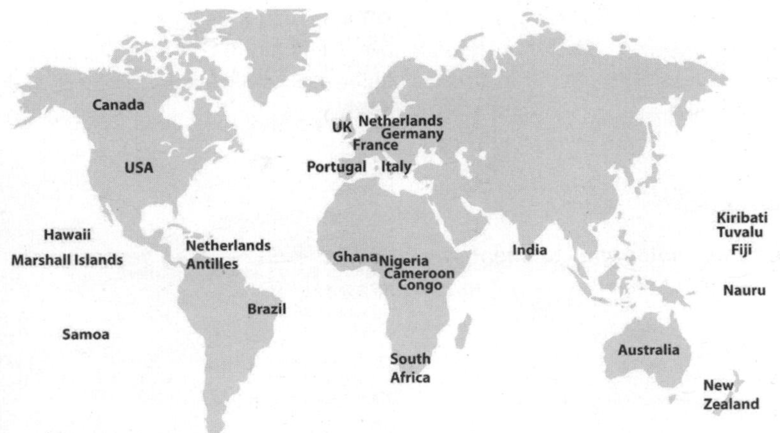

"*Strengthened my spiritual being and helped me with my Christian walk in life.*"

"*It contributed to my decision to become a deacon and quit drinking alcohol.*"

"*I enjoy the variety of different contributions for the notes, and that they are manageable in length. I generally find the notes refreshing and thought-provoking.*"

"*Gives me a structure to my daily devotional reading and frequently challenges my lifestyle and my theology!*"

"*I have found several of the writers this year have been inspirational, and I have felt enthused and excited by what they have said and the thoughts that have flowed from this. Some contributors have helped more than others, but I think it is the sense of honesty and renewed enthusiasm that has meant most to me.*"

"*On a number of occasions this year at a time of deaths associated with our congregation, a phrase in the morning readings has been most appropriate.*"

"*The IBRA readings gave me a firm belief in Jesus which has held me throughout my life. Such faith took me to Iran as an associate missionary (midwife) in my 20s and supported me through a difficult marriage. Now in old age, prayer and faith help me through illnesses, treatments and operations with minimum human support.*"

To find out more visit: **www.ibraglobal.org**

Where do you read your *FfTW*? Perhaps you have a favourite, unusual or comforting place to enjoy your Bible reading? Email **ibra@christianeducation.org.uk** to let us and your fellow readers know!

International Bible Reading Association partners and distributors

A worldwide service of Christian Education at work in five continents

HEADQUARTERS
IBRA
5–6 Imperial Court
12 Sovereign Road
Birmingham
B30 3FH
United Kingdom

www.ibraglobal.org

ibra@christianeducation.org.uk

SAMOA
Congregational Christian Church in Samoa
CCCS
PO Box 468
Tamaligi
Apia
Samoa

asst.gsec@cccs.org.ws / lina@cccs.org.ws

Congregational Christian Church in Tokelau
c/o EFKT
Atafu
Tokelau Island

hepuutua@gmail.com

Congregational Christian Church in American Samoa
P.O. BOX 1537
Pago Pago, AS 96799
American Samoa

gensec@efkasonline.org /
nfalealii@efkasonline.org

FIJI
Methodist Bookstore
11 Stewart street
PO Box 354
Suva
Fiji

mbookstorefiji@yahoo.com

Ekalesia Kelisiano Tuvalu Church Congregations in Suva, Kioa, Lautoka and Labasa
31 Ratu Sukuna Road
Nasese
Suva
Fiji

GHANA
Asempa Publishers
Christian Council of Ghana
PO Box GP 919
Accra
Ghana

gm@asempapublishers.com /
info@asempapublishers.com

NIGERIA
IBRA Nigeria
David Hinderer House
Cathedral Church of St David
Kudeti
PMB 5298 Dugbe
Ibadan
Oyo State
Nigeria

ibndiocese@yahoo.com

SOUTH AFRICA
Faith for Daily Living Foundation
PO Box 3737
Durban 4000
South Africa

ffdl@saol.com

IBRA South Africa
The Rectory
Christchurch
c/o Constantia Main and Parish Roads
Constantia 7806
Western Cape
South Africa

Terry@cchconst.org.za

DEMOCRATIC REPUBLIC OF THE CONGO
Baptist Community of the Congo River
8 Avenue Kalemie
Kinshasa Gombe
B.P. 205 & 397
Kinshasa 1
DR Congo

ecc_cbfc@yahoo.fr

CAMEROON
Redemptive Baptist Church
PO Box 65
Limbe
Fako Division
South West Region
Cameroon

evande777@yahoo.com

INDIA
All India Sunday School Association
House No. 9-131/1, Street No.5
HMT Nagar, Nacharam
Hyderabad
500076
Telangana
India

sundayschoolindia@yahoo.co.in

Fellowship of Professional Workers
Samanvay
Deepthi Chambers, Opp. Nin.
Tarnaka, Vijayapuri
Hyderabad 500 017
Telengana State
India

fellowship2w@gmail.com

Fresh from The Word 2024

Order and donation form

	Quantity	Price	Total
AA230205 *Fresh from The Word 2024*		£12.99	
10% discount if ordering 3 or more copies			
UK P&P			
Up to 2 copies		£3.95	
3–8 copies		£6.95	
9–11 copies		£8.95	
If ordering 12 or more copies please contact us for revised postage			
Western Europe P&P			
1 copy		£5.95	
If ordering more than 1 copy please contact us for revised postage			
Rest of the world P&P			
1 copy		£7.95	
If ordering more than 1 copy please contact us for revised postage			

Donation Yes, I would like to make a donation to IBRA's International Fund to help support our global community of readers.

£5.00 ☐	£10.00 ☐	£25.00 ☐	£50.00 ☐	Other ☐

TOTAL FOR BOOKS, P&P AND DONATION	

Title: ______ **First name:** ____________________ **Last name:** ____________________

Address: ____

____

Postcode: ____________________ **Tel.:** ____________________

Email: ____

Your order will be dispatched when all books are available. Payments in pounds sterling, please. We do not accept American Express or Maestro International. HOW WE USE INFORMATION ABOUT YOU AND RECIPIENTS OF YOUR INFORMATION: We will use your information in performance of your contract with us and the provision of our services to you including our legitimate interests. For further details please view our full privacy policy and your rights at www.ibraglobal.org/privacy

CARDHOLDER NAME: ________________________________

CARD NUMBER: ☐☐☐☐ ☐☐☐☐ ☐☐☐☐ ☐☐☐☐

START DATE: ☐☐ ☐☐ **EXPIRY DATE:** ☐☐ ☐☐

SECURITY NUMBER (LAST THREE DIGITS ON BACK): ☐☐☐

SIGNATURE: ________________________________

Card details will be destroyed after payment has been taken.

Please fill in your details on the reverse

Gift Aid declaration

giftaid it

If you wish to Gift Aid your donation please tick the box.

☐ I am a UK taxpayer and would like IBRA to reclaim the Gift Aid on my donation, increasing my donation by 25p for every £1. I understand that if I pay less income tax and/or capital gains tax than the amount of Gift Aid claimed on all my donations in that tax year, it is my responsibility to pay the difference.

Signature: ______________________ Date: ______________________

Thank you so much for your generous donation; it will make a real difference and change lives around the world.

Please fill in your address and payment details on the reverse of this page and send back to IBRA.

☐ **I enclose a cheque (made payable to IBRA)**

☐ **Please charge my MASTERCARD/VISA**

Please return this form to:

IBRA
5–6 Imperial Court
12 Sovereign Road
Birmingham
B30 3FH

You can also order through your local IBRA rep or from:

- Website: shop.christianeducation.org.uk
- Email: sales@christianeducation.org.uk
- Call: 0121 458 3313
- Ebook and Kindle versions are available from Amazon, Kobo and other online retailers.

Registered Charity number: 1086990